Surviving
Sexual Violence

Surviving Sexual Violence

A Guide to Recovery and Empowerment

Edited by Thema Bryant-Davis

ROWMAN & LITTLEFIELD PUBLISHERS, INC.
Lanham • Boulder • New York • Toronto • Plymouth, UK

Published by Rowman & Littlefield Publishers, Inc.
A wholly owned subsidary of The Rowman & Littlefield Publishing Group, Inc.
4501 Forbes Boulevard, Suite 200, Lanham, Maryland 20706
http://www.rowmanlittlefield.com

Estover Road, Plymouth PL6 7PY, United Kingdom

British Library Cataloguing in Publication Information Available

Library of Congress Cataloging-in-Publication Data

Surviving sexual violence : a guide to recovery and empowerment / edited by
Thema Bryant-Davis.
    p. cm.
  Includes bibliographical references and index.
  ISBN 978-1-4422-0639-7 (cloth : alk. paper) — ISBN 978-1-4422-0641-0
(electronic)
  1. Sexual abuse victims—Rehabilitation. 2. Sexual abuse victims—Psychology. I.
Bryant-Davis, Thema.
  RC560.S44S87 2011
  362.88—dc22

                                                                    2011013937

∞™ The paper used in this publication meets the minimum requirements of
American National Standard for Information Sciences—Permanence of Paper
for Printed Library Materials, ANSI/NISO Z39.48-1992.

Printed in the United States of America

Dedication

To my mother, Rev. Cecelia Williams Bryant, my first feminist role model, whose life is a testament that healing, recovery, growth, and empowerment are possible. Thank you for your fire.

Acknowledgments

Thank you to Shaquita Tillman and Monica Unique Ellis for your detailed administrative assistance in the compilation of this important text. Your dedication and spirit of excellence are appreciated as always. I am excited about the great paths that are ahead for each of you.

Contents

Part II: Paths of Recovery

Introduction

Thema Bryant-Davis

Sexual violence is a violation of survivors and society as a whole. It disrupts mental and physical well-being and devastates the fabric of social relationships. While many have written about the high global prevalence of sexual violence and its injurious consequences, less has been published about the multiple ways people can and do heal. Editing this book was important to me personally and professionally. I am a survivor of sexual violence, and I can honestly say the possibilities for my life did not end in the multiple moments of violation I have lived through. Additionally, I work as a licensed clinical psychologist and trauma researcher in the area of sexual violence. My work is based on the understanding that women and men, girls and boys around the globe have been sexually violated and yet many have found ways to move toward recovery and empowerment. This book is an acknowledgment of those who have started the healing journey as well as a resource for those who would like to get started on the path of reclaiming themselves and their lives.

The premise of this book is that survivors of sexual violence may develop pathology, but they also have incredible possibility to grow and live full lives. The book title speaks of survival because it is important to not centralize the mentality of victim but to know that survival is possible. It is also critical to not end at survival but to seek thriving. In other words, the healing pathways in this book aim to help people to not only reduce or eliminate post-trauma symptoms, but to also help survivors develop positive self-esteem, life purpose, relationships, and self-efficacy. In this way, the recovery process does not end at the point of cessation of symptoms of distress but moves through that place to the point of empowerment and life fulfillment.

There are diverse aspects of sexual violence. As a result, the beginning of this book provides an overview of the primary forms of violation one may have encountered. In reading through the prevalence and dynamics of these experiences, one will see similarities and differences. One important commonality is the abuse of power and the objectification of victims. While these forms of violence are sexual in nature, it is important to recall the clear issues of power and control that are the basis of these violations. Survivors of sexual harassment, trafficking, assault, and abuse all experience a level of dehumanization with the needs and desires of the perpetrator being prioritized over their rights to safety. There is no hierarchy of violation. In other words, it is critical that we avoid minimizing our experiences by comparing them to others. Whether you were sexually harassed, trafficked, assaulted, or abused, your trust was broken and your rights were violated. Recognizing that what happened to you should not happen to anyone is an important step in the recovery process.

Once the dynamics of these various types of sexual violation are described, the remainder of the book provides in-depth descriptions of various pathways to recovery and empowerment. These pathways include traditional psychotherapy (such as cognitive-behavioral, psychodynamic, and eye movement desensitization reprocessing) as well as nontraditional approaches (such as mind-body practice, spirituality, and expressive writing). This is the first book to include an in-depth description of these various pathways with a focus on sexual violence recovery. These chapters are authored by esteemed health professionals and scholars. I am pleased with the steps the authors have taken to make this resource accessible and applicable. Specifically, these chapters include both case studies of persons or groups of persons who have made use of these pathways as well as specific suggestions for those who would like to explore each pathway. A final but incredible asset of this text is that, as opposed to ignoring culture or segregating it into one chapter, the contributing authors explore the use of the various healing pathways within various cultural contexts, including but not limited to gender, ethnicity, socioeconomic status, and sexual orientation.

This resource guide is beneficial for counselors and survivors, as well as the support team of survivors. Regarding counselors, we can often get stuck in one orientation and approach to counseling. It is important to recognize the various ways that people heal, recover, and grow. This will allow us to adopt a strengths-based orientation that acknowledges and honors the diverse ways that people have survived. It will also allow for a more integrative approach that considers the possibility of referral and collaboration as well as the pursuit of continued education in various therapeutic methodologies.

For survivors, I would first like to thank you for picking up this text. I hope this guide serves as an important resource for your next steps toward healing and recovery. While you may be interested in reading a specific chapter, I would encourage you to read about all of the pathways. You may discover an interest in a new pathway that could be quite empowering. The reason the pathway chapters have suggestions within them is that it is important that you not only *read* about recovery but also take follow-up steps toward your empowerment. During the period of violation you were not in control, but you do have the ability to regain control over your life and shape the next stage of your journey. Sexual violence, in any form, is a devastating experience, but it does not have the final say in what your life will be nor what you will become.

For family members, romantic partners, and friends of survivors, I am glad that you are reading this book. Your support, belief, and presence make a huge difference in the lives of survivors. This guide can help you understand, in part, the experience of survivors as well as the various options that are available to them in the recovery process. It is also essential for you to listen to the survivor's experience, feelings, and thoughts, as the specifics of the trauma they endured will vary and be shaped by their personal history and the context they were in at the time of the violation. My hope is that this book will give you greater insight into both the struggles facing survivors and the possibilities for healing and growth.

I am pleased to share with you the expertise of both established and emerging authors. My hope is that you will find this body of work informative, insightful, and even inspiring. The aim of this book is to give you a sense of the urgent needs facing survivors and to highlight the phenomenal possibilities that survivors have for recovery and empowerment.

I

OVERVIEW OF SPECIFIC SEXUAL VIOLATIONS

1

Surviving Sexual Harassment: Coping With, Recognizing, and Preventing Unwanted Sexual Behaviors in the Workplace

NiCole T. Buchanan and Zaje A. Harrell

When most women reflect on their lives, they can recall at least one event that could be considered sexual harassment. For many, these events hearken back to high school, or earlier, and include comments made about her body, requests that she perform a sex act, or being groped by a boy, or group of boys, as she walked down the hallway. By college, a young woman may recall an instructor commenting on her body or hinting that she might discover her grade will improve if she will go on a date. By the time she finally enters the workforce, she may have a plethora of harassment experiences that have been so commonplace that few would recognize them as abusive. Once employed, she may be confronted by coworkers, bosses, and even supervisees that repeatedly make comments about her body, what sexual activities they would like to see her perform, or direct demands for sexual compliance that include the promise of a promotion if she does or a demotion if she refuses. Such experiences are not uncommon for the vast majority of girls and women, making sexual harassment one of the most common educational and occupational hazards girls and women face.

Many studies have substantiated that during their working lives, approximately half of all working women will experience at least one sexually harassing incident at work.[1,2] Those who have been sexually harassed are likely to experience a variety of negative psychological, health, and work/academic outcomes, such as depression, anxiety, and post-traumatic stress; job and supervisor dissatisfaction; diminished work productivity; and physical health problems.[3,4] Once harassment has ended, these symptoms often do not go away quickly and may persist for many years.[5] Sexual harassment is also directed toward men more frequently than previously assumed, and some of these men experience many of the same negative consequences as

7

women.[6] For example, approximately 15% of men have had at least one experience of sexual harassment at work,[7] and some environments are associated with even greater rates of male harassment (more than 35% of male military personnel experience some form of sexual harassment each year).[8] As further evidence of its occurrence, the Equal Employment Opportunity Commission, which investigates workplace discrimination complaints, reported that men filed 2,204 (15.9%) of the sexual harassment complaints reported in 2008.[9]

To date, sexual harassment research has largely examined the experiences of White adult working women and has focused little attention on the harassment experiences of other groups, such as working teen girls, harassed men, and ethnic minority women. Thus, questions remain regarding potential differences and similarities in the nature, frequency, and perceptions of sexual harassment across diverse groups of men and women. This chapter reviews current research findings on sexual harassment, including how it is defined as a behavioral and a legal construct, how men experience sexual harassment, and how sexual harassment is often infused with racial undertones when directed toward women of color (*racialized sexual harassment*).[10,11] Finally, the chapter concludes with an example of sexual harassment, representing the experiences of countless victims of harassment.

DEFINING SEXUAL HARASSMENT

Sexual harassment is both a psychological and a legal construct. Behavioral scientists define sexual harassment psychologically as unwanted gender-based comments and behaviors that the targeted person appraises as offensive, that exceeds his/her available coping resources, and/or that threatens his/her well-being.[12] Three subtypes of sexual harassment behaviors have been identified.[13,14] *Gender harassment* refers to nonsexual, negative, gender-based comments and behaviors, such as comments that women are not as smart as men or that certain jobs are "men's work" that women should not have. *Unwanted sexual attention* includes nonverbal and verbal comments, gestures, or physical contact of a sexual nature, such as repeated requests for dates or attempts to kiss or fondle someone against his/her will. *Sexual coercion* includes compelling someone to comply with sexual demands via job-related threats or benefits, such as promising a promotion if the worker is sexually cooperative or threatening to fire the employee if uncooperative. Sexual harassment can be perpetrated by employers, coworkers, or customers or can involve a subordinate sexually harassing his or her superior (*contrapower sexual harassment*).[15]

The legal framework defining sexual harassment is based upon precedent and evidence of threatening behaviors in the workplace. In *Meritor Savings*

Bank v. Vinson[16] the U.S. Supreme Court ruled that sexual harassment constitutes a form of sex discrimination and as such, is a violation of Title VII of the Civil Rights Act of 1964.[17] More specifically, they ruled that sexual misconduct can be defined as sexual harassment, even if the target did not suffer any tangible economic losses. Thus, sex-based discrimination includes circumstances in which unwanted negative, gender-based experiences become pervasive enough that an employee perceives it as hostile and/or it negatively affects his/her job performance (*hostile work environment*).[16,18,19] The second legal standard used to define sexual harassment is *quid pro quo* (equivalent to sexual coercion) and includes any attempt to coerce sexual interactions by threatening one's employment status.

CAUSES AND OUTCOMES OF SEXUAL HARASSMENT

The *Integrated Process Model of Sexual Harassment in Organizations* by Fitzgerald and colleagues[12,14] outlines how workplace sexual harassment is related to an organization's climate and job-gender context and then harms an employee's work, psychological, and physical health (see figure 1). In this model, organizational climate refers to the organization's tolerance of sexual harassment (e.g., harassment is modeled by superiors, harassers are not reprimanded). The job-gender context refers to a workgroup's ratio of men to women and whether the job is traditionally considered a man's or a woman's job. Workplaces that are generally tolerant of harassment, traditionally male-dominated occupations, and workgroups comprising more men than women typically have increased rates of harassment.

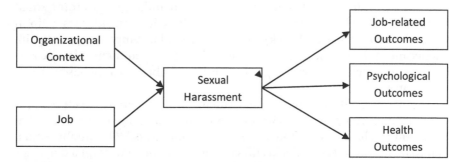

Figure. 1.1.   The integrated Process Model. The integrated process model of the antecedents and outcomes of sexual harassment in organizations (Fitzgerald et al., 1995b; 1997a). Fitzgerald, L.F., & Shullman, S. L. (1993). Sexual harassment: A research analysis and agenda for the 1990's. *Journal of Vocational Behavior, 42,* 5–27.

The integrated process model of sexual harassment also indicates that increased harassment is associated with a number of negative outcomes, such as lowered work satisfaction, increased absenteeism, depression, post-traumatic stress symptoms, and gastrointestinal problems.[4,21,22] Stress and appraisal theories[23] posit that how an individual perceives, or appraises, an event influences one's distress in response to an experience. How a target appraises a sexual harassment experience mediates the relationship between sexual harassment and negative outcomes.[24,25] The appraised severity of the harassment is affected by a variety of factors, such as being threatened or fearful as a result of the harassment,[26] the length of time over which one was sexually harassed, whether or not physical contact was made, and what type of harassment occurred. Harassment incidents that continue over a long period of time, occur frequently, and involve unwanted physical touch or sexual coercion are all associated with more negative appraisals of the harassment.[27] In addition to the harassment itself, factors related to who the perpetrator and target are also matter. For example, harassment by someone of higher organizational status is associated with more distress.[24] Further, being singled out for harassment versus knowing that harassment is also directed toward others in the workgroup is associated with worsened outcomes.[27] Among Black women, sexual harassment by White men was associated with greater distress than harassment by Black men, and experiences that included racialized sexual harassment further increased their distress.[28]

Sexual harassment harms those targeted,[29,30] and this harm may persist for years after the harassment has ended.[5] Many studies have documented the extensive physical and emotional costs for those who have been harassed. It is believed that costs to emotional well-being are directly related to harassment, whereas the physical health consequences are by-products of the increased psychological distress associated with sexual harassment.[20] More specifically, sexual harassment has been linked to gastrointestinal (heartburn, diarrhea, stomach pains), musculoskeletal (headaches; pain in joints, muscles, back, and neck), and cardiovascular symptoms (chest pain, tachycardia), headache, eyestrain, skin problems,[24,31] and chronic diseases, such as hypertension, neurological disorders, diabetes, cardiovascular diseases, and so on.[32]

The negative effect of sexual harassment on psychological well-being is far reaching. As a pervasive, chronic, and often traumatic event, sexual harassment can lead to symptoms of posttraumatic stress.[3,33,34] Initially, sexual harassment was not considered sufficiently traumatic to warrant a diagnosis of post-traumatic stress disorder (PTSD). Many researchers have challenged this assumption, arguing that sexual harassment meets the criteria for a diagnosable trauma as defined by the *Diagnostic and Statistical Manual of Mental Disorders, Fourth Edition* (DSM-IV).[35] If post-traumatic symptoms are examined, it is clear that the frequency and severity of post-traumatic stress symptoms are strongly associated with the frequency and severity of the sexual harassment experience.[3,4] This relationship is found when studying rates of harassment and discrimination across one's lifetime or only examining recent events and is found across situations (e.g., harassment in the workplace, in school, or by strangers in public).[5,20,33] Post-traumatic stress symptoms related to sexual harassment have also been documented across several studies and populations, such as college students,[3,4,36] Marines,[31] litigants,[34] Turkish women,[37] and Black women.[28,38] These studies show that sexual harassment is traumatic and commonly leads to symptoms of post-traumatic stress; therefore, a PTSD diagnosis is warranted when the criteria have been met.

Sexual harassment may also explain a portion of the difference in rates of depression and eating pathology among women and men. Women are twice as likely to develop depression[39] and more likely to experience sexual harassment compared to men.[40,41] Further, depression is higher among those who have experienced sexual harassment compared to their nonharassed counterparts, leading some to theorize that gender differences in the rates of certain disorders are related to women's higher risk of experiencing discrimination and sexual harassment.[42,43] Eating pathology and body dissatisfaction are also associated with sexual harassment, but this can occur for multiple reasons. Sexual harassment often damages self-esteem, particularly body-based self-esteem, which then puts one at risk for increased eating pathology (sexual harassment syndrome).[44,45] Sexual harassment also increases one's body scrutiny and dissatisfaction, which further increases one's risk for disordered eating.[45,46,47] Finally, when women's bodies are evaluated and objectified through sexual harassment experiences, targets may internalize this image (self-objectification) and spend increased time monitoring their bodies (self-objectification theory).[48] In turn, excessive body monitoring can increase body image distortion, shame, anxiety, restrictive eating, binge eating/bulimia,[49] and depression.[50,51,52]

Self-medicating via the misuse of cigarettes, prescription medications (e.g., sedatives and antidepressants), and alcohol are not uncommon among those who have been sexually harassed.[53,54] Clearly, many victims of sexual harassment use such substances to reduce their associated feelings of stress, depression, anxiety, hostility, and a perceived lack of control related to being sexually harassed.[53-55] These negative health behaviors used to cope with harassment are detrimental to long-term health.[56,57]

Work-related tasks and perceptions are also harmed by sexual harassment. For example, those who have been sexually harassed report increased absenteeism and lower job satisfaction, work productivity, supervisor satisfaction, and organizational commitment.[21,24,58] These behaviors not only reflect employee distress but also result in soaring organizational costs. The

U.S. Merit Systems Protection Board analyzed the costs of sexual harassment in terms of these negative work behaviors and determined that the U.S. government loses more than $327 million dollars every year due to factors such as employees' decreased productivity and absenteeism related to sexual harassment.[59] However, this figure is a vast underestimate of the true costs of sexual harassment because it does not include the cost related to the harasser (e.g., decreased productivity while engaging in harassment), changes in work behaviors by coworkers that have witnessed the harassment (e.g., decreased morale and productivity), or any of the costs of investigating, mediating, or litigating harassment charges.[60]

COPING WITH SEXUAL HARASSMENT

Problem-focused or emotion-focused coping strategies refer to a variety of cognitive or behavioral methods used to reduce the stress of a traumatic event.[23] Problem-focused strategies focus on managing or changing the situation (e.g., reporting the incident) while emotion-focused strategies attempt to manage one's own thoughts and feelings about the situation (e.g., avoiding thinking about it). Knapp and colleagues[61] proposed four categories of coping with sexual harassment: *avoidance-denial* (avoiding being physically close to the perpetrator or avoiding thinking about the harassment); *social support* (receiving emotional support and advice from others); *confrontation-negotiation* (directly communicating with the perpetrator that the harassment must end); and *advocacy-seeking* (reporting the perpetrator's behavior to appropriate individuals within the organization). The type of coping method one uses is influenced by characteristics of the target and perpetrator, the harassment, and his/her own cultural norms.[62] For example, more upsetting, frequent, and persistent harassment will result in the use of multiple strategies to try to end the harassment and decreased reliance on ignoring the perpetrator's behavior.[62,63,64] Those harassed by a superior, especially if they are fairly low in organizational status, are more likely to talk with trusted sources and eventually report the harassment than those harassed by coworkers.[63,64] Although rates of reporting sexual harassment remain extremely low overall,[65] women from collectivistic, patriarchal cultures are less likely to confront harassers than to try to avoid the perpetrator.[62] Among one sample of Black women, avoidance and denial were common, but as harassment increased in frequency and severity, they utilized additional coping strategies, including confrontation.[66] These findings reflect that coping with sexual harassment is a dynamic process,[67] and targets adapt their coping strategies in an attempt to end the harassment.

The question remains as to whether or not there are advantages to using certain coping strategies rather than others. Many organizations require that targets formally report sexual harassment to someone in authority within the company and more generally, many assume that confronting the perpetrator or filing a complaint are indicators that the target really did not want or enjoy the harassment. "Passive" responses, such as trying to avoid the harasser, are frequently viewed negatively; however, passive strategies often reflect well-thought, deliberate attempts to balance the harm of being harassed and the potential risks of angering or alienating the perpetrator and supporters (e.g., being ostracized by other coworkers, demoted, or fired).[63,67] In fact, over two-thirds of those who have voiced concerns about harassment faced retaliation as a result.[68] For example, among Black women in the military, those who filed formal complaints against their harassers experienced negative work outcomes; conversely, confronting the harasser (without filing a report) resulted in better psychological well-being.[66] Taken together, these studies indicate that the responses often assumed to be most appropriate may come with a high price to one's psychological and occupational well-being.

SEXUAL HARASSMENT AND WOMEN OF COLOR

Despite considerable progress over the past several decades, gender and racial inequalities remain across all sectors of the labor market; thus, working women of color are disadvantaged in the employment sector,[69,70] and this reality may influence how they are sexually harassed. Although sparse, theoretical and empirical work examining women of color and sexual harassment is growing, but many questions about their experiences remain unanswered.[71] *Double or multiple jeopardy* theory[72] informs much of this body of research and suggests that because women of color are marginalized across multiple domains due to their race and gender, they are at increased risk of being victimized. Thus, sexual harassment is likely to be more frequent and more severe for women with multiple intersecting marginalized identities.[73,74,75] A small, but growing, body of research supports this assertion that women of color experience more frequent and severe sexual harassment.[76-78]

Women of color are also at greater risk for experiencing more than one type of harassment (e.g., racial and sexual harassment). Little research has simultaneously measured multiple forms of harassment, but research with adult Black women[38] and Black, Asian, and multiracial college students[79] indicates that experiencing both sexual and racial harassment is associated with greater detriment to psychological, academic, and occupational outcomes. Moreover, because women of color cannot disaggregate their racial selves from their gendered selves, they are likely to experience harassment that addresses their race and gender concomitantly in the form of *racialized sexual harassment*.[10,11] Racialized sexual harassment is similar to, yet distinct from, racial and sexual harassment, making it impossible to discern where the racial harassment ends and the sexual harassment begins (e.g., calling someone a "Black bitch").[10,11] Thus, when sexual harassment is intertwined with multiple forms of workplace mistreatment, victims experience increased distress.[38,40,79]

SEXUAL HARASSMENT AND MEN

There is a paucity of research examining the sexual harassment experiences of men; yet men experience higher rates of sexual harassment than the small body of research would suggest.[6,8] Approximately 15% of men report at least one negative sexual harassment experience in the workplace.[9] Similar to research on women of color, data suggests that on average, Black men experience more sexual harassment compared to White men, particularly those with lower organizational status.[80] When men are harassed they are frequently targeted by other men,[59] and they experience all forms of sexual harassment.[6] However, research has also revealed that men frequently experience "not man enough" harassment—a type of gender harassment that targets men for failing to conform to male gender-role stereotypes—which has been associated with negative outcomes among harassed men.[81] "Not man enough" harassment may include saying he is not "a real man" if he performs traditionally female activities, such as cooking dinner or missing work to care for a sick child.

Findings regarding how men interpret and appraise sexual harassment have varied, and few have included "not man enough" harassment in examining men's appraisals. When examining the three primary categories of sexual harassment (gender harassment, unwanted sexual attention, sexual coercion), research suggests that sexual harassment from women is often appraised positively by men,[82,83] rarely evaluated as stressful or bothersome,[6,82] and associated with few changes in work or psychological outcomes, as compared to women.[84] Conversely, when men and women experience harassment that is similar in severity and frequency, men show detriment in work, psychological, and health outcomes that is on par with those of women.[40,41] Additional research must expand to include "not man enough" harassment, more severe forms of harassment, and same-sex harassment before strong conclusions about men's perceptions of sexual harassment can be made.

IN THEIR OWN WORDS:
AN EXAMPLE OF SEXUAL HARASSMENT

Below is an example of sexual harassment giving voice to the silenced whose stories are never told. It is a fictionalized example combining the autobiographical accounts of several women and representing a prototypical case rather than a specific woman or company.

After finishing graduate school I was excited about my new position. My supervisor, Dan, mentored me and led me to believe he was committed to my success. While working on the end-of-the-year fiscal reports, he asked me to join him to grab a bite to eat and discuss what work remained. At the restaurant, I felt somewhat uncomfortable by how close he sat to me and how many times his leg brushed against mine, but I dismissed these thoughts, thinking I was being too sensitive. As we left, we agreed to get to work early on Friday to meet our deadline.

Friday morning he started talking about how much he enjoyed spending time with me, how attracted he was to me, and how he wanted to help me rise in the organization. He then grabbed me around my waist and kissed me. He refused to stop as I begged him to let me go. His hand slipped inside my shirt; I yelled in surprise and managed to get out of his grasp. Moments later, his secretary knocked to let him know she had arrived and would bring his coffee shortly. I used the opportunity to get out of his office and avoided him the rest of the day.

I felt sick to my stomach and my heart started racing whenever someone passed my office. I could not sleep the next several nights and I worried about being fired the entire weekend. Monday morning I had to force myself to go into work. He called me into his office and began discussing how well the reports were done as if nothing had happened. As I turned to leave he said he had another urgent project for me and needed me to stay late to get it done on time. After everyone else had left, he started saying he was my special project and tried to kiss me again. I told him it was unacceptable and unprofessional. He apologized and left the office.

A few months later he started making comments about wanting to take me to a three-day conference and "show me a good time." I started getting sick to my stomach every time I saw him. When I told him I could not go, he said it was required as part of my position and I needed to be there if I wanted to keep my job. I was afraid of what he might do if we went out of town and I began having nightmares. I decided to report him to Human Resources, but after I did so, he began criticizing my work and telling coworkers that I lied about him to hide my poor performance. I talked to Human Resources again and a few days later received a negative performance review and was put on probation. A week later I was accused of losing an important client file and fired.

I have a new job at another company, but I have a hard time accepting mentoring or support, especially from my boss. I am still always "on guard" for him making advances and I cannot seem to relax. My work has suffered and I have lost faith that my efforts will be recognized and rewarded. That is the worst part. Not only did Dan sabotage my job with that firm, but he has robbed me of my ability to trust people at work. In addition to that, I cannot muster the desire to work as hard as I used to because I do not believe doing so will make any difference in how I am treated.

CONCLUSION

For the past three decades sexual harassment research has explored proper ways of defining sexual harassment, understanding why it occurs, and mitigating the associated risk factors and outcomes. Depression; post-traumatic stress; health problems; lower job satisfaction, work productivity, and supervisor satisfaction; increased absenteeism; and turnover have all been associated with sexual harassment, making it costly to those who are targeted and the organizations within which they work. Further, an increasingly diverse workforce requires greater attention to the needs and experiences of marginalized workers (e.g., women of color and gay and lesbian workers) who are likely to experience multiple types of harassment as well as fused forms of harassment that target them on the basis of multiple salient identities (e.g., racialized sexual harassment based on gender and race). Focusing on these factors will not only advance research on sexual harassment but will also better enable individuals to protect themselves and organizations to prevent harassment from occurring.

REFERENCES

1. Fitzgerald, L.F., & Shullman, S.L. (1993). Sexual harassment: A research analysis and agenda for the 1990s. *Journal of Vocational Behavior, 42,* 5–27.
2. Ilies, R., Hauserman, N., Schwochau, S., & Stibal, J. (2003). Reported incidence rates of work-related sexual harassment in the United States: Using meta-analysis to explain reported rate disparities. *Personnel Psychology, 56*(3), 607–631.
3. Avina, C., & O'Donohue, W. (2002). Sexual harassment and PTSD: Is sexual harassment diagnosable trauma? *Journal of Traumatic Stress, 15,* 69–75.
4. Willness, C.R., Steel, P., & Lee, K. (2007). A meta-analysis of the antecedents and consequences of workplace sexual harassment. *Personnel Psychology, 60,* 127–162.
5. Glomb, T.M., Munson, L.J., Hulin, C.L., Bergman, M.E., & Drasgow, F. (1999). Structural equation models of sexual harassment: Longitudinal explorations and cross-sectional generalizations. *Journal of Applied Psychology, 84,* 14–28.
6. Berdahl, J.L., Magley, V.J., & Waldo, C.R. (1996). The sexual harassment of men? Exploring the concept with theory and data. *Psychology of Women Quarterly, 20,* 527–547.
7. U.S. Merit Systems Protection Board (2004). *Issues of Merit.* Retrieved October 12, 2009 from http://www.mspb.gov/netsearch/viewdocs.aspx?docnumber=255 805&version=256094&application=ACROBAT
8. Antecol, H., & Cobb-Clark, D. (2001). Men, Women, and Sexual Harassment in the U.S. Military. *Gender Issues, 19,* 3–18.
9. Equal Employment Opportunity Commission. (2009). *Sexual Harassment Charges EEOC & FEPAs Combined: FY 1997–FY 2008.* Retrieved October 1, 2009 from http://www.eeoc.gov/stats/harass.html
10. Buchanan, N.T. (2005). The nexus of race and gender domination: The racialized sexual harassment of African American women. In P. Morgan & J. Gruber (Eds.), *In the Company of Men: Re-Discovering the Links between Sexual Harassment and Male Domination* (pp. 294–320). Boston: Northeastern University Press.

11. Buchanan, N.T., & Ormerod, A.J. (2002). Racialized sexual harassment in the lives of African American Women. *Women & Therapy, 25,* 107–124.

12. Fitzgerald, L.F., Swan, S., & Magley, V.J. (1997). But was it really sexual harassment? Legal, behavioral, and psychological definitions of the workplace victimization of women. In W. O'Donohue (Ed.), *Sexual Harassment: Theory, Research, and Treatment* (pp. 5–28). Needham Heights, MA: Allyn & Bacon.

13. Fitzgerald, L.F., Shullman, S.L., Bailey, N., Richards, M., Swecker, J., Gold, Y., et al. (1988). The incidence and dimensions of sexual harassment in academia and the workplace. *Journal of Vocational Behavior, 32,* 152–175.

14. Fitzgerald, L.F., Gelfand, M.J., & Drasgow, F. (1995). Measuring sexual harassment: Theoretical and psychometric advances. *Basic and Applied Social Psychology, 17,* 425–427.

15. Rospenda, K.M., Richman, J.A., & Nawyn, S.J. (1998). Doing power: The confluence of gender, race, and class in contrapower sexual harassment. *Gender & Society, 12,* 40–60.

16. *Meritor Savings Bank v. Vinson,* 477 U.S. 57 (1986)

17. Civil Rights Act, P.L. 88-352, 78 Stat. 241, Title VII, 42 U.S.C. 2000e 2(a) (1964).

18. Equal Employment Opportunity Commission. (1980). Guidelines on discrimination because of sex. *Federal Regulations, 43,* 74676–74677.

19. Hogler, R.L., Frame, J.H., & Thornton, G. (2002). Workplace sexual harassment law: An empirical analysis of organizational justice and legal policy. *Journal of Managerial Issues, 14,* 234–251.

20. Fitzgerald, L.F., Drasgow, F., Hulin, C.L., Gelfand, M.J., & Magley, V.J. (1997). Antecedents and consequences of sexual harassment in organizations: A test of an integrated model. *Journal of Applied Psychology, 82,* 578–589.

21. Munson, L.J., Hulin, C., & Drasgow, F. (2000). Longitudinal analysis of dispositional influences and sexual harassment: Effects on job and psychological outcomes. *Personnel Psychology, 53,* 21–46.

22. O'Connell, C.E., & Korabik, K. (2000). Sexual harassment: The relationship of personal vulnerability, work context, perpetrator status, and type of harassment to outcomes. *Journal of Vocational Behavior, 56*(3), 299–329.

23. Lazarus, R.S., & Folkman, S. (1984). *Stress, Appraisal, and Coping.* New York: Springer.

24. Langhout, R.D., Bergman, M.E., Cortina, L.M., Fitzgerald, L.F., Drasgow, F., & Williams, J.H. (2005). Sexual harassment severity: Assessing situational and personal determinants and outcomes. *Journal of Applied Social Psychology, 35*(5), 975–1007.

25. Swan, S., Fitzgerald, L.F., & Magley, V.J. (1996, March). *So what? Why did it bother her? Factors affecting women's perceptions of the severity of sexual harassment experiences.* Paper presented at the Association for Women in Psychology, Portland, OR.

26. Wright, C.V., & Fitzgerald, L.F. (2007). Angry and Afraid: Women's Appraisal of Sexual Harassment during Litigation. *Psychology of Women Quarterly, 31*(1), 73–84.

27. Hitlan, R.T., Schneider, K.T., & Walsh, B.M. (2006). Upsetting Behavior: Reactions to Personal and Bystander Sexual Harassment Experiences. *Sex Roles, 55*(3–4), 187–195.

28. Woods, K.C., Buchanan, N.T., & Settles, I.H. (2009). Sexual harassment across the color line: Experiences and outcomes of cross- vs. intra-racial sexual harassment among Black women. *Cultural Diversity and Ethnic Minority Psychology, 15*(1), 67–76.

29. Cantisano, G.T., Dominguez, J.F.M., & Depolo, M. (2008). Perceived sexual harassment at work: Meta-analysis and structural model of antecedents and consequences. *The Spanish Journal of Psychology, 11*(1), 207–218.

30. Chan, D.K.S., Lam, C.B., Chow, S.Y., & Cheung, S.F. (2008). Examining the job-related, psychological, and physical outcomes of workplace sexual harassment: A meta-analytic review. *Psychology of Women Quarterly, 32*, 362–376.

31. Shipherd, J.C., Pineles, S.L., Gradus, J.L., & Resick, P.A. (2009). Sexual harassment in the Marines, posttraumatic stress symptoms, and perceived health: Evidence for sex differences. *Journal of Traumatic Stress, 22*(1), 3–10.

32. Keskinoglu, P., Ucuncu, T., Yildirim, I., Gurbuz, T., Ur, I., & Ergor, G. (2007). Gender discrimination in the elderly and its impact on the elderly health. *Archives of Gerontology and Geriatrics, 45*, 295–306.

33. Berg, S.H. (2006). Everyday sexism and posttraumatic stress disorder in women: A correlational study. *Violence Against Women, 12*(10), 970–988.

34. Fitzgerald, L.F., Buchanan, N.T., Collinsworth, L.L., Magley, V.J., & Ramos, A.M. (1999). Junk logic: The abuse defense in sexual harassment litigation. *Psychology, Public Policy, and the Law, 5*, 730–759.

35. American Psychiatric Association. (1994). *Diagnostic and statistical manual of mental disorders* (4th ed.). Washington, D.C.: Author.

36. Rederstorff, J.C., Buchanan, N.T., & Settles, I.H. (2007). The moderating roles of race and gender role attitudes in the relationship between sexual harassment and psychological well-being. *Psychology of Women Quarterly, 31*, 50–61.

37. Wasti, S.A., Bergman, M.E., Glomb, T.M., & Drasgow, F. (2000). Test of the cross-cultural generalizability of a model of sexual harassment. *Journal of Applied Psychology, 85*, 766–778.

38. Buchanan, N.T., & Fitzgerald, L.F. (2008). The effects of racial and sexual harassment on work and the psychological well-being of African American women. *Journal of Occupational Health Psychology, 13*, 137–151.

39. Kessler, R.C. (2003). Epidemiology of women and depression. *Journal of Affective Disorders, 74*, 5–13.

40. Cortina, L.M., Fitzgerald, L.F., & Drasgow, F. (2002). Contextualizing Latina experiences of sexual harassment: Preliminary tests of a structural model. *Basic and Applied Social Psychology, 24*, 295–311.

41. Magley, V.J., Waldo, C.R., Drasgow, F., & Fitzgerald, L.F. (1999). The impact of sexual harassment on military personnel: Is it the same for men and women? *Military Psychology, 11*, 283–302.

42. Klonoff, E.A., Landrine, H., & Campbell, R. (2000). Sexist discrimination may account for well-known gender differences in psychiatric symptoms. *Psychology of Women Quarterly, 24*, 93–99.

43. Swim, J.K., Hyers, L.L., Cohen, L.L., & Ferguson, M.J. (2001). Everyday sexism: Evidence for its incidence, nature, and psychological impact from three daily diary studies. *Journal of Social Issues, 57*, 31–53.
44. Backhouse, C., & Cohen, L. (1978). *The secret oppression.* Toronto: Macmillan.
45. Larkin, J., Rice, C., & Russell, V. (1996). Slipping through the cracks: Sexual harassment, eating problems, and the problem of embodiment. *Eating Disorders: The Journal of Treatment & Prevention, 4*, 5–26.
46. Barker, E.T., & Galambos, N.L. (2003). Body dissatisfaction of adolescent girls and boys: Risk and resource factors. *The Journal of Early Adolescence, 23*(2), 141–165.
47. Larkin, J., & Rice, C. (2005). Beyond "health eating" and "healthy weights": Harassment and the health curriculum in middle schools. *Body Image, 2*, 219–232.
48. Frederickson, B., & Roberts, T. (1997). Objectification theory: Toward understanding women's lived experiences and mental health risks. *Psychology of Women Quarterly, 21*, 173–206.
49. Noll, S.M., & Fredrickson, B.L. (1998). A mediational model linking self-objectification, body shame, and disordered eating. *Psychology of Women Quarterly, 22*, 623–636.
50. Joiner, T.E., Wonderlich, S.A., Metalsky, G.I., & Schmidt, N.B. (1995). Body dissatisfaction: A feature of bulimia, depression, or both? *Journal of Social and Clinical Psychology, 14*, 339–355.
51. McKinley, N.M. (1998). Gender differences in undergraduates' body esteem: The mediating effect of objectified body consciousness and actual/ideal weight discrepancy. *Sex Roles, 19*, 113–123.
52. Stice, E., Hayward, C., Cameron R.P., Killen, J.D., & Taylor, C.B. (2000). Body-image and eating disturbances predict onset of depression among female adolescents: A longitudinal study, *Journal of Abnormal Psychology, 109*, 438–444.
53. Richman, J.A., & Rospenda, K.M. (2005). Sexual harassment and alcohol use. *Psychiatric Times, 22*(2). 48–53.
54. Zucker, A.N., & Landry, L.J. (2007). Embodied discrimination: The relation of sexism and distress to women's drinking and smoking behaviors. *Sex Roles, 56*, 193–203.
55. Rospenda, K.M., Richman, J.A., & Shannon, C.A. (2009). Prevalence and mental health correlates of harassment and discrimination in the workplace: Results from a national study. *Journal of Interpersonal Violence, 24*(5), 819–843.
56. Centers for Disease Control and Prevention. (2010). Health effects of cigarette smoking. Retrieved August 23, 2010 from http://www.cdc.gov/tobacco/data_statistics/fact_sheets/health_effects/effects_cig_smoking/
57. National Institute on Drug Abuse. (2002). Use of selected substances in the past month by persons 12 years of age and over, according to age, sex, race and Hispanic origin: United States, select years 1979–99. Retrieved April 12, 2002 from http://www.cdc.gov/nchs/products/pubs/pubd/hus/tables/2001/01hus063.pdf
58. Lapierre, L.M., Spector, P.E., & Leck, J.D. (2005). Sexual versus nonsexual workplace aggression and victims' overall job satisfaction: A meta-analysis. *Journal of Occupational Health Psychology, 10*, 155–169.

59. U.S. Merit Systems Protection Board (USMSPB). (1994). *Sexual harassment in the federal workplace: Trends, progress, continuing challenges.* Washington, D.C.: U.S. Government Printing Office.

60. Cortina, L.M., & Berdahl, J.L. (2008). Sexual harassment in organizations: A decade of research in review. In C. L. Cooper & J. Barling (Eds.), *Handbook of Organizational Behavior,* vol. 1, 469-497. Los Angeles: Sage Publications.

61. Knapp, D.E., Faley, R.H., Ekeberg, S.E., & Dubois, C.L.Z. (1997). Determinants of target responses to sexual harassment: A conceptual framework. *Academy of Management Review, 22,* 687–729.

62. Cortina, L.M., & Wasti, S.A. (2005). Profiles in coping: Responses to sexual harassment across persons, organizations, and cultures. *Journal of Applied Psychology, 90*(1), 182–192.

63. Bergman, M.E., Langhout, R.D., Cortina, L.M., Palmieri, P.A., & Fitzgerald, L.F. (2002). The (Un)reasonableness of Reporting: Antecedents and Consequences of Reporting Sexual Harassment. *Journal of Applied Psychology, 87,* 230–242.

64. Malamut, A.B., & Offermann, L.F. (2001). Coping with sexual harassment: Personal, environmental, and cognitive determinants. *Journal of Applied Psychology, 86,* 1152–1166.

65. Magley, V.J. (2002). Coping with sexual harassment: Reconceptualizing women's resistance. *Journal of Personality and Social Psychology, 83,* 930–946.

66. Buchanan, N.T., Settles, I.H., & Langhout, R.D. (2007). Black Women's coping styles, psychological well-being, and work-related outcomes following sexual harassment. *Black Women, Gender and Families, 1,* 100–120.

67. Magley, V.J., Fitzgerald, L.F., & Buchanan, N.T. (2000, April). Assessing coping with sexual harassment over time. In V.J. Magley (Chair), *Coping with sexual harassment: Layers of meaning.* Symposium conducted at the annual meeting of the Society for Industrial and Organizational Psychology, New Orleans, LA.

68. Cortina, L.M., & Magley, V.J. (2003). Raising Voice, Risking Retaliation: Events Following Interpersonal Mistreatment in the Workplace. *Journal of Occupational Health Psychology, 8,* 247–265.

69. Browne, I., & Misra, J. (2003). The intersection of gender and race in the labor market. *Annual Review of Sociology, 29,* 497–513.

70. Kim, J. (2006). Gender inequality in the U.S. Labor Market: Evidence from the 2000 Census. In M.F. Karsten (Ed.), *Gender, race, and ethnicity in the workplace: Issues and challenges for today's organizations* (pp. 269–290). Westport, CT: Praeger.

71. Buchanan, N.T., & West, C.M. (2009). Sexual Harassment in the Lives of Women of Color. In H. Landrine and N.F. Russo (Eds.), *Handbook of Diversity in Feminist Psychology: Theory, Research, and Practice.* Springer Publishing Company.

72. Beal, F.M. (1970). Double jeopardy: To be Black and female. In T. Cade (Ed.), *The Black woman: An anthology* (pp. 90–100). New York: Signet.

73. Bowleg, L., Huang, J., Brooks, K., Black, A., & Burkholder, G. (2003). Triple jeopardy and beyond: Multiple minority stress and resilience among black lesbians. *Journal of Lesbian Studies, 7,* 87–108.

74. DeFour, D.C., David, G., Diaz, F.J., & Thompkins, S. (2003). The interface of race, sex, sexual orientation, and ethnicity in understanding sexual harassment. In C.A. Paludi, M. Paludi (Eds.), *Academic and workplace sexual harassment: A*

handbook of cultural, social science, management, and legal perspectives (pp. 31–45). Westport, CT: Praeger Publishers/Greenwood Publishing Group.

75. Settles, I.H. (2006). Use of an intersectional framework to understand Black women's racial and gender identities. *Sex Roles, 54,* 589–601.
76. Berdahl, J.L., & Moore, C. (2006). Workplace harassment: Double jeopardy for minority women. *Journal of Applied Psychology, 91*(2), 426–436.
77. Buchanan, N.T., Settles, I.H., & Woods, K.C. (2008). Comparing sexual harassment subtypes for Black and White women: Double jeopardy, the Jezebel, and the cult of true womanhood. *Psychology of Women Quarterly, 32,* 347–361.
78. Nelson, N.L., & Probst, T.M. (2004). Multiple minority individuals: Multiplying the risk of workplace harassment and discrimination. In J.L. Chin (Ed.), *The psychology of prejudice and discrimination: Ethnicity and multiracial identity* (pp.193–217). Westport, CT: Praeger Publishers/Greenwood Publishing Group, Inc.
79. Buchanan, N.T., Bergman, M.E., Bruce, T.A., Woods, K.C., & Lichty, L.F. (2009). Unique and joint effects of sexual and racial harassment on college students' well-being. *Basic and Applied Social Psychology, 31,* 267–285.
80. Settles, I.H., Buchanan, N.T., & Colar, B.K. (under review). The impact of race and rank on the sexual harassment of Black and White men in the military. *Manuscript submitted for publication.*
81. Waldo, C.R., Berdahl, J.L., & Fitzgerald, L.F. (1998). Are men sexually harassed? If so, by whom? *Law and Human Behavior, 22,* 59–79.
82. Berdahl, J.L. (2007). The sexual harassment of uppity women. *Journal of Applied Psychology, 92,* 425–437.
83. Gutek, B.A. (1985). *Sex and the Workplace.* San Francisco, CA: Jossey-Bass.
84. Barling, J., Dekker, I., Loughlin, C., Kelloway, E., Fullagar, C., & Johnson, D. (1996). Prediction and replication of the organizational and personal consequences of workplace sexual harassment. *Journal of Managerial Psychology, 11,* 4–26.

2

Human Trafficking: Not an Isolated Issue

Michelle Contreras and Melissa Farley

Human trafficking is not an isolated issue. Rather it is a crime that intersects with some of the most challenging psychological issues that mental health professionals deal with. There is a complex relationship between human trafficking and sexual violence, domestic violence, political captivity, torture, and cults.[1-3] Human trafficking for the purpose of prostitution is sexual violence, a topic that we will discuss in this chapter. In order to understand the psychosocial needs of survivors, we will also discuss the overlaps between human trafficking, sexual violence, and prostitution. We will also briefly discuss the macro issues contributing to the proliferation of this crime, which explain some of the reasons why human trafficking is the global phenomenon that it is today.

Human traffickers search for victims who are vulnerable and desperate. The goal of the trafficker is to lure the person by presenting her* a false promise of a job that appears to have the potential of solving the victim's predicament. In some cases, even when the potential victim knows that the job will be degrading or even that she will be expected to prostitute, she doesn't picture just how bad it really will be. Furthermore, when a woman is trafficked for domestic servitude or sweatshop labor, she is usually sexually exploited in prostitution-like activities as well. The converse is also true: In Thai prostitution, for example, women are expected to wash laundry and prepare meals for sex buyers.

---

*Given that the majority of sex trafficking victims are women, we will use the feminine pronoun throughout this chapter to refer to the general victim population.

VULNERABILITIES TO
HUMAN TRAFFICKING AND PROSTITUTION

Risk factors. Prostitution and trafficking are rooted in social inequality: the inequality between men and women, between the rich and the poor, and between ethnic majorities and minorities.[4] The macro forces and individual risk factors contributing to human trafficking are multiple and relate to each other in complex ways. At their roots, risk factors include varying combinations of being young, poor, female, and being a member of a marginalized ethnic minority. Risk factors vary depending on the individual's country, region, city, community, and family and community supports. For example, in Latin America the growing problem of trafficking is exacerbated by sexist environments that discriminate against women and girls including by their physical and sexual abuse;[5] by limited economic opportunities for women;[6] by multinational corporations' demand for inexpensive labor; by sophisticated recruitment methods used by traffickers; by government corruption and disinterest in the protection of vulnerable people; immigration policies that force people into anonymity; unemployment; illiteracy; homelessness; drug and alcohol abuse; and gang membership.[7] A woman from Nicaragua described how her husband, a Salvadoran man, took her to live close to the Guatemalan border with Mexico shortly after they married. Every weekend he transported her to a Mexican brothel to be sold in prostitution. She escaped her husband/pimp/trafficker when he brought her to the United States to gain greater profits from the commercial sexual exploitation. She broke into tears when she recalled failed attempts to obtain help in Guatemala, stating, "One day I was fed up and decided to go to the police. I told them what was happening, and they laughed and told me I should shut my mouth and instead work on being an obedient wife. I wanted to kill myself, but my son kept me going." Three common characteristics of Central American cases of human trafficking are control and exploitation of victims including their delivery to sex trafficking markets across borders, lawless environments, and the rampant sex-based discrimination at all levels of society.

Limited economic opportunities. Women are increasingly channeled into prostitution as their opportunities for work in other sectors of the economy shrink. A prostituting Yemeni woman angrily accused her government of making her "worthless and of no value, oppressing us with these unstable conditions, moreover forcing us to indulge in actions that will haunt us for generations to come."[8] The prostitution of desperately poor women in Yemen may seem worlds apart from the prostitution of women and girls in the United States. But as globalized economies feminize poverty and as public health services and emergency networks collapse because of malignant governmental neglect, more U.S. women turn to prostitution to survive. This process of women's economic survival under the oppressive harm of poverty and conditions of war can not be described as a free choice to prostitute, as some would insist. The economic and social forces that channel young, poor, and ethnically marginalized women into prostitution are evident in post-Katrina New Orleans. One report pointed out that economic devastation of the hurricane increased prostitution and domestic trafficking into the region.[9]

Like domestically trafficked women, internationally trafficked women tend to be poor and unemployed and to come from countries that are in economic and social transition.[10] Trade liberalization policies have failed to diminish power imbalances between men and women, with impoverished women having dramatically less access to land, credit, and education than men, which places them at higher risk of vulnerability to pimps and traffickers.[11]

Ethnic and racial discrimination. Women's vulnerability to trafficking increases when they belong to an ethnically and/or racially marginalized group. A study that looked at the prevalence of lifetime violence and post-traumatic stress disorder of women prostituting in Vancouver, Canada, included 52% percent Aboriginal women, an overrepresentation in prostitution of Aboriginal women compared with less than 8% representation in the general population.[12] The authors point out that the same vulnerabilities of race, class, and gender that have been recognized as multiplicative risk factors for a wide range of health problems are also multiplicative risk factors for prostitution and conclude:

> In Canada, the triple force of race, class and sex discrimination disparately impacts First Nations [term of respect used by the authors to refer to people whose ancestors were the first nations of people in North America] women. Prostitution of Aboriginal women occurs globally in epidemic numbers with indigenous women at the bottom of a racialized sexual hierarchy in prostitution itself. (p. 17)[12]

The social forces that are assumed to cause human trafficking, such as poverty, human rights violations, gender disparity, and discrimination, are the same as those that channel women, men, and children into prostitution.[10,6] Magda, a Mayan Indian woman, described her trafficking experiences during the thirty-six-year armed conflict in Guatemala. Magda narrated how the soldiers kidnapped her from her village after killing her family. She described how they forced her to travel with them over the course of several weeks and used her to have sex with soldiers stationed in remote mountain areas. Reflecting on these traumatic childhood experiences, Magda said, "People saw me with them and they didn't do anything to help me. Maybe it's because I was an Indian girl. Maybe they would have helped if they saw a Ladina [term used to refer to westernized, biracial, or white Guatemalans] girl with a bunch of soldiers." This case illustrates the intersecting contextual factors of war, ethnic, racial, and gender-based discrimination that contribute to human trafficking.

The invisible coercions of prostitution are evident when we take a closer look at individual cases: the woman in India who worked in an office where she concluded that she might as well prostitute and be paid more for the sexual harassment and abuse that was expected of her anyway in order to keep her job; the teenager in California who said that in her neighborhood, "Boys grew up to be pimps and drug dealers and girls grew up to be 'hos." She was the third generation of prostituted women in her family. The woman in Zambia who said that five blow jobs paid for a bag of cornmeal and that this is how she could feed her children. The young woman sold by her parents at age sixteen into a Nevada legal brothel. Ten years later, she took six psychiatric drugs that tranquilized her so she could make it through the day selling sex. The narratives have a common thread: the women had extremely limited options for economic survival and all lived in cultures that were accepting of prostitution.

Sexual violence against women. Violence against women, which increases women's vulnerability to trafficking, is at pandemic levels. Conservative international statistics indicate that at least one of three women has been beaten, coerced into sex, or otherwise abused in her lifetime.[13] A World Health Organization study found that as many as 47% of women report that their first sexual experience was rape. In some communities laws prioritize family values over the rights of women to be free of sexual assault.[14] Every year, as many as five thousand women around the world are victims of honor killings—murders that are rationalized because a woman engaged in sex without community approval. Many societies have laws with loopholes that allow perpetrators to act with impunity. For example, in a number of countries, a rapist can go free under the penal code if he proposes to marry the victim, with women often blamed for having been raped by men.[15]

PROSTITUTION AND HUMAN TRAFFICKING UNDER THE LENS OF VIOLENCE AGAINST WOMEN

Women in prostitution suffer extremely high rates of violence from pimps and from men who buy them for sexual use. Farley and Barkan[16] found that among 130 people in prostitution interviewed in San Francisco 82% had been physically assaulted, 83% had been threatened with a weapon, and 68% had been raped while prostituting.

A Korean woman who was overwhelmed with credit card debt was led to believe by traffickers that if she traveled to the United States, she could work in the entertainment industry, quickly earn a lot of money, and then return home. A college student from a poor family who wanted to impress her new friends, You-Mi quickly generated $40,000 in debt. Naively believing traffickers who told her she would pour drinks as a hostess (but would not have to sell sex) for $10,000 a month in Los Angeles Korea Town, she was supplied a fake passport, and once in the United States and under the control of traffickers, she was moved between Los Angeles and San Francisco in massage parlors controlled by Korean organized criminals. In 2006 she prostituted fifteen hours a day at massage brothels with blacked-out windows and double metal security doors. You-Mi was allowed outside only if escorted by cabbies that were paid by the traffickers. Unable to speak more than a few basic sentences in English, she was unaware of where she was and dependent on her captors for food and shelter. You-Mi was isolated, terrorized, and prostituted in a massage brothel under prisonlike conditions of debt bondage. After a long struggle, she was finally recognized as a victim of trafficking.[17]

Regardless of the nature of the freely made, deceived, tricked, or coerced decision a woman makes to move to another country for prostitution, after she has actually moved she will be "recruited, transported and controlled by organized crime networks," Sullivan[18] wrote about Australian prostitution. The same is true in the United States. There is an evolving public awareness about the human rights violations of sex trafficking in the United States. This awareness and public outrage about trafficking, however, exists primarily for victims who have been transported across international borders.

Domestic trafficking—the sale of women in prostitution from poorer to more prosperous sex markets within a single country—can be as devastating for the women as international trafficking. This is true in countries where there is assumed to be significant wealth such as New Zealand and the United States as well as countries where there is more visible poverty such as India and Zambia.

> The apparently civilized transaction between elite prostitutes and their clients in luxury hotels is underpinned by the same logic that underpins the forcible sale of girls in a Bangladeshi brothel. This logic is premised on a value system that grades girls and women—and sometimes men and boys—according to their sexual value. (p. 247)[4]

Wherever there is a market, and wherever they can wrest control from other gangs or from local pimps, organized criminals run prostitution rings both inside countries and across international borders. Traffickers are businessmen who pay close attention to men's demand for prostitution. They obtain the women and girls who supply that demand wherever women are vulnerable because of economic factors and cultural practices that devalue women.

Although physical violence may or may not occur, in all cases of trafficking for prostitution, psychosocial coercion happens in contexts of sex and race inequality and under conditions of poverty or financial stress, and often a history of childhood abuse or neglect. Women may legally and seemingly voluntarily migrate from a poorer to a wealthier part of the world, for example with a work permit and the promise of a good job from a friend who turns out to be a trafficker. Once she has migrated, away from home and community support, she is dependent on traffickers and their networks. At that point the pimp/trafficker's psychological and physical coercion expands while her options for escape rapidly shrink.

Prostitution is the destination point for sex trafficking. Legal prostitution is a major contributing factor to the human rights violations of sex trafficking. Where prostitution is legal, states in effect say to the world: we accept the selling of women for sex; we consider pimps and traffickers to be sex entrepreneurs rather than organized criminals; we consider men who buy women for sex to be consumers of sexual services rather than predators. That same message is sent when governments look away from prostitution in their jurisdictions, refusing to enforce existing laws against buying and prostituting women.

There is widespread misunderstanding about the legal and conceptual differences between prostitution and trafficking.[19] Sex trafficking is not about transportation; rather, it involves coercive control. Any prostitution that involves third-party control or exploitation or pimping meets the definition of human trafficking. What is relevant is how she is abused in prostitution, the control of, sale and sexual use of a human being. Women who are used as maids or field workers are used in prostitution-like activities by traffickers. Women and girls are especially vulnerable to sexual abuse when used in domestic servitude.[20] An International Labor Organization (ILO) assessment in El Salvador found that two-thirds of girls in domestic service had been physically or psychologically abused, and many had also been sexually abused. The girls lived in constant fear of sexual advances from their employers, by the adult men in the extended family, the stronger children, or by other male workers of the household. When the girls became pregnant, they were often abandoned to the streets.[21] Not surprisingly, another ILO study on the sexual exploitation of Tanzanian girls found that many prostituted children were evicted by employers who had sexually abused them while they were working as domestic servants.[22]

PSYCHOLOGICAL CONSEQUENCES OF HUMAN TRAFFICKING AND PROSTITUTION

Exposure to violent and nonviolent forms of abuse. Traffickers frequently use a combination of nonviolent and violent forms of coercion like those used by perpetrators of domestic violence, torture, and cults.[2] Like abusive partners, traffickers alternate acts of kindness with unexpected abuse and degradation. Like cult leaders, traffickers isolate people and force victims to witness abuses perpetrated on others. Schwartz, Williams, and Farley[23] illustrate through case examples how traffickers and pimps use the same methods of mind control as those used by torturers to keep their victims under control including social isolation, sensory deprivation, deliberately induced exhaustion and physical debilitation, threats to self and family, occasional reprieves and indulgences, pimps and traffickers posturing as omnipotent, degradation, enforcing capricious rules, the deliberate creation of dissociated parts of the self who willingly prostitute, drugging and forced addiction, and forced pregnancy. Violent forms of abuse include physical and sexual abuse, often equivalent to the experiences of survivors of torture in the context of war. The Nicaraguan woman referred to earlier described how her trafficker deliberately broke one of her leg bones in order to prevent her escape. Another trafficked woman described how she was forced to service as many as thirty-five sex buyers a day, which kept her in a permanent state of exhaustion. "I couldn't even fully open my eyes sometimes," she stated. "I couldn't think, and sometimes I forgot where I was."

Related mental health problems. A nine-country study of prostitution found that 68% of women, men, and transgendered people in prostitution had post-traumatic stress disorder (PTSD), a prevalence that is comparable to that among battered or raped women seeking help and survivors of state-sponsored torture.[1] Across widely varying cultures on five continents the traumatic consequences of prostitution were similar whether prostitution was legal, tolerated, or illegal. Hossain and colleagues[24] interviewed 204 trafficked girls and women in seven European countries and found that 77% met criteria for PTSD with high comorbidity rates for depression and anxiety.

As a result of multiple experiences of betrayal by family, community, and governmental agencies, trafficking survivors and prostituted women have difficulties in establishing trusting relationships, which in turn presents many challenges for health care professionals. Loss of control can leave survivors of trauma feeling powerless and helpless.[25] Human trafficking victims lose control of many parts of their lives and may experience long-term relational consequences as a result. Treating this patient population poses unique challenges, as the therapy relationship will inevitably create a power differential.[26] Therefore, in cases of human trafficking and prostitution, therapists will also need to consider frameworks that address the relational abuses and lifetime social injustices that these populations have faced.

HUMAN TRAFFICKING ISSUES AND DEBATES

Victims of human trafficking and men who buy sex.
Trafficking victims have shared testimony regarding the ways in which traffickers used them as products to be bought, sold, and discarded. Dis-

cussing the torture and abuse used by traffickers, Sarson and MacDonald[28] described one young girl's testimony in which she told how her traffickers "rented her out" to local pedophiles. They also explain how traffickers, like pimps, exploit women and children to meet men's sexual needs.

Farley, Macleod, Anderson, and Golding's[27] interviews with sex buyers illustrate how men remove women's humanity in prostitution. Buying a woman in prostitution gives men the power to turn women into a living version of his masturbation fantasy. He removes those qualities that define her as an individual, and for him she becomes sexualized body parts. She then acts the part of the thing he wants her to be. For example, a sex buyer said prostitution was like "renting an organ for ten minutes." Another man said, "I use them like I might use any other amenity, a restaurant, or a public convenience."

As shocking as these observations may sound to those who have an idealized notion of prostitution, the buyers' descriptions closely match women's descriptions of prostitution. Prostituted women explain how it feels to be treated like a rented organ. "It is internally damaging. You become in your own mind what these people do and say with you. You wonder how could you let yourself do this and why do these people want to do this to you."[29] Women who prostitute have described it as "paid rape" and "voluntary slavery," and women exploited by traffickers use similar words. Prostitution is sexual harassment, sexual exploitation, and sometimes torture. A sex buyer's payment does not erase what we know about acts of sexual violence and rape.

A common myth is that sex buyers are harmless when it comes to prostitution. However, in the case of trafficking for the purpose of prostitution, the same sex buyers who purchase sex from allegedly "voluntary" prostitutes are also purchasing sex from trafficked women. One sex buyer said, "You get what you pay for without the 'no.'" Non-prostituting women have the right to say "no" and are legally protected from sexual harassment and sexual exploitation. But tolerating sexual abuse is the job description for prostitution and sex trafficking. Research shows that a majority of sex buyers refuse condoms, pay high prices to desperately poor women to not use condoms, or rape women without condoms.[30-31] In research comparing frequent and infrequent sex buyers, the men who most frequently used women in prostitution were also those most likely to have committed sexually aggressive acts against non-prostituting women.[32] In interviews with more than a hundred U.K. sex buyers, although a majority believed that most women have been lured, tricked, or trafficked into prostitution, they bought them anyway.[27]

Several studies have explored beliefs that sex buyers have about women's motivation to prostitute. A sex buyer stated, "All prostitutes are exploited. However, they also have good incomes." Some people have made the decision that it is reasonable to expect certain women to have sex with up to ten sex buyers a day in order to survive.[33] Women who have been trafficked for prostitution tell us that they perform sex acts with as many as twenty to thirty sex buyers a day. Those women most often are poor and most often are racially marginalized. A neocolonial economic perspective is enshrined in a Canadian prostitution tourist's comment about women in Thai prostitution, who stated, "These girls gotta eat, don't they? I'm putting bread on their plate. I'm making a contribution. They'd starve to death unless they whored." The sex buyer's sympathetic attitude avoids the question: Do all women have the right to live without the sexual harassment or sexual exploitation of prostitution—or is that right reserved only for those who have sex, race, or class privilege?

Human trafficking and the legalization of prostitution. All women should have the right to survive without prostituting and to live in environments that condemn the practices that make human trafficking possible. However, even when extensive research data shows that the women in prostitution are victims of pimps and traffickers, in cities where prostitution is illegal, the women themselves are the ones who are arrested, abused, and persecuted by local authorities. On the other end of the spectrum, in cities where prostitution is legal or decriminalized, prostituted women are left to fend for themselves against abusive pimps and traffickers, who are frequently networked with organized crime.

There is extensive evidence about the negative consequences of legal and decriminalized prostitution. Legal prostitution specifies where prostitution is permitted to take place, including municipal tolerance zones or red-light zones. Decriminalized prostitution removes all laws against pimping, pandering, and buying women in prostitution, and decriminalizes the person who is prostituted. Legal and decriminalized prostitution are similar in their effects. Pimp-like, the state collects taxes from legal prostitution. In decriminalized regimes, the old-fashioned pimps become legitimized entrepreneurs.[19]

In 2003, New Zealand passed a law that decriminalized selling sex, buying sex, and pimping. The New Zealand Prostitution Law Review Committee reported what happened after prostitution was decriminalized.[34] Seven years after the New Zealand law was passed, battles were still being waged about whose neighborhood prostitution would be zoned into. No one wanted prostitution next door. Prostitution was zoned into the neighborhoods of people who could not afford the legal fees to prevent it. The regulation of prostitution by zoning is a physical manifestation of the same social/psychological stigma that decriminalization advocates allegedly want to avoid. Whether in Turkish genelevs (walled-off multi-unit brothel complexes) or in Nevada brothels (ringed with barbed wire or electric fencing), women in state-zoned prostitution are physically isolated and socially rejected by the rest of society, and therefore more vulnerable to the crimes committed against them. The social stigma of prostitution persisted five years after decriminalization in New Zealand, according to the Law Review Committee. Moreover, after decriminalization in New Zealand, violence and sexual abuse in prostitution continued as before. According to the New Zealand Prostitution Law Review Committee, "The majority of sex workers felt that the law could do little about violence that occurred."[34] They found that after the law was passed, 35% of women in prostitution reported they were still coerced by sex buyers. Women prostituted in massage parlors who were under the control of pimps reported the highest rate of coercion. Five years after legally defining prostitution as work, the New Zealand law was unable to change the exploitive quasi-contractual arrangements that existed before prostitution was decriminalized. Most people in prostitution (both indoor and street) continued to mistrust police and did not report crimes committed against them.

Legalizing prostitution does not decrease violence against women in prostitution. For example, in Australia, where prostitution is legal in some provinces, the Australian Occupational and Safety Codes recommend classes in hostage negotiation skills for those in legal prostitution, reflecting the sex buyers' violence.[18] Human trafficking is also most prevalent wherever prostitution is legal or decriminalized. When prostitution is legal, pimps operate with impunity and sex buyers are welcomed. Trafficking of children has increased in New Zealand since decriminalization, especially the trafficking of ethnic minority Maori children. Reflecting increased organized crime since decriminalization, Auckland gangs have waged turf wars over control of prostitution. Since decriminalization, street prostitution has spiraled out of control, especially in New Zealand's largest city, Auckland. A 200% to 400% increase in street prostitution has been reported. After legalization of prostitution in Victoria, Australia, the number of legal brothels doubled. But the greatest expansion was in illegal prostitution. In one year there was a 300% increase in illegal brothels. Staff at a New Zealand agency providing prostitution exit strategies observed that there were twice as many sex buyers in the street since decriminalization. The sex buyers were more aggressive after prostitution was decriminalized, soliciting the agency's women staff members. Similar post-decriminalization increased aggression against women has been noted among Australian sex buyers.[19]

Human trafficking, prostitution and the concept of choice. The Dutch, and since then others, have posited essential differences between human trafficking and prostitution, but there is little evidence for this ideological viewpoint.[35] The arguments for legalizing prostitution depend on the strength of two arguments: that prostitution is a choice for those in it and that the harms of prostitution are decreased if it is legalized. However, prostitution and human trafficking overlap in many ways, strongly suggesting that the existence of one contributes to the proliferation of the other.

A review of many peer-reviewed studies and reports from agencies who offer direct services to those in prostitution and from policy experts reveals that only a tiny percentage of all women in prostitution are in prostitution after making a genuine choice between viable alternatives.[36] For most, prostitution is not a freely made choice, because the conditions that would permit genuine choice are not present: physical safety, equal power with buyers, and real alternatives. The very few who do choose prostitution are privileged by class or race or education. They usually have options for escape. Most women in prostitution do not have viable alternatives. They are coerced into prostitution by sex inequality, race/ethnic inequality, and economic inequality.

There is no evidence for the theory that legalization decreases the harm of prostitution. In fact, legalization increases trafficking, increases prostitution of children, and increases sex buyers' demands for cheaper or "unrestricted" sex acts.[37,18] Whether prostitution is legal or illegal, research shows that the poorer she is, and the longer she has been in prostitution, the more likely a woman is to experience violence.[38] The emotional consequences of prostitution are the same whether prostitution is legal or illegal, and whether it happens in a brothel, a strip club, a massage parlor, or on the street.[1]

Some governmental and some international laws address the intimate relationship between prostitution and trafficking. A United Nations document views trafficked women as victims, not criminals. The Palermo Protocol[39] declares that consent is irrelevant to whether or not trafficking has occurred. It encourages countries to develop legislative responses to men's demand for prostitution and establishes a method of international judicial cooperation that would permit prosecution of traffickers and organized criminals. The Palermo Protocol also addresses a range of other forms of sexual exploitation, including pornography.[40]

A decade ago, Sweden named prostitution as a form of violence against women that fosters inequality.[41] As a result Sweden criminalized sex buyers but decriminalized the person in prostitution. Iceland, Norway, and South Korea have now passed similar laws, with the United Kingdom passing legislation that moves in a similar direction, and Israel considering such a bill in 2011.

The Swedish government's evaluation of the effects of their law on prostitution shows that in a decade since the law was passed, street prostitution in Sweden decreased by 50%, although it has increased in neighboring countries during that same time.[42] There is no evidence that women have moved from street to indoor prostitution in Sweden. The intimate relationship between prostitution and trafficking is highlighted when buyers are criminalized. Sweden now has the fewest trafficked women in the European Union. The law interferes with the international business of pimping and the practice of buying sex. While there was initial resistance to the Swedish law, now more than 70% of the public support it. Women exiting prostitution use state-provided exit services. Not surprisingly, the report points out that the women out of prostitution favor the law, while women who are still exploited in prostitution are against the ban.

Whether or not it is legal, prostitution is extremely harmful for women. Women in prostitution have the highest rates of rape and homicide of any group of women ever studied.[43-44] They are regularly physically assaulted and verbally abused, whether they prostitute on the street or in massage parlors, brothels, or hotels. Sexual violence and physical assault are the norm for women in legal as well as illegal prostitution, and among trafficked women. A study of women in legal Dutch prostitution found that 60% of the women were physically assaulted, 70% were threatened with physical assault, 40% experienced sexual violence, and 40% had been coerced into legal prostitution.[38] The dilemma is not that there is no legal redress for coercion, physical assault, and rape in illegal prostitution. There are laws against those forms of violence. The dilemma is that once in prostitution, women cannot avoid sexual harassment, sexual exploitation, rape, and acts that are the equivalent of torture and that frequently meet U.S. and international definitions of human trafficking.

CONCLUDING THOUGHTS

With this data in mind, real differences between the experiences of women in prostitution and those who are trafficked are indistinguishable. The overlap between prostitution and human trafficking is becoming increasingly difficult to ignore. One study found that 89% of those in prostitution in nine countries on five continents desire to escape from prostitution.[1] In order to escape they need housing, education, jobs that provide a sustainable income, health care, and emotional support. We should all be working on providing women with alternatives to prostitution. Societies that fail to condemn the pimps, johns, and traffickers who promote prostitution, and who continue to view prostitution as a choice and an industry, are contributing to the proliferation of the abuses that make human trafficking possible.

REFERENCES

1. Farley, M., Cotton, A., Lynne, J., Zumbeck, S., Spiwak, F., Reyes, M.E., Alvarez, D., & Sezgin, U. (2003). Prostitution and trafficking in 9 countries: Update on violence and posttraumatic stress disorder. *Journal of Trauma Practice* 2(3/4), 33–74.
2. Hopper, E., & Hidalgo, J. (2006). Invisible chains: Psychological coercion of human trafficking victims. *Intercultural Human Rights Review, 1*, 185–209.

3. Stark, C., & Hodgson, C. (2003). Sister oppressions: A comparison of wife beating and prostitution. In M. Farley (Ed.), _Prostitution, trafficking and traumatic stress._ New York: Routledge.

4. Brown, L. (2000). _Sex slaves: The trafficking of women in Asia._ London: Virago.

5. Ugarte, M.B., Zarate, L., & Farley, M. (2003). Prostitution and trafficking of women and children from Mexico to the United States. In M. Farley (Ed.), _Prostitution, trafficking and traumatic stress._ New York: Routledge.

6. Ribando, C. (2005). _Trafficking in persons in Latin America and the Caribbean. Congressional Research Service._ (CRS Report No. RL33200). Washington, D.C.: Library of Congress. Retrieved from: www.oas.org/atip/Latin%20America/CRS%20 Dec%202005.pdf

7. Ribando Selke, C. (2009). _Trafficking in persons in Latin America and the Caribbean._ (CRS Report No. RL33200). Washington, D.C.: Library of Congress. Retrieved from http://www.fas.org/sgp/crs/row/RL33200.pdf

8. Almasmari, H. (2005). Poverty + Tourism = Prostitution. _Yemen Times_ 14 (892) Nov 7–9, 2005. Retrieved January 8, 2006 from http://yementimes.com/article. shtml?i=892&p=report&a=2

9. Bayhi-Gennaro, J. (2008). _Domestic minor sex trafficking: Baton Rouge/New Orleans, Louisiana._ Shared Hope International. PIP Printing: Arlington, VA. Retrieved from http://www.sharedhope.org/Portals/0/Documents/BatonRouge-NewOrleans_PrinterFriendly.pdf

10. Basu, S. (2005). The challenges of and potential solutions to the problem of the trafficking of women and children. In. K. Holt Barret & W.H. George (Eds.), _Race, culture, psychology, and law,_ (pp. 225–236). Thousand Oaks, CA: Sage Publications.

11. Sever, C., & Narayanaswamy, L. (2006). _Gender and trade: Supporting resources collection._ Sussex, UK: Institute of Development Studies. Retrieved from http://www.bridge.ids.ac.uk/reports/CEP-Trade-SRC.pdf

12. Farley, M., Lynne, J., & Cotton, A.J. (2005). Prostitution in Vancouver: Violence and the colonization of First Nations women. _Transcultural Psychiatry, 42_(2), 242–271.

13. Heyzer, N. (2003, April). Violence against women around the world. _The Zontian,_ 2002–2004 Biennial Issue Four.

14. Krug, E.G., Dahlberg, L.L., Mercy, J.A., Zwi, A.B., & Lozano, R. (Eds.) (2002). _World report on violence and health._ Geneva: World Health Organization. Retrieved from http://whqlibdoc.who.int/publications/2002/9241545615_eng.pdf

15. Coomaraswamy, R. (2002, January). _Integration of the human rights of women and the gender perspective: Violence against women._ Report of the Special Rapporteur on violence against women, its causes and consequences. E/CN.4/2002/93.

16. Farley, M., & Barkan, H. (1998). Prostitution, violence against women, and posttraumatic stress disorder. _Women & Health, 27_(3), 37–49.

17. May, M. (2006, October 6) San Francisco is a major center for international crime networks that smuggle and enslave. _San Francisco Chronicle._ Retrieved from http://www.sfgate.com/cgibin/article.cgi?f=/c/a/2006/10/06/MNGR1L-GUQ41.DTL&hw=meredith+may+sex+slaves&sn=005&sc=497. Cited in Farley, M. (2007). _Prostitution and trafficking in Nevada: Making the connections._ San Francisco: Prostitution Research & Education.

18. Sullivan, M.L. (2007). *Making sex work: A failed experiment with legalized prostitution.* North Melbourne: Spinifex.
19. Farley, M. (2009) Theory versus reality: Commentary on four articles about trafficking for prostitution. *Women's Studies International Forum, 32*(4), 311–315.
20. Kane, J. (2004). *Helping hands or shackled lives? Understanding child domestic labor and responses to it.* Geneva: International Labor Organization.
21. Godoy, O. (2002). *El Salvador: Trabajo infantil doméstico: Una evaluación rápida.* [El Salvador: Child domestic labor: A rapid evaluation]. Organización Internacional del Trabajo. Programa Internacional Para la Erradicación del Trabajo Infantil. Retrieved from http://white.oit.org.pe/ipec/documentos/elsal_tid.pdf
22. Kamala, E., Lusinde, E., Millinga, J., & Mwaitula, J. (2001). *Tanzania children in prostitution: A rapid assessment.* Geneva: International Labor Organization. Retrieved from http://www.childtrafficking.com/Docs/ilo_2001__child_prostitutio.pdf
23. Schwartz, H., Williams, J., & Farley, M. (2007). Pimp subjugation of women by mind control. In M. Farley (Ed.), *Prostitution and trafficking in Nevada: Making the connections.* (pp. 49–84) San Francisco: Prostitution Research & Education.
24. Hossain, M., Zimmerman, C., Abas, M., Light, M., & Watts, C. (2010). The relationship of trauma to mental disorders among trafficked and sexually exploited girls and women. *American Journal of Public Health, 100*(12), 2442–2449.
25. Herman, J.L. (1997). *Trauma and recovery: The aftermath of violence from domestic abuse to political terror.* New York: Basic Books.
26. Surrey, J. (1997). What do you mean by mutuality in therapy? In J. Jordan (Ed.), *Women's growth in diversity.* (pp. 42–49) New York: The Guilford Press.
27. Farley, M., Macleod, J., Anderson, L., & Golding, J. M. (2011, March 28). Attitudes and social characteristics of men who buy sex in Scotland. *Psychological Trauma: Theory, Research, Practice, and Policy.* Advance online publication. doi: 10.1037/a0022645
28. Sarson, J., & MacDonald, L. (2004, March). The many faces of torture. *Slide presentation at the 48th Session of the Commission on the Status of Women,* New York: United Nations.
29. Farley, M. (2003). Prostitution and the invisibility of harm. *Women & Therapy. 26*(3/4), 247–280.
30. Parker, R.G., Easton, D., & Klein, C. (2000). Structural barriers and facilitators in HIV prevention: A review of international research. *AIDS, 14,* S22–S32.
31. Wojcicki, J.M., & Malala, J. (2001) Condom use, power and HIV/AIDS risk: Sexworkers bargain for survival in Hillbrow/Joubert Park/Berea, Johannesburg. *Social Science & Medicine, 53,* 99–121.
32. Farley, M., Macleod, J., Anderson, L., & Golding, J. (in press). Attitudes and social characteristics of men who buy sex in Scotland. *Psychological Trauma: Theory, Research, Practice, and Policy.*
33. Cauduro, A., Di Nicola, A., Fonio, C., Nuvoloni, A., & Ruspini, P. (2009). Innocent when you dream: Clients and trafficked women in Italy. In Di Nicola, A., A. Cauduro, M. Lombardi, & P. Ruspini (Eds.). *Prostitution and human trafficking: Focus on clients.* (pp. 23–30). New York: Springer.
34. New Zealand Government. (2008). *Report of the Prostitution Law Review Committee on the Operation of the Prostitution Reform Act 2003.* (ISBN 978-0-478-29052-7). Wellington, New Zealand: Ministry of Justice.

35. Leidholdt, D.A. (2003), Prostitution and trafficking in women: An intimate relationship. In M. Farley (Ed.), *Prostitution, trafficking and traumatic stress*. New York: Routledge.

36. Farley, M. (2008) *Prostitution's hierarchy of coercion and coercion*. Graphic retrieved from http://www.prostitutionresearch.com/ProstitutionCoercionHierarchy.pdf

37. Raymond, J.G. (2003). Ten reasons for not legalizing prostitution and a response to the demand for prostitution. In M. Farley (Ed.), *Prostitution, trafficking, and traumatic stress*. (pp. 315–332). New York: Routledge. Also available at Coalition against Trafficking in Women website. http://www.catwinternational.org

38. Vanwesenbeeck, I. (1994) *Prostitutes' well-being and risk*. Amsterdam: VU University Press.

39. United Nations (2000) *Protocol to Prevent, Suppress and Punish Trafficking in Persons, Especially Women and Children, Supplementing the United Nations Convention Against Transnational Organized Crime*. Retrieved from http://www.uncjin.org/Documents/Conventions/dcatoc/final_documents_2/convention_%20traff_eng.pdf

40. Raymond, J.G. (2002). The New U.N. Trafficking Protocol. *Women's Studies International Forum 25*, 491–502.

41. Government Offices of Sweden. (1999). *Chapter 6: On sexual crimes*. (pp. 24–28). In the Swedish Penal Code. Sweden: Ministry of Justice. Retrieved from http://www.sweden.gov.se/content/1/c6/02/77/77/cb79a8a3.pdf

42. Government Offices of Sweden. (2010). *Against prostitution and human trafficking for sexual purposes*. Sweden: Ministry of Integration and Gender Equality. Retrieved from http://www.sweden.gov.se/sb/d/13420/a/151488

43. Hunter, S.K. (1993). Prostitution is cruelty and abuse to women and children. *Michigan Journal of Gender and Law*, 1, 1–14.

44. Potterat, J.J., Brewer, D.D., Muth, S.Q., Rothenberg, R.B., Woodhouse, D.E., Muth, J.B., Stites, H.K., & Brody, W. (2004). Mortality in a long-term open cohort of prostitute women. *American Journal of Epidemiology. 159*(8), 778–785.

3

Sexual Assault by Strangers and Nonintimate Associates

Kelly Cue Davis

OVERVIEW

Sexual contact that occurs without the consent of all parties involved has been broadly termed *sexual assault*. Anyone—men and women, boys and girls of all ages and backgrounds—can become a victim of a sexual assault. The present chapter focuses on sexual assaults that are committed by either someone the victim does not know (a stranger) or someone the victim knows but is not involved in an intimate relationship with, such as a friend, neighbor, or coworker. (A later chapter describes characteristics of sexual assaults that occur within dating and marital relationships.) Additionally, this chapter does not cover sexual assault incidents that may have occurred during childhood. This chapter details definitions of various forms of sexual assault, provides sexual assault prevalence rates, describes the dynamics of sexual assault situations, and delineates the potential effects of sexual assault on the victim.

DEFINITIONS

A variety of terms have been used to describe nonconsensual sexual behavior, including *sexual assault, sexual violence, sexual aggression, sexual abuse, sexual coercion, attempted rape,* and *completed rape.* The definitions for each of these terms may vary slightly from source to source. The terms are often used in a general way and are not usually reflective of specific legal terminology (which varies from jurisdiction to jurisdiction). Definitions for the terms used in this chapter are provided below.

As noted earlier, *sexual assault* refers to any type of sexual contact that is not consented to by one of the persons involved. This term thus has a fairly broad definition that includes a wide scope of behaviors ranging from nonconsensual sexual kissing or touching to nonconsensual oral, anal, or vaginal sex.[1] According to the Centers for Disease Control (CDC), the term *rape* refers to a completed nonconsensual sex act in which the perpetrator (person committing the rape) penetrates the victim's vagina, anus, or mouth with a penis, hand, finger, or other object.[2] In an *attempted rape*, the perpetrator attempts, but does not complete, the nonconsensual sex act. Finally, *nonconsensual* or *abusive sexual contact* is defined by the CDC as "intentional touching, either directly or through the clothing, of the genitalia, anus, groin, breast, inner thigh, or buttocks of any person without his or her consent, or of a person who is unable to consent or refuse" (p. 9).[2]

Consent generally means that at the time of the sexual activity, there were actual words or actions that indicated freely given agreement to have that sexual activity. Thus, if one's "agreement" is forced, coerced, or pressured, this is not considered "consent" because the agreement was not freely given.

> *"How can you not take 'no' for an answer? If they don't take 'no' for an answer, then they're raping you."*
>
> —Twenty-five-year-old African American woman

Moreover, the ability to give consent may be affected by a number of factors, including age (being a minor), temporary or permanent physical or mental disability, drug or alcohol intoxication (self-induced or forced), or language barriers. For example, a person who has passed out due to alcohol intoxication is not capable of providing consent to sexual intercourse or other sexual activity. Importantly, a lack of resistance to the assault (such as fighting back) does not indicate that the person consented to the sexual activity.

SEXUAL ASSAULT PREVALENCE

Sexual assault occurs all over the world and is present in all social, economic, ethnic, racial, religious, and age groups. While both men and women can be victimized by sexual assault, women are statistically more likely than men to experience such an incident. For example, according to the National Violence Against Women Survey (NVAWS), over three hundred thousand women and almost ninety-three thousand men are raped in the United States each year.[3] One of every six women and one in thirty-three men in the United States has been raped at some time in her or his life, with many of these individuals experiencing more than one rape incident over their lifetimes. Approximately 80% of women experience sexual assault, including unwanted verbal or physical coercion, while approximately 25% of women experience rape or attempted rape.[4] Another study found that 22% of women and 3.8% of men reported having experienced sexual assault as an adult.[5] Of the sexual assault victims in the 2006 National Crime Victimization Survey (NCVS), 89.3% were female compared with 10.7% male.[6] While both women and men can perpetrate sexual assault, men are statistically more likely than women to be sexual assault perpetrators. The NVAWS found that almost all of the female victims (99.6%) and the vast majority of male victims (85.2%) were raped by men.[3] Thus, the most typical sexual assault scenario involves a female victim and a male perpetrator.

Research indicates that most sexual assaults are committed by someone known to the victim, also known as *acquaintance rape*. The NCVS found that approximately 38% of the sexual assaults reported in 2006 were perpetrated by strangers, while 62% were perpetrated by someone known to the victim.[6] Rapes committed by strangers occurred in only 16.7% of the female victim cases and 22.8% of the male victim cases reported in the NVAWS. The NCVS also found that 58% of male victims and 64% of female victims knew their offender.[7] Female victims are more likely to be raped by a current or former intimate partner (often referred to as *date rape* or *marital rape*) than are male victims, who are more likely to be raped by acquaintances.[8]

SOCIOCULTURAL FACTORS

Age. Sexual assault is more likely to occur at younger ages. For example, the NVAWS found that more than half of female victims and almost three-fourths of male victims were raped before the age of eighteen. Young women between the ages of sixteen and twenty-four experience rape four times as much as other women.[9] Additionally, one study estimated that up to 25% of college women will be sexually assaulted *during their college-age years*.[10] Research also indicates that individuals who are sexually assaulted at a younger age are at a greater risk of being sexually revictimized later in life.[11]

"Looking back on it, I was so young when it happened. He really took advantage of that."

—Twenty-eight-year-old Latina woman

Although the majority of sexual assaults occur to the young, some older adults are also more vulnerable to experiencing a sexual assault. Because of barriers to reporting, it is difficult to gather a reliable estimate of the prevalence of elder sexual abuse.[12] As with other forms of sexual assault, elder sexual abuse may occur at the hands of strangers, acquaintances, family members, or partners. Additionally, vulnerable elder adults may also be assaulted by unrelated care providers and other residents in elder care settings. Most often, elder sexual abuse victims are female, physically frail, and may have dementia or other forms of cognitive impairment, thus increasing their vulnerability to assault.[13]

Race and ethnicity. The NVAWS found that racial/ethnic minority and nonminority women and men had approximately the same rates of experiencing rape (19% versus 17.9% for women; 3.4% versus 2.8% for men). However, when specific racial and ethnic backgrounds were examined, some important differences emerged. American Indian/Alaska Native women were more likely than women from any other group to have been raped during their lifetimes, with 34.1% reporting at least one rape experience. Mixed race women reported the second highest level of rape victimization (24.4%), followed by African American women (18.8%), non-Hispanic white women (17.9%), Hispanic white women (11.9%), and Asian/Pacific Islander women (6.8%).[3] Additionally, rates of sexual assault disclosure and reporting across different racial and ethnic backgrounds may vary due to cultural concerns and values, fear of racism, language barriers, immigration concerns, and lack of information regarding the U.S. legal system.

Sexual orientation. Although there is limited information about the rates of sexual assault against lesbian, gay, bisexual, and transgender (LGBT) individuals, researchers have estimated that 3% to 7% of LGBT individuals have experienced a bias-related sexual assault by either strangers or acquaintances.[14] Additionally, the rate of bias-related sexual assaults against LGBT individuals appears to be on the rise,[15] even though these incidents frequently go unreported to the legal system because of concerns about sexual orientation–related biases within that system.[14]

Disability. Estimates of sexual assault against individuals with either physical or developmental disabilities vary, but in general it appears that individuals with disabilities are significantly more likely to experience a sexual assault relative to the general population. For example, women with a disability are estimated to experience sexual assault at twice the rate of women without a disability.[16] Moreover, up to 83% of women and 32% of men with a developmental disability suffer sexual assault during their lifetimes.[16] Unfortunately, many of these cases may go undetected due to considerable reporting barriers.

SEXUAL ASSAULT REPORTING

Acquaintance rape is rarely reported to the police, even though many individuals will acknowledge their victimization in anonymous surveys. For example, only 19.1% of women and 12.9% of men reported their rape victimization to the police.[3] In fact, rape victims are statistically less likely to report rapes committed by acquaintances than rapes committed by strangers, perhaps due to concerns that they will not be believed by law enforcement officials or fears of being blamed for the incident. Indeed, fear of their rapist, shame and embarrassment, and not considering their rape a crime were the primary reasons survivors chose not to report their victimization to the police.[3]

> *"I never told anyone about what happened. He was my commanding officer. I thought that no one would believe me. I knew there was no way he would ever be punished for what he did to me."*
>
> —Sixty-five-year-old Caucasian woman

Even when reported to the police, only 37% of rapes resulted in criminal prosecution. When extrapolated to all women who reported being raped since the age of eighteen, only 7.8% of rapists were prosecuted, 3.3% were convicted of a crime, and 2.2% of rapists were ultimately incarcerated. In sum, the vast majority of sexual assaults and rape incidents in the United States each year go unreported, uninvestigated, unprosecuted, and unpunished.

SEXUAL ASSAULT DYNAMICS

Although every sexual assault situation is different, many sexual assaults have certain characteristics in common. For example, the majority of sexual assaults occur in private settings like a home or car rather than a public setting,[3] with the bulk of these assaults occurring at night. For both male and female victims, the majority of rape incidents involve one perpetrator.[3] That noted, assaults involving more than one perpetrator ("gang rapes") often result in more severe outcomes than do individual assaults.[17]

Perpetrator tactics. Sexual assault perpetrators may use a variety of tactics to try to gain compliance from their victims during the assault, including verbal coercion, threats of physical harm, and actual physical violence. Verbally coercive tactics include the following: telling lies and making false promises, threatening to spread false rumors, engaging in continual verbal pressure, showing displeasure, being critical of the victim, and getting angry.[18] Physical violence can include slapping or hitting, kicking, biting, choking, hitting with an object, beating, and using a weapon.[3]

A perpetrator may use multiple tactics during an assault. For example, one survey of young women aged eighteen to twenty-four who reported experiencing at least one incident of sexual assault found that 61% reported being pressured to have intercourse through either words or actions that did not involve actual threats of physical harm, while 32% reported that the perpetrators threatened to physically harm them.[19] Fifty-seven percent reported that they were physically held down during the assault, while 40% noted that the perpetrator used his larger physical size as a means of intimidation. Twenty-six percent reported being physically injured during the assault. These tactics also vary by perpetrator-victim relationship, in that sexual assaults perpetrated by strangers are typically more likely to involve the use of a weapon and result in physical harm than are assaults perpetrated by known individuals.[20]

Alcohol and drugs. One contributing factor to the occurrence of sexual assault is alcohol. Research has consistently found that a majority (55% to 74%) of acquaintance sexual assault incidents involves alcohol use by male perpetrators, female victims, or both.[21,22] In her extensive review of rape avoidance studies, Dr. Sarah Ullman concluded that completed rapes are more likely when both victim and offender have been drinking than when both are sober.[23] Importantly though, the presence of alcohol in a sexual assault situation does not justify or excuse the assault itself.

Alcohol use might increase the risk of sexual assault through a variety of pathways. Intoxicated victims may be less likely to perceive that they are at risk for sexual assault, and thus may be less likely to take precautionary measures when intoxicated than when sober.[24] Additionally intoxicated victims may be less able to resist an assault effectively, particularly at higher levels of drinking.[25]

> *"We were at a party and had both been drinking. When he said he wanted to get to know me better, we went to one of the rooms to talk. I never really thought something like this would happen. I mean, he seemed like a nice enough guy. I never really felt like I was in danger until it was too late. I was too drunk to stop him."*
>
> —Twenty-two-year-old Caucasian woman

Intoxicated perpetrators may be more likely to use alcohol as an excuse for their actions and may believe that intoxication justifies sexual aggression. They may also be more likely to misperceive their victim's sexual interest and whether consent has been given, particularly if the victim has also been drinking.[26] Finally, some perpetrators may intentionally provide their victims with alcoholic drinks in order to facilitate their sexual access. Alcohol may increase the risk of sexual assault whether consumed voluntarily by the victim or consumed due to deliberate attempts by the perpetrator to incapacitate the victim.

Other drugs may also be used to facilitate the occurrence of sexual assault. In particular Rohypnol and GHB (gamma hydroxybutyrate) have been widely discussed in the media as drugs that may be surreptitiously slipped into a victim's drink to incapacitate the victim. However, other drugs may also increase the occurrence of sexual assault, including marijuana, cocaine, barbiturates, and hallucinogens. One study found that marijuana was the drug most frequently used in rapes that involved the consumption of drugs by the victim, accounting for 73% of the drug-involved assaults.[27] Additionally, gang rapes are more likely than individual rapes to involve drug use by the victim.[17]

THE CONSEQUENCES OF SEXUAL ASSAULT

Sexual assault may adversely affect the physical and mental health of its victims. However, although many survivors of sexual assault experience high levels of distress in response to sexual assault, other survivors appear fairly resilient in the face of experiencing such an assault. This diversity in outcomes may be attributable to personal characteristics of the survivor, his or her level of social support, or the characteristics of the assault itself.[28] In addition to the consequences for the victims, sexual violence can also adversely affect the victim's family and friends, as well as the community as a whole. The next section of this chapter reviews our current understanding of the effects of sexual assault on its victims and their larger communities. Please note, however, that not all individuals will necessarily experience any or all of these consequences. For those that do, their experiences of these effects may range from mild to severe.

Physical and sexual health consequences. Many sexual assault victims experience physical injuries during the assault itself, with female rape victims (31.5%) being about twice as likely as male rape victims (16.1%) to report being physically injured.[3] Of those injured, the vast majority (74%) reported experiencing relatively minor injuries, such as scratches, bruises, or welts. About 14% of those injured suffered a broken bone or dislocated joint, while less than 10% reported cuts and knife wounds, internal injuries, muscle injuries, and/or chipped or broken teeth. Only 36.2% of female rape victims reported that they received medical treatment.[3]

Many victims also experience sexual and reproductive health consequences from sexual assault. According to one study, 50% to 90% of victims experience some form of genital injury from the assault, such as bruising, inflammation, tenderness, abrasions, and lacerations.[29] Additionally, women with a sexual assault history are more likely than women without a sexual assault history to report experiencing severe pain during menstruation, excessive menstrual bleeding, and sexual dysfunction.[30] Between 3% and 20% of victims acquire a sexually transmitted infection through sexual assault involving penetration.[3,31] Among women of reproductive age, approximately 5% of those raped became pregnant from the assault, with more than 32,000 pregnancies resulting from rape each year.[32]

"I'm scared I may have caught something from him. I'm too afraid to get tested."

—Forty-year-old Asian American woman

Psychological and behavior-related health consequences. Sexual assault may lead to numerous psychological and behavioral health problems. While every assault survivor responds differently, common psychological consequences of sexual victimization include fear, depression, anxiety, post-traumatic stress, decreased self-esteem, sleep problems, suicidal and self-harm behaviors, trust issues, and fear of intimacy.[5,33,34] Some of these consequences may be short-term reactions to the assault, while others may result in longer-term effects. That is, for some individuals, these symptoms subside approximately three months after their assault, while for others they may continue until help is received.[5] Although many of these consequences may not rise to the level of a diagnosable psychological disorder, they may still result in clinically significant symptoms for the sexual assault survivor. According to the NVAWS, 33% of female rape victims and 24.2% of male rape victims reported that they received mental health counseling regarding their rape.[3]

"I get afraid of my emotions. I try to tell myself: 'I've put that behind me; I don't think about that now.' But I do think about it—all the time."

—Twenty-five-year-old Caucasian man

Sexual assault may also increase high-risk behaviors that can negatively impact a victim's physical health. For example, survivors of sexual assault are more likely to use and abuse alcohol, cigarettes, illicit drugs, and prescription drugs as a way of coping with the trauma they have experienced.[35] Individuals who have experienced sexual assault may also be more likely to engage in unhealthy diet-related behaviors, including extreme fasting, vomiting, overeating, diet pill abuse, and overutilization of health services.[36]

"Every day when I get home from work, I start to feel depressed. I want to feel good. I want to feel different. So I drink."

—Forty-seven-year-old Caucasian woman

Additionally, research indicates that some survivors of sexual assault are more likely to engage in high-risk sexual behavior. Such behavior can include having multiple sex partners, choosing unhealthy sex partners (such as someone with HIV), not negotiating for or using condoms, or trading sex for money or drugs.[35] Although these behaviors may provide temporary relief to victims struggling to cope with their sexual victimization, they also may ultimately increase their likelihood of experiencing other health problems.

Financial consequences. High rates of sexual assault not only take a toll on victims, but have economic implications as well. One study estimated that in 2003, the costs of rape were approximately $460 million in the United States alone.[37] These costs include medical and mental health care and the costs of lost productivity. The NVAWS found that 19.4% of female and 9.7% of male rape victims lost time from work due to the rape, possibly to cope with the aftermath of the assault, receive medical or mental health treatment, or attend to legal matters.[3] Thus, the sequelae of sexual assault not only affect the survivor and his or her loved ones, but also the greater community.

CONCLUSION

Sexual assault is a significant public health problem in the United States and worldwide. Although certain groups may be more at risk for experiencing a sexual assault, it can happen to anyone regardless of cultural, economic, religious, or social background. In addition to the broader costs to society, sexual assault can have dramatic negative consequences for its victims, including impact on their physical health, their sexual and reproductive health, and their psychological and behavioral health. Despite these harmful effects, survivors of stranger and acquaintance sexual assault can benefit greatly from positive support from others, including friends, family, helping professionals, and other community resources. These paths to recovery are detailed in later chapters.

REFERENCES

1. Abbey, A., Zawacki, T., Buck, P.O., Clinton, A.M., & McAuslan, P. (2001). Alcohol and sexual assault. *Alcohol Research and Health, 25*, 43–51.
2. Basile, K.C., & Saltzman, L.E. (2002). *Sexual violence surveillance: Uniform definitions and recommended data elements*. Atlanta, GA: National Center for Injury Prevention and Control, Centers for Disease Control and Prevention.
3. Tjaden, P., & Thoennes, N. (2006). *Extent, nature, and consequences of rape victimization: Findings from the National Violence Against Women Survey*. (No. 210346). Washington, D.C.: U.S. Department of Justice.
4. Koss, M.P., Gidycz, C.A., & Wisniewski, N. (1987). The scope of rape: Incidence and prevalence of sexual aggression and victimization in a national sample of higher education students. *Journal of Consulting & Clinical Psychology, 55*, 162–170.

5. Elliott, D.M., Mok, D.S., & Briere, J. (2004). Adult sexual assault: Prevalence, symptomatology, and sex difference in the general population. *Journal of Traumatic Stress, 17,* 203–211.

6. U.S. Department of Justice. (2008). *Criminal victimization in the United States, 2006 statistical tables: National Crime Victimization Survey.* (NCJ 223436). Washington, D.C.: U.S. Department of Justice. Retrieved August 1, 2010 from http://bjs.ojp.usdoj.gov/content/pub/pdf/cvus06.pdf

7. Bureau of Justice Statistics. (2008, December). *Bulletin: National Crime Victimization Survey, Criminal Victimization, 2007.* (NCJ 224390). Washington, D.C.: U.S. Department of Justice. Retrieved July 31, 2010 from http://bjs.ojp.usdoj.gov/content/pub/pdf/cv07.pdf

8. Tjaden, P., & Thoennes, N. (2000). *Extent, nature, and consequences of intimate partner violence: Findings from the National Violence Against Women Survey.* (No. 181867). Washington, D.C.: U.S. Department of Justice.

9. Humphrey, S., & Kahn, A. (2000). Fraternities, athletic teams and rape: Importance of identification with a risky group. *Journal of Interpersonal Violence, 15*(12), 1313–1322.

10. Fisher, B.S., Cullen, F.T., & Turner. M.G. (2000). *The sexual victimization of college women.* Washington, D.C.: U.S. Department of Justice. Retrieved August 2, 2010 from http://www.ncjrs.org/pdffiles1/nij/182369.pdf

11. Gidycz, C., Coble, C., Latham, L., & Layman, M. (1993). Sexual assault experience in adulthood and prior victimization experiences. *Psychology of Women Quarterly, 17,* 151–168.

12. Burgess, A.W., Ramsey-Klawsnik, H., & Gregorian, S.B. (2008). Comparing routes of reporting in elder sexual abuse cases. *Journal of Elder Abuse & Neglect, 20,* 336–352.

13. Holt, M.G. (1993). Elder sexual abuse in Britain: Preliminary findings. *Journal of Elder Abuse & Neglect, 5*(2), 63–71.

14. Gentlewarrior, S. (2009). *Culturally competent service provision to lesbian, gay, bisexual and transgender survivors of sexual violence.* Retrieved August 4, 2010 from http://new.vawnet.org/Assoc_Files_VAWnet/AR_LGBTSexualViolence.pdf

15. National Coalition of Anti-Violence Programs (2008). *Anti-lesbian, gay, bi-sexual and transgender violence in 2007.* Retrieved August 1, 2010 from http://www.avp.org/publications/reports/documents/2007HVReportFINAL_002.pdf

16. Elman, R.A. (2005). *Confronting the sexual abuse of women with disabilities.* Retrieved July 31, 2010 from http://new.vawnet.org/Assoc_Files_VAWnet/AR_SVDisability.pdf

17. Ullman, S.E. (1999). A comparison of gang and individual rape incidents. *Violence and Victims, 14,* 123–133.

18. Koss, M.P., Abbey, A., Campbell, R., Cook, S., Norris, J., Testa, M., et al. (2007). Revising the SES: A collaborative process to improve assessment of sexual aggression and victimization. *Psychology of Women Quarterly, 31,* 357–370.

19. Holcombe, E., Manlove, J., & Ikramullah, E. (2008). *Forced sexual intercourse among young adult women.* Child Trends. Retrieved August 2, 2010 from www.childtrends.org

20. Ullman, S.E., & Siegel, J.M. (1993). Victim-offender relationship and sexual assault. *Violence and Victims, 8,* 121–134.

21. Testa, M., & Livingston, J.A. (1999). Qualitative analysis of women's experiences of sexual aggression: Focus on the role of alcohol. *Psychology of Women Quarterly, 23*(3), 573–589.
22. Ullman, S.E., & Brecklin, L.R. (2000). Alcohol and adult sexual assault in a national sample of women. *Journal of Substance Abuse, 12*, 1–16.
23. Ullman, S.E. (2007). A 10-year update of "review and critique of empirical studies of rape avoidance." *Criminal Justice Behavior, 34*(3), 411–429.
24. Davis, K.C., George, W.H., & Norris, J. (2004). Women's responses to unwanted sexual advances: The role of alcohol and inhibition conflict. *Psychology of Women Quarterly, 28*(4), 333–343.
25. Abbey, A., BeShears, R., Clinton-Sherrod, A., & McAuslan, P. (2004). Similarities and differences in women's sexual assault experiences based on tactics used by the perpetrator. *Psychology of Women Quarterly, 28*, 323–333.
26. Abbey, A., McAuslan, P., & Ross, L.T. (1998). Sexual assault perpetration by college men: The role of alcohol, misperception of sexual intent, and sexual beliefs and experiences. *Journal of Social and Clinical Psychology, 17*(2), 167–195.
27. McCauley, J., Ruggiero, K.J., Resnick, H.S., Conoscenti, L.M., & Kilpatrick, D.G. (2009). Forcible, drug-facilitated, and incapacitated rape in relation to substance use problems: Results from a national sample of college women. *Addictive Behaviors, 34*, 458–462.
28. Yuan, N.P., Koss, M.P., & Stone, M. (2006). *The Psychological Consequences of Sexual Trauma.* Retrieved July 20, 2010 from http://new.vawnet.org/Assoc_Files _VAWnet/AR_PsychConsequences.pdf
29. Sommers, M.S. (2007). Defining patterns of genital injury from sexual assault: A review. *Trauma, Violence, & Abuse, 8*, 270–280.
30. Golding, J.M., Wilsnack, S.C., & Learman, L.A. (1998). Prevalence of sexual assault history among women with common gynecologic symptoms. *American Journal of Obstetrics and Gynecology, 179*, 1013–1019.
31. Jenny, C., Hooton, T.M., Bowers, A., Copass, M.K., Krieger, J.N., Hillier, S.L., Kiviat, N., Corey, L., Stamm, W.E., & Holmes, K.K. (1990). Sexually transmitted diseases in victims of rape. *New England Journal of Medicine, 322*, 713–716.
32. Holmes, M., Resnick, H.S., Kilpatrick, D.G., & Best, C.L. (1996). Rape-related pregnancy: Estimates and descriptive characteristics from a national sample of women. *American Journal of Obstetrics and Gynecology, 175*, 320–325.
33. Herman, J.L. (1992). *Trauma and recovery: The aftermath of violence—from domestic abuse to political terror.* New York: Basic Books.
34. Resick, P.A., & Schnicke, M.K. (1993). *Cognitive processing therapy for rape victims: A treatment manual.* Sage Publications: Newbury Park, CA.
35. Martin, S.L., & Macy, R.J. (2009). *Sexual violence against women: Impact on high-risk health behaviors and reproductive health.* Retrieved July 31, 2010 from http:// new.vawnet.org/Assoc_Files_VAWnet/AR_SVReproConsequences.pdf
36. Brener, N.D., McMahon, P.M., Warren, C.W., & Douglas, K.A. (1999). Forced sexual intercourse and associated health-risk behaviors among female college students in the United States. *Journal of Consulting and Clinical Psychology, 67*, 252–259.
37. Max, W., Rice, D.P., Finkelstein, E., Bardwell, R.A., & Leadbetter, S. (2004). The economic toll of intimate partner violence against women in the United States. *Violence & Victims, 19*, 259–272.

4

Marital Rape and Sexual Violation by Intimate Partners

A. Monique Clinton-Sherrod and Jennifer Hardison Walters

Marriages and other romantic relationships are often complex and sprinkled with peaks and valleys; however, few individuals anticipate sexual violence as a possible trauma resulting from their intimate relationship. Romantic relationships are complex by the very nature of intimacy experienced by the two individuals. The sexual aspects of the relationship often are among the most personal and cherished times for partners; however, in some cases what should be healthy and caring expressions of love may take a violent turn, resulting in the sexual violation of a partner perpetrated by another partner. Given that research indicates a woman is raped every six minutes in the United States[1] and one out of every two females will be sexually assaulted in her lifetime,[2] addressing sexual violence in all relationship contexts should be a national priority. While a sizable amount of attention has been focused on stranger, dating, and acquaintance sexual assaults, far less has been placed on sexual assault within long-term, committed relationships. This chapter provides an overview of what is known about sexual assault that occurs between married couples and committed intimate partners.

Throughout this chapter, both *rape* and the more encompassing terms of *sexual assault* and *sexual violence* will be used, primarily based on the original terminology used in the research cited. However, the definitions of these terms will be consistent, with rape referring to the legal definition of nonconsensual or forced anal, oral, or vaginal penetration and sexual assault encompassing a range of contact and noncontact, unwanted sexual behaviors (including rape).[3] The chapter includes information on survivors from both heterosexual and gay and lesbian intimate relationships; however, very limited information is presented outside of married heterosexual relationships due to the fact that there has been so little research on sexual violence within these other types of intimate relationships.

Far too often the label of rape has been narrowly viewed as perpetrated by strangers or, even more recently, acquaintances. Oftentimes intimate partners and spouses are misperceived as the least likely offenders in this form of violence, or sexual perpetration by a spouse or an intimate partner is minimized and viewed as less severe compared with sexual violations perpetrated by nonintimates. A variety of individual, couple, community, and societal factors contribute to the interpretation and understanding of sexual violence that occurs within marriages and intimate relationships; however, many of the views around this issue are grounded in historical context.

LEGAL HISTORY AND THEORETICAL GROUNDING

Historically, the legal definitions of rape have excluded married female spouses. This stems from various English laws, including (1) laws that viewed a woman's contractual obligation to her husband in marriage as including unlimited sexual access for her partner; (2) early views of women as the property of their husbands and arguments that an individual can not be charged for violating his own property; and (3) arguments that viewed the marriage as uniting a couple as one and in such cases, a man cannot violate himself.[4] As recently as the early 1990s, state laws did not consider marital rape a crime and gave exemptions to spouses when it came to rape laws applied to nonspousal offenses. The following excerpt from North Carolina law (in existence until 1993) serves as an example of such a statute: "*A person may not be prosecuted under this article if the victim is the person's legal spouse at the time of the commission of the alleged rape or sexual offense unless the parties are living separate and apart* (North Carolina General Statute 14-27.8)."[5] From early dictates on marital rape, a woman's entry into marriage was deemed a contract that bound her to her husband, including any sexual demands that he might make—in essence, dissolving any prospects of her voicing a marital rape concern because of a lack of legal grounds to do so.

Additional barriers included general social resistance to addressing the issue—prevalent views maintained (and sometimes still do) that sexual violence among intimate partners was a private matter, that assertions of such challenged the institution of marriage, and that women might use false claims of marital rape in vindictive ways.[6,7] With these many barriers to establishing legal avenues for survivors of marital rape, change was slow but eventually occurred through growing feminist advocacy efforts initiated in the early 1970s.[8] Changes have occurred in all states to provide grounds for women to take legal actions against their spouses for rape; however, these laws vary from state to state. Thirty-two states still maintain partial exemptions to legal statutes that essentially legally allow marital rape (and in some cases rape among cohabiting couples) under certain circumstances without consequences (e.g., when a spouse is unable to give consent).[9,10] Challenges remain—the severity of punishment and reporting periods for intimate partner and nonintimate partner rape vary, with nonintimate partner rape often resulting in longer time periods for reporting the crime and more severe sentencing statutes.[11]

The limited societal focus on sexual violence in intimate relationships is also apparent in the conceptual development of the issue from a research perspective. Sexual violation in long-term relationships has yet to be examined with a theoretical model that takes a comprehensive perspective encompassing individual, couple, and societal factors that may impact these traumatic experiences. Feminist theories of intimate partner sexual violence perpetration assert that control and dominance issues are the driving forces for sexual violence. In related perspectives, social constructionist[12] and sex role socialization[13] theories are grounded in traditional roles of power or traditional sex role beliefs. Each of these theories attempts to explain the important underlying forces at play with sexual violence; however, as previously noted, there remains limited exploration of more comprehensive theoretical models that consider a socioecological perspective incorporating the various layers of individual, couple, and societal contributing factors.[11]

PREVALENCE

While the myth that sexual violence is most often perpetrated by a stranger persists, the National Violence Against Women Survey (NVAWS) found that 62% of women who were sexually victimized reported that the offender was a past or present partner.[1] Various factors, such as study methodology, definition used, and underreporting, have influenced abilities to develop an agreed-upon overall prevalence rate of rape and other forms of sexual violence;[14] however, findings from community and college studies suggest a stable estimated prevalence rate of rape at 15% for U.S. women since the 1980s. Findings specifically on married women suggest that 10% to 14% of married women are raped by their husbands in the United States.[15]

In a review on marital rape, Martin et al.[11] summarize the different types of marital sexual violence and related prevalence rates. Their findings conclude that this type of intimate partner violence can take one of two forms based on tactics used by the offender: (1) nonphysical sexual coercion, which is most frequent and involves coercive tactics that stem from social (e.g., traditional beliefs about spousal sexual responsibilities) and interpersonal (e.g., use of resources or power to coerce desired sexual behaviors from a spouse) factors and (2) threatened or forced sex categories that can be further grouped based on extent of co-occurring forms of violence and motives of the offender.[16] Studies involving clinical and national samples have found a range of nonphysical sexual coercion from 36% to 61%.[8,17] Threatened or forced sex has been reported at much lower rates among available samples, with ranges from 4% to 48% among married women.[17,18]

Discrimination does not exist in terms of who may be exposed to sexual violence; however, available data clearly indicates that women are disproportionately affected by rape and other forms of sexual violence.[1] Women have been the focus of the majority of research in this area and often from a heterosexual relationship perspective, with less attention given to men and gay or lesbian individuals who may be victims of intimate partner–perpetrated sexual violence. For men, NVAWS findings indicate that 2.9% of men were raped; however, unlike women, sexual violations were most often by a nonintimate male, with intimate partner–perpetrated violence 18% of the time among raped men.[1] Sexual violence has also been found in the limited number of studies on gay and lesbian intimate relationships and as summarized by Christopher and Pflieger (2007), findings indicate that more than 50% of lesbians and 4.7% of gay men have survived sexual violence. However, in the NVAWS, sixty-seven out of eight thousand gay male respondents reported rape by a male, and there were no reports of adult rape of lesbian women by another woman.[1]

These findings highlight the alarmingly high rates of sexual violence, particularly among women. As indicated, however, these existing data have limitations in how fully they capture the extent of sexual violence. The availability of nationally representative data remains limited to a few studies that vary in terms of methods and definition of sexual violence. As well, research has placed even less focus on subgroups such as gay and lesbian intimate relationships. This concern with prevalence data is also compounded by the fact that many survivors never disclose their experience.[8]

UNDERSTANDING FACTORS ASSOCIATED WITH SEXUAL VIOLENCE IN COUPLES

Sexual violence within intimate relationships has been shown to occur across a diverse range of possible survivors with various ethnic, racial, age, sexual orientation, and physical ability categories; however, studies yield some insights into particular characteristics found at individual, dyadic, and societal levels that are related to these occurrences. We explicitly note that no characteristic or behavior of survivors of sexual violence excuses the offender's behavior, yet empirical research that sheds light on factors that may place an individual at greater risk for victimization or perpetration is important to consider, given its utility for providing guidance on prevention and intervention efforts.

Individual-Level Factors

Empirical findings indicate a high level of overlap of individual factors related to sexual violence offenders in stranger or intimate relationships. They include characteristics such as low social conscience, permissive attitudes, low levels of empathy, hypermasculinity attitudes, beliefs in rape myths, and perpetration of other forms of violence.[19-24] Researchers purport that many of these attitudinal and behavioral factors that lead to a greater disposition to offend often co-occur with prior exposure to violence as a child, whether through experiencing childhood abuse or witnessing abusive behavior between parents or caregivers, which may lay a foundation for later adult behavior in relationships (Dean & Malamuth, 1997). Attempts have been made to categorize individual offenders by the pattern of sexual violence they exhibit within relationships. More recent approaches, however, have attempted to gain better insights into this behavior and in turn improve prevention and intervention efforts by considering the wide range of environmental, couple, and situational factors that may impact sexual violence perpetration.[25]

For survivors of intimate partner sexual violence, violence spans across sociodemographic and geographic boundaries,[26] but a few studies have identified distinct factors that may place some survivors at greater risk. For example, in a community sample of women, low sexual refusal assertiveness, drug use, and prior intimate partner victimization predicted intimate-partner sexual victimization, while heavy episodic drinking and number of sexual partners predicted victimization from nonintimates.[27] Studies assessing demographic characteristics have found that marital rape can occur across the life span, but at least one study found that first-time rapes within a marriage occur most often before the age of twenty-five.[26] Earlier research often reported mixed findings on greater risk for lower versus higher social class backgrounds, often because of a more limited focus on class.[16,26] However, more recent research has highlighted the increased risk and more lethal forms of violence among low-income women, especially when considering compounded effects of race and gender.[28]

Survivors of intimate partner sexual violence are found across all racial and ethnic groups as well; however, African American and American Indian/Alaska Native women have been found to have slightly higher rates compared with white, Latina, and Asian women.[26,29,30] Additionally, immigration status has been found to be associated with risk. This increased risk may stem from several issues, including the continuance of inequitable gender roles inherent in their own cultures, financial barriers to leaving such relationships, and possible challenges with partners who may threaten deportation or use other coercive tactics.[31,32] Other factors found to potentially impact risk for sexual violence include geographic location, with recent findings indicating increased risk for partners in rural areas;[33,34] attachment styles, with anxiously attached partners more frequently reporting consent to unwanted sexual relations (Impett & Peplau, 2002); and physical conditions or related issues such as pregnancy, physical illness, and recent hospital discharge.[35,36]

Relationship Factors

When we discuss sexual violence in the context of intimate relationships, it is also important to consider characteristics of the couple that may increase risk for sexual violence. Many of these associated factors revolve around dynamics that create power issues within the relationship. These may include ill-matched power dynamics such as financial or educational status discrepancies, lack of dating experience for one partner, low relationship satisfaction, large age discrepancies between partners, perceived investment in the relationship, fear of losing a partner, level of commitment, and conflict and ambivalence about the future of the relationship.[11,16,21,29,37]

One of the most consistent predictors of an initial experience of sexual violence in an intimate relationship is the existence of other forms of physical abuse within the relationship.[38-40] For example, findings from the NVAWS indicate that past physical and sexual violence offenses by a partner increase the likelihood of future violence offenses against a partner. An additional commonly reported risk factor for sexual violence and other forms of intimate partner violence is substance use (particularly alcohol) by one or both partners.[42] Findings reveal that the prevalence of alcohol use among married or cohabitating male batterers is higher as compared to appropriate comparison samples.[43]

Social Factors

Social and environmental factors remain key domains as well in the continued perpetration and acceptance of sexual violence within long-term intimate relationships. The peer network of the offender is often a strong influencing factor in the initiation and continuance of violence within an intimate relationship. If an offender's network of friends condone violence against women through their own behavior or attitudes, an offender's behavior is more likely to go unchecked, resulting in increased risk for sexual abuse of a partner.[33,34] Many of the peer network's and individual offender's beliefs and attitudes are shaped by general societal norms regarding sexual violence in general and specifically in intimate relationships. Survivors are faced with societal perceptions that often minimize the severity and need for consequences for perpetrators of sexual violence within long-term relationships.[35,44] This unfortunately can even carry over to survivors' perceptions of sexual offenses as well, with findings indicating that subgroups of survivors may only define their experiences as rape if their partners used force or have a greater likelihood of labeling an incident as rape if the offender was a stranger as compared to an intimate partner.[8,44]

CONSEQUENCES OF SEXUAL VIOLENCE IN INTIMATE RELATIONSHIPS

Survivors of sexual assault in intimate relationships often experience both short- and long-term effects that include psychological and physical impacts. Individual survivors' experiences are unique, and thus there is no one pattern of what aftermath may result; however, research findings lead us to some frequent experiences among survivors.

Psychological Effects

Survivors of rape and other forms of sexual violence have reported a litany of negative psychological outcomes. The outcomes range from post-traumatic stress disorder (PTSD), suicidality and depression, to substance abuse.[45,46] Survivors often report elevated risk for and experience of these types of outcomes. These experiences are often further compounded by increased feelings of anxiety, anger, humiliation, and guilt.[15,16,26] Additionally, survivors are often at greater risk of sexual revictimization and health risk behaviors such as increased tobacco, alcohol, and drug use.[47-51] Psychological effects on survivors can also influence future intimate relationships when leaving the offending partner, including challenges with trust, sexuality, and ultimate goals of initiating and sustaining healthy relationships.[37,52]

Physical Effects

Survivors of sexual violence perpetrated by a cohabitating partner or spouse often experience more severe forms of physical injuries, as compared with stranger or acquaintance sexual violence.[53,54] Physical effects may include vaginal and anal injuries, cuts, bruises, soreness, broken bones, black eyes, stabbings, and torn muscles.[32,46] Many of these physical consequences often result in chronic physical ailments and gynecological problems such as pelvic pain, miscarriages, and increased risk for sexually transmitted diseases.[55,56] Often the gynecological-related health consequences for survivors relate back to power issues with an abusive partner. For example, a survivor's attempts at condom use for risk protection from sexually transmitted diseases or pregnancy may actually result in abusive behavior by a partner and unprotected sexual violence that increase the survivor's health risk.[57] However, as with psychological impacts of sexual violence perpetrated by intimate partners, the physical consequences can also vary along a spectrum of possible impacts based on the survivor's individual experience.

CONCLUSION

This chapter highlights several lingering issues in research on rape and other forms of sexual assault in intimate relationships. A need remains for more research and more consistency in methods, definitions, and procedures in determining the number of survivors who have experienced sexual violence from a partner. It is critical that attention be paid not only to heterosexual females in this determination, but a particular focus is necessary for subgroups such as gay and lesbian couples, men who are survivors, racial/ethnic minorities, and persons from varying socioeconomic backgrounds and geographically diverse areas. Additionally, further efforts are necessary for continued development of theoretical and conceptual models on sexual violence that is inclusive of the many factors that can impact this trauma.

A critical component of combating sexual violence is changing societal views on this issue. A collective effort from researchers, practitioners, and the general public will be required to effectively implement broader community-level strategies that address norms that perpetuate acceptance of sexual violence within intimate relationships, particularly with long-term or married couples. These efforts will be most impactful with continued focus on changing policy and statutes that do not apply equal consequences for nonintimate and intimate sexual violence. Only with such changes will we be able to effectively provide resources for survivors (psychological, physical, and legal) that provide support and not revictimization when help seeking occurs and eventually eliminate the need for such resources.

REFERENCES

1. Tjaden, P., & Thoennes, N. (2006). *Extent, nature and consequences of rape victimization: Findings from the National Violence Against Women Survey.*
2. Sheffield, C.J. (1994). Sexual terrorism. In J. Freeman (Ed.), *Women: A feminist perspective* (pp. 110–127). Mountain View, CA: Mayfield.
3. Koss, M., & Achilles, M. (2008). Restorative justice responses to sexual assault. Retrieved July 27, 2010 from http://www.vawnet.org/Assoc_Files_VAWnet/AR_RestorativeJustice.pdf

4. Barshis, V.G. (1983). The question of marital rape. *Women's Studies International Forum, 6*(4), 383–393.
5. North Carolina General Statute 14–27.8 (1979, c. 682, s. 1; 1987, c. 742; 1993, c. 274.) No defense that victim is spouse of person committing act.
6. Augustine, R. (1991). Marriage: The safe haven for rapists. *Journal of Family Law, 29*, 559–590.
7. Caringella-MacDonald, S. (1988). Parallels and pitfalls: The aftermath of legal reform for sexual assault, marital rape, and domestic violence victims. *Journal of Interpersonal Violence Against Women, 3*, 174–189.
8. Basile, K.C. (1999). Rape by acquiescence: The ways in which women "give in" to unwanted sex with their husbands. *Violence Against Women, 5*, 1036–1058.
9. Monson, C.M., & Langhinrichsen-Rohling, J. (1998). Sexual and nonsexual marital aggression: Legal considerations, epidemiology, and an integrated typology of perpetrators. *Aggression and Violent Behavior, 3*(4), 369–389.
10. National Clearinghouse House for Marital and Date Rape. (2005). State law chart. Retrieved July 27, 2010 from www.ncmdr.org
11. Martin, E.K., Taft, C.T., & Resick, P.A. (2007). A review of marital rape. *Aggression and Violent Behavior, 12*(3), 329–347.
12. Muehlemhard, C.L., & Kimes, L.A. (1999). The social construction of violence: The case of sexual and domestic violence. *Personality and Social Psychology Review, 3*, 234–245.
13. Simonson, K., & Subich, L.M. (1999). Rape perceptions as a function of gender-role traditionality and victim-perpetrator association. *Sex Roles, 40*, 617–634.
14. United States Government Accountability Office. (2006). *Prevalence of Domestic Violence, Sexual Assault, Dating Violence and Stalking: Briefing to Congressional Committee.*
15. Bergen, R.K., & Bukovec, P. (2006). Men and intimate partner rape—Characteristics of men who sexually abuse their partner. *Journal of Interpersonal Violence, 21*(10), 1375–1384.
16. Finkelhor, D., & Yllo, K. (1985). *License to rape: Sexual abuse of wives.* New York: The Free Press.
17. Finkelhor, D., & Yllo, K. (1988). Rape in marriage. In M.B. Straus (Ed.), *Abuse and victimization across the life span* (pp. 140–152). Baltimore: The Johns Hopkins University Press.
18. Basile, K.C. (2002). Prevalence of wife rape and other intimate partner sexual coercion in a nationally representative sample of women. *Violence and Victims, 17*, 511–524.
19. Petty, G.M., & Dawson, B. (1989). Sexual aggression in normal men: Incidence, beliefs, and personality characteristics. *Personality and Individual Differences, 10*, 355–362.
20. Sullivan, J.P., & Mosher, D.L. (1990). Acceptance of guided imagery of marital rape as a function of macho personality. *Violence and Victims, 5*, 275–286.
21. Frieze, I.H. (1983). Investigating the causes and consequences of marital rape. *Signs: Journal of Women in Culture and Society, 8*, 532–553.
22. Malamuth, N.M., Linz, D., Heavey, C.L., Barnes, G., & Acker, M. (1995). Using the confluence model of sexual aggression to predict men's conflict with women: A 10-year follow-up study. *Journal of Personality and Social Psychology, 69*, 353–369.

23. Christopher, F.S., Owens, L.A., & Stecker, H.L. (1993). An examination of men and women's premarital sexual aggressiveness. *Journal of Social and Personal Relationships, 10,* 511–527.

24. Rapaport, K., & Burkhart, B.R. (1984). Personality and attitudinal characteristics of sexually coercive college males. *Journal of Abnormal Psychology, 93,* 216-221.21. Frieze, I. H. (1983). Investigating the causes and consequences of marital rape. *Signs: Journal of Women in Culture and Society, 8,* 532–553.

25. Monson, C.M., Langhinrichsen-Rohling, J., & Taft, C.T. (2009). Sexual aggression in intimate relationships. In K.D. O'Leary & E.M. Woodin (Eds.), *Psychological and physical aggression in couples: Causes and interventions.* (pp. 37–57). Washington, D.C: American Psychological Association.

26. Russell, D. (1990). *Rape in marriage.* Bloomington: Indiana University Press.

27. Testa, M., VanZile-Tamsen, C., & Livingston, J.A. (2007). Prospective prediction of women's sexual victimization by intimate and nonintimate male perpetrators. *Journal of Consulting and Clinical Psychology, 75*(1), 52–60.

28. Sokoloff, N.J., & Dupont, I. (2005). Domestic violence at the intersections of race, class, and gender: Challenges and contribution to understanding violence against marginalized women in diverse communities. *Violence Against Women, 11*(1), 38–64.

29. Tjaden, P., & Thoennes, N. (2000). Prevalence and consequences of male-to-female and female-to-male intimate partner violence as measured by the National Violence Against Women Survey. *Violence Against Women, 6*(2), 142–161.

30. Vogel, L.C., & Marshall, L.L. (2001). PTSD symptoms and partner abuse: Low income women at risk. *Journal of Traumatic Stress, 14,* 569–584.

31. Dasgupta, S.D. (2005). Women's realities: Defining violence against women by immigration, race, and class. In N. J. Sokoloff & C. Pratt (Eds.), *Domestic violence at the margins: Readings on race, class, gender, and culture.* (pp. 56–70). Piscataway, N.J.: Rutgers University Press.

32. Bergen, R.K. (2006). Marital rape: New research and directions. Retrieved July, 18, 2010 from http://new.vawnet.org/Assoc_Files_VAWnet/AR_MaritalRapeRevised.pdf

33. DeKeseredy, W.S., Donnermeyer, J.F., Schwartz, M.D., Tunnell, K.D., & Hall, M. (2007). Thinking critically about rural gender relations: Toward a rural masculinity crisis/male peer support model of separation/divorce/sexual assault. *Critical Criminology, 15*(4), 295–311.

34. DeKeseredy, W.S., & Joseph, C. (2006). Separation and/or divorce sexual assault in rural Ohio: Preliminary results of an exploratory study. *Violence Against Women, 12,* 301–311.

35. Browne, A. (1993). Violence against women by male partners: Prevalence, outcomes, and policy implications. *American Psychologist, 48*(10), 1077–1087.

36. Campbell, J.C. (1998). Abuse during pregnancy: Progress, policy, and potential. *American Journal of Public Health, 88,* 185–187.

37. Christopher, F.S., & Pflieger, J.C. (2007). Sexual aggression: The dark side of sexuality in relationships. *Annual Review of Sex Research, 18,* 115–142.

38. Marshall, A.D., & Holtzworth-Munroe, A. (2002). Varying forms of husband sexual aggression: Predictors and subgroup differences. *Journal of Family Psychology, 16,* 286–296.

39. Dienemann, J., Boyle, E., Baker, D., Resnick, W., Wiederhorn, N., & Campbell, J.C. (2000). Intimate partner abuse among women diagnosed with depression. *Issues in Mental Health Nursing, 21,* 499–513.
40. DeMaris, A. (1997). Elevated sexual activity in violent marriages: Hypersexuality or sexual extortion? *The Journal of Sex Research, 34,* 361–373.
41. Johnson, H. (2003). The cessation of assaults on wives. *Journal of Comparative Family Studies, 34,* 75–91.
42. Foran, H., & O'Leary, K.D. (2008). Alcohol and intimate partner violence: A meta-analytic review. *Clinical Psychology Review, 28*(7), 1222–1234.
43. Julian, T.W., & McKenry, P.C. (1993). Mediators of male violence toward female intimates. *Journal of Family Violence, 8*(1), 39–56.
44. Ullman, S.E., & Siegel, J.M. (1993). Victim-offender relationship and sexual assault. *Violence and Victims, 8*(2), 121–134.
45. Brown, A.L., Testa, M., & Messman-Moore, T.L. (2009). Psychological consequences of sexual victimization resulting from force, incapacitation, or verbal coercion. *Violence Against Women, 15*(8), 898–919.
46. Campbell, R. (2008). The psychological impact of rape victims. *American Psychologist, 63*(8), 702–717.
47. Amstadter, A.B., Resnick, H.S., Nugent, N.R., Acierno, R., Rheingold, A.A., Minhinnett, R., et al. (2009). Longitudinal trajectories of cigarette smoking following rape. *Journal of Traumatic Stress, 22*(2), 113–121.
48. Resnick, H.S., Acierno, R., Amstadter, A.B., Self-Brown, S., & Kilpatrick, D.G. (2007). An acute post-sexual assault intervention to prevent drug abuse: Updated findings. *Addictive Behaviors, 32*(10), 2032–2045.
49. Acierno, R., Resnick, H.S., Flood, A., & Holmes, M. (2003). An acute post-rape intervention to prevent substance use and abuse. *Addictive Behaviors, 28*(9), 1701–1715.
50. Macy, R.J. (2008). A research agenda for sexual revictimization: Priority areas and innovative statistical methods. *Violence Against Women, 14*(10), 1128–1147.
51. Breitenbecher, K.H. (2001). Sexual revictimization among women. A review of the literature focusing on empirical investigations. *Aggression and Violent Behavior, 6*(4), 415–432.
52. Kilpatrick, D.G., & Acierno, R. (2003). Mental health needs of crime victims: Epidemiology and outcomes. *Journal of Traumatic Stress, 16,* 119–132.
53. Stermac, L., Del Bove, G., & Addison, M. (2001). Violence, injury, and presentation patterns in spousal sexual assaults. *Violence Against Women, 7,* 1218–1233.
54. Stermac, L., Du Mont, J., & Dunn, S. (1998). Violence in known-assailant sexual assaults. *Journal of Interpersonal Violence, 13,* 398–412.
55. El-Bassel, N., Gilbert, L., Krishnan, S., Schilling, R.F., Gaeta, T., Purpura, S., et al. (1998). Partner violence and sexual HIV-risk behaviors among women in an inner-city emergency department. *Violence and Victims, 13*(4), 377–393.
56. Campbell, J.C., & Soeken, K.L. (1999). Forced sex and intimate partner violence: Effects on women's risk and women's health. *Violence Against Women, 5,* 1017–1035.
57. Wingood, G.M., & DiClemente, R.J. (1997). The effects of an abusive primary partner on the condom use and sexual negotiation practices of African-American women. *American Journal of Public Health, 87*(6), 1016–1018.

5

War and Sexual Violence in the Military

Janet C'de Baca

Women have served in the military since the American Revolution[1] with the stipulation they not be assigned to ground combat units (e.g., the infantry, special operations commandos, tank crews). Things began to change, and in the 1990s, Congress lifted the ban on women flying combat aircraft and serving on combat ships. Today, women soldiers in Iraq and Afghanistan are serving in support units as truck drivers, mechanics, medics, military police, helicopter pilots, and so on. About 180,000 (14% of total soldiers deployed) women soldiers are deployed in Iraq and Afghanistan.[2] However, warfare in Iraq and Afghanistan includes improvised explosive devices, mortar attacks, suicide bombs, and rocket-propelled grenades. Both front-line and support units find themselves under attack and in battle because of this guerrilla warfare. Combat-related traumas include being shot at or ambushed, being wounded or injured, knowing someone who was seriously injured or killed, and taking care of the wounded and dead. Women soldiers are increasingly among the wounded and killed in combat. As of February 2010, 658 women soldiers have been wounded in action and 124 killed in action.[3,4]

In addition to combat events, female soldiers are exposed to sexual assault and other military sexual traumas, as are male soldiers. Data from the U.S. Department of Veterans Affairs (VA) universal screening program, which asks all veterans receiving care at the VA whether they experienced sexual trauma during their military service, indicates about one in five women (20%) and one in one hundred (1%) men responded "yes."[5] The term *military sexual trauma* (MST) is defined by the Department of Veterans Affairs[6] as "sexual harassment that is threatening in character or physical assault of a sexual nature that occurred while the victim was in the military, regardless of geographic location of the trauma, gender of victim, or the relationship to the perpetrator."

Among traumatic events, rape and combat exposure pose the highest risk for development of post-traumatic stress disorder (PTSD).[7,8,9] Kang and colleagues[10] reported sexual assault and harassment during military service continued to be associated with PTSD in both female and male veterans even after controlling for combat exposure. They reported the risk of developing PTSD associated with MST at 5.41 and the risk associated with high combat exposure at 4.03 for female veterans. For males, these numbers were 6.21 and 4.45, respectively. These findings suggest sexual assault by another soldier is the greater contributor to PTSD. For women, serving in a war zone can be particularly risky. Women soldiers have to deal with combat trauma and the potential for sexual assault.

What are the types of violence endured by women in uniform? In 2009,[11] 3,230 military sexual assaults were reported, an increase of 11 percent from fiscal year (FY) 2008. The 2006 Gender Relations Survey of Active Duty Members[12] defines unwanted sexual contact as sexual touching (i.e., intentional touching of genitalia, breasts, or buttocks), sexual intercourse, oral or anal sex, or penetration by a finger or object. Among active duty women and men completing the survey, 7% and 2%, respectively, experienced unwanted sexual contact. Unwanted sexual touching was the most frequent MST experienced by women (78%), followed by attempted sexual intercourse (41%), completed sexual intercourse (17%), attempted oral sex, anal sex, or object penetration (24%), and completed oral sex, anal sex, or object penetration (17%). Among men experiencing unwanted sexual contact, 66% reported unwanted sexual touching; 27% attempted and 12% completed sexual intercourse; and 26% attempted and 12% completed oral sex, anal sex, or object penetration. Sexual harassment is defined as crude/offensive behavior, unwanted sexual attention, and sexual coercion, and was reported by 34% of the women and 6% of the men completing the Gender Relations Survey of Active Duty Members. Fifty-two percent of these women reported crude/offensive behavior, followed by unwanted sexual attention (31%) and sexual coercion (9%). Female gender clearly confers a greater risk for sexual trauma during military service;[13] thus, this chapter will mainly focus on women soldiers.

What about women soldiers in combat situations? Combat areas of interest where women soldiers have served include Bahrain, Iraq, Jordan, Lebanon, Syria, Yemen, Egypt, Djibouti, Kuwait, Oman, Qatar, Saudi Arabia, United Arab Emirates, Iran, Pakistan, Afghanistan, and Kyrgyzstan. According to the Department of Defense annual report for FY 2008, 241 sexual assaults occurred in combat areas of interest, a 38 percent increase over the prior reporting period.[14] In FY 2009, this number increased by 16 percent to 279. If we look just at Iraq and Afghanistan, in FY 2008, 141 sexual assaults were reported in Iraq and 22 in Afghanistan, a 26% increase over FY 2007. And in FY 2009, there were 175 reports of sexual assault in Iraq and 40 in Afghanistan.[11] Officials attribute the increasing numbers to the 2005 enactment of the Sexual Assault Prevention and Response (SAPR) program to encourage increased reporting of the crime, not to an increase in sexual assault.[11] The Department of Defense report estimates only 10 to 20% of assaults are reported, or, put another way, 80% to 90% of sexual assaults go unreported by both female and male victims. This differs from the civilian population, where about a third of rapes/sexual assaults are reported to the authorities.[15]

Why is the report rate so low? The military legal system may contribute to the low reporting rate. If a sexual assault is reported to medical personnel, military police, or sometimes even a military chaplain, the assault must be reported to the command.[16] The report then becomes part of her military record, and the soldier does not have the benefit of confidentiality. Once reported, the commander has the authority to decide if the case goes forward to court-martial. The commander also assigns the prosecuting and defense Judge Advocate General Corps (JAG) attorneys, oversees the investigation, and may have the ultimate say in any disciplinary action.[16] With this system, the potential for abuse of power is evident, as is the possibility of conflict of interest in the event both the victim and perpetrator are under the same command. Additionally, MST victims may not have adequate legal representation. Though JAG attorneys are qualified to practice military law, they may not be familiar with the laws of the state where the assault occurred. Also, the JAG office functions as prosecutor and at the same time defense counsel, another potential for conflict of interest.[16]

The SAPR program created a "restricted option" of reporting sexual assault. Restricted reporting allows women to confidentially access medical care and advocacy services without initiating an investigation. While the restricted option seems positive, the downside is that unless charges are filed, the perpetrator is protected, and as a result he may even gain confidence in his ability to get away with rape. The challenges for female active duty servicewomen to report are different than for civilian women. In the civilian world, knowing how to make a sexual assault report has been simplified, where a woman calls 9-1-1 or goes to an emergency room or police station. Whichever she chooses, her confidentiality is protected, and charges will be filed. In the military, since the SAPR program was instituted, she may contact the local sexual assault response coordinator, victim advocate, or a health care provider. Or she may contact her chain of command or law enforcement (military or civilian). However, if she reports to her chain of command or law enforcement, an investigation will be initiated and she will not have the option to make a restricted report.[16]

There are a number of fear-based reasons for not reporting a sexual assault.[17] A woman working in any male-dominated field may have a fear of retaliation, harassment, or career disruption, particularly prevalent in the military. She may fear she will not be believed and hence labeled a troublemaker. She may feel her choice to join the service means she should not complain. Not wanting anyone to know about the sexual assault is a frequently cited reason. The lack of confidentiality, the concern she will be the target of gossip, and potentially ostracism or ridicule are not unrealistic. Then there is the possibility she will be removed from her unit, thus losing an important support system. In the military the mission is of utmost importance. She may not report because of guilt feelings about jeopardizing the mission and the cohesiveness of her unit. Or she may be strongly encouraged to keep silent about the assault to maintain unit cohesion.[18] She may have been violating a rule when the assault occurred, such as underage drinking or fraternization. These behaviors could result in severe consequences.[19]

Another reason for not reporting MST is the belief nothing will be done about it. Sacks[19] identified a list of factors considered by a commander when deciding how to dispose of an offense. These include the character and military service of the accused, possible improper motives of the accuser, reluctance of the victim or others to testify, and the availability and admissibility of evidence. Historically, rape victims are reluctant to testify, and MST can and often does occur without witnesses. In the military, only 8% of cases investigated result in prosecution of the perpetrator, and about 80% of those perpetrators convicted still receive an honorable discharge. The rape victim may then have to return to work with her perpetrator.

Other reasons for not reporting MST include believing the incident was not important enough to report, that reporting it would take too much time and effort, or believing the sexual assault is just part of being in the military.[12,20,21] If a woman believes being assaulted is "just part of being in the military," military culture is doing a disservice to women who serve our country.

What sociocultural factors set the stage for MST? Myths about rape are still prevalent, even in today's society.[22] Some common myths suggest that sexual assault is provoked by the victim; victims ask for it by their actions, behaviors, or by the way they dress; most rapes are reported by women who "change their minds" afterward or who want to "get even" with a man; and once a man gets sexually aroused, he can't just stop. And within the military, there is also the myth that false reports of MST are common,[19] and there are negative perceptions about women soldiers who report MST. Examples of negative perceptions are that women do not belong in the military; female soldiers are less valuable because they cannot engage in front-line combat; sexual harassment is what you get when a woman tries to do a man's job; and rape is inevitable when women are in the company of large groups of men who are on deployment without easy access to consensual sex.[19] Myths that keep men silent about being sexually assaulted suggest that men can't be sexually assaulted by women; men can't be sexually assaulted because they are able to defend themselves; only gay men are sexually assaulted; and erection or ejaculation during sexual assault means you "really wanted it" or consented to it, which can feed into distressing issues of self-doubt about sexuality and manliness. Sixty percent of men felt the incident was not important enough to report, and 47% did not want anyone to know about the incident.[12]

Misogyny is defined as a cultural attitude of hatred, dislike, or distrust for females simply because they are female. Military culture has been described as misogynistic,[23,24] as revealed in common military language. For example, drill instructors routinely denigrate recruits by calling them ladies, girls, bitches, and pussies. This is not limited to drill instructors. Sexist insults permeate the everyday speech of soldiers. Pornography, including violent pornography, is prevalent, and then there are the misogynist rhymes (Jody calls)[25,26] commonly used during drills. For example, Burke's book cites this Naval Academy chant: Who can take a chainsaw; Cut the bitch in two; Fuck the bottom half; And give the upper half to you . . . .[24]

Are certain women at higher risk? Risk factors for MST include entering the military at a younger age and being of enlisted rank, with lower education, a negative home life, and a history of sexual assault.[12,27] Lipari and colleagues[12] report that women in the Army and junior enlisted members were more likely than women in other services or of higher rank to experience unwanted sexual contact. The offender was most likely male and a military coworker (54%) or a military person of higher rank (52%). The most likely place for the unwanted sexual contact was at a military installation, while at work. Only about a third of women report the use of alcohol and/or drugs at the time of the trauma by either the perpetrator or the female soldier. About a third of women experiencing unwanted sexual contact reported they were sexually harassed before the assault.

About a third of the women completing the Gender Relations Survey of Active Duty Members reported sexual harassment. Again, junior enlisted women in the Army were more likely than women in other services to experience sexual harassment.

What makes MST in a combat zone more stressful? Military personnel, including military police and medical staff, may not be trained to handle sexual assault cases. They may accept common myths regarding sexual assault; for example, it wasn't rape if there are no physical injuries, a man cannot rape his wife, or men cannot be raped. They may not be trained in the dynamics of sexual assault (e.g., rape is rarely a crime of passion; it is a way to dominate, humiliate, control) or in performing a sexual assault examination, including carefully collecting and preserving evidence. The consequences of a sexual assault can include a sexually transmitted infection and, for women, the risk of getting pregnant. In a conflict zone, access to emergency contraception, antibiotics, and abortion may be extremely limited. In addition, female soldiers fighting in countries where women are expected to be in more traditional roles, such as Middle Eastern countries, are treated with disdain and are at higher risk for sexual assault by civilian males if not accompanied by male soldiers.[28]

It is more difficult in the military for a female soldier to avoid her assailant if he is also a soldier, especially if stationed on a remote combat base.[16] In the military, the mission is of utmost importance. Command might decide it is in the best interest of the mission to not separate the female sexual assault victim from her perpetrator. She may feel threatened by or actually experience additional attacks in the context of the mission. Escaping or even avoiding her assailant may not be possible. Imagine having to show respect for the man who assaulted you or to have to rely on him for basic needs or depend that he will support you in a conflict situation.

In war, the need to trust fellow soldiers takes on high importance. Being victimized by a fellow soldier intensifies the sense of betrayal. The traumas of combat exposure and sexual persecution are often borne alone. Women frequently serve in a platoon with few or no other women, experiencing loneliness instead of the camaraderie that every soldier depends on for comfort and survival.[29]

CONCLUSION

The consequences for women with MST are increased difficulty with social and career readjustment.[1] Sadly, significant numbers of women who report a sexual assault are discharged from service against their wishes. They are misdiagnosed with adjustment disorder, personality disorder, and preservice existing PTSD, making them ineligible for military service and effectively ending their careers.[30] MST is a risk factor for homelessness, with 40 percent of homeless women veterans having experienced a sexual assault in the military.[31] Women veterans with MST have been found to be nine times more likely to develop PTSD then women with no sexual assault history[32] and four times more likely when compared to civilian women with sexual assault. MST is the primary causal factor of PTSD for women; combat experience is the primary predictor of PTSD for men.[33] Other common physical ailments frequently co-occurring with PTSD include depression, substance abuse, somatization, obesity, and suicidal behaviors.[34] Therefore, the problem of sexual assault and sexual harassment in the military is a primary concern for women who have served their country, both in and out of combat settings. Despite the efforts made by the military, it continues to be a primary issue challenging females serving in the military. The health costs for these women as veterans is pervasive both in medical and psychiatric care. Health care costs for women veterans with MST are higher than for women veterans without MST.[32]

Presently, of the approximate 1.7 million women serving in our military, 30% to 45% report military sexual trauma and 4% to 31% report combat exposure.[35] The results are and will be large numbers of female veterans at risk for psychological problems (PTSD, depression, anxiety) and medical problems (gastrointestinal, sexual, obesity), who will be dependent on the health care system.

REFERENCES

1. Katz, L.S., Bloor, L.E., Cojucar, G., & Draper, T. (2007). Women who served in Iraq seeking mental health services: Relationships between military sexual trauma, symptoms, and readjustment. *Psychological Services, 4*(4), 239–249.
2. Department of Defense (2008). *Active duty military personnel by rank/grade.* Retrieved November 3, 2010 from http://siadapp.dmdc.osd.mil/personnel/MILITARY/rg0809f/pdf
3. Department of Defense (2009). *Military casualty information.* Retrieved November 3, 2010 from http://siadapp.dmdc.osd.mil/personnel/CASUALTY/castop.htm
4. Leland, A., & Oboroceanu, M.J. (2010). *American war and military operations casualties: Lists and statistics.* Congressional Research Service, 7-5700, www.crs.gov, RL 32492
5. Department of Veterans Affairs National Center for PTSD (2007). Retrieved October 27, 2010 from http://www.ptsd.va.gov/public/pages/military-sexual-trauma-general.asp
6. Veterans Health Administration (2004). *Veterans Health Initiative: Military Sexual Trauma.* Retrieved October 21, 2010 from http://www1.va.gov/vhi/docs/MST_www.pdf
7. Kessler, R.C., Sonnega, A., Bromet, E., Hughes, M., & Nelson, C.B. (1995). Post-traumatic stress disorder in the National Comorbidity Survey. *Archives of General Psychiatry, 52*(12), 1048–1060.
8. Wolfe, J., Sharkansky, E., Read, J., Dawson, R., Martin, J., & Quimette, P. (1998). Sexual harassment and assault as predictors of PTSD symptomatology among US female Persian Gulf War military personnel. *Journal of Interpersonal Violence, 13,* 40–57.
9. Fontana, A., Litz, B., & Rosenheck, R. (2000). Impact of combat and sexual harassment on the severity of posttraumatic stress disorder among men and women peacekeepers in Somalia, *Journal of Nervous and Mental Disorders, 188,* 163–169.
10. Kang, H., Dalager, N., Mahan, C., & Ishii, E. (2005). The role of sexual assault on the risk of PTSD among Gulf War veterans. *Annals of Epidemiology, 15*(3), 191–195.
11. Department of Defense Sexual Assault Prevention and Response (2010). *Fiscal Year 2009 Annual Report on Sexual Assault in the Military.* Retrieved October 12, 2010 from http://www.sapr.mil/media/pdf/reports/fy09_annual_report.pdf

12. Lipari, R.N., Cook, P.J., Rock, L.M., & Matos, K. (2008). *2006 Gender relations survey of active duty members.* Defense Manpower Data Center Report No. 2007-022. Arlington, VA.

13. Street, A.E., Vogt, D., & Dutra, L. (2009). A new generation of women veterans: Stressors faced by women deployed to Iraq and Afghanistan. *Clinical Psychology Review, 29,* 685–694.

14. Department of Defense Sexual Assault Prevention and Response (2009). *Fiscal Year 2008 Annual Report on Sexual Assault in the Military.* Retrieved on October 8, 2010 from: http://www.sapr.mil/media/pdf/reports/dod_fy08_annual_report _combined.pdf

15. Rennison, C.M. (2002). *Rape and sexual assault: Reporting to police and medical attention, 1992–2000.* NCJ 194530. Washington, D.C.: U.S. Department of Justice, Bureau of Justice Statistics.

16. Mullins, C. (2005). Understanding sexual assault in the United States Military Culture. In *Connections: A Bi-annual Publication of the Washington Coalition of Sexual Assault Programs.* Fall/Winter 2005.

17. Gaudiano, N. (2005). Air Force issues long-awaited report on sexual assault issues. In *Connections: A Bi-annual Publication of the Washington Coalition of Sexual Assault Programs.* Fall/Winter 2005.

18. Kilpatrick, D.G. (1983). Rape victims: Detection, assessment and treatment. *Clinical Psychology, 36*(4), 92–95.

19. Sacks, S. (2005). Sexual assault and the military: A community sexual assault program's perspective. In *Connections: A Bi-annual Publication of the Washington Coalition of Sexual Assault Programs.* Fall/Winter 2005.

20. Healing Pathways Manuscript_12.5.10.doc.Government Accountability Office. *Military Personnel: DOD's and the Coast Guard's Sexual Assault Prevention and Response Programs Face Implementation and Oversight Challenges,* GAO-08-924. Washington, D.C.: August 29, 2008.

21. Valente, S., & Wight, C. (2007). Military sexual trauma: Violence and sexual abuse. *Military Medicine, 172*(3), 259–265.

22. Suarez, E., & Gadalla, T.M. (2010 Nov). Stop blaming the victim: A Meta-analysis on rape myths. *Journal of Interpersonal Violence, 25*(11), 2010–2035. Epub 2010 Jan 11.

23. Morris, M. (1996) By force of arms: Rape, war, and military culture. *Duke Law Journal, 45*(4), 651–692.

24. Burke, C. (2004). *Camp All-American, Hanoi Jane, and the high-and-tight: Gender, folklore, and changing military culture.* Boston: Beacon Press.

25. Van Ness, N. (2008). *Perceived as "dykes, whores, bitches": 1 in 3 military women experience sexual abuse.* Retrieved November 3, 2010 from http://www.thewip.net/ contributors/2008/05/perceived_as_dykes_whores_bitc.html

26. Benedict, H. (2007). *The private war on women soldiers.* Retrieved on October 8, 2010 from http://www.salon.com/news/feature/2007/03/07/women_in_military

27. Suris, A., & Lind, L. (2008). Military sexual trauma: A review of prevalence and associated health consequences in veterans. *Trauma, Violence & Abuse, 9*(4), 250–269.

28. Jordan, E. (2010). *How women will end the war in Afghanistan.* Retrieved November 3, 2010 from http://www.marieclaire.com/celebrity-lifestyle/articles/living/ women-soldiers-afghanistan

29. Benedict, H. (2009). *The lonely soldier: The private war of women serving in Iraq.* Boston, MA: Beacon Press.
30. Information on military sexual trauma: Some statistics (2009, June), Retrieved October 8, 2010 from http://helpforveterans.blogspot.com/2009/06/some-statis tics.html
31. Williamson, V., & Mulhall, E. (2009). *Invisible wounds: Psychological and neurological injuries confront a new generation of veterans.* New York: Iraq and Afghanistan Veterans of America.
32. Suris, A., Lind, L., Kashner, T.M., Borman, P.D., & Petty, F. (2004). Sexual assault in women veterans: An examination of PTSD risk, health care utilization, and cost of care. *Psychosomatic Medicine, 66,* 749–756.
33. Street, A.E., Stafford, J., Mahan, C.M., & Hendricks, A. (2008). Sexual harassment and assault experienced by reservists during military service: Prevalence and health correlates. *Journal of Rehabilitation Research and Development, 45*(3), 409–420.
34. Skinner, K.M., Kressin, N., Frayne, S., Tripp, T.J., Hankin, C.S., Miller, D.R., & Sullivan, L.M. (2000). The prevalence of military sexual assault among female Veterans Administration outpatients. *Journal of Interpersonal Violence, 15*(3), 291–310.
35. Zinzow, H.M., Grubaugh, A.L., Monnier, J., Suffoletta-Maierle, S., & Frueh, B.H. (2007). Trauma among female veterans: A critical review. *Trauma, Violence, & Abuse, 8*(4), 384–400.

6

Multiple Perpetrator Sexual Assault: Risk Factors, Effects, and Help-Seeking

Shaquita Tillman

DEFINITION AND PREVALENCE

Gang rape, group rape, and *multiple perpetrator rape* are all terms used variously in the research literature to describe incidences of sexual assault in which there are two or more assailants. The term *gang rape* dates back to the 1970s and 1980s and is the term most commonly referenced in the literature. Further, it remains the most preferred concept among some academics. Ullman,[1-2] one of the pioneers in the field examining sexual assault (both individual and multiple assailant) generally uses the term *gang rape* to refer to "a rape of a woman by multiple men" (p. 50). Her rationale for using this term is multifold: First, she would like to maintain consistency with previous literature, and second, it clearly denotes the distinction between rapes committed by "one man against one victim." In her more recent work, Ullman[2] acknowledges that the term *gang* has other connotations, specifically to established "street gangs," which exist prior to and following the sexual assault and are often involved in other criminal and noncriminal acts together. With this in mind, Ullman includes rapes committed by "street gangs" under the umbrella term *gang rape.*

However, Horvath and Kelly[3] argue that the concept of "gang rape" is not all encompassing and prevents delineation between the types of groups of men that may be perpetrating the assaults, and furthermore may serve to disguise these variations. As such, the term *group rape* entered into academic discourse more recently, and indeed is associated with attempts to overcome the limitations of "gang rape." Typically, "group rape" is defined and used very broadly to refer to attacks committed by two or more offenders.[4] In sum, studies have used varying terminology to name and define the offense, from *gang rape* to *group rape*.[2,4] Consequently, whichever terminology has been used, the findings about the basic characteristics of the offense are variable. Nevertheless, the most frequently occurring size of the group fluctuates from two[5] to four,[6] which is consistent with earlier estimations about co-offending more generally, which proposed that the modal number of perpetrators in a crime incident is two or three.[7]

Not surprisingly, varying terminology across the literature has compounded the problems encountered in estimating accurately the prevalence and incidence of multiple perpetrator sexual assaults; therefore, researchers cannot state with certainty the extent of the sexual assaults involving multiple perpetrators. However, it is likely that, as for other kinds of sexual assault, the figures available underestimate the problem.[8] To date, research indicates that the rate of multiple perpetrator sexual assault range from under 2% in student populations to up to 26% in police samples.[9]

The prevalence of sexual assault in prison populations is more difficult to determine, as our society and researchers largely ignore rape of inmates. Nevertheless, some research has been done in this area. In a sample of 538 inmates (486 men and 42 women) in a Midwestern prison system, the researchers found that approximately 50% of the participants had been forced to have intercourse (vaginal, anal, and/or oral), with one-fourth of the cases qualifying as gang rape.[10] Of the male victims, 50% said that only one perpetrator was involved, 30% said two or three persons, 10% said four or five persons, 6% said six to ten persons, and 4% said eleven to twenty-six persons; for the female victims one incident involved a single perpetrator, and two incidents involved three or four perpetrators.[10] Furthermore, the researchers found that in these worst case incidences the perpetrator(s) of the assault were most often male.[10]

In addition, a growing body of literature has increasingly been able to capture some of the associated characteristics of multiple assailant sexual assaults. As an example, in a descriptive study comparing multiple perpetrator and individual rape incidents among a large, urban-area sample of community-residing female sexual assault victims, Ullman[2] found that in regard to situations prior to the assault, more victims of multiple perpetrator sexual assault were at parties/bars or walking outdoors before the attack, whereas victims of single-offender rape were more often at home or on a date. In this same study, multiple perpetrator sexual assaults were more likely to occur indoors, to be committed by strangers, and to involve violence including verbal threats, weapons, and physical injuries; further, these offenses were also more likely to involve substance use and victim resistance than single-offender rapes.[2] In addition, victims in this sample reported more nonforceful and forceful verbal resistance and more fleeing but less forceful physical resistance during the assault as compared with single-offender rapes.[2] Finally, Ullman[2] found that oral and/or anal penetration was more likely in sexual assault with multiple assailants, as was physical injury.

In an effort to gain a better understanding of this devastating phenomenon, this author examined the risk factors, psychological sequelae, and disclosure and help-seeking patterns among survivors of multiple perpetrator sexual assaults. First the author describes at-risk populations and situations in which the likelihood of experiencing multiple perpetrator sexual assaults is heightened. Next the author identifies the emotional and psychological effects that may develop in the aftermath of sexual assault. Then the author addresses experiences of disclosure and help seeking (to both informal and formal networks) among survivors of sexual assault. Finally, counseling and policy implications are provided. Of note, in the current work, the author will primarily focus on sexual assault with multiple assailants in which the perpetrators were male and the victim is female in nonprison populations.

AT-RISK POPULATIONS

Multiple perpetrator rape is a ubiquitous public health concern; however, there are populations who are increased risk of experiencing this atrocious act(s). Adolescence is a high-risk period for attempted and completed sexual assaults; approximately one-third of sexual assault victims in the United States report sexual violence during this developmental stage. Ullman's study[1] comparing individual and multiple perpetrator rape reported to Chicago police indicated that victims and offenders of multiple perpetrator sexual assaults tended to be younger and unemployed. These findings are critically important given that adolescent sexual assault is associated with an increased vulnerability for a range of mental health problems. Specifically, longitudinal study findings indicate that sexual assault during adolescence is associated with increased risk of post-traumatic stress disorder (PTSD), major depression, and substance abuse disorders.[11]

Individuals with a prior trauma history are also vulnerable to multiple perpetrator sexual assaults. In particular, a history of previous traumatic experiences is related to increased vulnerability to multiple assailant sexual assaults among women. In Ullman's investigation[2] she found that in a sample of 1,084 community-residing female victims of sexual assault (multiple-offender cases; $n = 176$, 17.9% of the sample) and with single-offender cases ($n = 807$), the majority of the women had experienced a lifetime traumatic event (90%), but multiple perpetrator sexual assault victims experienced an average of 3.72 traumatic events, whereas individual rape victims experienced 3.05 traumatic events, $t (1, 216) = -3.27, p = .001$. Furthermore, more than half of the sample had child sexual abuse histories, and multiple perpetrator rape victims were marginally more likely to have experienced child sexual abuse ($p < .007$).[2]

Finally, researchers are increasingly recognizing that a substantial proportion of assaults involve alcohol and other substances and may differ from assaults where alcohol or other drugs are not involved.[12] An estimated half to three-quarters of sexual assaults involve alcohol use.[13-14] Approximately one in twenty women (4.7%) reported being raped in 119 schools surveyed in 2001. Nearly 72% of the victims experienced rape while intoxicated. White women under twenty-one years of age, residing in sorority houses, using illicit drugs, drinking heavily in high school, and attending college with high rates of heavy episodic drinking were at higher risk of rape while intoxicated.[15] The amount of alcohol that perpetrators or victims consumed during assault was linearly related to the type of sexual assault committed and to how much aggression was used by perpetrators during the assault.[16]

Drug-facilitated sexual assaults have also been on the rise over the last decade, involving what is often referred to as "date rape" or club drugs. Gamma-hydroxybutyrate, methylene-dioxy-methamphetamine, and ketamine hydrochloride and its components are among the most popular drugs used for this purpose. Use of these chemical substances is increasingly frequent among youth, especially during all-night dance parties and at clubs. Perpetrators choose these drugs because they act rapidly, diminish inhibition, produce relaxation of voluntary muscles, and give the victim lasting anterograde amnesia for events that occur under the influence of the drug.[17]

EFFECTS OF SEXUAL ASSAULT

Researchers have identified a myriad of psychological effects of sexual assault on women. Burgess and Holmstrom's classic study[18] first described rape trauma syndrome in sexual assault survivors, and more recent studies have documented numerous psychological consequences of rape (e.g., depression, anxiety, sexual problems) including PTSD.[19-21] An alarming 17% to 65% of women with a lifetime history of sexual assault develop PTSD.[22] Many (13%–51%) meet diagnostic criteria for depression.[22-24] An overwhelming majority of sexual assault victims develop fear and/or anxiety (73%–82%)[25] and 12% to 40% experience generalized anxiety.[26-27] Approximately 13% to 49% of survivors become dependent on alcohol, whereas 28% to 61% may use other illicit substances.[2,28] Further, it is not uncommon for victims to experience suicidal ideation (23%–44%)[29] and 2% to 19% may attempt suicide.[30] It is also important to note that some research has shown that multiple perpetrator rape incidents may be more serious and lead to more harmful consequences.[1]

As an example, in a sample of community-residing women, more than two-thirds of victims had PTSD, and gang rape victims had a marginally greater likelihood of current PTSD ($p < .004$) than single-offender victims.[2] Additionally, trauma histories, perceived life threat during the assault, post-assault characterological self-blame, avoidance coping, and negative social reactions from others were all related to greater PTSD symptom severity.[2]

PTSD and substance use often co-occur in sexual assault victims' lives. Reviews suggest significant comorbidity of PTSD and substance abuse/drinking problems, particularly in female trauma survivors.[31] The self-medication hypothesis has been variously used to explain this relationship and proposes that victims suffering from PTSD may use alcohol to reduce PTSD symptoms.[32] While this form of coping may temporarily reduce trauma symptoms, in the long run, it may result in chronic PTSD. Similarly, multiple factors have been identified to better understand the relationship between PTSD and drinking problems, including trauma histories, social support, coping, self-blame, alcohol expectancies, and drinking to cope with distress. As an example, trauma histories and child sexual abuse are related to greater risk of both PTSD and drinking problems in women.[31]

Suicide ideation and attempts are another adverse consequence of sexual assault among female victims. In a study examining correlates of serious suicidal ideation and attempts in a diverse urban community sample of women adult sexual assault (ASA) survivors, the researchers found that experiencing ASA by multiple assailants was associated with greater serious suicidal ideation.[33] Multiple perpetrator sexual assaults often involve more completed rapes; in this same study completed rapes were associated with more reports of suicide attempts. This suggests that more severely traumatized women are at greater risk of suicidality and should be targeted for intervention.[33]

In addition, sexual functioning and relationships are altered following sexual violence. Research indicates that the frequency of sexual contact decreases after sexual assault. Up to a year postassault, survivors experience diminished satisfaction and pleasure in sexual activities. Some victims develop sexual problems, such as fear and arousal and desire dysfunction that could persist for years after the assault. Young age, a known assailant, and penetration during the assault were found to have a strong association with sexual problems. Furthermore, emotions such as anger toward self and shame and guilt felt during and immediately after the assault might be predictive of later sexual problems.[34]

DISCLOSURE AND HELP SEEKING

Disclosure and help-seeking behaviors following sexually assault are critical first steps in healing and recovery. Sexual assault victims have extensive postassault needs and may seek support from multiple formal social systems for assistance: Approximately 26% to 40% of victims report the assault to the police and pursue prosecution through the criminal justice system, 27% to 40% seek medical care and medical forensic examinations, and 16% to 60% obtain mental health services.[1,2,35-37] Researchers also found that increased levels of distress symptoms predicted seeking social support from both informal and formal support networks.[38] In a more recent study, research findings indicate that in terms of postassault outcomes, victims of multiple perpetrator sexual assaults were no more likely to disclose assault to anyone than single-offender victims.[2] In this same study, individual and multiple assailant sexual assault victims did not differ in number of informal support sources told, but of disclosers, multiple perpetrator rape victims were more likely to report to police and medical authorities and to seek counseling postassault.[2] Moreover, multiple perpetrator rape victims reported no differences in average positive social reactions received when disclosing assault but did receive more negative social reactions (M = 1.30) than individual rape victims (M = .98), t (1,780) = –5.22, p = .000.[2] Given these findings, it is important to note that what happens in one instance of seeking support has implications for further help seeking and distress.

CONCLUSION

Provided the greater levels of violence, sexual acts, and poorer assault aftermath that are markers of multiple perpetrator sexual assaults, more resources are needed to improve treatment and support to the victims. Research findings documenting victim's experiences with support systems following multiple perpetrator sexual assaults suggest targeting interventions toward police, medical, and mental health sources for this high-risk group of victims. Implications of these findings should be used to inform policy, treatment, and prevention strategies targeting sexual assaults with multiple assailants. At the individual level, public education efforts must emphasize that victims' experiences of sexual assault are not universal. Multiple perpetrators can victimize males and females, and the victims are likely to respond in diverse ways. However, education efforts must emphasize that certain groups are at increased risk for being sexually assaulted by multiple assailants (e.g., adolescents). In addition, rape awareness programs need to provide information for informal support providers about the varied reactions survivors may exhibit. These programs should also emphasize to informal support providers that positive reactions such as emotional support and tangible aid are helpful for recovery, and negative reactions, such as blame, may overshadow any positive efforts, particularly for survivors of multiple perpetrator sexual assault.

REFERENCES

1. Ullman, S. (1999). A comparison of gang and individual rape incidents. *Violence and Victims, 14,* 123–133.
2. Ullman, S. (2007). Comparing gang and individual rapes in a community sample of urban women. *Violence and Victims, 22*(1), 43–51.
3. Horvath, M., & Kelly, L. (2009). Multiple perpetrator rape: Naming an offense and initial research findings. *Journal of Sexual Aggression, 15*(1), 83–96.
4. Porter, L., & Alison, L. (2004). Behavioral coherence in violent group activity: An interpersonal model of sexually violent gang behavior. *Aggressive Behavior, 30,* 449–468.
5. Porter, L.E., & Alison, L.J. (2006). Examining group rape: A descriptive analysis of offender and victim behavior. *European Journal of Criminology, 3,* 357–381.
6. Bijelveld, C., Weerman, F., Looije, D., & Hendriks, J. (2007). Group sex offending by juveniles: Coercive sex as group activity. *European Journal of Criminology, 4,* 5–31.
7. Shaw, C., & McKay, H. (1931). Male juvenile delinquency as group behavior. In *Report on the Causes of Crime*, No. 13. Washington, D.C.: National Commission on Law Observance and the Administration of Justice.
8. Fisher, B., Daigle, L., Cullen, F., & Turner, M. (2003). Reporting sexual victimization to the police and others. *Criminal Justice and Behavior, 30,* 6–38.
9. O'Sullivan, C. S. (1991). Acquaintance gang rape on campus. In A. Parrot & C. Bechhofer (Eds.), *Acquaintance rape: The hidden crime* (pp. 140–156). New York: Wiley.
10. Struckman-Johnson, C., Struckman-Johnson, D., Rucker, L., Bumby, K., & Donaldson, S. (1996). Sexual coercion of reported by men and women in prison. *Journal of Sex Research, 33*(1), 67–76.
11. Kilpatrick, D., Ruggiero, K., Acierno, R., Saunders, B., Resnick, H., & Best, C. (2003). Violence and risk of PTSD, major depression, substance abuse dependence, and comorbidity: Results from the National Survey of Adolescents. *Journal of Consulting and Clinical Psychology, 71,* 692–700.
12. McCauley, J., Ruggiero, K., Resnick, H.S., Conoscenti, L., & Kilpatrick, D. (2009). Forcible, drug-facilitated, and incapacitated rape in relation to substance use problems: Results from a national sample of college women. *Addictive Behaviors, 34,* 458–462.
13. Abbey, A., Zawacki, T., Buck, P., Clinton, A., & McAuslan, P. (2004). Sexual assault and alcohol consumption: What do we know about their relationship and what types of research are still needed? *Aggression and Violent Behavior, 9,* 271–303.
14. Roy-Byrne, P., Russo, J., Michelson, E., Zatzick, D., Pitman, R.K., & Berliner, L. (2004). Risk factors and outcome in ambulatory assault victims presenting to the acute emergency department setting: Implications for secondary prevention studies in PTSD. *Depression and Anxiety, 19,* 77–84.
15. Mohler-Kuo, M., Dowdal, G., Koss, M., & Wechsler, R. (2004). Correlates of rape while intoxicated in a national sample of college women. *Journal of Studies on Alcohol, 65,* 37–45.

16. Abbey, A., Clinton-Sherrod, A., Meauslan, R., Zawaki, T., & Buck, P. (2003). The relationship between the quantity of alcohol consumed and the severity of sexual assaults committed by college men. *Journal of Interpersonal Violence, 18,* 813–833.

17. Schwartz, R., Milteer, R., & Lebeua, M. (2000). Drug-facilitated sexual assault ("date rape"). *Southern Medical Journal, 93,* 558–561.

18. Burgess, A., & Holmstrom, L. (1978). Recovery from rape and prior life stress. *Research in Nursing and Health, 1,* 165–174.

19. Foa, E., & Riggs, D. (1993). Posttraumatic stress disorder and rape. In J.M. Old-ham & A. Tasman (Eds.), *Review of psychiatry* (Chapter 11). Washington, D.C.: American Psychiatric Press.

20. Frieze, I.H. (2005). *Hurting the one you love.* Thousand Oaks, CA: Sage.

21. Resick, P.A. (1993). The psychological impact of rape. *Journal of Interpersonal Violence, 8,* 223–255.

22. Clum, G., Calhoun, K., & Kimerling, R. (2000). Associations among symptoms of depression and posttraumatic stress disorder and self-reported heath in sexually assaulted women. *Journal of Nervous and Mental Disease, 188,* 671–678.

23. Acierno, R., Brady, K., Gray, M., Kilpatrick, D.G., Resnick, H., & Best, C.L. (2002). Psychopathology following interpersonal violence: A comparison of risk factors in older and younger adults. *Journal of Clinical Geropsychology, 8,* 13–23.

24. Dickinson, L.M., deGruy, F.V., Dickinson, W.P., & Candib, L.M. (1999). Health-related quality of life and symptom profiles of female survivors of sexual abuse in primary care. *Archives of Family Medicine, 8,* 35–43.

25. Ullman, S.E., & Siegal, J.M. (1993). Victim-offender relationship and sexual assault. *Violence and Victims, 8,* 121–134.

26. Siegel, J., Golding, J., Stein, J., Burnam, M., & Sorensen, S. (1990). Reactions to sexual assault: A community study. *Journal of Interpersonal Violence, 6,* 229–246.

27. Winfield, I., George, L., Swartz, M., & Blazer, D. (1990). Sexual assault and psychiatric disorders among a community sample of women. *American Journal of Psychiatry. 147,* 335–341.

28. Ullman, S., & Brecklin, L. (2002). Sexual assault history, PTSD, and mental health service seeking in a national sample of women. *Journal of Community Psychology, 30,* 261–279.

29. Petrak, J., Doyle, A., Williams, L., Buchan, L., & Forster, G. (1997). The psychological impact of sexual assault: A study of female attenders of a sexual health psychology service. *Sexual and Marital Therapy, 12,* 339–345.

30. Davidson, J., Hughes, D., George, L., & Blazer, D. (1996). The association of sexual assault and attempted suicide within the community. *Archives of General Psychiatry, 53,* 550–555.

31. Stewart, S., & Israeli, A. (2001). Substance abuse and co-occurring psychiatric disorders in victims of intimate violence. In C. Wekerle and A. Hall, (Eds.), *The violence and addiction equation,* Hogrefe and Huber, New York, 98–122.

32. Epstein, J., Saunders, B., Kilpatrick, D., & Resnick, H. (1998). PTSD as a mediator between childhood rape and alcohol use in adult women. *Child Abuse and Neglect, 22,* 223–234.

33. Ullman, S., & Nadjowski, C. (2009). Correlates in suicide ideation and attempts in female adult sexual assault survivors. *Suicide and Life-threatening Behavior, 39*(1), 47–57.

34. Van Berlo, W., & Ensink, B. (2000). Problems with sexuality after sexual assault. *Annual Review of Sex Research, 11,* 235–257.
35. Campbell, R., Ahrens, C., Sefl, T., Wasco, S.M., & Barnes, H.E. (2001). Social reactions to rape victims: Healing and hurtful effects on psychological and physical health outcomes. *Violence & Victims, 16,* 287–302.
36. Ullman, S. (1996). Correlates and consequences of adult sexual assault disclosure. *Journal of Interpersonal Violence, 11,* 554–571.
37. Ullman, S., & Filipas, H. (2001). Correlates of formal and informal support seeking in sexual assault victims. *Journal of Interpersonal Violence, 16,* 1028–1047.
38. Starzynski, L.L., Ullman, S.E., Filipas, H.H., & Townsend, S.M. (2005). Correlates of women's sexual assault disclosure to informal and formal support sources. *Violence & Victims, 20,* 417–432.

7

Understanding Child Sexual Abuse: Prevalence, Multicultural Considerations, and Life Span Effects

Anneliese A. Singh and April Sikes

Child sexual abuse is a widespread problem in the United States and globally. Depending on the particular study and definition used, estimates of the prevalence of child sexual abuse in the United States vary greatly from 2% to 62%.[1] In 2008, the National Child Abuse and Neglect Data System (NCANDS) of the Children's Bureau reported 69,184 children (9.1% of all confirmed cases of child maltreatment) in the District of Columbia, Commonwealth of Puerto Rico, and the fifty states were victims of sexual abuse.[2] Despite this figure, it is believed that a substantial number of child sexual abuse cases remain unreported.

There has been significant work in developing a comprehensive definition of child sexual abuse, which is "any completed or attempted (noncompleted) sexual act, sexual contact with, or exploitation (i.e., noncontact sexual interaction) of a child" (see[3], pp. 14–16, for a full definition). A uniform definition provides researchers, practitioners, and advocates with a consistent manner in which to achieve best practices in understanding the prevalence of child sexual abuse across diverse communities, the context in which child sexual abuse occurs, and strategies for survivor healing.[4-5]

Children of every age, gender, sexual orientation, educational and socioeconomic status, and racial/ethnic group can encounter sexual abuse. According to Prevent Child Abuse America,[6] at least 20% of American women and 5% to 16% of American men experienced some form of sexual abuse as children. Although statistics indicate that girls are more frequently the victims of sexual abuse, it is also prevalent among boys.[7] For example, in the United States one in six boys will be sexually abused before reaching adulthood.[8] The highest risk for sexual abuse of boys includes those younger than the age of thirteen, who are youth of color, are not residing with their fathers, are of low socioeconomic status, and are disabled.[7] In 2008, sexual abuse victims for all racial groups were reported as 10.3% White, 9.0% Native American or Pacific Islander, 8.3% Hispanic, 6.8% African American, 6.6% Asian, 5.2% American Indian, and 5.2% Multiple Race.[2] Other alarming sexual abuse facts include (a) the median age for reported sexual abuse is nine years old,[9] (b) 90% of child sexual abuse victims know the perpetrator in some way; 68% are abused by family members,[10] (c) sexually abused children are often victims between the ages of eight and twelve years,[11] (d) 20% of child sexual abuse victims are under the age of eight,[12] (e) more than 60% of pregnant teens have been sexually abused,[12] and (f) most child sexual abuse is committed by men; women are the abusers in 14% of cases reported against boys and 6% against girls,[13] and most of them identify themselves as heterosexuals.[14]

CHILD SEXUAL ABUSE
AND MULTICULTURAL CONSIDERATIONS

In addition to further refining a definition of child sexual abuse, its prevalence, and its effects, researchers have increasingly begun to examine how survivors of child sexual abuse who hold diverse identities experience abuse and healing.[15,16,5] Numerous social locations contextualize the experience of child sexual abuse. This section will explore the specific multicultural considerations associated specifically with gender, race/ethnicity, sexual orientation, socioeconomic status, and disability. Other important identities also intersect with child sexual abuse experiences (e.g., immigration status, national origin) that are beyond the scope of this chapter. However, the influence of the intersection of various identities for child sexual abuse survivors will be explored.

Gender. Considerable research reveals gender-related differences among child sexual abuse victims. For example, the literature suggests that sexual abuse is more prevalent amongst girls[1,17,18] and that girls are more likely than boys to have their abuse substantiated by Child Protective Services.[19] However, boys are believed to be equally at risk for sexual victimization [20] but are more hesitant and less likely to disclose than girls.[20-22] The stigma against homosexuality,[19,20,14] being labeled helpless,[20] loss of self-esteem,[14] and fear of violence retaliation[19,14] make boys less likely to report the abuse than girls. Additionally, a sexually abused boy may have been warned that he will be responsible for any bad things that happen to his family if he discloses the abuse.[20] Sexually abused girls that are pressured into silence may share this concern. Other gender differences include (a) boys who are sexually abused often come from single-parent homes than do girls[20]and (b) a boy is more likely to be victimized by his mother than is a girl,[20] and (c) boys are more likely to experience anal and oral intercourse than girls.[23]

Research consistently indicates that sexual abuse has numerous and profound effects. Specifically, sexually abused boys and girls tend to display more behavioral problems, emotional problems, academic difficulties, suicidal tendencies, disordered eating behaviors, substance use, and sexual risk taking than their nonabused peers.[24,1,17,20] In a study examining the gender differences in outcomes of male and female teenagers who self-reported a history of sexual abuse, Chandy et al.[24] found male adolescents with a history of sexual abuse tended to report performing below average and had a high or very high dropout risk when compared to female adolescents, were at higher risk than females in delinquent activities (e.g., beating up another person, group fights, running away from home, stealing), sexual risk taking (e.g., frequency of intercourse, use of contraception), and marijuana use. On the other hand, female adolescents showed higher risk for suicidal involvement (e.g., attempts, thoughts), disordered eating, and frequent alcohol use.

When considering how gender and child sexual abuse intersect, transgender individuals are often an ignored and misunderstood group. Transgender people are those whose sex assigned at birth (female or male) is not in alignment with their internal sense of gender identity and expression. Although the literature with transgender people and child sexual abuse is nascent, there is some evidence that transgender youth and adults of color experience high rates of abuse.[25-26]

Race/ethnicity. There are several important considerations related to race/ ethnicity and child sexual abuse. A primary factor in this regard is that if rates of child sexual abuse are underreported in general, with regard to racial/ethnic minorities underreporting is exacerbated.[27] Researchers have found an inconsistent relationship between child sexual abuse and race/ ethnicity across various studies. For instance, Ullman and Filipas[28] examined the relationship between race/ethnicity and child sexual abuse for 461 female college students and found significant differences across ethnicity for the severity and prevalence of abuse—in addition to differences in the survivor-perpetrator relationship and healing from child sexual abuse. A study of White American, African American, and Hispanic American child sexual abuse survivors found no significant differences in terms of reporting or recognizing child sexual abuse.[16] Despite inconsistent findings regarding child sexual abuse and race/ethnicity, there appears to be commonality across racial/ethnic groups that child sexual abuse survivors often know their perpetrators.[29]

An additional consideration with regard to race/ethnicity is that research has indicated the disclosure of child sexual abuse by child survivors during forensic interviews can be a racialized experience. Researchers, for instance, examined the influence of race/ethnicity of the interviewer and child in disclosing child sexual abuse in an urban setting and found higher rates of disclosure among cross-race than same-race pairs.[30] However, issues of racism may become a major factor influencing other components of child sexual abuse. For example, researchers have postulated that African Americans have long histories of interacting with unjust legal and social service organizations, which may deter them from seeking help for child sexual abuse, as there may be more severe consequences for survivors, families, and perpetrators.[31] In addition, the primacy of collectivistic values in many diverse racial/ethnic groups (e.g., Asian American/Pacific Islander, Latino/a, African heritage, Native American) may become a major factor in how child sexual abuse survivors who are people of color experience and heal from child sexual abuse.[32] Survivors may not disclose their abuse because of their fear of how their family may be viewed negatively as a result—or fear that they may be ostracized by their family and/or community. For instance, if a family is already struggling with the deleterious effects of racism, a survivor who was abused by a family member may not want to bring additional stress or "shame" to the family.

Sexual orientation. Lesbian, gay, and bisexual (LGB) individuals experience higher rates of child sexual abuse than their heterosexual counterparts.[33-34] Researchers suggest that this increased prevalence requires further investigation, especially examining how sexual orientation and potential related gender identity variance may become risk factors for abuse.[35] Scholars have noted that LGB adolescents are at higher risk in general for violence and homelessness due to the "hazard of stigma" in the form of homophobia.[36]

For many LGB survivors of child sexual abuse, there is the added pressure of negotiating misinformation that somehow their abuse history "caused" them to be LGB. In addition, LGB adolescents are more likely than their heterosexual counterparts to attempt suicide related to internalized homophobia and experiencing societal heterosexism. The Massachusetts 2006 Youth Risk Survey suggested these youth are almost four times more likely to attempt suicide than their heterosexual counterparts, so LGB adolescents who may have a child sexual abuse history face additional barriers to their healing—from family rejection and homelessness to increased rates of depression, drug abuse, and engaging in unprotected sex.[37]

Socioeconomic status (SES). Research is mixed in terms of child sexual abuse and SES. For instance, in a recent study examining male- and female-perpetrated child sexual abuse in terms of family structure, 40% of victims of female-perpetrated sexual abuse came from households where the total annual family income was less than $15,000.[38] However, 20% of victims of female-perpetrated sexual abuse came from households with incomes more than $58,000 compared to 6.8% for male-perpetrated violence. According to the Third National Incidence Study of Child Abuse and Neglect,[39] children from the lowest-income families were eighteen times more likely to be sexually abused. Based on these conflicting findings, further study of this issue is needed to determine the relationship between SES and child sexual abuse.

Disability. Increased occurrences of sexual abuse among children with disabilities are well documented.[40,22,41,18] The literature suggests children with disabilities experience sexual abuse at higher rates than those children in the general population.[40-41] Sullivan and Knutzon[41] found that children with disabilities were three times more likely to be sexually abused than children without disabilities. In addition, Sullivan and Knutzon found that preschool-age disabled children experience significantly more sexual abuse than disabled children in elementary, middle, and secondary school age groups. In the same study, differences by gender and type of disability were found, with significantly more females than males with disabilities and those identified as having behavior disorder most likely to experience child sexual abuse.

Child sexual abuse and intersecting identities. Attention has increased for the importance of investigating how the various identities (e.g., race/ethnicity, gender, etc.) intersect and influence mental health.[42] These intersections of identities are complex to consider but are a critical component of understanding the experience of child sexual abuse—especially for those who have multiple historically marginalized identities. For instance, recent studies have explored the relationship between sexual orientation and race/ethnicity as mitigators of post-traumatic stress disorders (PTSD) for child sexual abuse survivors.[43] Balsalm et al.[44] examined the relationship between race/ethnicity and sexual orientation for 669 child sexual abuse survivors who were LGB and found Latino American and Asian American participants experienced higher rates of abuse than their White American and African American counterparts. In another study of intersecting identities, Tonmyr, Mery, and MacMillan[45] examined the rate of child sexual abuse among women living with disability for a community sample of 4,243 women between fifteen and sixty-four years old and found 40% had experienced child abuse, although child sexual abuse was not significantly related to physical disability for the women in this study.

EFFECTS OF CHILD SEXUAL ABUSE ACROSS THE LIFE SPAN

Although many mental health concerns may result from experience(s) of child sexual abuse, particular diagnoses may be relevant to those seeking to understand child sexual abuse and work with survivors. Depression and anxiety disorders may be common experiences for survivors of child sexual abuse.[46] Because many survivors of child sexual abuse experience disruption in their ability to regulate their affect,[47] many are at risk for developing substance abuse or substance dependence disorders.[48] In addition, child sexual abuse survivors may develop PTSD, experience intrusive thoughts about their abuse, become hypervigilant to abuse-related stimuli, and develop avoidance strategies such as numbing and dissociation. There are also those survivors whose trauma experiences may have put them at risk for developing borderline personality disorder.[49] Although the negative consequences of child sexual abuse are important to understand thoroughly, there has been a recent focus over the past ten years on the resilience experiences of survivors.[50,51,5] Resilience may be understood as a survivor's ability to "bounce back" from adversity despite difficult experiences and may include both individual and collective components of resilience that may assist survivors in healing from child sexual abuse.[32]

Childhood and adolescence. Children and adolescents exposed to sexual abuse are at great risk for physical, social, and psychological challenges. Sexual abuse has been linked to a variety of negative consequences including disordered eating,[52] suicidal behaviors,[52,17] and sexual risk behaviors.[53] Ackard and Neumark-Sztainer[52] found that for girls and boys, experiencing a single form or more than one form of sexual abuse was associated with significantly higher rates of vomiting, taking diet pills, binge eating, skipping meals, and taking laxatives than for peers who were not sexually abused. In addition, they found that those reporting multiple forms of sexual abuse reported the highest rates of suicide attempts (52.9% girls; 58.5% boys). Similarly, Martin et al.[17] found that sexually abused adolescents were much more likely to report *"thoughts about killing themselves,"* to have *"made plans,"* to have *"made threats,"* to have *"deliberately hurt themselves,"* and to claim attempt(s) to kill themselves, than nonabused. In a recent study, adolescents with a history of child sexual abuse were significantly more likely to have had sex in the last ninety days, engaged in unprotected sex, and supported fewer advantages of using condoms.[53]

According to Lovett,[54] "The effects of child sexual abuse are quite variable and are influenced by a number of factors including the extent and nature of abuse, age of child, relationship to the perpetrator, violence involved, and other aspects of the child's life" (p. 581). These "factors" increase the likelihood that a child or adolescent will experience multiple short- and long-term consequences as a result of sexual abuse. Furthermore, exposure to abuse during childhood or adolescence increases the risk for difficulties in adulthood.[55]

Effects during adulthood. Adult survivors of child sexual abuse struggle with many of the short- and long-term consequences that child and adolescent survivors face. As discussed in the previous section, adult survivors similarly develop coping resources that developed to manage past experiences of trauma.[47,48] The American Psychiatric Association reviewed the literature on the effects of child sexual abuse for adult survivors and identified increased rates of depression, autoimmune disorders (e.g., fibromyalgia), disordered eating, obesity, and addictive behaviors. For those survivors whose trauma symptoms rise to the level of a PTSD diagnosis, additional symptoms include hypervigilance, avoidance and numbing, and reexperience of the abuse.[56] For these reasons, scholars have called for a holistic approach to healing for child sexual abuse survivors that includes attention to a wide range of physical and emotional effects for adult survivors.[57,48]

The American College of Obstetricians and Gynecologists[58] outlined seven categories that may overlap with one another: emotional reactions, PTSD symptoms, self-perceptions, physical and biomedical effects, sexual effects, interpersonal effects, and social functioning. For instance, some adult women survivors of child sexual abuse may experience long-term effects in the form of disordered eating, self-injurious behavior, and dissociative disorders[59]—all behaviors that develop in an attempt to regulate emotional dysregulation that may result from these traumatic experiences.[47] In addition, child sexual abuse survivors may experience long-term somatization effects, where they experience physical pain as a result of their abuse.[60]

CHAPTER SUMMARY

This chapter provided an overview of both the definition and prevalence of child sexual abuse, in addition to multicultural considerations and the issues that survivors of child sexual abuse encounter over the life span. Although important strides have been made in practice, research, and advocacy with child sexual abuse survivors, significant gaps in our knowledge of these areas with regard to survivors from historically marginalized groups continue to exist.

REFERENCES

1. Hunter, S.V. (2006). Understanding the complexity of child sexual abuse: A review of the literature with implications for family counseling. *The Family Journal, 14*, 349–358.
2. U.S. Department of Health and Human Services, Administration on Children, Youth and Families. (2010). *Child Maltreatment 2008*. Washington, D.C.: U.S. Government Printing Office.
3. Leeb, R.T., Paulozzi, L., Melanson, C., Simon, T., & Arias, I. (2007). Child maltreatment surveillance: Uniform definitions for public health and recommended data elements, Version 1.0. Atlanta, GA: Centers for Disease Control and Prevention, National Center for Injury Prevention and Control.

4. Singh, A.A., Hays, D.G., & Ancis, J. (2007). Sexual abuse (childhood). In J. Ancis (Ed.), *The complete women's psychotherapy treatment planner* (pp. 130–139). Hoboken, N.J.: Wiley & Sons.

5. Singh, A.A., Hays, D.G., Chung, Y.B., & Watson, L.S. (2010). Resilience strategies of South Asian women who have survived child sexual abuse. *Violence Against Women, 16*, 444–458.

6. Prevent Child Abuse America. (2002b). *Fact sheet: Sexual abuse of children.* Retrieved from http://member.preventchildabuse.org/site/DocServer/sexual_abuse .pdf?docID=126

7. Prevent Child Abuse America. (2002a). *Fact sheet: Sexual abuse of boys.* Retrieved from http://member.preventchildabuse.org/site/DocServer/sexual_abuse_of _boys.pdf?docID=127

8. Mitchell, M.W. (2010). Child sexual abuse: A school leadership issue. *The Clearing House, 83*, 101–104.

9. Georgia Center for Child Advocacy. (n.d.). *About us.* Retrieved from http://www .georgiacenterforchildadvocacy.org

10. Childhelp. (n.d.). *National Child Abuse Statistics.* Retrieved from http://www .childhelp.org/pages/statistics

11. Hinkelman, L., & Bruno, M. (2008). Identification and reporting of child sexual abuse: The role of elementary school professionals. *The Elementary School Journal, 108*, 376–391.

12. Darkness to Light. (2010). *Child sexual abuse statistics.* Retrieved from http:// www.d2l.org/site/c.4dICIJOkGcISE/b.6143427/k.38C5/Child_Sexual_Abuse _Statistics.htm

13. U. S. Department of Veterans Affairs, National Center for PTSD. (2007). *Child sexual abuse.* Retrieved from http://www.ptsd.va.gov/public/pages/child-sexual -abuse.asp

14. Valente, S.M. (2005). Sexual abuse of boys. *Journal of Child and Adolescent Psychiatric Nursing, 18*, 10–16.

15. Ligiero, D.P., Fassinger, R., & McCauley, M. (2009). Childhood sexual abuse, culture, and coping: A qualitative study of Latinas. *Psychology of Women Quarterly, 33*, 67–80.

16. Lowe, W., Pavkov, T.W., Casanova, G.M., & Wetchler, J. (2005). Do American ethnic cultures differ in their definitions of child sexual abuse? *American Journal of Family Therapy, 33*, 147–166.

17. Martin, G., Bergen, H.A., Richardson, A.S., Roeger, L., & Allison, S. (2004). Sexual abuse and suicidality: Gender differences in a large community sample of adolescents. *Child Abuse & Neglect, 28*, 491–503.

18. Titus, J.C. (2009). Gender differences in victimization among youths with and without hearing loss admitted to substance abuse treatment. *Journal of the American Deafness & Rehabilitation Association, 43*, 7–33.

19. Maikovich-Fong, A.K., & Jaffee, S.R. (2010). Sex differences in childhood sexual abuse characteristics and victims' emotional and behavioral problems: Findings from a national sample of youth. *Child Abuse & Neglect, 34*, 429–437.

20. Nielsen, T. (1983). Sexual abuse of boys: Current perspectives. *Personnel & Guidance Journal, 62*, 139–142.

21. O'Leary, P.J., & Barber, J. (2008). Gender differences in silencing following childhood sexual abuse. *Journal of Child Sexual Abuse, 17*, 133–143.

22. Paine, M.L., & Hansen, D.J. (2002). Factors influencing children to self-disclose sexual abuse. *Clinical Psychology Review, 22,* 271–295.
23. Fontanella, C., Harrington, D., & Zuravin, S.J. (2000). Gender differences in the characteristics and outcomes of sexually abused preschoolers. *Journal of Child Sexual Abuse, 9*(2), 21–40.
24. Chandy, J.M., Blum, R.W., & Resnick, M.D. (1996). History of sexual abuse and parental alcohol misuse: Risk, outcomes, and protective factors in adolescents. *Child and Adolescent Social Work Journal, 13,* 411–432.
25. Grossman, A.H., D'Augelli, A.R., Howell, T.J., & Hubbard, S. (2006). Parents' reactions to transgender youths' gender nonconforming expression and identity. *Journal of Gay & Lesbian Social Services, 18,* 3–16.
26. Singh, A.A., & McKleroy, V.S. (in press). "Just getting out of bed is a revolutionary act": The resilience of transgender people of color who have survived traumatic life events. *International Journal of Traumatology.*
27. Kenny, M.C., & McEachern, A.G. (2000). Racial, ethnic, and cultural factors of childhood sexual abuse: A selected review of the literature. *Clinical Psychology Review, 20,* 905–922.
28. Ullman, S.E., & Filipas, H.H. (2005). Ethnicity and child sexual abuse experiences of female college students. *Journal of Child Sexual Abuse, 14,* 67–89.
29. Cuevas, C.A., & Sabina, C. (2010). *Final report: Sexual Assault Among Latinas (SALAS) Study.* Washington, D.C.: National Institute of Justice.
30. Springman, R.E., Wherry, J.N., & Notaro, P.C. (2006). The effects of interviewer race and child race on sexual abuse disclosures in forensic interviews. *Journal of Child Sexual Abuse, 15,* 99–116.
31. Abney, V.D., & Priest, R. (1995). African Americans and sexual child abuse. In L.A. Fontes (Ed.), *Sexual abuse in nine North American cultures: Treatment and prevention* (pp. 11–30). Thousand Oaks, CA: Sage Publications.
32. Singh, A.A. (2010). Helping South Asian women use resilience strategies in healing from sexual abuse: A call for a culturally relevant model. *Women and Therapy, 32*(4), 361–376.
33. Balsalm, D.R., Rothblum, E.D., & Beauchaine, T.P. (2005). Victimization over the life span: A comparison of lesbian, gay, bisexual, and heterosexual siblings. *Journal of Consulting and Clinical Psychology, 73,* 477–487.
34. Corliss, H.L., Cochran, S.D., & Mays, V.M. (2002). Reports of parental maltreatment during childhood in a United States population-based survey of homosexual, bisexual, and heterosexual adults. *Child Abuse & Neglect, 26,* 1165–1178.
35. Triffleman, E.G., & Pole, N. (2010). Future directions in studies of trauma among ethnoracial and sexual minority samples: Commentary. *Journal of Consulting and Clinical Psychology, 78,* 490–497.
36. Saewyc, E.M., Skay, C.L., Pettingell, S.L., Reis, E.A., Bearinger, L., Resnick, M., Combs, L. (2006). Hazards of stigma: The sexual and physical abuse of gay, lesbian, and bisexual adolescents in the United States and Canada. *Child Welfare, 85,* 195–213.
37. Ryan, C., Huebner, D., Diaz, R.M., & Sanchez, J. (2009). Family rejection as a predictor of negative health outcomes in White and Latino lesbian, gay, and bisexual young adults. *Pediatrics, 123,* 346–352.
38. Peter, T. (2009). Exploring taboos: Comparing male- and female-perpetrated child sexual abuse. *Journal of Interpersonal Violence, 24,* 1111–1128.

39. Sedlak, A.J., & Broadhurst, D.D. (1996). Executive summary of the third national incidence study of child abuse and neglect. Retrieved from http://www.childwelfare.gov/pubs/statsinfo/nis3.cfm

40. Kvam, M.H. (2005). Experiences of childhood sexual abuse among visually impaired adults in Norway: Prevalence and characteristics. *Journal of Visual Impairment & Blindness, 99*, 5–14.

41. Sullivan, P.M., & Knutson, J.F. (2000). Maltreatment and disabilities: A population-based epidemiological study. *Child Abuse & Neglect, 24*, 1257–1273.

42. Chun, K.S.K., & Singh, A.A. (in press). The bisexual youth of color intersecting identities development model: A contextual approach to understanding multiple marginalization experiences. *Journal of Bisexuality.*

43. Andres-Hyman, R.C., Cott, M.A., & Gold, S.N. (2004). Ethnicity and sexual orientation as PTSD mitigators in child sexual abuse survivors. *Journal of Family Violence, 19*, 319–325.

44. Balsalm, K.F., Lehavot, K., Beadness, B., & Circo, E. (2010). Childhood abuse and mental health indicators among ethnically diverse lesbian, gay, and bisexual adults. *Journal of Consulting and Clinical Psychology, 78*, 459–468.

45. Tonmyr, L., Jamieson, E., Mery, L.S., & MacMillan, H.L. (2005). The relationship between childhood adverse experiences and disability due to physical health problems in a community sample of women. *Women & Health, 41*, 23–35.

46. Gibb, B.E., Chelminski, I., & Zimmerman, M., 2003). Childhood emotional, physical, and sexual abuse, and diagnoses of depressive and anxiety disorders in adult psychiatric outpatients. *Depression and Anxiety, 24*, 256–263.

47. Briere, J. (2002). Treating adult survivors of severe childhood abuse and neglect: Further development of an integrative model. In J.E.B. Myers, L. Berliner, J. Briere, C.T. Hendrix, T. Reid, & C. Jenny (Eds.). (2002). *The APSAC handbook on child maltreatment* (2nd ed., pp. 175–202). Newbury Park, CA: Sage Publications.

48. Wilson, D.R. (2010). Health consequences of childhood sexual abuse. *Perspectives in Psychiatric Care, 46*, 56–64.

49. Widom, C.S., Czaja, S.J., & Paris, J. (2009). A prospective investigation of borderline personality disorder in abused and neglected children followed up into adulthood. *Journal of Personality Disorders, 23*, 433–446.

50. Breno, A.L., & Galupo, M.P. (2007). Sexual abuse histories of young women in the U.S. child welfare system: A focus on trauma-related beliefs and resilience. *Journal of Child Sexual Abuse, 16*, 97–113.

51. Edmond, T., Auslander, W., & Elze, D. (2006). Signs of resilience in sexually abused adolescent girls in the foster care system. *Journal of Child Sexual Abuse, 15*(1), 1–28.

52. Ackard, D.M., & Neumark-Sztainer, D. (2003). Multiple sexual victimizations among adolescent boys and girls: Prevalence and associations with eating behaviors and psychological health. *Journal of Child Sexual Abuse, 12*, 17–37.

53. Houck, C.D., Nugent, N.R., Lescano, C.M., Peters, A., & Brown, L.K. (2010). Sexual abuse and sexual risk behavior: Beyond the impact of psychiatric problems. *Journal of Pediatric Psychology, 35*, 473–483.

54. Lovett, B.B. (2007). Sexual abuse in the preschool years: Blending ideas from object relations theory, ego psychology, and biology. *Child & Adolescent Social Work Journal, 24*, 579–589.

55. Sikes, A., & Hays, D.G. (2010). The developmental impact of child abuse on adulthood: Implications for counselors. *Adultspan Theory Research & Practice, 9,* 26–35.

56. American Psychiatric Association. (2000). *Diagnostic and statistical manual of mental disorders* (4th ed.). Washington, D.C.: Author.

57. Walker, E., Holman, T., & Busby, D. (2009). Childhood sexual abuse, other childhood factors, and pathways to survivors adult relationship quality. *Journal of Family Violence, 24,* 397–406.

58. American College of Obstetricians and Gynecologists. (2010). *Adult manifestations of childhood sexual abuse.* Retrieved from http://www.aaets.org/article120 .htm.

59. Wise, S., Florio, D., Benz, D.R., & Geier, P. (2007). Ask the experts: Counseling sexual abuse survivors. *Annals of the American Psychotherapy Association, 10,* 18–21.

60. Modestin, J., Furrer, R., & Malti, T. (2005). Different traumatic experiences are associated with different pathologies. *Psychiatric Quarterly, 76,* 19–32.

II

PATHS OF RECOVERY

8

Cognitive and Behavioral Treatments for Sexual Violence

Diane T. Castillo

PAST VIEWS OF TRAUMATIC EVENTS

Effective treatments for traumas will be identified, but first it is important to examine how attitudes toward traumas have evolved over the years in our society. It has only been in the last thirty years that traumatic events have been recognized by the mental health community as the cause of psychological symptoms and in more severe cases, psychological diagnoses. Recognition first began with large numbers of Vietnam War Veterans presenting to therapists with psychological symptoms after their return from combat in Vietnam. When combat Veterans from past wars presented with fatigue and anxiety symptoms, these were first labeled "combat fatigue," "shell-shocked," or "warrior's heart";[1] then labels were directly related to the Vietnam War, like "Post-Vietnam Syndrome." In a hallmark research project, the National Vietnam Veterans Readjustment Study,[2] a set of symptoms was documented as the direct result of the Veterans' combat experiences. This set of symptoms was identified as post-traumatic stress disorder or PTSD, and this diagnosis started being used in 1980.[3] Soon after, researchers and therapists discovered that PTSD symptoms were caused not only by combat, but by any type of life-threatening event, such as rape, natural disaster, or severe automobile accident. While having a label for PTSD symptoms helps therapists, many people feel uncomfortable receiving a psychiatric diagnosis; however, the value of having a label validates and legitimizes the individual's experience of a trauma. Our society has a long history of invalidating trauma survivors by "blaming the victim" even when family and friends believe they are being supportive. An example of a less-direct way of dismissing or invalidating a survivor is telling them to "pull yourself up by your own bootstraps" or "try to forget about it and move on." More direct and damaging messages of blaming the victim are "get over it," "you shouldn't have gone out with him" in a rape trauma, or calling a Vietnam Veteran a "baby killer," as was often done during the Vietnam War. Therefore, having the PTSD label for symptoms after the experience of a trauma acknowledges that the person was truly helpless in the situation and responsible neither for the event nor for the symptoms that occurred afterward. Since the inception of the PTSD diagnosis, it has been documented that after a rape or other trauma, people may experience PTSD but may also experience other psychological symptoms as well.

PSYCHOLOGICAL REACTIONS TO RAPE—POST-TRAUMATIC STRESS DISORDER AND OTHER SYMPTOMS

Any number of psychological symptoms can and do occur at high rates soon after a rape or sexual assault. In fact, it has been reported[4] that one week after a rape, up to 94% of women experienced PTSD symptoms. The percentage dropped to 65% after one month, continued to drop to 47% after three months, and after one year, ended up between 15% and 25%. It is quite common to have psychological symptoms after a rape. While this chapter emphasizes PTSD and its treatment, it is important to recognize that there are many reactions to trauma, such as anxiety, depression, irritability, suicidal thoughts, and alcohol/drug use. Feelings of worthlessness that contribute to depression may occur, as might anxiety about being around people or going to work. And the survivor may use alcohol or drugs to help manage anxiety symptoms, nightmares, or poor sleep. While a number of different symptoms occur after a rape, the most common are PTSD symptoms.

There are a total of seventeen PTSD symptoms[5] within the three categories labeled re-experiencing, avoidance and numbing, and hyperarousal. It is most important to seek the advice of a therapist if symptoms interfere with work, social relationships, school, or everyday activities, and particularly if symptoms persist a year after the trauma. This chapter will refer to rape survivors as women, only for the sake of brevity; males are also the victims of rape and benefit from the same treatments that will be described.

Most Effective Treatments for Post-Traumatic Stress Disorder

Over thirty years of research has been conducted on different types of therapies for the diagnosis of PTSD and/or specific PTSD symptoms. When these studies were compiled and reviewed,[6,7] the results revealed two therapies were consistently the most effective in treating PTSD. The two most effective therapies for PTSD are cognitive therapy and exposure therapy. A form of each will be described in detail in the remainder of this chapter. Briefly, the cognitive therapies help the person change or modify negative thoughts/beliefs that occur as the result of a rape in order to improve emotions; exposure therapies help the woman safely revisit the memory of the trauma repeatedly in her mind with the goal of processing the painful emotions associated with a rape. It is important to note that other therapies have also been found to be helpful in reducing PTSD symptoms, such as relaxation therapy, assertiveness training, and stress inoculation therapy. Also, other approaches not considered psychotherapy, such as yoga, meditation, and spirituality, target the overall well-being of the individual and are also important in creating a balance within the individual and her recovery. Other chapters will provide details on approaches that supplement or balance the exposure and cognitive therapies. Finally, it is important to recognize that each individual has a cultural background, ethnic or other, and some ethnicities offer specific methods for healing the effects of traumas. Therefore, it is important to balance the strongest therapies with approaches that seem most helpful to the individual.

COGNITIVE RESTRUCTURING

Cognitive restructuring is a therapy that focuses on "restructuring" or changing negative thoughts to improve problem emotions. Very simply, the theory is that thoughts—also called cognitions—create emotions or feelings. For example, the thought "I'm a loser" will create feelings of sadness or depression. The thought "I'm a success" will create happy, positive feelings. Cognitions are thoughts, beliefs, ideas, attitudes, values, and even the stream of thoughts that run in our heads continuously. *Cognitions, thoughts,* and *beliefs* are terms that will be used interchangeably throughout the chapter. Thoughts can be positive, negative, and neutral. They may be current or may be long-standing, such as attitudes, morals, and ideals. Cognitions or beliefs about ourselves and the world begin forming during childhood and may change with new experiences, as we age and mature. How we view ourselves is based on thoughts created by parents, important people, and significant experiences, both positive and negative. Thus, cognitions are very powerful in influencing how we think about ourselves, our world, and the direction of our lives. Cognitive therapy is about "listening" to the thoughts in our heads; identifying the negative, erroneous, or judgmental thoughts; and changing them to more realistic, positive, or even neutral thoughts. In the example above, the thought "I'm a loser" creates feelings of depression;

to change the depression, the therapy suggests changing the thought to "I'm successful at some things." Note that the second thought is not the opposite of "I'm a loser," leading to "I'm the most successful person in the world," but rather to a more realistic belief to create positive and hopeful feelings. Recognizing the link between our thoughts and feelings is essential,[8,9] and many self-help books[8] have been written to guide individuals in identifying negative thoughts, modifying them, and thus improving feelings. The book *Feeling Good: The New Mood Therapy* by David Burns[9] and the supplemental workbook[10] are written for nonprofessionals and specifically target depression. The workbook contains many useful exercises that can be used to target PTSD symptoms in rape survivors as well.

Cognitive therapy has a long history of research supporting its effectiveness with different psychological problems or problem emotions, such as depression, anxiety, and anger.[11] In the PTSD arena, cognitive therapy has been identified as one of the two most effective treatments for PTSD. Negative or irrational beliefs/thoughts develop after a life-threatening event or trauma such as rape. The type and extent of negative beliefs that develop after a rape are influenced by beliefs prior to the rape, beliefs about the rape, and society's or family's messages toward the woman and about rape in general. Recovery after a rape will be influenced by these messages. Attitudes and beliefs about women, including roles and relationships with men, can make the aftershock of a rape worse. For example, if a woman grows up believing that she is responsible for her family's problems, she will most likely blame herself after being raped for "letting it happen." It is important to note that most people tend to blame themselves after a trauma even if the trauma is not as personal as a rape. This self-blame is reinforced with society's message of "blame the victim" and will further negatively impact a woman after a rape. Society's messages about women experiencing rape have varied over the years. Long ago, society clearly blamed women for being raped by bringing into focus how they dressed seductively, "teased" a man, or enjoyed the sex, all messages suggesting women somehow "caused" the rape. Regarding men who have been raped, society's messages are just as harsh in the opposite direction, such as "men can't be raped." Therefore common negative beliefs of the man are "Why did they pick me? I must look gay; they must think I wanted it." For both male and female rape victims, these are all negative, irrational, distorted beliefs, and how strongly a woman or man believes these thoughts will determine the severity of the negative feelings after a rape. Negative beliefs or messages persist unless they are actively challenged or questioned. The beliefs held prior to and after a rape contribute to the severity of symptoms and/or recovery. Cognitive therapy works by examining one's beliefs, challenging and changing negative or distorted beliefs as a way of improving feelings and lessening symptoms.

Cognitive Processing Therapy

One specific and highly developed cognitive restructuring therapy for trauma survivors is Cognitive Processing Therapy (CPT).[12] CPT will be described in detail in this chapter because it is one of the most widely used cognitive therapies for PTSD. The manual *Cognitive Processing Therapy for Rape Victims* is written for trained therapists, and while a brief description and a few suggestions will be offered in this chapter, a trained CPT therapist should be consulted to obtain the full, positive effects of the therapy.

Like general cognitive therapies, CPT teaches the rape survivor how to listen to thoughts, challenge the irrational/distorted thoughts, and change them to more realistic ones. However, CPT[12] goes further to identify five belief themes that are often negatively altered after a rape. The five themes are beliefs about (1) safety, (2) trust, (3) power/control, (4) esteem, and (5) intimacy. CPT is an extensive, twelve-session therapy, and the full version includes writing in detail about the rape event twice. CPT-C is the version where the trauma writing is omitted; writing is a form of exposure, which will be described in detail in the second part of this chapter. The first seven sessions of CPT teach the rape survivor the causal link between thoughts and feelings and to progressively develop skills for questioning and challenging negative beliefs. The negative beliefs are called "automatic thoughts" or "stuck points" that result after a rape. A list of challenging questions helps determine if the belief is negative or distorted. The goal is to change the negative thought to a more adaptive, realistic belief. An example of a challenging question is "Are you thinking in all-or-none terms?" (pg. 69)[12] All-or-none thinking is a common cognitive distortion in PTSD because it represents the dualistic, life/death nature of the trauma. Examples of other types of general cognitive distortions can be found in Burns's[8] book. Work on the five themes begins with a homework assignment to write at least one page on how the rape affected beliefs on each theme, beginning with safety. The client brings the writing to the session and reads aloud the writing, and the therapist and client analyze it for distorted, negative, or judgmental thoughts. Using worksheets, each distorted thought is challenged and modified to an alternative, more realistic thought. The client is asked to rehearse the process of checking, challenging, and changing thoughts, as well as practicing the new, adaptive thoughts. Thoughts are examined for those held before the rape, whether positive or negative; those developed after the rape; and thoughts about self and others. This chapter will provide only a few common examples for illustration.

Safety. Beliefs and thoughts about safety are important because the rape violated a woman's sense of safety. The rape is a life-threatening event that produced fear and helplessness. Rape occurs in a range of situations; it can be from childhood through adulthood, and it can range from extremely violent with physical injuries to more subtle coercion by someone in

power. It can be a single episode or a series of rapes in an ongoing relationship. For example, if the woman is raped as an adult by a coworker at
a company party one evening and had a troubled past (growing up beaten
by her mother and father, unsupported, in poverty, possibly molested as a
child), then her safety beliefs might be "I'm never safe and I never will be.
Everyone is out to hurt me." The link between thoughts and feelings is the
key here. In her present life, the "I am never safe" thoughts create feelings of
anxiety, panic, and fear. The degree of anxiety will depend on the strength
of the negative thought. Each day that she walks out of her home with the
"I am never safe" thought, she creates feelings of anxiety. The anxiety can
be immobilizing, leading to daily functioning problems, such as avoiding
work and relationships, and potentially creating a need to use drugs or
alcohol to manage these intense feelings. The goal of CPT is to lower the
intensity anxiety by modifying the "I am never safe" thought. Remember,
it is not possible to erase or eliminate feelings, but they can be lowered to
manageable levels; extreme levels of emotions cause problems. The figure below shows how the automatic thoughts might come up in various
situations, such as getting ready to go to the grocery store. The automatic
thought may end up creating so much anxiety that the woman decides not
to pursue the activity. The change thought is more realistic, allows for the
possibility of not-so-safe situations, and gives the woman the opportunity
to use judgment in creating safety.

The change thought of "Not everyone is dangerous; I can keep myself
safe" creates feelings of moderate anxiety and some calm. The calm, moderate anxiety feelings make it possible to function at daily tasks, such as
grocery shopping or going to work. In this example, the absolute words
like *never* create an expectation that generalizes the terror and danger of the

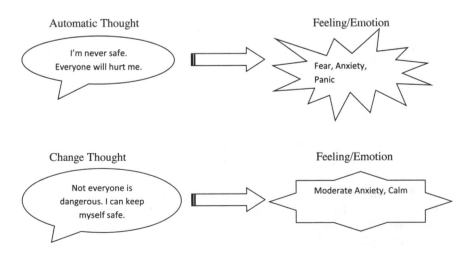

rape to relatively safe situations like going to work or the grocery store. The absolute words create terror in everyday activities. "Everyone is dangerous" is also a distorted belief, because although the rapist was dangerous, the absolute of "everyone" dismisses even the safe people in the woman's life, resulting in her treating safe people similarly to the rapist.

Trust. Beliefs about trust impact a woman after a rape because the rape violated trust beliefs, whether the perpetrator was a friend, family member, or stranger. The betrayal of trust of a friend or family member is obvious because of the expectation for love and trust; the stranger may violate her trust of the world. Let's take the earlier example of the woman with the troubled past. Her previous betrayals of trust by loved ones will bring in beliefs such as "I should have known better; I can't trust myself. Nobody can be trusted" when raped by the coworker. The loss of trust in one's self can undermine the core of our being and the sense that we can keep ourselves safe in a world that is sometimes dangerous. It is important to understand that perpetrators are extremely skilled at manipulating women by first creating a seemingly safe situation, and then by making it impossible for the woman to leave or protect herself before the danger is realized. Instead of the belief that "perpetrators are skilled manipulators" the rape victim believes "I should have known better; I can't trust myself," which creates feelings of doubt and fear. To lower the intensity of the emotion, the change thought can be "Rapists are good manipulators and can't be trusted." Notice that the blame has appropriately shifted from the rape survivor to the perpetrator. It should be noted that in this chapter we refer to male perpetrators and female victims because it is most common; however, it is also important to remember that sexual assault can be perpetrated by both males and females against any individual. It is important to note also that rape is a crime and an exertion of power and not to be minimized as merely a sexual act.

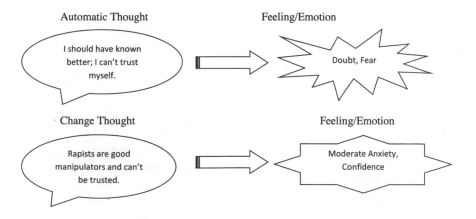

Automatic Thought	Feeling/Emotion
I should have known better; I can't trust myself.	Doubt, Fear

Change Thought	Feeling/Emotion
Rapists are good manipulators and can't be trusted.	Moderate Anxiety, Confidence

Trust beliefs about others focus on external situations and/or people. An example might be "Men can't be trusted," which create feelings of fear and anxiety in daily life, as men make up half of the population. This belief does not account for already-established trust in others nor will it allow a woman to develop new relationships. The change thought "Some people are more trustworthy than others. Not all men rape. I can practice trust by opening up to others slowly to make sure I don't get hurt" will help the woman gain perspective on existing relationships and create calmer feelings and the ability to function in life effectively. As you might have noticed, the five themes can and do overlap, as between trust and the previous theme of safety. Most of the five themes overlap to some degree, and while the separation between the five may seem arbitrary, the separation is intended to help understand the link between thoughts and feelings.

Power/control. Beliefs and thoughts about power and control are based in the feeling of helplessness the woman experienced during the rape, because of the inescapable, life-threatening nature of the situation. Extreme helplessness often translates into the need for control or power after rape. A rape survivor may exert excessive control in relationships, home, and work, which can interfere with functioning in these areas. While control may create a sense of predictability and safety for the survivor, it can also result in rigidity and compulsive behaviors. The minor tasks of everyday life are treated with the same life/death intensity as the rape, oftentimes creating crises where none exist. Negative power/control beliefs in the previous example might be "I must be in control [and if I'm not somebody will die].If someone else is in control, I will get raped again." The thought in the brackets suggests that the woman might not be aware of this thought, but it is "in the back of her head." The "somebody will die" thought is quite powerful and creates feelings of terror and fear, which interfere with daily functioning, in developing and/or maintaining intimacy in existing relationships. While the woman may outwardly acknowledge there is not a threat of death

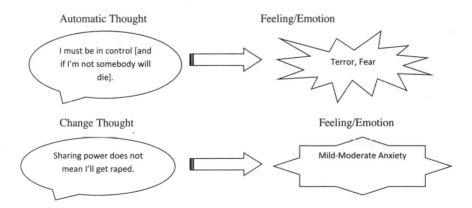

in daily situations like going to the grocery store, her behavior will reflect the life/death intensity in the situation.

Change thoughts can be "Sharing power does not mean I'll get raped again. Some people die, but I can be careful; I can't control everything." The feelings created by the change thoughts are calm and create mild to moderate anxiety.

Esteem. Negative thoughts regarding self-esteem are core to recovery because the act of rape is a deeply personal attack. It is common for a rape survivor to blame herself, especially if everyone else is blaming her. Common negative beliefs about esteem are "What's wrong with me? Why can't I get over this? Nobody else has this problem." There are many different versions of negative self-blame, and it is important to examine those that are specific to each individual. Negative self-esteem beliefs create feelings of sadness and depression, which can be debilitating.

To lessen the intensity of the depression, the change thought can be "I did all I could; my reactions are normal." The changed thoughts will create feelings of confidence and hope. Negative thoughts around esteem are typically associated with depression, and here is where the overlap of depression and PTSD symptoms is noted. Burns's[8] exercises directly target depression and negative self-beliefs about esteem and can help with PTSD as well.

Intimacy. Thoughts about intimacy are typically associated with sexual intimacy, which is negatively affected because the rape was aggression of a sexual nature. While some people minimize rape as "just sex," it is an act of violence and aggression and is against the law. However, because the violence involved sex, negative beliefs about sexual intimacy develop in the woman, like "Sex is dangerous; I can't cuddle or he'll want sex and then I won't be able to stop him." These thoughts create feelings of fear and typically arise when the woman is about to become physically or emotionally close to another person.

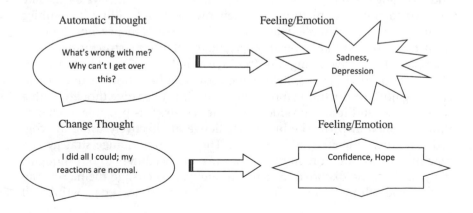

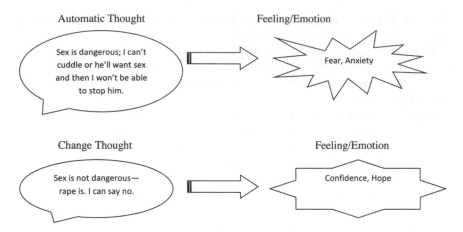

The change thought is "Sex is not dangerous—rape is. I can say no." The changed thoughts produce feelings of hope and confidence in the woman. It is important to note that women who have been raped often struggle with sexual intimacy because having sex, even when it is safe, triggers memories of the rape. Those that have overcome difficulties engaging in sex have done so by having patience with themselves and having a patient, accepting partner. Improvement in sexual functioning begins with listening for distorted thoughts about sex, separating the rape thoughts from the safe-sex thoughts, challenging negative thoughts, and creating adaptive thoughts.

Practical suggestions. Again, if a rape survivor continues to have PTSD or other symptoms after a rape, especially if the symptoms persist beyond a year, she should seek professional treatment from a trained CPT therapist. While cognitive restructuring or CPT is an effective therapy intended to treat PTSD, the process of listening to negative thoughts and challenging and changing them is not a new concept, and most people have used some form of cognitive restructuring on their own without calling it cognitive restructuring. For example, when you tell yourself "I'm just not going to think that way anymore," you are engaging in cognitive restructuring. Other examples of cognitive change are "positive affirmations" used in general or alcohol recovery programs. Rehearsing positive affirmations is not technically cognitive restructuring, but rather replacing a negative thought with a positive one, and it also produces positive results. It is possible to change thoughts on your own. The biggest challenge in effectively using the cognitive restructuring strategy is practice. The cognitive change strategy is a type of hard work that requires the practice of "listening" to our thoughts daily to catch the distorted, negative thoughts and change them. You can remind yourself by setting a timer to "listen" three times a day, writing all the thoughts down in a journal, and reviewing them at the end of the day. If you chose to use a journal to jot down your thoughts, you will need to sort through and pick out the distorted or negative thoughts for change; identify new, positive, or neutral thoughts; and practice the new thoughts in your head daily. An important point here is that many thoughts become like habits. We often repeat the same negative thought in our head regularly, and change requires repeating and practicing the new thoughts to counter the old, distorted, negative ones. Cognitive restructuring is a very powerful tool to improve PTSD and other symptoms, but it must be done daily. This work is much like starting a diet or exercise program. Unless you set a routine to do it, the change will not happen. If you do, however, you will be surprised at the improvement you will see in your life. Do not hesitate to contact a therapist to help you through the process.

EXPOSURE THERAPY

Exposure therapy addresses the heart of PTSD symptoms by going directly to the trauma memory with the guidance of a therapist. In exposure therapy, the client revisits the memory of the trauma in her mind, describing the event repeatedly in the therapist's office. The goal of exposure therapy is to help the woman experience and process emotions that occurred during the trauma but were not allowed out because of the danger of the situation. Many therapies help manage specific PTSD symptoms, such as medications to help with sleep and nightmares or relaxation/breathing to help with anxiety, but exposure therapy directly addresses the link between the trauma and the symptoms. As noted earlier, traumas are life-threatening events, where the individual experiences the most intense emotions of her life. An important part of survival during the trauma event requires the individual to "shut down" or numb these intense emotions. The logical time to process these emotions would be soon after the trauma has ceased and the individual is safe once again. However, most often the community surrounding the woman does not support talking about the experience or only encourages the woman to provide factual information as in a police report, if she reports it at all. The "police report" narrative typically discourages the expression of emotions and is technical in nature. An important part of healing is experiencing the painful, fearful emotions of the trauma in a safe manner. Unfortunately, family members also discourage victims of sexual assault from expressing emotions after a rape, primarily because of their own discomfort. For example, the husband does not want to hear details of his wife being raped because of his own sense of helplessness and inability to protect her. Sometimes in an attempt to support the woman, family members and friends will suggest the woman "try not to think about

it," which only serves to further invalidate her experience rather than helping her heal. The result is the woman reacts to memories and triggers of the
rape by continuing to shut down the intense emotions, as she still does not
feel safe. The woman may also suppress emotions because of time or family
commitments, such as her responsibilities as a parent or the need to return
to work. She may not have the benefit of therapy or support or be afforded
the time to heal.

The consequence of "pushing down" or numbing of emotions is PTSD.
As noted earlier, most people experience PTSD symptoms after a trauma,
but most individuals' symptoms resolve within a year. It is believed that
those people with natural support systems who talk about their experiences
afterward are less likely to continue to have symptoms.[2] Those that continue
to hold in the emotions by avoiding thinking or talking about the rape or
avoiding places that remind them of the rape are those that continue to
be bothered by PTSD, which can last a lifetime. Additionally, women who
blame themselves or think negatively about themselves or their symptoms
also continue to have symptoms. PTSD symptoms, most obviously nightmares and flashbacks, are signs that the emotions of the trauma have not
been processed. Revisiting the trauma memory in exposure therapy allows
the individual to process the emotions of the life-threatening event. Here is
an example of how exposure works with a fearful event. Let's say a young
boy, age four, is taken to the beach by his mother every day. The little boy
loves visiting the beach and playing in the sand and water. One day a strong
wave catches him by surprise and knocks him over. He is frightened and
may even swallow a little water, but his mother is close by to ensure his
safety. The next day, when his mother prepares him for the beach, he begins
to cry and fuss, not wanting to go. The mother, in all her wisdom, insists
on taking him; however, on the first day she walks with him far away from
the water. The next day he fusses, but she again insists on taking him and
continues to do so daily despite his protests. Each day his protests lessen
and she also takes him closer and closer to the water until he eventually returns to his normal state and once again loves going to the beach. Now let's
rewind this example and the next day after the incident the mother gives
in to his protests, feeling badly for him after the difficult experience, and
doesn't take him back. The third day, his protests worsen, and the fourth
his protests escalate further. The mother, thinking she is saving him from an
uncomfortable situation, never takes him back to the beach. The result is,
while the little boy feels better in the moment in not going back, in the long
run, he grows into an adult with a fear of water and dislike of the beach.
The example shows the philosophy behind exposure therapy. The example
is taken from everyday life and the way we use exposure to face challenges,
such as going to job interviews, giving speeches, and going to the dentist.
In other words, we have all engaged in one type of exposure or another.

Prolonged Exposure

Prolonged Exposure (PE; see client manual *Reclaiming Your Life from a Traumatic Experience—Workbook* for details)[13,14] is the most developed model of exposure therapy for PTSD and is considered the standard of care in providing exposure therapy. Therapists across the country are being trained in PE[15] because of the positive results found in its application with all types of trauma, even traumas that occurred years ago. Like CPT, PE therapy is a time-limited treatment. It consists of ten, ninety-minute individual sessions with a therapist trained specifically in the PE protocol. PE consists of education, breathing retraining, and two types of exposure therapy—imaginal and in vivo, or real life.

Education and breathing retraining. Education and breathing retraining are provided in the first two sessions. Education on how exposure therapy works is essential, as understanding the therapy will help an individual complete it. There may be times when the individual may want to stop the therapy. Education starts with an explanation of habituation, which simply means "to get used to something," particularly an uncomfortable something. An example of habituation is going to the same scary movie multiple times. The first time a scary movie is watched, it creates the feeling of fear, possibly a fun kind of fear, as we have chosen to watch it. However, if the same scary movie is watched twenty times in two weeks, by the twentieth time there would no longer be fear, but rather boredom. The fear would have progressively decreased with each viewing of the movie. This is called habituation. The same thing happens with a trauma memory. In the original rape, the emotions were overwhelming and terrifying, and the woman could have died. When the memory of the rape returns, women experience similarly intense, fearful emotions, but going back to the memory repeatedly, like the movie, will allow habituation of these feelings.

Education is also provided about the role of avoidance in keeping PTSD symptoms alive. While avoidance is one of the symptoms of PTSD, it is a strategy used to lessen uncomfortable anxiety. When avoidance is examined more closely, essentially it works in the short run but not the long run. Just as with the little boy on the beach, immediate avoidance after the incident lessened his anxiety but had long-term negative consequences. In another example, say a woman's child needs milk for cereal the next morning, and she must go to the store, but going to the store makes her quite anxious. She thinks, "I'll go this afternoon at 2," and as 2 o'clock gets closer, her anxiety starts to build. It continues to build until 2 o'clock arrives; she makes the decision not to go to the store. Immediately after her decision, her anxiety drops and she feels better. So avoidance worked to reduce her anxiety, but only in the short run. In the long run, she feels badly because her child has no milk for his cereal and she feels like a bad parent. Another long-term consequence is that it is harder to go to the store later when she has no alternative and must go. In the example, the woman felt the immediate positive effects of deciding to avoid but then experienced the longer-term negative effects of avoidance. In therapy, it is also noted that while avoidance has been used as a strategy by the individual over the many years since the trauma, it has not been successful in eliminating the PTSD.

Another part of education is teaching the woman to "measure" her anxiety using a scale called the subjective unit of distress (or discomfort) scale or SUDS. The SUDS is a rating scale that ranges from 0, which is without any anxiety, to 100, which is the highest anxiety/fear, such as that experienced during the rape. A middle event is identified and rated a 50 (which will always remain a 50), such as going to the accountant to get income taxes done. The main value of using a SUDS measure is that it marks improvement during the imaginal and in-vivo activities and demonstrates the gains during therapy for the woman.

Finally, breathing retraining is a relaxation method used to help manage anxiety but is discouraged during exposure sessions. It is used at different times during the week between sessions. While relaxation methods, including breathing retraining, are helpful with the anxiety symptoms of PTSD, the goal of in-vivo and imaginal exposure is to allow anxiety to increase and lower on its own. Engaging in breathing or any other exercise during the imaginal or in-vivo exposures may create the message that the memory is truly dangerous and a coping strategy like relaxation must be used.

Imaginal and in-vivo exposure. PE is based on the theory that intense emotions are created during a rape or trauma, and these intense emotions require processing. PTSD symptoms are natural responses until processing occurs. The two factors that cause PTSD to persist are avoidance of trauma reminders and negative beliefs associated with the trauma. There are two types of avoidance, and they are easily recognizable: (1) avoidance of memories or thoughts of the trauma and (2) avoidance of people, places, or things that are reminders of the rape. The reason avoidance is so common is that avoidance is a natural response to pain. For example, when we touch a hot stove, we immediately pull our hand away. This type of avoidance is useful in keeping damage to a minimum. However, avoidance of emotional pain associated with the memory of a rape causes more problems in the future, as it does not allow for the emotional processing necessary for such a significant event. The two main treatment components of PE—imaginal and in-vivo exposure—allow experiencing of the emotional pain in systematic ways that promote healing of the trauma memory. The second factor that maintains PTSD symptoms is negative thinking around the trauma memory. Thoughts such as "It's my fault this happened. If only I would have said no. Why can't I just let it go? I must be going crazy. Nobody else has these problems" are common, inaccurate thoughts and serve to keep the PTSD symptoms active.

Imaginal exposure. Imaginal exposure directly addresses avoidance by having the woman face the memories and release the emotional pain. The symptoms of nightmares, flashbacks, and/or intrusive thoughts are signals that the emotional pain, fear, and anxiety associated with rape have not been processed. Avoidance is defined as any type of distraction used by the woman when a memory of the rape comes up, with or without reminders. Avoidance can occur in any number of ways, such as leaving the room, turning on the TV, or even drinking alcohol. Facing the memory or permitting the memory of the rape allows her to experience the unprocessed feelings of fear and pain. A useful metaphor is the book example. It is used here to highlight how the trauma emotions are not processed. Let's say our life experiences are represented in a book, with each chapter consisting of different times in our life. The first few chapters might represent all our childhood experiences, the next our teens, the next college, and so on. You can easily read through (remember) the chapters in all parts of your life before and after the rape. However, when you reach the chapter on the rape, you quickly slam the book closed. This occurs each time the book opens to the rape chapter; the chapter cannot be read through, and the memory is never processed. Exposure therapy is opening up the chapter and reading through each painful experience of the trauma over and over, so eventually the rape chapter becomes like all the other chapters in the book. While the rape memory will always produce significant feelings, these feelings are approachable and not overwhelming. The book metaphor helps demonstrate how, in people with PTSD, the memory of the rape is set apart from all other life experiences.

In an imaginal therapy session, the therapist helps the woman identify her worst trauma, if there is more than one. Next, the woman is asked to close her eyes and describe the memory of the rape in the present tense, recalling as many details as possible. A specific starting and ending point are identified, and when she completes the description, or narrative, she is asked to return to the beginning and repeat it. She is instructed to include sights, sounds, smells, thoughts, and feelings as she describes the rape. The repetitions of the same trauma narrative continue for forty-five to sixty minutes in the therapy session. The effect of imaginally repeating the trauma, in the present tense, in the therapist's office, week after week, essentially allows all the feelings the woman experienced in the rape to come out. All the feelings of fear, terror, betrayal, pain, and anger, as well as others, emerge. The emergence of these feelings may result in tears, but most important they emerge, are released, and are processed. Another effect of imaginal exposure is allowing for corrective information. While most trauma survivors believe they remember all the details of the rape or trauma, particularly because the nightmares and flashbacks are recalled so vividly, individuals tend to store the memory away with self-blame labels, among other cognitive distortions. As the memory is repeated, and the variety of emotions arise, greater details of the rape are also remembered, which allow for corrective information. The inaccurate thoughts become corrected simply by a repeated imaginal review of the trauma narrative (not cognitive restructuring, as in the previous section). For example, the woman who initially blamed herself for a gang rape when she was eleven years old realizes she did nothing to cause the rape and could not have been to blame only after she visits the memory repeatedly. The imaginal exposure is conducted in sessions three through ten, and during each imaginal session, the SUDS ratings are taken by the therapist every five minutes. Additionally, the session is tape-recorded, and the woman is instructed to listen to the tape daily, rating her pre-, peak, and postanxiety levels using the SUDS measure. This repetition of imaginal review each week and listening to the rape daily allows the woman to fully engage the memory with all the painful details and all the difficult emotions surrounding the event and thus allows healing of the traumatic memory. The description of imaginal exposure may sound terrifying to someone who has been through a trauma like rape; however, it is important to keep in mind that while there may be a temporary increase in nightmares or anxiety, the overall symptoms will improve. The woman is reminded that the imaginal exposure is just bringing back a memory, and while the actual trauma was life threatening, recalling the memory will not hurt her. The uncomfortable feelings are real, but the image is a memory.

In-vivo exposure. The in-vivo exposure also consists of facing one's fears, but it is done in real-life situations. The in-vivo exposure involves going to places or engaging in activities that have been avoided since the trauma. Most people who have experienced a trauma avoid crowded places because they feel unsafe due to the unpredictability of a large crowd. Other avoided situations are those that remind the woman of the rape. In our earlier example where the woman was raped by a coworker at a company party, the woman would avoid interacting with coworkers including her rapist, going to parties, and going out during the night. The biggest problem with avoided situations is that they multiply. In other words, the number and types of avoided situations increase over time. Years after the rape, she may now avoid restaurants, convenience and grocery stores, and athletic events, none of which were directly related to the trauma. This is called generalization, and the way it happens is illustrated by the following example. Let's say the woman who was raped by a coworker at a party happens to be at a convenience store when she has a flashback of the rape. She escapes from the store, isolates, and never returns to the convenience store because the convenience store has now become a reminder of her rape. As time goes on, more situations become associated or connected with the memory of the rape, and they too are avoided. The woman's world continues to shrink, and she is less able to function in these everyday situations because they too have become reminders of the rape.

In-vivo exposure involves creating a list of all these avoided situations. The situations are specific to each individual and should include a range of anxiety-producing events from mild to high. Once the list is complete, each item is rated with the SUDS measure. With the guidance of the therapist, two or three situations in the 40 to 60 anxiety range are selected for practice from daily to a few times during the week. For example, the woman might rate going to the grocery store at 2 in the afternoon as a 55. She would then be asked to go the grocery store every day and stay in the store for a minimum of thirty minutes or until her anxiety drops to half of its peak, whichever comes first. She would rate her anxiety with the SUDS before going into the store for pre levels, then again when she completed the activity for peak and post levels. While the activity itself is important, the rating is also important because it will eventually provide concrete evidence of her anxiety lowering. While the numbers may not seem lower from day to day, they do lower with continued practice over a two-week period of time. The lower numbers provide self-confidence and confidence in the process. When her anxiety has dropped sufficiently and is no longer problematic for that particular situation, she selects a different avoided activity in which to engage. The more often the activity is done, the more quickly her anxiety lowers. Remember that avoidance is a PTSD symptom and individuals will tend to avoid doing the homework exercises, and it is important *not* to extend the in-vivo activities over long periods, but rather to do them daily and frequently. The grocery store example illustrates the importance of daily in-vivo exposures. If the woman goes daily for two weeks, her anxiety may start at 40, go up to 60, and come down to 55 on the first day. Each day these numbers will continue to lower until after two weeks or fourteen days, her numbers may be 10 pre, 20 peak, and 10 post. If she did the same activity every other day, she would achieve the same results in one month; if she did the exercise once a week, it would take fourteen weeks or 3 1/2 months to improve. Not only does stretching the exercise out slow improvement, but it also encourages the person to continue to use avoidance as a coping strategy. Therefore, doing the in-vivo activities as frequently as possible (at least daily) will result in improvement more quickly. Once one activity is completed, another is assigned from the list.

Practical suggestions. This section on exposure therapy and PE is intended to provide a general description of how this therapy works and is *not* intended as a guide to use this therapy on your own. It is extremely important *not* to jump into your trauma memories based only on the direction in this chapter. While exposure therapy seems intuitively appealing and straightforward, traumatic memories should only be brought back with a trained therapist, because unforeseen problems can arise. The therapist has training and skill in dealing with potential problems and can help you get through the traumatic memories in a successful manner. Having said that, it is likely you can recall having done some minor levels of exposure in your life at various times with nontraumatic experiences. It is important to recognize that you have already done lower levels of "in-vivo" exposure, even though it was not technically therapy. Think back to situations where you forced yourself to do something uncomfortable, like giving a speech or taking a test. The more often you did it, the easier it became and the less anxiety you experienced. Therefore, you can set goals and tackle relatively easy activities that can be completed on your own with the understanding that you must seek professional help should you get overwhelmed. Another very easy activity to implement is using the SUDS measure. It takes little effort and can give you tremendous payoff. You can check your own SUDS numbers at almost any time of the day. Getting your SUDS levels throughout the day or when you go to an activity (pre/peak/post) will help you start the process of healing and lay a useful foundation when you begin therapy.

CASE STUDY

Ellie is a twenty-three-year-old Hispanic female Veteran who was raised in a small Southwestern community by both parents and with one younger brother. She was sexually abused by an uncle (mother's older brother) from the age of eight through eighteen. The abuse began as fondling and developed into vaginal rape by the time she was in her teens. She reported that the sexual abuse/assault occurred about once or twice a month when she and her brother would stay with her uncle and aunt at their house or when the uncle and aunt would come to her house to babysit. The aunt would leave her alone with the uncle while she took the brother to church. Ellie tried to tell her mother when Ellie was about ten, but was not believed. Her father was away from home frequently and when he was home, he drank heavily. Ellie joined the military to get away from home but was raped by another soldier. Since her discharge, she has been completely isolated and no longer dates. Her only close relationship is with her brother, and she avoids her friends because "all they do is drink and hang out at bars." She works full-time as a clerk in a hospital but stays away from her coworkers. She feels like she cannot trust anyone, especially men. When not working, she spends her time at home alone with her dog. Her symptoms include weekly nightmares about the rape, intrusive memories about the rape, feeling anxious and depressed most of the time, poor sleep, getting only two to three hours of sleep a night, irritability, and poor concentration. She began drinking alcohol daily to help manage her anxiety and panic symptoms, but she ended up feeling more depressed.

Cognitive therapy for Ellie. Ellie has many negative thoughts about the world, herself, and life from the sexual traumas. She isolates because she has thoughts like "people are not safe; men are dangerous," which create feelings of anxiety. Thoughts about trust are "no one can be trusted, not even family," also creating feelings of anxiety when she is at work and causing distance in relationships. Negative power/control beliefs might be "I must be in control or I'll get hurt again." Esteem thoughts might be "What did I do to cause this? I'll never get better." Thoughts about intimacy might be "When you love someone, they hurt you." The negative thoughts in Ellie's head that were created by the trauma may not be immediately apparent, and the challenge for Ellie and her therapist will be to examine how she thinks about herself and her world. Once Ellie begins the process of challenging and changing these distorted, negative beliefs, her emotions will improve, as will her relationships and general functioning.

Exposure therapy for Ellie. Exposure therapy for Ellie would consist of helping Ellie to understand the importance of why she needs to go back to the trauma memory, noting how Ellie's past avoidance has worked only in the short run but has left her with many problems in the long run. An index trauma or the worst sexual assault would be identified for imaginal exposure. This might be difficult because of the many times her uncle abused her. There is likely one specific type of rape situation from her childhood that would be selected to go over repeatedly in imaginal exposure. If Ellie's SUDS levels lower sufficiently on the first index trauma, but her PTSD symptoms persist, a second trauma can be identified on which to conduct imaginal exposure. Often the imaginal exposure on a second or third trauma progresses more quickly than the first, and Ellie would experience generalization of anxiety reduction to other traumas. Ellie would also develop her in-vivo, or real-life, hierarchy of avoided situations to tackle in her homework, like her social isolation. She might be asked to go to the grocery store every day at the same time and rate her SUDS anxiety pre, peak, and post, looking for improvement after two weeks. She might also be assigned homework of walks around her neighborhood daily with her dog, rating her SUDs. It is important for Ellie to start with easier, manageable activities to give her evidence that this approach works and confidence in herself. She can then progress to more difficult ones on her list. The combination of imaginal and in-vivo exposures with Ellie can provide improvement in PTSD within as few as three months.

The key for Ellie and victims of sexual violence is to address the PTSD and anxiety symptoms as soon as the woman feels safe to do the work. Some women think they are too old or the trauma happened too long ago. They should know that the length of time since the trauma does not matter and these therapies can be effective soon after a sexual assault or thirty years later.

CHAPTER SUMMARY

Sexual violence or rape is a traumatic experience that can have a devastating psychological impact on women and men. The psychological symptoms can range from mild anxiety or depression to severe symptoms, such as suicidal thoughts, PTSD, and/or alcohol/drug abuse or dependence. Most women will experience psychological symptoms after a rape, and while most get better, a certain percentage will not. Fortunately, two well-developed, effective therapies can help those with PTSD symptoms even years after one trauma or many traumatic events. These two therapies, Cognitive Processing Therapy and Prolonged Exposure Therapy, have had a tremendously positive impact on rape survivors and have created hope for healing. These two very different therapies tackle PTSD and offer reassurance to the rape survivor. Understanding the foundation of these two therapies is important because a survivor can choose the therapy that is most comfortable, and knowledge can set the stage for healing when the time is right to start treatment. The important message is that there is hope with two effective treatment options for healing the devastating effects of rape.

RECOMMENDED READINGS

Feeling good: The new mood therapy. David Burns, 1999. New York: Morrow.
The feeling good handbook. David Burns, 1999. New York: Penguin Putnam Inc.
Reclaiming your life from a traumatic experience—workbook. Barbara O. Rothbaum, Edna B. Foa, & Elizabeth A. Hembree, 2007. New York: Oxford University Press.
Reclaiming your life after rape: Cognitive-behavioral therapy for posttraumatic stress disorder. Barbara O. Rothbaum & Edna B. Foa, 1999. New York: Oxford University Press.

REFERENCES

1. Williamson, V., & Mulhall, E. (2009).Invisible wounds: psychological and neurological injuries confront a new generation of Veterans. Iraq and Afghanistan Veterans of America, Issue Report, 1–23.
2. Kulka, R.A., Schlenger, W.E., Fairbank, J.A., Hough, R.L., Jordan, B.K., Marmar, C.R., & Weiss, D.S. (1988). *Contractual Report of Findings from the National Vietnam Veterans Readjustment Study: Volume I: Executive Summary, Description of Findings, and Technical Appendices.* Research Triangle Institute. Research Triangle Park, NC.
3. American Psychiatric Association (1980). *Diagnostic and statistical manual of mental disorders* (3rd ed.). Washington, D.C.: Author.
4. Rothbaum, B.O., Foa, E.B., Riggs, D.S., Murdock, T., & Walsh, W. (1992). A prospective examination of post-traumatic stress disorder in rape victims. *Journal of Traumatic Stress, 5,* 455–475.

5. American Psychiatric Association (1994). *Diagnostic and statistical manual of mental disorders* (4th ed.). Washington, D.C.: Author.
6. Cahill, S.P., Rothbaum, B.O., Resick, P., & Follette, V.M. (2009). Cognitive-behavioral therapy for adults. In E.B. Foa, T.M. Keane, M.J. Friedman, & J.A. Cohen (Eds.), *Effective treatments for PTSD: Practice Guidelines from the International Society for Traumatic Stress Studies* (pp. 139–222). New York: The Guilford Press.
7. Institute of Medicine (2008). *Treatment of posttraumatic stress disorder: An assessment of the evidence.* Washington, D.C.: The National Academies Press.
8. Burns, D. (1999a). *Feeling good: The new mood therapy.* New York: Morrow.
9. Kanfer, F.H., & Schefft, B.K. (1988).*Guiding the process of therapeutic change.* Research Press, Champaign, IL.
10. Burns, D. (1999b). *The feeling good handbook.* New York: Penguin Putnam Inc.
11. Olatunji, B.O., & Hollon, S.D. (2010).The current status of cognitive behavioral therapy for psychiatric disorders. *Psychiatric Clinics of North America, 33*, xiii–xix.
12. Resick, P.A., & Schnicke, M.K. (1996). *Cognitive processing therapy for rape victims: A treatment manual.* Newbury Park, CA: Sage Publications, Inc.
13. Rothbaum, B.O., Foa, E.B., & Hembree, E.A. (2007). *Reclaiming your life from a traumatic experience—Workbook.* New York: Oxford University Press.
14. Rothbaum, B.O., & Foa, E.B., (1999). *Reclaiming your life after rape: Cognitive-behavioral therapy for posttraumatic stress disorder.* New York: Oxford University Press.
15. Foa, E.B., Hembree, E.A., & Rothbaum, B.O. (2007). *Prolonged exposure therapy for PTSD: Emotional processing of traumatic experiences—Therapist guide.* New York: Oxford University Press.

9

Rape Crisis Centers: Serving Survivors and Their Communities

Jessica Shaw and Rebecca Campbell

In the 1970s, the anti-rape movement emerged with two key foundations: (1) violence against women is used for the social control of women; and (2) women can help one another with the transformation from victim to survivor.[1] Consequently, rape crisis centers (RCCs) were born. This chapter will review the environmental, political, and social factors that culminated in the creation of RCCs and their successive development, the services currently offered by most RCCs, and their effectiveness and impact on communities. To do this, the chapter is divided into six sections. The first section will review the history of the anti-rape movement and its role in the creation of RCCs. Additionally, we will briefly explore how RCCs have changed over the years as their surrounding environments changed. The second section will present the different services offered by RCCs and how these organizations partner with other systems to provide comprehensive services to survivors, their families, and their communities. The third and fourth sections of the chapter will provide an in-depth examination at two specific services, counseling and medical advocacy, and their effectiveness and impact on those served and partnering agencies. (For more in-depth reviews of legal advocacy, see Campbell, 2006,[2] and Campbell, Dworkin, & Cabral, 2009[3]). Finally, the last two sections of the chapter discuss the future of RCCs as we move forward and reviews next steps survivors can take to access RCC services.

THE DEVELOPMENT OF RAPE CRISIS CENTERS

Today, there are more than 1,200 RCCs in operation throughout the United States.[4] It took time to get here, however. The first RCCs emerged through grassroots organizing and volunteering in the 1970s with the intention of providing direct service and creating social change.[1,5] Many of the first centers, brought about by the emotion and passion of feminist activists, were run out of women's homes with donated materials.[6,7,8,9,10] These early RCCs aimed for new models of practice that placed women at the center of all efforts and were staffed by community volunteers who did not have traditional licensing in counseling or professional service backgrounds.[1,6,11,12] They believed in and practiced shared power and decision making as opposed to implementing a top-down organizational model, where an executive director or executive board makes most of the decisions that affect those who work under them.[13] Organizations were not dependent upon or affiliated with parent organizations, but instead were freestanding.[6] Women joined these organizations because they were committed to the movement, that is, to providing direct service and making change in their communities and society at large. This model seemed to work, and the number of RCCs increased throughout the United States.[6]

As time went on, many of the original leaders left the movement after years of struggling to meet their goals and an overcommitment to their cause.[1,12] New staff who placed less emphasis on politics came on board, resulting in varied visions for the structure and function of RCCs.[1,9,12,13] Additionally, providing comprehensive services to the many women who came forward reporting rape on such a limited budget was becoming increasingly difficult.[11] With limited financial resources, many RCCs turned to government funding and began to apply for and receive funds from Law Enforcement Assistance Administration (LEAA) and United Way.[1,6,9,10,11,12] These changes to funding impacted RCCs in a number of ways. First, government funding often required a board of directors, executive directors, and program coordinators to oversee the use of their funds.[11] This caused a shift from the original shared decision making and shared power to a top-down approach.[6] Additionally, government funding sources wanted professionally certified personnel to act as direct service providers as opposed to women who originally joined such centers to empower others and make change.[6,7] Finally, government funds were not infinite. RCCs had to compete for limited funds, which brought about the need for affiliation.[14] RCCs became affiliated with or were absorbed into existing agencies.[1,8,10,12] The changes in personnel, finances, and organizational structure transformed RCCs from organizations run by local community members who shared decision-making power and who were working for bigger, more groundbreaking change to social service agencies.

These changes, however, were not uniform across all RCCs and happened in varying degrees over several years.[6] For example, of ninety RCCs receiving government funds in 1978, only 43% had boards of directors.[9] Some organizations opted for overseeing committees instead, attempting to maintain their feminist collective ideology.[6] Throughout the 1980s, more RCCs emerged, and the variation among them grew.[12] Gornick et al.[12] surveyed a sample of fifty nationally representative RCCs and developed four typologies: (a) centers resembling the original feminist collectives of the early 1970s, (b) centers resembling more mainstream social service programs, (c) centers embedded in other social service or mental health agencies, and (d) programs based in hospitals or emergency departments. These structural differences accounted for differences in practice. Independent centers were more politically active than affiliated centers. Additionally, collectively run centers were more service oriented than hierarchical centers.[1,12] In addition to differences in structure accounting for differences in practice, there are differences between centers formed during the peak of the anti-rape movement, in 1978 or earlier, and centers formed after that time. Campbell et al.[11] found that the older centers were more likely to participate in activities that aimed to make "big picture" change, or social change, such as marches where women reclaim their right to walk alone at night or education initiatives that encourage people to challenge the way things are. These centers were also more likely to practice participatory decision making. Older centers also had larger budgets and more staff. While younger centers were less likely to engage in public demonstrations, such as taking to the street for a march or protest, they were more likely to be involved in political lobbying. All of this seems to suggest that RCCs have adapted their strategies, structure, and function to the times so as to ensure survival.[6]

RAPE CRISIS CENTERS AS SERVICE PROVIDERS

While there have been many changes to the structure, strategies, and function of RCCs over the years, their direct services have essentially stayed the same. Most RCCs provide free, short-term crisis intervention services.[15] Current funding sources (e.g., state Victims of Crime Act funds) often require that three basic services are offered: (a) 24-hour crisis hotline—trained volunteers and staff provide crisis counseling, information, and referrals to a wide variety of community resources via telephone, 24 hours a day; (b) counseling (group, individual, support groups)—licensed professionals, paraprofessionals, and volunteers provide counseling services to address the sexual violence experienced by survivors; and (c) legal and medical advocacy—trained volunteers and staff accompany and assist survivors as they obtain emergency medical care, report their assault, and move through the criminal justice system.[15] Even if RCCs do not receive such funds, it is likely that they offer the same services. In Campbell et al.'s[11] study of 168 RCCs in 1995, all had a rape hotline and almost all (95%) offered medical, police, and court advocacy even though they were not receiving any assistance or funds from the Violence Against Women Act of 1994. Additionally, most all of the centers offered crisis intervention and individual short-term counseling with nearly half providing long-term counseling and counseling in group settings. Both volunteers and paid staff work together to provide these services. Volunteers frequently staff crisis hotlines and provide some advocacy, while counseling services are most frequently provided by licensed professionals.[11] Of the three basic services offered, legal and medical advocacy prove to be the most challenging for center staff and volunteers.[6,16,17] Advocacy will be discussed in more depth in the next section, where we take a critical look at what it entails, its effectiveness, and its impact on survivors and partnering agencies. Additionally, we will return to counseling in the final section of this chapter to discuss different techniques or strategies and their effectiveness in working with rape survivors.

In addition to providing direct services to survivors and their families, RCCs engage in community organizing and help communities become active to make larger social change and spread awareness within their communities. Many of these efforts serve two main purposes, education and action. RCCs engage in many different activities in an attempt to educate. First, they assist mainstream organizations with training. RCCs assist in training police recruits on rape, visit schools to teach sections of health education courses, and train prosecutors on questioning perpetrators and victims.[6] Second, RCCs create and distribute materials on rape and related topics to the media and the community at large.[6] These materials cover a variety of topics and can be created for survivors (e.g., list available resources and natural reactions to rape), for their loved ones (e.g., how to be a supporter), and for a variety of other stakeholders. Third, RCCs engage in community outreach. For example, RCC staff attend community events where they can interact with and provide community members with information and resources. Finally, many RCCs provide prevention programming. Many times, this programming is offered in schools and other institutions.[6] As opposed to risk reduction programming or direct service, prevention programming can target the root cause, including gender roles and gender inequities. While older RCCs (i.e., centers established before 1979) are more likely to provide programming that focuses on the underlying causes of rape, such as gender inequities, it is found across RCCs.[11]

While many of these educational efforts are taken on with the end goal of action, many RCCs also take direct action. First, RCCs work to build community connections and partnerships to improve the response to rape. RCCs help to create or collaborate with sexual assault nurse examiner (SANE) programs to improve how survivors are treated and responded to when they access medical care.[6,18] Additionally, RCCs frequently help organize sexual assault response teams (SARTs) that engage different community members from different backgrounds (e.g., nurses, lawyers, police officers, advocates, etc.) to create a community-wide response to rape, improve existing services, or develop new programs.[6] Second, RCCs participate in or help organize social change activism and public demonstrations. Campbell et al.[11] found that nearly three-quarters of the 168 RCCs surveyed participated in events like the Take Back the Night March, the Clothesline Project, or victim rallies. Finally, RCCs take action by lobbying elected politicians, thus affecting policy outcomes and creating legal reform.[6,11,19,20,21,22]

The steady increase in the number of RCCs in the United States and the funds supporting these centers suggests that these centers and their valuable services are not likely to fade out.[6,23] The research to date has not yet examined how RCC services are responsive to the needs of women of different races, ethnicities, cultures, abilities, and other facets of social location. As this literature develops, RCCs must be ready to develop their services accordingly. Next, we will turn our attention to specific services, their effectiveness, and their impact on survivors and communities.

MEDICAL ADVOCACY SERVICES

Providing medical advocacy for survivors remains one of the most challenging tasks for RCC staff and volunteers.[6,16,17] Rape victim advocates assist survivors as they seek services following their assault. Through this work, rape victim advocates aim to prevent "the second rape," or secondary victimization—insensitive, victim-blaming treatment from system personnel that mirrors and elevates the trauma of the initial rape.[2,6,24,25,26,27,28,29,30] The rape victim advocate's job is twofold—improve direct service delivery and stop secondary victimization.

While rape victim advocates can work with survivors as they navigate different social systems, their work within the medical system will be of primary focus here. Following a sexual assault, rape victims may need emergency medical care for a number of reasons. Victims may have suffered physical injuries during the assault such as cuts, bruises, or lacerations. A medical exam can help to detect and treat these injuries. Semen, blood, hair, fiber, or other forensic evidence can be collected during the exam (often termed a "rape kit") to aid in later prosecution if desired. Additionally, many women have concerns regarding sexually transmitted infections (STIs) and pregnancy. Hospital staff can provide information and preventive treatments to attend to these concerns.[31]

Rape victims often experience long waits in hospital emergency departments for these services, and during that wait, they are not to eat, drink, or urinate as it can destroy evidence of the assault.[32,33,34] When finally seen by medical personnel, survivors often receive very brief explanations of what will occur and why.[31,32,35] Frequently, evidence collection procedures are performed incorrectly, as hospital emergency department personnel do not receive adequate training, while those with training do not conduct exams frequently enough to maintain their aptitude.[32,33,36]

Most rape survivors seeking medical services receive a medical forensic exam and forensic evidence collection kit (70%–81%), but fewer receive comprehensive health care services.[37,38] For example, less than half receive information of the risk of pregnancy (40%–49%).[38,39] Additionally, between 20% and 43% of victims are able to gain access to and obtain emergency contraception to prevent pregnancy.[37,38,39,40] Approximately one-third of victims receive information on the risk of STIs and HIV from the assault and between 34% and 57% actually receive medication to treat and/or prevent STIs.[37,38,39,40,41]

In addition to the invasive nature of the exam and gaps in service delivery, many victims report the experience as cold, impersonal, and detached.[2,37,42] While medical personnel may find questions regarding prior sexual history, sexual response during the assault, what they were wearing prior to the assault, and their actions prior to or during the assault necessary, rape survivors find them very upsetting, and they can result in a negative impact on victims' mental health.[37,42] As a result of contact with medical personnel following an assault, most rape survivors reported feeling bad about themselves (81%), guilty (74%), depressed (88%), violated (94%), nervous or anxious (91%), distrustful of others (74%), and reluctant to seek further help (80%).[37,42] Rape survivors who place their trust in the medical system, only to experience a "second rape," risk the possibility of additional distress.[43]

Rape victim advocates can be instrumental in preventing many of these common problems and gaps in medical services for victims. Studies show that RCC victim advocates increase the likelihood victims will be able to obtain needed services and that advocates prevent secondary victimization. In terms of medical service delivery, Campbell and Bybee[25] found that 82% of survivors who had the assistance of an advocate during their hospital emergency department care received an exam, 70% of those working with an advocate received information on pregnancy, 38% received emergency contraception, 67% received information on STIs, and 79% received STI-preventive antibiotic treatment. These rates are higher than what is typical in the other studies of victims' experiences in hospital emergency departments. Additionally, Campbell[2] found similar results when comparing survivors who worked with an advocate to those who did not work with an advocate at two different hospitals during the same six-month period. Women who had the assistance of a rape victim advocate were significantly more likely to receive information on STIs (72% versus 36%), were more likely to receive information on HIV (47% versus 24%), were more likely to receive STI prophylaxis (86% versus 56%), and were more likely to receive emergency contraception to prevent pregnancy (33% versus 14%) than women who did not have the assistance of an advocate. Both of these studies suggest that advocates improve medical service delivery for rape survivors.

As previously mentioned, the advocate's role is not only to improve service delivery, but also to prevent secondary victimization. Wasco, Campbell, Barnes, and Ahrens[44] found that survivors who worked with an advocate reported less distress after contacting the medical system, as compared to survivors who did not work with an advocate. Similarly, Campbell,[2] in comparing the experiences of survivors who had the assistance of an advocate with survivors who did not have the assistance of an advocate over the same six-month period, found that hospital staff were more likely to refuse to conduct a medical exam and/or evidence collection kit when the survivor did not have the assistance of an advocate (36% versus 36%). Additionally, survivors who did not have the assistance of a medical advocate were more likely to report being treated coldly or impersonally (69% versus 36%), were more likely to be asked how they were dressed at the time of the assault (48% versus 28%), were more likely to be asked about their prior sexual history (73% versus 44%), and were more likely to be asked if they responded sexually to the assault (20% versus 3%) than survivors who did work with an advocate. Finally, survivors who did not have the assistance of an advocate were more likely to report blaming themselves (82% versus 54%), and to state that they were reluctant to seek further help (91% versus 67%). These studies, combined, suggest that RCC medical advocates not only improve service delivery but also decrease survivors' experiences of secondary victimization.

While medical advocates improve survivors' interactions with medical system personnel, their work cannot be done alone. It is crucial that RCC advocates create and continue to develop partnerships with medical care providers. SANEs are specifically trained to attend to the medical and psychological needs of rape survivors. SANE programs were designed to avoid the problems of traditional emergency medical care by having specially trained nurses who provide twenty-four-hour-a-day, immediate-response care to sexual assault survivors in both hospital and nonhospital settings.[43] Many SANE programs work with their local RCC so that RCC medical advocates can be present during the exam to provide support to the survivor.[33,34,45,46,47,48,49] Additionally, SANEs frequently are called upon to provide factual witness testimony or expert testimony.[50,51] When a SANE provides testimony, they act as a witness, not as an advocate. For this reason, having both a SANE and RCC medical advocate working together to attend to the needs of a rape survivor resolves any role conflict.[43]

COUNSELING SERVICES

RCCs frequently provide counseling services to help survivors, and sometimes supporters of survivors, address the sexual violence they have experienced.[6,15,32] RCCs are perhaps the most visible and accessible source for rape survivors' mental health services, as they frequently provide both individual and group counseling free of charge and do not require health insurance.[6,32,52] While little is known about the types of counseling/therapy offered by RCCs, recent literature notes the prevalence of both cognitive-behavioral therapy (CBT) and a feminist and/or empowerment theoretical orientation.[32]

The ways in which sexual assault affects women's well-being is diverse— quite simply, there is no "one way" victims react to such a devastating crime. While psychological symptoms vary during recovery, many victims experience guilt, shame, fear, embarrassment, tension, crying spells, anxiety, an exaggerated startle response, depression, anger (both generalized and directed toward men), discomfort in social situations, rapid mood swings, and/or impaired memory and concentration.[52] Years later, survivors are more likely to have a serious psychiatric diagnosis such as major depression, drug abuse and dependence, generalized anxiety, post-traumatic stress disorder, and obsessive-compulsive disorder.[53,54,55] All of these responses may prompt a survivor to seek out counseling services. They may also seek such services as they begin to disclose their experience to others and as they attempt to build new and foster old relationships.

Having identified survivors' needs for counseling services, we can now turn to frequently used approaches. As mentioned, little is known about RCC counseling practices. However, CBT and feminist therapy emerge as the most commonly used approaches. CBT involves systematic exposure to traumatic memories and cognitive reinterpretation of the events.[56] It can include systematic desensitization, flooding, prolonged exposure treatment, and stress inoculation training. CBT works on the assumption that remembering and visualizing feared situations can help to gradually reduce anxiety.[57] CBT techniques demonstrate effectiveness in reducing fear-related symptoms; however, other factors critical to rape recovery, such as reducing self-blame and increasing social support, are not focused upon in CBT, and their effectiveness in attending to these issues is not known.[58,59,60,61]

Feminist therapeutic approaches, alternatively, focus on longer-term symptoms like guilt, shame, and self-blame. They employ shared goal setting, the identification of rape as a social issue as opposed to a personal problem, and focus on gender inequities.[15,62,63,64,65] Because feminist therapy places a focus on self-blame, guilt, and shame, group therapy is often preferred.[13] This setting can break down feelings of isolation, help to develop supportive relationships, and promote sharing of experiences. This, of course, may not be ideal for all survivors, as preexisting psychological problems may interfere with their ability to participate in a group.[66] In comparing those in feminist therapy to those in traditional counseling, Hutchinson and McDaniel[67] found that those in feminist therapy showed larger improvements in regard to feelings of guilt and self-blame. Morgan[68] found similar results among a group of female survivors of childhood sexual abuse as compared to a control group. CBT and feminist therapy do not need to be used in isolation. Rather, it is common for practitioners to combine different models and techniques to attend to immediate and long-term effects of rape.

While the specific techniques and orientations employed by RCCs are not always explicitly identified, they seem to be working. Wasco and colleagues[15] aimed to evaluate RCC services in Illinois. Seventy-six recipients of RCC sexual assault counseling services completed a survey before and after counseling. Survey results indicated an increase in well-being and coping and lower levels of post-traumatic stress symptoms from the precounseling survey to the postcounseling survey. Additionally, Howard et al.,[64] in comparing post-traumatic stress disorder symptoms before and after counseling among victims receiving rape crisis counseling services, found reductions in distress levels and self-blame over time and an increase in social support, sense of control, and self-efficacy. These studies are promising and indicate that RCC counseling services are working. However, additional research further exploring the techniques and methods employed is necessary.

LOOKING FORWARD

The changes in RCCs over the years may initially suggest that they aren't working, that something is amiss. However, this is not the case. RCCs' continuous change and adaptation illustrates their ability to evolve with the times and to maintain their role in supporting and serving survivors of sexual assault and their communities. When RCCs emerged, they aimed to provide direct services to survivors of sexual assault. Through the decades, they have continued to place survivors and their needs at the center of direct service, and they are making a difference. Historically, the number of RCCs and the funds supporting these centers have typically increased over time, but more recent data suggest that many agencies still identify funding as the single most important challenge, and some RCCs are experiencing financial cutbacks.[6,23,69] It is likely that we will see additional change. RCCs may undergo another wave of transformation in their organizational structure, or we may see changes in funding sources or financial dependence. RCCs will take these changes in stride, as they always have, and will continue with their commitment to survivors of sexual assault, to their communities, and to making change.

CASE STUDY

Lisa just got to the hospital. She's not exactly sure of what she just experienced, but she knows it didn't feel right. She decided to come to the hospital just to get checked out, to make sure that everything is okay, and maybe to get a better understanding of what happened. After checking in at the emergency department, Lisa is taken to private room in the back of the emergency room. As she waits for the nurse, a woman with a bag walks into the room.

The woman explains to Lisa that she is an advocate from the local RCC. She tells Lisa that she is there to provide her with information and resources, to answer any questions she has, and to support her through the process. She then asks Lisa if she would like her to stay. Lisa says yes. The advocate pulls up a chair next to Lisa and asks her if she needs anything, perhaps a warm blanket. Lisa nods, and the advocate leaves the room, shortly returning with the blanket. The advocate then asks Lisa if she wants to talk while they both wait for the nurse to come in. Lisa agrees, and the advocate takes out an envelope that has pamphlets from different organizations in their community that provide services to survivors of sexual assault. The envelope also contains a pamphlet on victims' rights and crime victim compensation. There are handouts that Lisa can give to close family and friends to help them understand how they can support her and what she might be feeling. Lisa tells the advocate that she's not exactly sure what happened to her and she might not need all of that. The advocate tells her that either way, she can take it with her just in case she needs it; these services are always available and she can choose to use them in the future, or not.

The nurse comes into the room and gives Lisa an overview of the medical forensic exam, explaining step-by-step what she will do and why. As she finishes explaining the exam, the advocate interjects and tells Lisa that she can do all of the exam, parts of the exam, or not do it at all if she's not comfortable with part of it, and that she has the right to say no to any of it. Lisa feels okay with this. She's hesitant about the exam, but decides to go ahead with it because she knows she can stop at any time.

The nurse then asks if Lisa would like to talk to the police and file a report of what happened. Lisa turns to the advocate. The advocate tells Lisa that there is no mandatory reporting in her state, that it is absolutely her decision if she talks to the police. The advocate further explains that this would be the first step in the legal process. Filing a police report does not mean that Lisa has to pursue prosecution, but it makes it a lot easier if she decides to later. Still, it is Lisa's decision. Lisa decides that she does not want to file a report, and the advocate tells her that's fine. She tells Lisa that if she changes her mind later, the RCC can provide an advocate to go with her to the police station.

The exam then begins. The nurse does a good job of explaining to Lisa each thing she is doing before she does it. If she forgets, the advocate reminds her and asks her to explain it to Lisa. There are some parts of the exam that Lisa doesn't like, but decides that it is okay to do them. Other parts of the exam are too much and Lisa decides she does not want them done. The advocate tells her that's fine, and the nurse respects her decision. After the exam, the advocate gives Lisa some new clothes to wear home because Lisa decided to let the nurse collect her clothes as evidence. The advocate asks Lisa if she has any final questions. Lisa says no. After Lisa is discharged, the advocate walks out with her, and Lisa returns home.

Several months later, Lisa has put the experience behind her. While it is still very much a part of her, she doesn't think about it quite as much and feels as though she has moved on. She never found a need to go to counseling or use any of the other services the advocate told her about. She recently started a new job. She's looking forward to the change. Some of her old coworkers were there the night it happened. Even though they didn't say anything to her about what happened that night, she knew that they knew and was sure that they talked about it sometimes.

The first few weeks at her new job are great. She is meeting new people and learning a lot. It's challenging, but in a good way. One afternoon, her coworkers invite her to happy hour. She declines, saying she has plans already, and says that she'd love to go next time. Lisa is surprised by her own response. She doesn't have plans. She's not quite sure why she responded the way she did. When she gets home that night, she is still thinking about what happened. She realizes she's worried about getting close to coworkers again and felt like she had to do this to keep herself safe. Lisa didn't like feeling this way and wasn't sure if it was normal. She continued to think about this over the next few days and finally decided to call the RCC. She remembered the advocate telling her that people use their services even if they aren't exactly sure what happened to them and that she should contact them even if she's not sure what she needs. Lisa calls the RCC and sets up an appointment with a counselor there. She is nervous but decides it can't hurt to go.

At the first session, Lisa is a bit uncomfortable talking about what happened. She still feels it was her fault, that she should have done something differently, and that perhaps she was making a big deal about nothing. She feels as though there is something wrong with her, that she's not normal now. The counselor listens to her and together, they work through many of these things over the next couple of weeks. After several sessions, the counselor asks Lisa what she would think about attending a support group. She tells Lisa that she is not alone in how she is feeling and thinks she may benefit from hearing other people's stories. It might help her to understand that she is having a perfectly normal response for what she experienced. Lisa decides to give it a try.

Lisa is nervous for the first session and a bit uncomfortable. She doesn't know if the other women will have similar stories. She worries that what she experienced isn't "real" enough. Through the group sessions, she learns that she is not alone. While she is saddened to hear that other women had to go through this too, it helps her to understand that she is not the problem, that she is not broken. Lisa starts to understand that she did not choose what happened to her and it is not her fault. Going to group therapy has helped Lisa understand that the process of healing will take time, but now she is going with others instead of alone.

WHAT CAN YOU DO?

- *Locate your local RCC.* Your local RCC operates to serve survivors, supporters, and their communities. They are only effective if people are aware of and access their services. RAINN, the Rape, Abuse, and Incest National Network, is a great place to start. RAINN is the nation's largest anti–sexual violence organization. You can visit their website, www.rainn.org, to find your local RCC. Additionally, you can call their national sexual assault hotline at 1-800-656-HOPE. You will be directly connected to the RCC closest to you.
- *Call your local RCC's hotline.* The hotline is there for you. Staff and volunteers cover the hotline twenty-four hours a day to provide crisis intervention and information. Many people that call the hotline aren't quite sure how to label their experience. That's okay. If it didn't feel right, it probably wasn't. Hotlines are for supporters too.
- *Schedule a counseling appointment.* Recovery takes time, and healing is possible. RCC counselors are there to support you as you begin this process.
- *Attend a support group.* You are not alone. Support groups provide a safe space for people with similar experiences to come together, talk, process, and support one another. Many RCCs provide support groups for survivors, loved ones of survivors, and other supporters. Contact your local RCC to find out if and when they host support groups.
- *Participate in community events.* RCCs began as grassroots organizations and still thrive on community involvement and activism. Many RCCs hold multiple community events throughout the year—Take Back the Night marches, Clothesline Projects, 5K races—contact your local RCC

to find out what events are coming up and how you can get involved. It's okay if you're not ready to lead the march; simply showing up is more than enough. In coming together, we can make change.

• *Volunteer.* RCCs still depend on the commitment and passion of dedicated individuals to provide services and make change. They are always looking for volunteers to provide advocacy services for survivors, to work the crisis hotline, to help out at community events, to provide education and outreach services, and to staff their resource libraries. Contact your local RCC to find out how you can help. Working with sexual assault survivors is both rewarding and challenging. Volunteering with your local RCC may be an empowering experience, but it should not be used in place of therapy or counseling. Taking care of yourself is most important. If you choose to volunteer, collaborate with others at your RCC to develop self-care techniques and ways to support one another.

REFERENCES

1. Matthews, N.A. (1994). *Confronting rape: The feminist anti-rape movement and the state.* New York: Routledge.
2. Campbell, R. (2006). Rape survivors' experiences with the legal and medical systems: Do rape victim advocates make a difference? *Violence Against Women, 12,* 1–16.
3. Campbell, R., Dworkin, E., & Cabral, G. (2009). An ecological model of the impact of sexual assault on women's mental health. *Trauma, Violence, and Abuse, 10*(3), 225–246.
4. National Sexual Violence Resource Center, 2010; personal communication
5. Riger, S. (1994). Challenges of success: Stages of growth in feminist organizations. *Feminist Studies, 20,* 275–300.
6. Campbell, R., & Martin, P.Y. (2001). Services for sexual assault survivors: The role of the rape crisis centers. In C. Renzetti, J. Edleson, & R. Bergen (Eds.), *Sourcebook on violence against women* (pp. 227–241). Thousand Oaks, CA: Sage.
7. Collins, B.G., & Whalen, M.B. (1989). The rape crisis movement: Radical or reformist? *Social Work, 34,* 61–63.
8. Schechter, S. (1982). *Women and male violence.* Boston: South End Press.
9. O'Sullivan, E.A. (1978). What has happened to rape crisis centers? A look at their structure, members, and funding. *Victimology, 3,* 45–62.
10. Pride, A. (1981). To respectability and back: A ten-year view of the anti-rape movement. In F. Delacoste & F. Newman (Eds.), *Fight back: Feminist resistance to male violence.* Minneapolis: Cleis Press.
11. Campbell, R., Baker, C.K., & Mazurek, T. (1998). Remaining radical? Organizational predictors of rape crisis centers' social change initiatives. *American Journal of Community Psychology, 26,* 465–491.
12. Gornick, J., Burt, M.R., & Pittman, K.J. (1985). Structure and activities of rape crisis centers in the early 1980s. *Crime and Delinquency, 31,* 247–268.

13. Koss, M.P., & Harvey, M.R. (1991). *The rape victim: Clinical and community interventions.* Newbury Park, CA: Sage.
14. Byington, D.B., Martin, P.Y., DiNitto, D.M., & Maxwell, M.S. (1991). Organizational affiliation and effectiveness: The case of rape crisis centers. *Administration in Social Work, 15,* 83–103.
15. Wasco, S.M., Campbell, R., Howard, A., Mason, G., Schewe, P., Staggs, S., & Riger, S. (2004). A statewide evaluation of services provided to rape survivors. *Journal of Interpersonal Violence, 19,* 252–263.
16. Campbell, R. (1996). [Unpublished field notes from interviews with 20 rape survivors]. East Lansing: Michigan State University.
17. Martin, P.Y. (1997). Gender, accounts, and rape processing work. *Social Problems, 44,* 464–482.
18. Ledray, L. (1999). *Sexual assault nurse examiners (SANE): Development and operations guide.* Washington D.C.: Department of Justice, Office for Victims of Crime.
19. Berger, R.J., Searles, P., & Neuman, W.L. (1988). The dimensions of rape reform legislation. *Law and Society Review, 22,* 329–357.
20. Fischer, K. (1989). Defining the boundaries of admissible expert testimony on rape trauma syndrome. *University of Illinois Law Review,* pp. 691–734.
21. Schmitt, F., & Martin, P.Y. (1999). Unobtrusive mobilization by an institutionalized rape crisis center: "All we do comes from victims." *Gender & Society, 13,* 364–384.
22. Martin, P.Y., DiNitto, D., Byington, D., & Maxwell, M.S. (1992). Organizational and community transformations: The case of a rape crisis center. *Administration in Social Work, 16,* 123–145.
23. Martin, P.Y. (1999). *Rape processing work in organization and community context.* Unpublished manuscript, Florida State University, Department of Sociology.
24. Campbell, R. (1998). The community response to rape: Victims' experiences with the legal, medical, and mental health systems. *American Journal of Community Psychology, 26,* 355–379.
25. Campbell, R., & Bybee, D. (1997). Emergency medical services for rape victims: Detecting the cracks in service delivery. *Women's Health, 3,* 75–101.
26. Madigan, L., & Gamble, N. (1991). *The second rape: Society's continued betrayal of the victim.* New York: Macmillan.
27. Frohmann, L. (1991). Discrediting victims' allegations of sexual assault: Prosecutorial accounts of case rejections. *Social Problems, 38,* 213–226.
28. Martin, P.Y., & Powell, R.M. (1994). Accounting for the second assault: Legal organizations' framing of rape victims. *Law and Social Inquiry, 19,* 853–890.
29. Matoesian, G.M. (1993). *Reproducing rape: Domination through talk in the courtroom.* Chicago: The University of Chicago Press.
30. Williams, J.E. (1984). Secondary victimization: Confronting public attitudes about rape. *Victimology, 9,* 66–81.
31. Martin, P.Y. (2005). *Rape work: Victims, gender, and emotions in organization and community context.* New York: Routledge.
32. Campbell, R. (2008). The psychological impact of rape victims' experiences with the legal, medical, and mental health systems. *American Psychologist, 63,* 702–717.

33. Littel, K. (2001). Sexual assault nurse examiner programs: Improving the community response to sexual assault victims. *Office for Victims of Crime Bulletin, 4,* 1–19.

34. Taylor, W.K. (2002). Collecting evidence for sexual assault: The role of the sexual assault nurse examiner (SANE). *International Journal of Gynecology and Obstetrics, 78,* S91–S94.

35. Parrot, A. (1991). Medical community response to acquaintance rape—Recommendations. In A. Parrot & L. Bechhofer (Eds.), *Acquaintance rape: The hidden crime* (pp. 304–316). New York: Wiley.

36. Plichta, S.B., Vandecar-Burdin, T., Odor, R.K., Reams, S., & Zhang, Y. (2006). The emergency department and victims of sexual violence: An assessment of preparedness to help. *Journal of Health and Human Services Administration, 29,* 285–308.

37. Campbell, R. (2005). What really happened? A validation study of rape survivors' help-seeking experiences with the legal and medical systems. *Violence & Victims, 20,* 55–68.

38. Campbell, R., Wasco, S.M., Ahrens, C.E., Sefl, T., & Barnes, H.E. (2001). Preventing the "second rape": Rape survivors' experiences with community service providers. *Journal of Interpersonal Violence, 16,* 1239–1259.

39. National Center for Victims of Crime & National Crime Victims Research and Treatment Center. (1992). *Rape in America: A report to the nation.* Arlington, VA: National Center for Victims of Crime.

40. Amey, A.L., & Bishai, D. (2002). Measuring the quality of medical care for women who experience sexual assault with data from the National Hospital Ambulatory Medical Care Survey. *Annals of Emergency Medicine, 39,* 631–638.

41. Rovi, S., & Shimoni, N. (2002). Prophylaxis provided to sexual assault victims seen at U.S. emergency departments. *Journal of American Medical Women's Association, 57,* 204–207.

42. Campbell, R., & Raja, S. (2005). The sexual assault and secondary victimization of female veterans: Help-seeking experiences with military and civilian social systems. *Psychology of Women Quarterly, 29,* 97–106.

43. Campbell, R., Patterson, D., & Lichty, L. (2005). The effectiveness of sexual assault nurse examiner (SANE) programs: A review of psychological, medical, legal, and community outcomes. *Trauma, Violence, & Abuse, 6,* 313–329.

44. Wasco, S.M., Campbell, R., Barnes, H., & Ahrens, C.E. (1999, June). *Rape crisis centers: Shaping survivors' experiences with community systems following sexual assault.* Paper presented at the Biennial Conference of the Society for Community Research and Action, New Haven, CT.

45. Hatmaker, D., Pinholster, L., & Saye, J. (2002). A community-based approach to sexual assault. *Public Health Nursing, 19,* 124–127.

46. Lang, K. (1999). *Sexual assault nurse examiner resource guide for Michigan communities.* Okemos: Michigan Coalition Against Domestic and Sexual Violence.

47. Rossman, L., & Dunnuck, C. (1999). A community sexual assault program based in urban YWCA: The Grand Rapids experience. *Journal of Emergency Nursing, 25,* 424–427.

48. Seneski, P. (1992). Multi-disciplinary program helps sexual assault victims. *The American College of Physician Executives,* pp. 417–418.

49. Smith, K., Homseth, J., Macgregor, M., & Letourneau, M. (1998). Sexual assault response team: Overcoming obstacles to program development. *Journal of Emergency Nursing, 24*, 365–367.

50. Ledray, L. (1998). Sexual assault: Clinical issues, SANE expert and factual testimony. *Journal of Emergency Nursing, 24*, 284–287.

51. Ledray, L., & Barry, L. (1998). SANE expert and factual testimony. *Journal of Emergency Nursing, 24*, 3.

52. Koss, M.P., Bailey, J.A., Yuan, N.P., Herrera, V.M., & Lichter, E.L. (2003). Depression and PTSD in survivors of male violence: Research and training initiatives to facilitate recovery. *Psychology of Women Quarterly, 27*, 130–142.

53. Burnam, A., Stein, J. Golding, J., Siegel, J., Sorenson, S., Forsythe, A., & Telles, C. (1988). Sexual assault and mental disorders in a community population. *Journal of Consulting and Clinical Psychology, 56*, 843–850.

54. Kilpatrick, D.G., Best, C.L., Veronen, L.J., Amick, A.E., Villeponteaux, L.A., & Ruff, G.A. (1985). Mental health correlates of criminal victimization: A random community survey. *Journal of Consulting and Clinical Psychology, 53*, 866–873.

55. Koss, M.P. (1993). Rape: Scope, impact, interventions, and public policy responses. *American Psychologist, 48*, 1062–1069.

56. Foa, E., Riggs, D., & Gershuny, B. (1995). Arousal, numbing, and intrusion: Symptom structure of PTSD following assault. *American Journal of Psychiatry, 152*, 116–120.

57. Foa, E., Steketee, G., & Rothbaum, B.O. (1989). Behavioral/cognitive conceptualizations of post-traumatic stress disorder. *Behavior Therapy, 20*, 155–176.

58. Foa, E., Rothbaum, B.O., Riggs, D.S., & Murdock, T.B. (1991). Treatment of post-traumatic stress disorder in rape victims: A comparison between cognitive-behavioral approaches and counseling. *Journal of Consulting and Clinical Psychology, 59*, 715–723.

59. Frank, E., Anderson, B., Stewart, B.D., Dancu, C., Hughes, C., & West, D. (1988). Efficacy of cognitive behavioral therapy and systematic desensitization in the treatment of the rape victim. *Behavior Therapy, 19*, 403–420.

60. Resick, P.A., Jordan, C.G., Girelli, S.A., Hutter, C.K., & Marhoefer-Dvorak, S. (1988). A comparative study of behavioral group therapy for sexual assault victims. *Behavior Therapy, 19*, 385–401.

61. Resick, P.A., & Schnicke, M.K. (1992). Cognitive processing therapy for sexual assault victims. *Journal of Consulting and Clinical Psychology, 60*, 748–756.

62. Edmond, T. (2006, February). *Theoretical and intervention preferences of service providers addressing violence against women: A national survey.* Paper presented at the Council on Social Work Education Conference, Chicago, IL.

63. Goodman, L.A., & Epstein, D. (2008). *Listening to battered women: A survivor-centered approach to advocacy, mental health, and justice.* Washington, D.C.: American Psychological Association.

64. Howard, A., Riger, S., Campbell, R., & Wasco, S.M. (2003). Counseling services for battered women: A comparison of outcomes for physical and sexual abuse survivors. *Journal of Interpersonal Violence, 18*, 717–734.

65. Ullman, S.E., & Townsend, S.M. (2008). What is an empowerment approach to working with sexual assault survivors? *Journal of Community Psychology, 36*, 1–14.

66. Sprei, J., & Goodwin, R.A. (1983). The group treatment of sexual assault survivors. *Journal for Specialists in Group Work, 8,* 34–46.

67. Hutchinson, C.H., & McDaniel, S.A. (1986). The social reconstruction of sexual assault by women victims: A comparison of therapeutic experiences. *Canadian Journal of Community Mental Health, 5,* 17–36.

68. Morgan, T. (2000). Psychological change in group therapy experienced by women survivors of childhood sexual abuse. *Dissertation Abstracts International, 60,* 4898.

69. Macy, R., Giattina, M., Parish, S., Crosby, C. (2010). Domestic violence and sexual assault services: Historical concerns and contemporary challenges. *Journal of Interpersonal Violence, 25*(1), 3–32.

10

Eye Movement Desensitization and Reprocessing for Sexual Assault

Diane Clayton

"Pain in this life is not avoidable, but the pain we create avoiding pain is avoidable."

—R.D. Laing, M.D.

VICTIMS OF SEXUAL ASSAULT

In a traumatic event, the body's natural reaction is the "fight, flight, freeze, or collapse" response. Memories of sexual molestation affect the victim's behavior, self-esteem, motivation, and general beliefs they have about themselves. It is not unusual for untreated sexual assault victims to use avoidant behaviors to inhibit these overwhelming and disturbing memories. They often engage in compulsive behaviors and may turn to substance abuse.[1]

In my thirty-two years of treating recovering female addicts, I have observed that 75% had a history of sexual abuse. These victims feel dirty, think of themselves as unlovable, and may experience some form of sexual dysfunction, ranging from lack of sexual desire to compulsive sexuality. The younger and more chronic the sexual abuse, the more fragmented and fragile is the victim's personality structure.

Using eye movement desensitization and reprocessing (EMDR), the therapist is able to guide the client through these painful memories. Thoughts and feelings of worthlessness and powerlessness are replaced by those of worth and dignity. The victim stance is replaced by healthy self-awareness and stability.

WHAT IS EYE MOVEMENT
DESENSITIZATION AND REPROCESSING?

In this chapter we are going to explore the complex model of EMDR. It is a phase-oriented approach to therapy based on principles and protocols designed to move the recipient of treatment through a process that is extremely prescriptive, and empowering.

EMDR is a rapid, safe, and effective psychotherapeutic modality when used in the treatment of sexual assault and other trauma-induced pathologies. It was discovered in 1987 by Francine Shapiro, Ph.D., while she was researching ways to reduce stress. Dr. Shapiro noticed that after rapid eye movements a disturbing event in her own life was no longer as disturbing. She believed she had tapped into a natural healing process much like the body's attempt to heal a wound.[2]

It was initially named eye movement desensitization. After further research, Dr. Shapiro published the first study[3] addressing symptoms of post-traumatic stress disorder found in combat veterans and rape victims. This study revealed that after only three to five sessions the symptoms of post-traumatic stress disorder (hypervigilance, flashbacks, and nightmares) were extinguished.

For these tortured souls, the war was finally over and the rape had finally ended. This was as important a discovery for mental health counseling as the laser had been for surgery. From these humble beginnings EMDR has evolved into a therapeutic modality that is effectively used in treating everything from anxiety to dissociation.

In 1990, Dr. Shapiro noticed more was happening than just desensitization. It was as if a digestion of the memory had taken place. The participants had stopped reacting to the event with overwhelming anxiety but had metabolized and integrated the experience. The name was changed to eye movement desensitization and reprocessing.[2]

EMDR has many components of other therapies: cognitive, behavioral, psychodynamic, family systems, and experiential, just to name a few. All of these components are found in the procedures and protocols in EMDR and work faster than any of the therapies do individually. EMDR is combined with other modalities in the treatment of complex post-traumatic stress disorder such as ego state therapy.[4]

It has become one of the most researched psychotherapies. Most research has been on simple trauma as opposed to complex trauma. Information regarding research can be found on the website of the EMDR International Association at http://emdria.org and the Francine Shapiro Library at http://emdr.nku.edu. The *Journal of EMDR Practice and Research* is dedicated to publishing EMDR's newest findings.

HOW DOES EYE MOVEMENT
DESENSITIZATION AND REPROCESSING WORK?

Despite its proven effectiveness, EMDR has been criticized by some, perhaps because it is not known exactly *how* it works. Several theories have been postulated. Dr. Shapiro uses the language of neuropsychology to explain her theory. Her explanation is called adaptive information processing (AIP) theory. The AIP model proposes that the unconscious is composed of stored memories that guide us automatically like a well-worn path. These unprocessed memories are networked with or linked to certain other memories, emotions, and distorted thoughts and beliefs, and they elicit physiologic sensations. These emotions, thoughts, and feelings then arise in the present and cause disturbances.

Processing these memories frees the individual to respond more appropriately in the present. How EMDR accomplishes this "processing" is still a matter of debate in the scientific community. However, this therapeutic model guides treatment planning and predicts clinical outcome consistently in EMDR. The client is able to connect to more positive information that was previously blocked from awareness by traumatic memories.

Researchers have referred to EMDR as going beyond a talking cure and checking into emotions and bodily sensations while noticing mental content.[5] EMDR gets behind words and taps into the unconscious. PET scans after EMDR showed an increase in prefrontal lobe activity. Before EMDR, PET scans revealed more activity in the limbic system. These results indicate that the client is functioning in the present rather than reacting from emotionality and events from the past.

Laboratory studies of eye movements[6] have revealed effects on memory components. These studies have revealed that the following changes take place after eye movements:

- Decreased vividness of memory images and related thoughts
- Decreased emotionality related to memory images
- Physical changes such a lowering of the heart rate, skin conductance, and increased heart rate variability
- Increased cognitive recall of words and early childhood memories
- Increased episodic memory

THE EIGHT PHASES OF EYE MOVEMENT
DESENSITIZATION AND REPROCESSING

The "treatment goal for the individual is to get the most profound and comprehensive results in the shortest period while maintaining a stable client within a balanced family and social system."[7]

EMDR is a client-centered, complex, eight-phase approach to psycho-therapy. The more extensive the abuses, the more extended are the different phases. The sessions are generally ninety minutes long. The following description characterizes the EMDR protocol, though the particulars are unique to each individual.

Phase I: History and Treatment Planning

During the first phase of treatment the therapist takes an extensive history, if this is not too overwhelming for the client. It is essential to establish rapport and build trust in this phase. When someone has had an extensive sexual abuse history, they may have difficulty talking about the event or in some cases remembering the event. The psyche protects itself by creating amnesia barriers when an event is too overwhelming.[8]

Many victims blame themselves instead of their abuser and feel shame and humiliation about what has happened to them.[9] They may experience self-loathing and have difficulty talking to anyone about such a traumatic, life-changing event. The therapist may get only parts of the story at this time if the client is too overwhelmed.

The therapist then determines if the client is appropriate for EMDR and if the client is emotionally stable enough at this point for processing. *Stable* implies that the client is functioning and living in a stable environment. The client is screened for dissociation. According to *Diagnostic and Statistical Manual of Mental Disorders, Fourth Edition* (DSM-IV), "the essential feature of dissociative disorders is a disruption or alteration in the usually integrated functions of consciousness, memory, identity or perception of the environment. The disturbance or alteration may be sudden or gradual, and transient or chronic."[10]

Dissociation is a defensive pattern used by victims of complex trauma that enables the blocking of memories that are too overwhelming. While EMDR does not cause dissociation, it does bring it to the forefront if it exists in the individual. Using the standard protocol in EMDR with this population will destabilize and open up an overwhelming response. Screening is a safety precaution. The client may need more rapport building and be resistant to working on these memories immediately.

Phase II: Preparation

Trauma is stored in fragments in the memory and locked in with the feelings, sounds, smells, and body sensations, as if frozen in time. EMDR processing releases a lot of emotional tension, and the client may abreact during processing.

Phase II prepares the client for processing. A concise but thorough consent briefing is completed in which the client is carefully informed of what to expect in treatment and reassured that control over the process rests entirely with them. Self-control techniques are taught. When processing, the client will experience the trauma again, but in a very short period of time, while being oriented to safety in the present.

The method of bilateral stimulation (BLS) is chosen. BLS is one of the features that make EMDR a unique therapy. Bilateral eye movements, hand taps, or sounds are employed while the client assesses the disturbing memories. The client follows the therapist's fingers or a light bar designed to move the eyes rhythmically back and forth. Tapping or sounds may also be used to stimulate processing. The therapist chooses the type of BLS most fitting to the client's individual needs.

If the client has had extensive abuse, the preparation phase will be extended and ego-strengthening exercises will be used to prepare the client and help establish the courage to face their trauma.

Phase III: Assessment

The goal of this phase is choosing the target memory to be processed first. There may be several targets, but the first is chosen based on what the client feels ready to process. Generally the earliest memory that started the negative beliefs about the self, known as the touchstone event, is identified with the present triggers and symptoms. Beliefs often espoused by sexual assault victims are "I am not lovable" or "I am not good enough."

The client identifies a memory and brings forth the image that represents the worst part of the memory. The negative belief about the self is contrasted with what the client would like to think about the self and compared to how true the positive statement is in the present.

The client is asked to identify the emotions associated with the memory and how disturbing these emotions are in the present. This is rated on a scale of 0 to 10, referred to as the subjective units of disturbance scale.[11]

The client then focuses on the body sensation associated with the memory. After this baseline information is gathered the client is ready to move to the fourth phase, desensitization.

Phase IV: Desensitization

This is the phase where processing begins. The client holds the disturbing memory, the negative cognition, and body sensations in mind while the therapist starts the bilateral stimulation (BLS).

The client allows whatever internal experience is happening for them to emerge as they hold the memory. Through observing the client's face while processing, the therapist determines when is a good time to give the client a break from processing by saying, "Take a deep breath and blank out the memory." The therapist requests that the client share their experience. There are no right or wrong answers. The client shares what they have experienced internally and then returns to the last part of the memory, processing more with BLS.

When the client starts processing the event or events, the individual focuses on what happened but does not remain fixated on the event while processing. Information may emerge that the client had forgotten. Positive connections start to occur. The client moves through the different memory channels related to the event. Processing may plateau at different points, and the client is taken back to the target memory.

The therapist acts as a facilitator and stays out of the way of the processing. Only if the client gets stuck or derailed does the therapist intervene. The goal is to move the processing along until the memory channels are cleared and the disturbance is brought down to 0 or 1.

The client is taught to just observe and let whatever happens happen, like watching the scenery from a train. The processing follows, using targets from the past, present and future. Anticipatory anxiety about the event in the future is processed along with the past and present targets. Much of what happens for the client is free association. This is where tapping into unconscious material allows the client to get beyond words and make a connection, giving insight not readily achieved through talk therapy.

Phase V: Installation

Installation involves taking the positive belief identified in the assessment phase and pairing it with the identified trauma memory. Bilateral stimulation is added to reinforce the positive belief changed from the negative cognition.

The client holds the original image and the positive belief about the self before starting the eye movement sets. The installation continues until the client feels that the positive cognition is true. The client is asked to rate their belief on a scale of 1 (false) to 7 (totally true). This is referred to as the validity of cognition scale.

Phase VI: Body Scan

After the desensitization of the negative cognition and the installation of the positive belief, a body scan is taken. It consists of having the client scan down their body mentally, noticing any residual tension while thinking about the original target and the positive belief about the self. If tension exists, it is processed with bilateral stimulation.

Phase VII: Closure

This is the last phase completed before the client leaves the session. The client is instructed to keep a log of memories along with the cognitions, emotions, body sensations, and level of disturbance. This teaches the client that they are larger than the events in their lives and to observe themselves without acting. The log is used to determine the direction of the next session.

If the client is continuing to experience some disturbance at the end of the session, then a full debriefing is completed. The client uses self-control techniques and is grounded to the present. The goal is always to have the client leave in better shape than when they came into the session.

Phase VIII: Reevaluation

When the client returns for the next session, the processing that was completed in the previous session is evaluated. If the positive cognition has continued to be valid and the memory is no longer disturbing, then the log may be used to determine a new target for processing.

Research has shown that fidelity to the protocol is necessary to get the desired results in treatment. One should seek a therapist trained in programs approved by EMDR International Association. This serves as the governing body overseeing the training and education in EMDR. New and innovative strategies are researched as part of their mission.

ONGOING IMPACT OF SEXUAL ASSAULT

Sexual assault victims may experience anxiety, phobias, panic, and/or depression. The longer an individual goes without treatment, the more impact the trauma and avoidance behavior will have on the victim's life and affect the decisions they make in the present.

The victim engages in self-defeating behavior with unintended negative consequences. Processing allows new connections to be made so decisions in the present are clear and not colored by the past trauma and avoidance. Failing to attend treatment creates a domino effect, creating more pain and low self-esteem.

Sexual assault is so much more than the event itself. The person is left with feelings of helplessness, powerlessness, self-blame, and shame. Bad choices after the event create more feelings of self-loathing.

Post-traumatic stress untreated can last for a lifetime, leaving the victims with chronic symptoms and loss of potential for a happy life. The following case is an example of the effects of delayed treatment.

THE CASE OF EMILY

In 2006, Emily was drugged and kidnapped by a sexual predator and raped repeatedly for two days. The drug left her paralyzed for a period of time. After escaping from the predator she felt dirty and blamed herself. Emily is a white, middle-class, female, thirty-six years old, and divorced; her life changed overnight from this event.

She had met the man in a restaurant on a date, and while she was in the bathroom, he put something in her drink that caused her to feel disoriented. He then offered to give her a ride home. Unable to drive, she accepted his offer. While unable to move from the effects of the drink, she was trapped in her house with this man.

After the terror and repeated rape, she blamed herself and started acting out her feelings of self-blame and -loathing. For two years after the event Emily used alcohol and drugs to numb her pain. She was arrested numerous times over a two-year period. On the last occasion of her arrest, she was kept in jail for a month. After this happened she sought treatment.

The psychiatrist recognized that Emily was not alcohol dependent but suffering from post-traumatic stress disorder. After six sessions of EMDR, Emily processed through the rape, her feelings of being dirty, and the humiliations of being arrested. She stopped drinking and using drugs and returned to her former functioning self. She had been competent and successful before the rape. The two-year delay in treatment had been costly both emotionally and financially to Emily. From a recent contact she reports her life is going well. The treatment effects have held over time.

EARLY-LIFE IMPACT OF SEXUAL ABUSE

Ongoing sexual abuse before the age of six, mixed with other life instabilities, may lead to complex post-traumatic stress disorder.[4] The personality fragments into different ego states to accommodate the needed duality of existence. This may happen when sexual abuse is perpetrated by unstable parenting figures.

A distant mother and raging alcoholic father that sexually abuses create overwhelming fear, insecurity, and confusion in a child, creating inadequate attachment.

Children often identify with their parents, and if one is an abuser, the child's survival is dependent upon the abuser. The child labels itself as bad, rather than the parent, to ensure its own survival. The child will punish itself. Ironically, in order to feel safe from harm, the child may abuse herself. The child often experiences emotional deregulation and may engage in self-harm such as cutting.

Dissociation runs on a spectrum. Splitting of the personality may result. To protect itself, the psyche may develop alternative ego states. The following case is an example of ego splitting.

THE CASE OF MARIA

Maria is a forty-two-year-old divorced female of first-generation Spanish/ Italian descent with a sixteen-year-old son. She is an educated business-woman, beautiful and bright. She began experiencing flashbacks and terrible nightmares six years ago. When the flashbacks occurred, she thought she was losing her mind. She started seeking treatment, and over the course of four years, she received many different diagnoses, depending on how she presented at the time of her appointments. One diagnosis was attention deficit disorder, and she was placed on medication. Several more diagnoses followed. None of the treatments she received improved her hopeless mood or improved her ability to function. She had shut down and isolated herself.

Due to nightmares and flashbacks, Maria became fearful of staying in her home. She spent a good deal of her resources staying in hotels to feel safe. After four years of missed diagnoses and failed treatment, she entered EMDR treatment.

In the flashbacks were childhood memories of being sexually fondled by her father for as long as she could remember. He had been a "gypsy" and was raised in a culture where he had learned to steal and had been sexually molested himself. Maria's abuse was ritualistic in nature. Objects had been inserted into her vagina. She remembered the pain being so unbearable that she would escape into a fantasy in her mind. It was like she would leave her body and look down upon the event. Her parents had told her she was special and that she would be ahead of the other girls her age. Her father was an erratic alcoholic, and her mother was rejecting and emotionally distant.

The memories of the molestations had been buried. Maria had difficulty sleeping for most of her life. She did not understand why she had such difficulty. When the memories started surfacing, she asked her parents, who denied any such thing ever happened. This further reinforced her fear that she was losing her mind. Her parents cut off their relationship with her after the confrontation. She felt abandoned and had little reason to live. After doing some research, she found her suspicions were well founded. Her father had been arrested for fondling another child. Other buried memories returned.

When she was a child, because of her father's erratic behavior, the family was ostracized by the community where they lived. Other children were not allowed by their parents to play with Maria. She had attended many schools, never able to maintain friendships. She felt alienated and rejected. Her friendships would abruptly end as people in the neighborhood witnessed her father's behavior. As a small child, she recalled being taken to many different hospitals on numerous occasions for urinary infections. Most of the abuse occurred before the first grade.

After some time in treatment Maria started to trust her judgment that her flashback memories were real. Because of her dissociation, she had memory lapses and would often awaken in a childlike state. This was terrifying. Sometimes she would find work she had done that she did not remember doing. She felt very young and small and did not remember how to use phones or computers or respond to e-mails. Awakening from the nightmares was difficult. She knew she was not herself and struggled to get back to her normal functioning. Aware of her condition, she understood when she switched from an adult to a childlike state.

After Maria was stabilized and was taught grounding techniques, she started EMDR processing. For the first time in her life she started sleeping through the night. She processed old memories, and the pieces of her life started to make sense, like pieces in a puzzle. She started to feel more control over her life. She became more hopeful.

Prior to treatment she had planned to commit suicide when her son completed high school. After two years of treatment she had worked thought much of the painful memories.

Because of the insecurity she felt in the attachment and bonding experience with her parents, she has not yet overcome her fear of connecting to people. She has difficulty in relationships. Either she tends to cling or run away from them. Her attachment is a disorganized one. She is now working on this problem and is more hopeful about her future.

Utilizing grounding techniques and orienting herself to be present most of the time, she has realized her potential to be a high-functioning adult.

COMPLICATION IN PROCESSING

Victims while in processing often get stuck around beliefs regarding responsibility, safety, and choices.[2] A cognitive interweave is brought into EMDR processing when the client has difficulty in these areas. A cognitive interweave created by Dr. Shapiro may be a statement or giving of information to the client needed to move the processing.

The therapist integrates the new information with BLS. Clients have difficulty feeling safe in the present, particularly sexual abuse victims. Many were threatened at the time of the assault and may feel that if they disclose what happened, they will be harmed. Victims, particularly children, have fear of disclosure. Although the person may be an adult now, the fear of disclosure is still locked in the body and psyche.

Victims of pedophiles experience confusion in processing regarding responsibility because pedophiles groom their victims before abuse. The pedophile may be generous financially, provide nurturing, and make the child feel special. A loyalty and bond develops between the victim and predator.

The experience of an assault combined with having their abuser provide positive things for them creates a trauma bond.[9] The victim may willingly participate, feeling they owe the perpetrator. Reenactment is a common behavior for the victim. The female victim may compulsively go from one abusive relationship to another if treatment does not occur.

Because of the developed loyalty to the perpetrator, the child fails to disclose, feels confused about their participation, and blames herself. This creates a "double bind" for the victim. Processing is more difficult because of these confused feelings. Psychoeducation for the victim regarding grooming behavior relieves some of the confusion. The following case is an example.

THE CASE OF SARA

Sarah is now in her twenties, a white, single, poor female from a southern state. She is experiencing anxiety and depression. She grew up in a single-parent family where her mother was weary with two jobs and had little time to spend with her. She had experienced emotional deprivation and loneliness as a child and teenager. When she was in high school, her gym teacher had taken some interest in her. The teacher would invite her to her home and showed special interest in her.

After a while the teacher started soliciting sexual favors from Sara. It left her with feelings of self-loathing and self-hatred. She started cutting herself. Later, when in EMDR therapy, she was stuck feeling that the gym teacher was the only one who had cared about her. To give up the belief meant that she was unlovable and unworthy. Sara could not win with either cognition. It took months for the client to work through her stuck processing.

EMDR WITH COMPLEX TRAUMA

EMDR can be very powerful in moving the victim to trauma resolution. It can also be destabilizing if processing ensues too quickly and the standard protocol not modified. Complex trauma with EMDR has not been researched as completely as single events. The current research indicates that using Resource Development installation, titrating the trauma in processing, and extending the preparation phase produces the best results.[12] Hypnosis, ego state therapy, and cognitive therapy combined with EMDR strategically helps the client to develop a higher level of affect tolerance. This is needed for the client to tolerate the abreactive responses commonly experienced in EMDR processing.

More research is needed on complex trauma and EMDR. Many pioneer therapists are forging ahead and developing techniques in stabilization and processing with EMDR, keeping the client oriented to the present. Dr. Shapiro initially recognized the EMDR Dissociative Disorder Task Force[13] to make recommendations and guidelines outlined in her second-edition text.[2]

THEORY OF STRUCTURAL DISSOCIATION OF THE PERSONALITY

Theory of structural dissociation of the personality (TSDP) postulates that the personality of traumatized individuals is unduly divided in two basic types of dissociative subsystems or parts. One type involves dissociative parts primarily mediated by daily life action systems or motivational systems. The other type involves dissociative parts, fixated in traumatic memories, primarily mediated by the defense action system. The more severe and chronic the trauma, the more dissociative parts can be expected to exist.[8] This theory helps to guide the use of EMDR with complex trauma and dissociative disorders.

In sexual assault the victim attempts to integrate the experience. The ability to integrate preserves their mental health and guides them in an action plan. When integration is unsuccessful, the survivor may split off the emotional part of the self from what presents as the apparent normal part. The greater the trauma, the more fragmented are the parts of the self.[8] This means in treatment that longer preparation is required to not overwhelm an already-stressed system that could totally decompensate without creating a structure for treatment.

Structural dissociation is found to exist in different categories: primary, secondary, and tertiary. Primary dissociation involves all forms of trauma and includes post-traumatic stress disorder. There is some splitting of the apparent normal self and emotional parts. In secondary dissociation there are more emotional parts and one apparent normal self. In tertiary disassociation there are many parts of self as a result of more traumas.[8] An incorrect diagnosis and premature processing can be a disaster for the client. While EMDR is very effective, a healthy respect for its impact is important for the therapist and the client. Treatment must be phase oriented with much preparation and stabilization. The standard protocol described above must be altered to accommodate the complexity of the individual.

In summary EMDR is a powerful, effective psychotherapeutic modality that is still evolving with new research for treating all traumatic disorders. There is hope for those that prior to EMDR had poor prognosis for recovery. With EMDR used by a well-trained therapist there is a light at the end of the tunnel. The client can hope to have a full recovery and have the quality of life possible before trauma. Fidelity to certain phases of the protocol is important. The client must be ready to face their trauma and prepare to be empowered by the process.

REFERENCES

1. Abel, N.J., & O'Brian, J.M. (2010). EMDR treatment of comorbid PTSD and alcohol dependence. *Journal of EMDR Practice and Research, 4*(2), 50–59.
2. Shapiro, F., (2001) Eye movement desensitization and reprocessing, basic principles, protocols, and procedures (2nd ed.). New York: Guilford Press.
3. Shapiro, F. (1989b). Eye movement desensitization: A new treatment for post-traumatic stress disorder. *Journal of Behavior Therapy and Experimental Psychiatry, 20,* 211–217.
4. Forgash, C. (2008). Healing the heart of trauma and dissociation with EMDR and ego state therapy. New York: Springer Publishing Company.
5. van der Kolk, B., McFarlane, A., & Weisaeth, L. (1996). *The effects of overwhelming experience on mind, body, and society.* New York: Guilford Press.
6. Propper, R., & Christman, S. (2008). Interhemispheric interaction and saccadic horizontal eye movements. *Journal of EMDR Practice and Research, 2*(4), 269–281.
7. EMDRIA.org, Definition of EMDR, Revised 10/25/09.
8. van der Hart, O., Nijenhuis, E., & Solomon, R. (2010). Dissociation of the personality in complex trauma-related disorders and EMDR: Theoretical considerations. *Journal of EMDR Practice and Research, 4*(2), 76–92.
9. Carnes, P. (1997). *The betrayal bond.* FL: Health Communications, Inc.
10. American Psychiatric Association (1994). *Diagnostic and statistical manual of mental disorders* (4th ed.). Washington, D.C.: Author.
11. Wolpe, J. (1958). *Psychotherapy by reciprocal inhibition. Stanford, CA: Stanford University Press.*
12. Korn, D. (2009). EMDR and the treatment of complex PTSD: A review. *Journal of EMDR Practice and Research, 3*(4), 1465–1487. 13. Fine, C., Luber, M., Paulsen, S. Puk, G., Rouanzoin, C., & Young, W. (1995). A general guide to the use of EMDR in the dissociative disorders: A task force report. In Shapiro, *Eye movement desensitization and reprocessing: Basic principles, practices and procedures.* New York: Guilford Press.

11

Family Systems and Recovery from Sexual Violence and Trauma

Amy Tuttle

> The core experiences of psychological trauma are disempowerment and disconnection from others. Recovery, therefore, is based upon the empowerment of the survivor and the creation of new connections. Recovery can take place only within the context of new relationships; it cannot occur in isolation. In her [his] renewed connections with other people, the survivor re-creates the psychological facilities that were damaged or deformed by the traumatic experience (p. 133).[1]

> . . . Relationships are central to health and key to treatment (p. 391).[2]

> Multisystemic, resilience-oriented practice approaches help families and communities expand their vision of what is possible through collaboration, not only to survive trauma and loss but also to regain their spirit to thrive (p. 224).[3]

The fields of psychotherapy and psychology have provided survivors and mental health professionals with unique and multiple paths to recovery and healing. Though many of the "paths" and approaches have traditionally focused on healing the survivor, family-oriented treatments and interventions have provided a multisystemic, relational approach to facilitating this process. This chapter will examine a family systems understanding of the process of recovery from sexual violations and traumas. A family systems perspective and the systemic effects on the individual, couple, and family will be explored, and strategies for healing, case examples, and recommendations for survivors, family members, and mental health professionals will be presented.

FAMILY SYSTEMS ORIENTATION

A family systems orientation supports the notion that families are "causative in generating or maintaining symptoms," a perspective that facilitated the development of the field of family therapy (p. 12).[4] Differing from traditional psychodynamic approaches that focused on the intrapsychic, the past, and the individual, systemically orientated approaches conceptualize change and healing from an interactional, process-oriented perspective.

From a family systems perspective, every individual is relational; "a competent identity does not develop in isolation, but in constant relationship to others," and when an individual experiences trauma or violence, others, including family members, are impacted (p. 27).[5] Several characteristics highlight how a family systems–oriented perspective serves to describe problem development, change, and healing. These include (a) recognizing processes of overt and covert forms of communication, (b) viewing interactional dynamics from a process-oriented perspective in which patterns and structure are highlighted, and (c) attending to the connection between social context and the interaction and interrelatedness between individuals and the family.

Early family researchers, such as Don Jackson and Jay Haley, contended that instead of examining only the intrapsychic and biological contributions to problems, one must consider interactional, process, and relational-related dynamics; specifically, *how* one communicates. For instance, in their early studies on schizophrenia, they challenged the perspective that biological and other internal processes supported the diagnosis and in turn developed interventions that addressed family roles, rules, and structure. They asserted that "one cannot not communicate," as communication is essential to understanding the system, and thus, "communication implies a commitment and thereby defines the relationship" (p. 51).[6] Similarly, family scholars, such as Jay Haley and Salvador Minuchin, highlighted the interactional characteristics of systems. They supported the notion that problems develop and are maintained in the relationships within families, and therefore, solutions and change are managed by reorganizing family structure, power, and hierarchy; altering communication patterns; and identifying alternative meanings and perspectives.

Lastly, interactions and relationships are connected in a social context. The self is social and exists in social interaction with others; thus the mind is inseparable from the context around it. This socially constructed idea of self cannot be thought of as residing within an individual, but rather is created and maintained between people. From this perspective everyone is inherently relational, and models of therapy emphasize the interpersonal and interactional creation of meaning and experience. Thus, individuals and families may also be viewed as functioning within larger social systems (e.g., family of origin, communities, and larger systems), and they are impacted by dominant social discourses.[7,8] This view of self is popular among contemporary family therapists who base their work on social constructionist theories.[9,10,11]

FAMILIES, LARGER SYSTEMS, AND SOCIOCULTURAL CONTEXTS

During the late 1970s and early 1980s, issues of gender and culture began to emerge in the field of family therapy, and family scholars began to acknowledge that all families are influenced and reliant upon other systems as well as sociocultural and political contexts.[12] Not only are we challenged us to *re-vision* family systems theory, but we must also address and revise how we are defining and describing a *family*. Traditional notions of family and family intervention must "make room for the unspoken structures, the cultural, racial, class- and gender-biased hierarchies that are the underpinnings of our society" and "think of families in terms of the communities they live in" (p. 6).[12]

By expanding our vision of families and acknowledging the realities in which families exist, it is important to integrate contextual issues into conversations, treatment, and healing practices to enhance the change process. For instance, Minuchin and Aponte highlighted intervention with diverse and poor families, Boyd-Franklin and Lindblad-Goldberg published literature on multisystemic and ecosystemic approaches and interventions, and Hare-Mustin, Walters, Carter, Papp, and Silverstein published on gender and feminist critiques of the field. These family scholar pioneers opened the space to integrate issues of spirituality (e.g., Walsh), immigration (e.g., Falicov), cultural and family of origin (e.g., Garcia-Preto, Moore Hines), and diverse family structure (e.g., Nealy) into healing from multigenerational trauma, sexual violence, and other forms of abuse.

Changes within society and family therapy opened the possibility for inclusion of the cultural aspects of the family into healing from sexual violence and trauma. In this process, families and mental health professionals may consider sociocultural and political forces that impact the recovery process and work to expose "dominant cultural norms that have contributed to the client's abuse and oppression" (p. 15).[13] Further, issues of gender, culture, sexual violence and trauma, and sociocultural implications and meanings of victimization must be considered, and issues of masculinity and sexuality ought to be considered to avoid dominant social discourses leading to isolation and oppression.

FAMILY SYSTEMS AND RECOVERY FROM TRAUMA

Consistent with family systems theory, trauma and violence inflicted on an individual impacts not only that individual, but the immediate family members, extended family members, and future generations.[14] Researchers[13,15,16] have addressed reactions of family members and a disruption in the structure of the family when a child experiences physical and medical traumas, and literature[17,18] has highlighted the influence of childhood sexual abuse on trust and intimacy in relationships with family members and friends. These researchers have supported the idea that though one individual may directly experience a violent or traumatic incident, family members and others may be affected by the event, thus resulting in a form of secondary trauma. Secondary trauma may be experienced by an individual whose family member (or significant other) is violated or has experienced some type of traumatic event.[19,20] Barnes (1998, 2005)[19,20] and Pfefferbaum (1997)[21] have addressed the systemic nature of trauma response and experiences of parents when a child is violated or traumatized. This notion of systemic traumatic stress results from the "sudden demands imposed on each member of the family system and the resultant change in relationship patterns" (p. 83).[20] This secondary trauma not only affects the parents, but other members of the family, family structure, roles, and organization. Therefore, intervention and healing invites a family systems orientation and involvement and support of the entire family and community.[22]

Family Systems Recovery Process

Survivors, families, and communities must develop more effective strategies for navigating through the healing process to develop alternative, family-oriented ways to relate to the sexual violence and trauma. Integrating literature from a family systems perspective and supporting inclusion of family in the healing process,[19,20,23,3,22] family systems recovery from sexual violence and trauma invites two core areas of exploration: (1) sharing experiences related to the violence and abuse and (2) identifying the role of culture and context.

Stories of trauma. Consistent with a family systems perspective, survivors *and* family members are impacted by the trauma of sexual violence and abuse. Survivors experience the direct emotional and physical symptoms, and family members experience secondary trauma; thus, the system experiences systemic related trauma.[20] For instance, those in relationship with one who has been sexually abused or violated may experience guilt, fear, and helplessness related to the inability to protect another and prevent the violent act or abuse. Therefore, each member of the family system may experience the negative emotional and psychological consequences of the traumatic event.

Sharing stories and expressing experiences about the traumatic event and related emotional and psychological symptoms assist the survivor and family members in healing by acknowledging and processing their experiences related to the event.[23,3,22]

> When painful or unacceptable feelings can't be expressed and supported, or when differences are viewed as disloyal or threatening, there is a higher risk of somatic and emotional disturbance, destructive behavior, and substance abuse (p. 214).[3]

Further, Johnson (2004) writes that expression of emotion organizes "interactions between the couple [and family] as music organizes a dance" (p. 500).[24] Therefore, sharing stories and experiences of the violent, traumatic event open up possibility for a deeper level of trust, intimacy, and connection in relationships while creating alternative meanings and ways to understand the trauma or abuse incident.

As noted above, expression of experience is important to the healing process. However, *how* survivors and family members communicate their experiences and the effects of a traumatic event provide insight into the organization and structure of the family, highlighting possible destructive relational patterns. As literature on the impact of child trauma and violence contends, the family structure and roles may be impacted by the traumatic event. Thus, as experiences and stories are shared, *how* the family communicates and interacts is important to address. For instance, if a member of the family is distant and aloof, the traumatic event may shift or even highlight their role in the family. A shift in role or structure has the potential to reengage the distant, aloof member in the family system. On the other hand, if a shift doesn't occur, additional intervention may be initiated to increase family support and connection. Sharing experiences and stories of the effects of the trauma provides family members opportunity to engage and support all members.

Just as sharing stories of how the survivor and family members have managed through the crisis is important to healing and recovery, so is the process of sharing stories and experiences of how the family and survivor have developed the courage and strength to cope with the trauma. Themes of hope, resilience, and strength are important to examine[25,26,3] and may be introduced and explored in the conversation. Stories of resilience and courage provide opportunities to further explore the meaning of the event and develop healing family rituals and resources.

Role of sociocultural and contextual issues. Sociocultural and contextual issues are a significant part of a survivor's and family member's experience.[23,3,22] Sociocultural influences provide insight into how the survivor and family members approach, understand, and thus heal from the trauma, highlighting the influence of gender, culture, and dominant social discourses on each person and the family. Further, sociocultural influences on the structure of the family and roles of individual members may be explored to assist with the healing process.

Sociocultural issues may provide the survivor and family with ways to understand the effects of the trauma and assist in the identification of internal and external resources. Further, survivors and family members may reflect on relational connections and possible opportunities to strengthen and reconnect with their sense of spirituality, extended family members, supportive systems, and community resources.

Family Systems Recovery Process: Tasks

Family members and survivors' collaborative recollection of the effects of violence and trauma on the family and related sociocultural issues rebuild and strengthen relational connections in family relationships. These connections not only increase support, but also provide opportunity to further examine individual and family resources, acknowledge the event and the resilience of the family, and identify possibilities for the future. To facilitate this process of healing, survivors and family members may work toward (a) identifying, exploring, and integrating internal and external individual, family, and community resources; (b) acknowledging the event and resilience of the family to utilize in the healing process;[23,3] and (c) extending resources, strengths, and family stories of resilience into the future.

Internal and external resources. Mental health clinicians and family members must provide opportunities for exploration of individual, family, and community internal and external resources. By providing a safe place to express memories and experiences of the trauma, as well as inviting exploration of strength, courage, and resilience, family members, friends, mental health professionals, and members of the community can assist in the healing process and expose the internal and external resources required for change and recovery.

Individual and family system internal resources and strengths assist with building resilience in the family system. These may include courage, hopefulness, faith, and spirituality. In addition to internal resources, external resources and relationships or connections with extended family members, friends, and the community are important to identify and utilize. External resources may include relationships with others or involvement in a faith or spiritual community. Possible questions to access internal and external resources include:

1. How have you (survivor and family members) managed to get to this point?

2. Tell me about your (survivor and family members) courageous attitude in getting you here?
3. What do you and your family members do when things aren't going well? What do you and your family members do in time of crisis?
   a. Have you or family members turned to religion, faith, spirituality, and/or a higher power? How has this helped in the past? How can it help now?
4. What strengths do you (survivor and family member) have that have assisted in this situation?
   a. How have you used it? How did you get it?
   b. Who helped to notice that strength? Who was the first to notice this strength in you?
   c. Who else in the family has that strength? How does that strength show itself in the family?
   d. What strengths have others noticed?
5. Who do you (survivor and family members) turn to in time of crisis?
   a. Why did you turn to this person or group? How were they helpful? How can they be helpful now?

Acknowledge the event and the family's resilience. As survivors and family members share their experiences and stories of abuse and trauma, it is important to listen for internal and external resources that may highlight individual and family resilience. Family resilience may be acknowledged in stories of survival and strength and through the development of family healing rituals. Family healing rituals, for example, are structured actions or activities that highlight a developmental or family transition or transformation.[27,28] They may be developed to acknowledge and heal from a trauma and may integrate the family's cultural heritage and customs. For instance, communities and families celebrate holidays and participate in activities, such as candlelight vigils, funerals, and memorial services, to remember an event. These ritualized activities provide opportunities to remember the positive and negative effects of an event. The following questions may be introduced to assist families in developing family healing rituals:

1. What are some of the customs or rituals your family uses to acknowledge important events or holidays in the family? How does your family celebrate and remember events?
   a. How can you and your family use this custom/ritual to remember this event?
   b. What are the positive aspects or areas of growth and strength you and your family can acknowledge? Are there negative aspects or stories you'd like to "remember" during the ritual?

    c. How can you use parts of your cultural heritage to develop a family activity or ritual?
2. How and what would you like to remember (positive and negative aspects) next month? Next year? In the future?

Extending meaning and connection into the future. Survivors' and family members' healing process may include identifying how they can grow and possibly learn from the events and effects of the trauma and violence. Deeper meanings and relationships can result, thus increasing support and understanding. Families may draw upon internal and external resources, strengths, and relationships to facilitate this process. Examining alternative ways to understand the violent, traumatic event may expand meaning and consequences of the event and invite a more fulfilled future. Questions to access possible alternative meanings and envision these alternatives in the future include:

1. What have you (survivor and family member) learned? How do you see yourself and your family using this in the future?
2. How are you (survivor and family member) and your family members different? Given these differences, how do you see yourself and your family members in a year from now, five years from now, etc.?
3. Who have you (survivor and family member) felt most supported by? Who have you reconnected with? Who has surprised you with their support?

FAMILY HEALING ACTIVITIES

Family healing activities support the family recovery process and promote healing for the survivor and family. These activities and exercises may be initiated and performed by the survivor, family member, mental health professional, or community member. Further, these activities highlight the impact of the traumatic event on family relationships, interactions, and communication and attend to the influence of the social context.

Assess the Role of the "Family" Members and Community

As we consider a family systems understanding of sexual violence and trauma, we need to remember that "children [and families] need more than one or even two adults to raise them, and adults need more than one or two close relationships to get them through life" (p. 7).[12] Therefore, it is important to consider who else may be involved in the healing process, including extended family members, friends, and others in the community. These others may serve as witnesses to the stories of resilience and provide insight into other strengths and resources the individual or family may be unable to notice.

For instance, a European American single mother, Carol, entered therapy to address the sexual abuse of her two daughters, Anna, age thirteen, and Beth, age fifteen. The girls were sexually abused by their stepfather for over ten years, and he was recently convicted and incarcerated for the abuse. As the therapist explored the reason for treatment, the family's support network was explored. The therapist learned that Carol was very connected to her church "family." The therapist and family members explored how the church "family" supported them before and after the abuse was disclosed. Each person in the family reflected on feeling "better" when they ask their faith community to pray for their strength and healing. Carol stated that she often meets for Bible study on Thursday nights and the girls shared their experiences in the weekly youth group. Specifically, Anna said that there are times at the end of the youth group meetings in which the youth director asks for prayer requests. Anna and her family suggested that Anna ask the youth director to pray for strength and healing in her family. Together, the family identified the people in the church they can "lean on" for continued support.

Construct a Trauma, Resources, and Recovery Family Genogram

Family scholars, such as Murray Bowen and Monica McGoldrick, provide a visual method of exploring and documenting intergenerational trauma and resilience within the family. The genogram, family diagram, or family tree provides families with visual representation of who is in the family, including important events in the family and identifying intergenerational patterns of trauma, abuse, and violence.[29] In addition to documentation and assessment of trauma, a genogram may include strengths and resources and may invite opportunities for sharing stories of strength and resilience.

Alicia, a Mexican American woman in her late fifties, was struggling with her fifteen-year-old granddaughter, Bernadette. Alicia stated that she has cared for "Bernie" since she was three because her daughter was heavily involved in substance abuse. In the last three years, Bernadette became involved in substance abuse, and Alicia, a devout Roman Catholic, attempted to implement and enforce strict rules; however, Bernie continued to "rebel."

Alicia and Bernie met with a family therapist at a community mental health agency to address Alicia's concerns, and the therapist initiated a family genogram. The therapist began the interview by asking questions about who was in the family, characteristics of members, relationships and interactions, immigration and racism experiences, crises and traumas, abuse, and resilience and strengths. Questions asked included:

1. Who is in your family? What are their names, ages, occupations, and three characteristic of each person?
2. Who is closest in the family? Most distant? Is there conflict in the family?
3. What types of abuse were/are present in the family?
4. When did the family immigrate to this country? What stories have been passed down about this experience?

Alicia and Bernie were very engaged in constructing the genogram, as it provided an indirect way to discuss their family's challenges and strengths. Specifically, the genogram provided a way for the family to identify, acknowledge, and discuss several family patterns, including an intergenerational pattern of domestic violence, substance use, sexual abuse, and relationship violence. The recognition of the family's intergenerational patterns of sexual violence and the relationships between traumas and negative coping strategies provided insight, relational connection, empathy, and healing in Alicia and Bernie's relationship.

Share Stories of the Experience and Stories of Resilience and Survival

Survivors and families may build support and connection between one another as they share their individual and family experiences of the trauma.[23,3] These stories may be shared in a formal setting, such as in a family or group therapy session, or informally at the family home or other appropriate location. Some prompts to begin the storytelling process may include:

1. How has the sexual violence or trauma impacted you and the family?
2. What do you recall about your experience and the experience of other family members?
3. Is there a feeling or memory that seems more significant than others?
4. How has this event changed your family, positively and negatively?
5. What have you and your family learned about yourself? Others? The strength of your family?
6. If you were going to give this entire experience (highlighting the negative effects as well as what was learned and how you and the family have grown) a title, what might it be?
7. What are you most proud of in yourself and others in your family?
8. What would you share with another family going through something similar about your experiences?

Develop Family Rituals

Family rituals may serve as powerful tools in the healing process to acknowledge the negative effects of the trauma, as well as the individual and family strengths, resources, and processes of resilience.[27,28] Survivors and their families may draw upon cultural and spiritual values to assist with mourning losses, expressing emotions, and creating a new path or vision for the future. These rituals may be celebrated or memorialized by extended family members, friends, and those in the community. When developing family rituals, it is important to consider intervals that are most appropriate and convenient for the family (e.g., monthly, annually, or once). Some family rituals created by families include:

- Sara and her partner Jennifer remember sexual assault victims at a monthly "ceremony." Sara was sexually assaulted three years ago by a former partner. Sara's physical scars healed after a few weeks; however, the emotional and psychological effects continue to remain a part of her relationships. Specifically, Sara and Jennifer and their "family" (friends, not biological family members) meet once a month to remember Sara's assault and the sexual assault of unnamed others. They memorialize the assaults by lighting candles at sundown at the local park. Several survivor stories are read and the ceremony concludes with a moment of silence.
- The Nakamura-Ito family meets annually to remember the internment of the Japanese Americans during World War II at the eldest son's home during the first weekend in December. The family members sit around the dining room table and recall the positive and negative stories passed down from their parents about their experiences in "camp." Each year, new stories and recollections seem to emerge. After the conversation and storytelling, the family members pass around pictures of their parents in "camp." This time of sharing is followed by a traditional Japanese meal and games and activities initiated by the children.

Seek Family and Couple Therapy

Survivors and their families may engage in many healing activities; however, there are some instances in which additional support will enhance the healing process. In these situations, it is suggested that family and/or couple therapy is initiated. To access resources for family systems–related therapy, families may visit http://www.therapistlocator .net/index.asp.

"WE *CAN* DO THIS": FROM STORIES DOMINATED BY ABUSE TO A FAMILY STORY OF RESILIENCE

The following clinical excerpts apply a family systems orientation when encountering issues of sexual violence and trauma. The case descriptions are not an exhaustive review of the therapeutic process; instead highlights of treatment are included to demonstrate how this clinician approached sexual violence and trauma from a family systems perspective. The treating clinician worked with the family for a total of five years and met with the family in different contexts, including couple and family therapy. Information has been changed to protect the identity of the family members.

A biracial, heterosexual married couple, Arturo, a Latino male age forty-seven, and Kim, a Korean American female age thirty-two, were referred for couple therapy and parenting skill building by their county caseworker after their three children (Alex, age thirteen; Kara, age eleven; and Martha, age ten) were removed from their care due to suspected physical and sexual abuse and neglect. Arturo and Kim agreed that they would benefit from couple and parenting skill building; however, they specifically complained of problems in their intimate relationship and struggles with physical and emotional intimacy. "We don't have enough sex" was Arturo's complaint, while Kim expressed wanting to feel "closer" to her husband and children.

Couple/Intimacy Issues

The therapist utilized the family genogram to access historical, relational, and trauma-related information. The family genogram exposed abuse and violence in Arturo's and Kim's families of origin. Arturo reported growing up in an intense, hostile family. He disclosed that he was exposed to violence between his parents and, as the oldest, took the "brunt" of it. He was often the "scapegoat" among his siblings to receive "beatings" by his father. "When my dad was angry, we all knew it. He took it out on my mom and me, but we were all afraid. He yelled, swore, threw things, and hit and beat me and my mom. She took it, though . . . and so did I. We took it for the others. If he was hitting us, he wasn't hitting the younger kids."

Patterns and themes in Arturo's family of origin reflected hostility and violence. Arturo recalls memories of his grandfather speaking harshly to his grandmother and states, "I was scared of him. He wasn't a big man, but he was powerful. We [siblings] tried to keep our distance." He added that besides the hostility he witnessed, his grandparents didn't express much emotion; "they didn't even seem to like each other." Arturo shared stories of his family's immigration to the United States, stating, "We were always running scared, from our parents, from immigration. . . ."

Kim, on the other hand, told stories of her Korean-born parents and their immigration to the United States. She stated her family was best described as a "reserved, passive" family; "we are quiet and pretty unassuming." Kim stated that oftentimes her father would not overtly express his happiness or even his disappointment, but she "just knew" what he was experiencing, and thus, she "just knew" how to respond appropriately. Kim's grandparents lived in Korea, and she knew very little about them. Kim recalls her mother talking about her immigration to the United States: "Mama [Kim's grandmother] was sad when we left. She wanted us to stay in Korea, but she knew Daddy [Kim's father] had a good opportunity to build the business." Her mother and father didn't share many stories about their parents, and there were few pictures. In addition, Kim rarely witnessed her parents showing affection toward one another, stating, "I just knew they loved each other. I mean, Daddy worked so hard for us and Mommy was always making sure me and Daddy were cared for."

As the genogram process continued, additional themes of violence and abuse emerged. Kim stated that when she was in junior high school she was sexually assaulted by a "family friend," her father's business associate. She was afraid to disclose the abuse to her family for fear of not being believed, and she doubted her role in the event, feeling like it was "my fault." However, Kim wrote about the incident in her diary. While cleaning Kim's room, her mother found and read her diary. Kim's mother confronted her about the "story" in her diary, and Kim "broke down" and told her what had happened. Initially, her mother seemed to doubt Kim's account of the abuse; however, she became upset and tearful as Kim disclosed the details. Later that evening when Kim's father arrived home from work, her mother told him about the abuse. He "refused" to believe the sexually violent event occurred. "I was sitting at the kitchen table and he kept asking me, 'Why would *he* do this? He's a good man. If this happened, why would he do this to you?'" After the intense "questioning," the family never spoke of the incident again.

Kim and Arturo engaged in the family genogram process and shared their stories and experiences of the traumatic abuse and violent events of their childhood, many of which the couple had never discussed. Kim shared stories of family silence around issues of abuse and violence, while Arturo reflected on his parents' intense and oftentimes hostile interactions. Conversations about their own abuse histories opened the door to explore the abuse and violence within their immediate family system. Specifically, Kim talked about the hostility and violence between her and Arturo, Arturo disclosed his role in physically abusing the children, and Kim shared her reaction to the sexual abuse of her daughter. Kim said,

"When the social worker told me Martha was molested by the babysitter, I was horrified. I didn't want to believe it, I wanted to question her. [tearful] But it happened to me . . . it happened to me . . . I haven't talked or even thought about this for so long . . . I remember when I was raped . . . I remember being scared . . .I remember Daddy . . . I remember feeling so alone . . . I think I still feel so alone . . ."

Through the genogram process, the therapist identified several patterns of abuse and Arturo's and Kim's struggles with trust and intimacy. In an effort to explore these issues and begin the healing process, the therapist utilized the genogram to open conversations about how their abuse histories impact current functioning. The therapist also facilitated alternative, more effective ways for the couple to communicate and express their emotions. For instance, the therapist encouraged Kim to express her emotions and experiences related to the sexual assault while Arturo actively listened. The therapist supported Arturo in reflecting what he heard, paying particular attention to Kim's emotions and his reaction to her disclosures. His empathy and validation of her experience invited compassion, and "compassion begins to act as an antidote to negative emotions like shame and validate the worth of the wounded partner" (p. 500).[24] Further, the therapist and couple explored structure, roles, and communication styles in their families of origin and how these patterns replicated themselves in their immediate family. Many conversations, insights, and reenactments were initiated to facilitate shifts in how they related to and communicated with one another, and they were able to experience alternative, more effective ways of communicating and relating.

Though the genogram promoted insight and understanding, the therapist referred Kim for specialized treatment to address her response to the trauma, referring her for eye movement desensitization and reprocessing treatment, and they continued to explore their struggle with intimacy and trust in relationships.

Parenting

The family of origin patterns of abuse and violence shaped and influenced how Kim and Arturo functioned as a couple and as parents. These intergenerational patterns of abuse were transmitted to the family they created, resulting in a conflictual couple relationship and a parenting style that included the use of physical violence and abuse. Due to family of origin patterns and struggles in their couple relationship, Kim and Arturo were challenged in how they parented their children. Their lack of connection and fear of intimacy created distance and distrust in the couple *and* parenting relationship.

As Kim and Arturo began to trust themselves and each other and heal from the abuse and violence in their pasts, they began to reconnect and strengthen their couple relationship and enhance their ability to tolerate and engage in an intimate relationship. This process invited new possibilities for parenting, and Kim and Arturo were able to confront the physical and sexual abuse of their children. Through their healing, rather than avoiding, denying, or becoming intensely emotional, they developed several strategies to utilize when dealing with their children. Some of these strategies included:

1. Providing a safe, supportive, nonviolent home for their children. Clearly communicating expectations (verbally and in writing on behaviors charts) and creating nonviolent forms of discipline.
2. Allowing their children to share their stories, experiences, and emotions related to the abuse without interruption or "trying to clarify why it happened." Instead, letting the child share their account.
3. Acknowledging and showing compassion and empathy toward their children. For instance, as the child shares his/her experiences or emotions, parents turn and face them, reflect back what was shared, highlight their emotions, and comment on a specific strength or resource (internal and/or external).
4. Highlighting and ensuring their children's sense of safety by saying something such as, "You are safe, we are safe, and Mommy and Daddy are here for you."
5. Listening for and verbalizing their individual strengths and courage.
6. Focusing on where to go from here and what they can do about the situation now.
7. Identifying systems of support and specific people/places to go to for strength and support.
8. Inviting others to witness their courage and strength. The child identifies those who may serve as witnesses (e.g., family members, friends) and, with the child's permission, she/he is invited to share their successes and courage.

Family Treatment

As couple therapy progressed, Kim and Arturo increased their levels of intimacy and trust and developed more adaptive communication styles and parenting techniques. This progress facilitated family therapy interventions that supported healing from the effects of past as well as more recent incidents of violence and abuse. The couple was able to "practice" new strategies and interventions with their children and reorganize interactions around support and safety, versus violence and abuse. The parents initiated activities and games that opened the space for emotional expression and conversations about "how things used to be." Thus the children began to trust the parents and openly communicate their experiences, fears, and hopes for the future. As time progressed, the family stories shifted from those of the negative effects of the trauma to stories of how the family copes, their strengths, and the resilience in each member. For instance, in the later stages of therapy, the family engaged in a mutual family drawing. In this intervention, each family member contributed to a "picture" of the family, each taking a turn to add to the "family portrait." Martha drew her parents sitting at the table playing a game and Kara drew her brother helping her with her homework. The drawing highlighted the themes of increased cohesion and trust within the family, and a shift from a family saturated in abuse and violence to a resilient, connected family.

Termination

At the end of treatment, the family and therapist engaged in some discussion of their progress and healing process. The therapist assisted in developing a family ritual and asked how they might "remind" each other of what they've learned. Together, the family members discussed ways to "remember" their progress and strengths when things "got tough." They decided that they would write down family and individual strengths on small pieces of paper. These pieces of paper would be placed in a jar labeled "Being Strong." They decided that additional "strengths" could be added at any time. On Sunday nights before bed, the family agreed to sit at the dining room table and take turns reading several "Being Strong" statements.

RECOMMENDATIONS FOR SURVIVORS AND THEIR FAMILIES

Sexual violence and trauma not only impacts the individual, but the family system, relationships, and communication. Therefore, when a family member discloses a sexually violent/abusive experience, there are several recommendations as to how to cope with and heal from the violation.

1. Provide emotional support and empathy.
2. Contact local law enforcement.
3. Seek professional psychological services.
4. Ensure victim(s) and others are safe from harm.
5. Enlist support of family members.
6. Engage in family healing recovery processes and activities as described in the above sections.

CONCLUSION

Recovery from sexual violence and trauma is essential to the continued growth and development of individuals, families, and communities. A violent act, traumatic experience, or abusive relationship not only impacts the oppressor and oppressed, but it impacts the whole, including those with whom the persons interact and future generations. Therefore, mental health professionals, communities, and families must identify ways to assist in healing to ensure all become *survivors* of trauma and violence. Further, communities and families must unite to influence those in positions of power to create systemic changes in public policy and legislation related to consequences of violent and abusive acts, treatment and intervention programs, and support for individuals, families, and communities.

Families and communities play a significant role in healing and recovery from sexual violence and trauma. Embracing a systemic, family-oriented perspective serves to engage others in the healing process for the survivor, family, and community. ". . . In struggling to make meaning, in reaching out to others, and in active coping efforts, people [families and communities] tap into resources that they may not have drawn on otherwise, and gain new abilities and perspectives on life" (p. 218).[3]

REFERENCES

1. Herman, J. (1997). *Trauma and recovery*. New York: Basic Books.
2. Silverstein, R., Buxbaum Bass, L., Tuttle, A.R., Knudson-Martin, C., & Huenergardt, D. (2006). *What does it mean to be relational? A framework for assessment and practice, 45*, 391–405.
3. Walsh, F. (2007). Traumatic loss and major disasters: Strengthening family and community resilience. *Family Process, 46*, 207–227.
4. Wynne, L.C., Shields, C.G., & Sirkin, M.I. (1992). Illness, family theory, and family therapy: Conceptual issues. *Family Process, 31*(1), 3–18.
5. Beavers, W.R. (1977). *Psychotherapy and growth: A family systems perspective*. New York: Brunner/Mazel.
6. Watzlawick, P., Beavin Bavelas, J, & Jackson, D.D. (1967). *Pragmatics of human communication: A study of interactional patterns, pathologies, and paradoxes*. New York: Norton.
7. Boyd-Franklin, N., & Bry, B. (2000). *Reaching out in family therapy: Home-based, school and community interventions*. New York: Guilford.
8. Lindblad-Goldberg, M., Dore, M.M., & Stern, L. (1998). *Creating competence from chaos: A comprehensive guide to home-based services*. New York: Norton.
9. Anderson, H. (1997). *Conversations, language, and possibilities: A postmodern approach to therapy*. New York: Basic Books.
10. Fishbane, M.D. (2001). Relational narrative of the self. *Family Process, 40*, 273–292.
11. Gergen, K. (1994). *Realities and relationships: Sounding in social construction*. Cambridge, MA: Harvard University Press.
12. McGoldrick, M., & Hardy, K.V. (2008). *Re-visioning family therapy: Race, culture, and gender in clinical practice* (2nd ed.). Guilford Press: New York.

13. Burke Draucker, C. (2003). Unique outcomes of women and men who were abused. *Perspectives in psychiatric care, 39*(1), 7–16.

14. Danieli, Y. (1998). *Intergenerational handbook of multigenerational legacies of trauma.* New York: Plenum Press.

15. Hoekstra-Weebers, J.E., Jaspers, J.P.C., Kamps, W.A., & Klip, E.C. (1998). Marital dissatisfaction, psychological distress, and the coping of parents of pediatric cancer patients. *Journal of Marriage and the Family, 60*, 1012–1021.

16. Noojin, A.B., Causey, D.L., Gros, B.J., Bertolone, S., & Carter, B.D. (1999). The influence of maternal stress resistance and family relationships on depression in children with cancer. *Journal of Psychosocial Oncology, 17*, 79–97.

17. Maltz, W., & Holman, B. (1987). *Incest and sexuality: A guide to understanding and healing.* Lexington, MA: Lexington Books.

18. Westerlund, E. (1992). *Women's sexuality after childhood incest.* New York: Norton.

19. Barnes, M.F. (1998). Treating burnout in families following childhood trauma. In C.R. Figley (Ed.), *Burnout in families: Secondary trauma stress in everyday life* (pp. 177–185). Boca Raton: CRC Press.

20. Barnes, M.F. (2005). When a child is traumatized or physically injured: The secondary trauma of parents. In D.R. Catherall (Ed.), *Family stressors: Interventions for stress and trauma* (pp. 77–94). New York: Brunner-Routledge.

21. Pfefferbaum, B. (1997). Posttraumatic stress disorder in children: A review of the past 10 years. *Journal of the American Academy of Child and Adolescent Psychiatry, 36*, 1503–1511.

22. Walsh, F., & McGoldrick, M. (2004). *Living beyond loss: Death in the family* (2nd ed.). New York: Norton.

23. Walsh, F. (2002). A family resilience framework: Innovative practice applications. *Family Relations, 51*, 130–137.

24. Johnson, S. (2004). Facing the dragon together: Emotionally focused couples therapy with trauma survivors. In D.R. Catherall (Ed), *Handbook of stress, trauma, and the family* (pp. 493–512). New York: Brunner-Routledge.

25. Brom, D., Pat-Horenczyk, R., & Ford, J.D. (Eds.). (2009). *Treating traumatized children: Risk, resilience, and recovery.* New York: Routledge.

26. Courtois, C.A., Ford, J.D., & Cloitre, M. (2009). Best practices in psychotherapy for adults. In C.A. Courtois (Ed.), *Treating complex traumatic stress disorder: An evidence-based guide* (pp. 82–103). New York: Guilford Press.

27. Imber-Black, E. (2003). *Rituals in families and family therapy.* New York: Norton.

28. Palazzoli, S. (1974). *Self-starvation: From the intrapsychic to the transpersonal approach to anorexia nervosa.* London: Human Context Books.

29. McGoldrick, M., Gerson, R., & Petry, S. (2008). *Genograms: Assessment and intervention.* New York: Norton.

12

Feminist Counseling as a Pathway to Recovery

Carolyn Zerbe Enns

Feminist therapy is an approach to recovery that emphasizes an egalitarian counseling relationship, goals that are consistent with achieving equality in the full range of human relationships, and a perspective that explores the sociocultural, ecological context in which life issues are experienced. Feminist counseling highlights the "personal as political," which means that personal issues are seen as connected to the social structure in which we live and have implications for social as well as personal change. This set of assumptions has significant implications for how healing after sexual violence is viewed by feminist counselors.

Feminist therapists think of symptoms of individual distress, including the consequences of sexual violence, as survival mechanisms. They see clients who have experienced violence as coping with their life challenges to the best of their ability, and the psychological challenges associated with the aftermath of sexual violence represent "normal" reactions to abnormal circumstances. In other words, feminist therapists believe that "not all symptoms are neurotic. Pain in response to a bad situation is adaptive, not pathological" (p. 90).[1] This perspective means that the therapist treats the client as her (or his) own best expert, and together, a counselor and client work as partners to uncover issues and promote healing. The client's efforts to contend with the consequences of violence often appear as disorienting symptoms. The job of the client and counselor is to sort out how to transfer or redirect the personal energy that results in these symptoms toward methods of achieving health and resolution.

The words *feminist* or *feminism* are sometimes assumed to be relevant only to women, and even more specifically, white women. As black feminist bell hooks's[2] book title notes, however, *Feminism is for everybody.*

Inclusive feminisms involve a commitment to ending all forms of oppression and are attentive to the intersections of racism, classism, colonialism, heterosexism, ethnocentrism, ageism, ableism, sexism, and other forms of inequality. Although sexual violence is disproportionately perpetrated by men against women,[3] both men and women can be survivors of sexual violence and both men and women can be perpetrators of sexual violence. These understandings are central to the content of this chapter.

CASE STUDY: WHY FEMINIST THERAPY?

The following personal experience conveys why I believe a feminist approach is a necessary option for healing. Shortly after I identified myself as a feminist counselor, I worked with a woman who had been raped and then revictimized in an unequal psychotherapy experience. Some weeks into our work together, my client (who I will refer to as Anne) disclosed details about a previous experience with therapy that Anne had initiated after she had been raped by someone who had broken into her home. Her traditional psychoanalytically trained therapist suggested that at some deep and nonconscious level, she had experienced a type of masochistic pleasure during the rape. Although this psychotherapy had occurred about ten years prior to our work together, it was still very much on her mind. Anne was confused and angered about the feedback she had received, and mystified about how an event that was so devastating could have been construed by her therapist as an act that gave her masochistic satisfaction. Rather than helping her cope effectively with the aftermath of sexual violence, her psychotherapist had contributed to self-blame and self-questioning attitudes that had kept her in a state of psychological paralysis. I was shocked and appalled by Anne's story and conveyed my distress that a therapist would propose such an outrageous hypothesis. During the ensuing weeks, we spent much time challenging the rape myths that had been reinforced by this experience. Her trust slowly increased as we challenged myths, worked to understand her experience within the context of a culture that supports blaming victims, and developed new and productive tools for reaching her goals.

The therapist my client had seen worked from a classical psychoanalytic model that viewed women as passive, narcissistic, and masochistic. This triad of "feminine" traits had its origins in Sigmund Freud's[4] views about the differences between the sexes and was further developed by some of his followers, including women psychoanalysts such as Helene Deutsch.[5] With regard to masochism, this approach proposed that women may unconsciously seek out pain and suffering, and may become attuned to these experiences of pain through childbirth and other life experiences. Freud's original ideas about women were not the only ones to support negative views. In the area of intimate violence, an influential article from the 1960s was titled "The Wifebeater's Wife"[6] and proposed that a husband's aggression fulfilled the wife's masochistic needs to maintain equilibrium through a relationship that cycled between passivity and aggression. It is important to note that since the 1960s, feminists have worked to correct these biases and have proposed psychoanalytically informed feminisms that are compatible with feminist counseling practices.

The views described in the previous paragraph reveal the biases embedded in early psychological theories. In her groundbreaking book titled *Women and Madness*, Phyllis Chesler[7] compared the traditional therapy relationship to that of a patriarch and patient. She described the traditional psychotherapy encounter as "just one more instance of an unequal relationship, just one more opportunity to be rewarded for expressing distress and to be 'helped' by being (expertly) dominated" (p. 140). The client's belief in her helplessness and dependency on an all-knowing figure is reinforced in such a relationship. This scenario is consistent with the negative therapy experience I summarized in the case study, in which a therapist imposed a narrow view of sexual violence on his client by suggesting that she had at some level seen her rape as fulfilling a masochistic need. To counteract these views, feminist mental health workers who were influenced by the women's movement of the 1960s and 1970s proposed new forms of therapy and recovery. These feminist therapies emphasized the importance of consciousness-raising about how inequality influences problems. They also proposed healing approaches that valued women's perspectives and empowered them to take control of their own lives as well as change social systems that serve victims of violence.

In response to the efforts of feminists, rape crisis centers and domestic violence shelters also emerged as places where victims of violence could experience validation and recovery in safe environments. Feminist mental health workers identified acts of sexual violence as events that traumatize and challenge one's sense of meaning and safety in the world, and labeled predictable patterns of symptoms as rape trauma syndrome[8] and battered woman syndrome.[9] These descriptions connected the personal and political by showing how violence, which is learned by the perpetrator from the culture, can shatter an individual's sense of safety and trigger disorienting personal symptoms. More specifically, the survivor's personal pain is not the result of some type of inner weakness or pathology, but the consequence of a society that tolerates violence. The personal repercussions of violence tell us about the need for political and social change. Early activists also clarified how violence can lead to changes in a person's internal self-structure and result in learned helplessness, avoidance behaviors, emotional numbness or other distortions of emotions, jarring nightmares or flashbacks, or disrupted cognitive experiences such as self-blame and confusion. Many of these reactions are now reflected in the diagnostic category of post-traumatic stress disorder (PTSD),[10] which identifies patterns of emotions, cognitions, and behaviors that often follow traumatic events of many types.

Feminist approaches have grown in influence and diversity over the past forty years. The following sections focus on the social context of violence, phases of trauma and recovery, the feminist counseling relationship, assessment in feminist counseling, and feminist interventions.

THE SOCIAL CONTEXT OF SEXUAL VIOLENCE

Sexual violence is a global issue, and survivors of sexual violence live in societies in which sexual violence myths are rampant and permeate popular culture. Survivors are at risk for internalizing these messages, often at an unconscious level. Challenging these social beliefs is a major aspect of working toward wholeness. These myths include the belief that victims secretly desire to experience sexual violence, that women "ask" for assault by acting or dressing in seductive ways, that sexual assault is primarily a consequence of men's stronger desire for sex, or that the perpetrator didn't really mean to assault the victim. Other myths include notions that victims exaggerate the impact of sexual assault, that victims should be able to "get over it" quickly, or that only strangers can be perpetrators of sexual violence. Furthermore, those who do not fight back physically but seek to survive assault through other methods are not seen as "real" victims, and victims who bring charges against perpetrators are often defined as trying to get back at men for various imagined wrongs from the past.[11,12,13,14]

The first myth on the list, the belief that women secretly desire to be violated, is consistent with the rape myth held by the therapist I described in the case study, pointing to the degree to which myths are widespread and can revictimize those who experience assault and other forms of sexual violence. The presence of these myths also underlines the reason a sociocultural, ecological perspective is central to recovery from sexual violence. During feminist therapy, therapists typically explore the ways in which the victim/survivor has internalized negative beliefs about sexual violence, and help the client challenge these beliefs. Therapists may also counter these myths by providing information based on research about the realities of rape. Unfortunately, the legal system and even well-intentioned persons in one's support system often convey victim-blaming attitudes that make it difficult for survivors to transcend the power of sexual violence myths.[15,16,17]

Patricia Rozée[18] identified "normative" or condoned rape in 97% of the thirty-five societies she examined. Normative sexual violence takes on a variety of different forms such as marital rape, exchange rape (rape as a bargaining tool), punitive rape (rape designed to punish a family or group), ceremonial rape (e.g., rape as an introduction to womanhood), rape as a weapon of war, and acquaintance or date rape.[19,20] Sexual violence may also reinforce male status over women or the power of one ethnic group over another. Although the right to experience freedom from violence is recognized as a fundamental human right, evidence indicates that sexual violence is a global health burden[21] with major implications for both physical and psychological health. In other words, the personal act of violence has political implications. Thus, feminist therapy, which recognizes the link between the personal and political, is an important foundation for working toward healing. From a feminist perspective, change needs to occur at individual, interpersonal, family, community, national, and global levels.[22,23,24]

PHASES OF RECOVERY FROM A FEMINIST PERSPECTIVE

Recovering from sexual violence often involves a long-term process. Survivors often (but not always) experience a series of predictable stages during their journey toward wholeness, and knowledge of these common experiences may decrease self-blame and increase patience toward oneself.[25] As noted in the previous section, sexual violence occurs in a social context in which myths about sexual violence are widespread. Thus, the first phase represents presexual violence events and sociocultural beliefs. These realities may contribute to women's fears about freedom of movement even before acts of sexual violence occur. Given the power of this cultural climate and the fact that those who experience sexual violence are also likely to be revictimized by inadequate legal, medical, and social support services, this social context represents the first phase of a phase approach to understanding sexual violence and its impact on individuals.

The second phase consists of acts of sexual violence, including the specific sequence of events that occurred before, during, and after sexual violence.[26] At this point, immediate survival and escape are the central concerns of the victim/survivor. In the case of a specific incident of rape, these events tend to occur over a relatively circumscribed time span. In contrast, when the individual is a victim of long-term sexual harassment or intimate violence, physical escape may not be possible, and mental coping skills for dealing with ongoing violence may become priorities. The different interpersonal contexts of long-term and shorter-term interpersonal violence have an impact on the nature of a survivor's immediate coping needs and symptoms.

Crisis and feelings of disorganization typically follow sexual violence. Although reactions to violence vary, one early study found that 94% of all rape victims experienced significant traumatic stress symptoms in the immediate aftermath of sexual violence.[27] Acute reactions of distress are common, and a recent study found that three months after surviving rape, 45% of victims met PTSD criteria.[28] Another study found that among women survivors who experienced PTSD, 52% also experienced depression.[29]

Following an acute phase, individuals tend to cope by getting back to "normal" life as quickly as possible. This period may be marked by efforts to avoid thinking about violence by practicing forms of denial or minimizing the impact of the violence.[30] However, the types of coping mechanisms used by victims/survivors vary substantially, with some individuals more likely to use adaptive, problem-focused coping than avoidance or denial.[31] When individuals experience long-term sexual violence, they are more likely to experience dramatic, complex changes in self-image or emotional experience or idealize perpetrators in order to cope with violence from which they were/are unable to escape physically.[32]

Although denial and pretending that nothing has happened are frequent coping mechanisms, they are difficult to maintain for long periods, in large part because of the psychological and stress-related costs of these alternatives. As a result, victims often find themselves reliving scenes related to violence or finding that it becomes more difficult to control or "contain" their reactions.[33] It is not unusual for individuals to avoid seeking counseling until they experience the disorienting symptoms associated with this phase. During this phase, the counselor and client work on remembering and processing the fragments and details of sexual violence for the purpose of creating a new story in which the survivor gains increasing control and perspective.[34] A final phase can be referred to as resolution and integration. The survivor finds ways to place sexual violence within a larger perspective, often making a transition from feeling victimized to experiencing a sense of greater empowerment. Survivors may also find meaning and purpose by engaging in prevention, social change, and activism that contribute to a safer world for others.[35]

The past events, current circumstances, and learned patterns of behavior of a woman contribute to significant diversity with regard to how women react, cope, and experience distress and recovery. The "phases" described in this section provide only one example of how crisis and healing may unfold. Some phases may not be present, and the ordering of typical reactions may vary, reflecting the many individual and cultural differences among victims and survivors. The following sections provide greater detail about the type of counseling relationship, assessments, and interventions that help individuals move effectively through these phases of recovery.

THE FEMINIST THERAPY COUNSELING RELATIONSHIP

During the twenty-first century, a wide range of counseling approaches have emphasized the importance of a collaborative partnership as a foundation for successful psychotherapy and recovery. Feminist therapists were some of the first mental health workers to identify an egalitarian relationship as central to successful recovery. In order to counteract the negative impact of sexual violence, a counseling relationship marked by safety is essential.

To convey respect for their clients, feminist therapists believe that it is important to be aware of their personal values and to be well informed about the potential life experiences of diverse groups of women, such as women in poverty, lesbians, adolescent girls, women of color, and older women. Feminist therapists typically communicate their feminist values to their clients while also conveying their respect for a client's worldview, personal experiences, and values. More specifically, feminist counselors convey their belief that persons working toward recovery from violence are competent and capable persons who, despite current coping difficulties, have many insights that will contribute to their healing. Although clients have often learned to question their competence or defined their own behaviors as "crazy," the therapist helps clients to gradually redirect their energies from battling symptoms toward enhancing positive coping. The role of the therapist is to act as a knowledgeable guide and resource person to clients as they eradicate "patient identities," redirect perceived weaknesses into strengths, and generate plans for building new skills.

The feminist counselor seeks to model communication skills such as genuineness, confrontation, self-disclosure, empathy, and congruence as methods for establishing egalitarian relationships. When clients enter counseling, they often feel isolated and inadequate and may believe that the counselor is an all-powerful expert. In such instances, the counselor may use brief self-disclosure statements to communicate that she (or he) is a human being who must also work to resolve problems and difficulties or who may have worked through the effects of violence or broken trust. When a client has the opportunity to see the counselor as a coping role model, psychotherapy is demystified, and an egalitarian climate is reinforced.[36,37] In addition to being a coping role model, the therapist provides a climate of safety and one in which the client can express the full range of her or his emotions without needing to fear that his or her reactions and feelings may overwhelm the counselor. Given the fact that disconnection and disempowerment are major markers of sexual violence, a therapeutic relationship that supports open expression, relational support, validation, and safety is central to the healing process.

In general, feminist therapists work toward implementing a reciprocal model of influence in which counselors share power, avoid making decisions for the client, and communicate confidence in the client's decision-making skills.[38,39,40] The counselor participates as a colleague in order to ensure that the client develops problem-solving skills that will help her (or him) become her (or his) own therapist in the future. Although the feminist counselor works toward eliminating artificial boundaries and models egalitarian behaviors that support a client's negotiation of effective relationships both within and outside of counseling, the feminist counselor remains mindful that she or he brings skills and expertise to the relationship and shares these skills generously and respectfully.[41,42,43]

As part of the egalitarian relationship, the feminist counselor works together with the client to clarify goals, ensure that the client and counselor maintain a clear focus in their work, and minimize the risk of misunderstandings. When goals are clearly specified, clients are able to take greater responsibility for their change and evaluate progress regularly. Clients have more information about what they can expect from the counselor and what the therapist expects of the client.[44] This predictability can also help the survivor recover from the disorientation and violation associated with sexual violence. As the counseling relationship evolves, the client is likely to assume a more active and collaborative role in decision making and is able to take higher levels of responsibility within counseling and within their daily lives.

Many feminist counselors also provide their clients with written rights and responsibilities statements, which include descriptions of their approach to counseling, areas of strength or expertise, views about how feminism influences their counseling practice, as well as expectations about the client's role in counseling. Depending on a client's specific needs, expectations for the client may involve participating in homework assignments, trying out specific types of coping skills, disclosing intense or suicidal feelings if they emerge, or raising questions on occasions when the client disagrees with the counselor. An important aspect of informed consent involves creating an environment in which the client can feel comfortable about asking questions about the direction and focus of counseling. To counteract the disempowerment they experienced as victims of violence, clients need to know that "they have rights and privileges that do not disappear no matter how frightened or vulnerable they feel" (p. 166).[45] In addition, "the therapist is committed to the protection of those rights and sees the empowerment of the client as integral rather than incidental to the therapy process itself" (p. 166).

ASSESSMENT IN FEMINIST COUNSELING

Comprehensive assessment allows the counselor and client to gain a complete sense of the client's background and history, symptoms, and coping skills and strengths. It is crucial for the counselor to understand the symptoms that disrupt survivors' experiences as well as the resources and strengths they have used to cope with life difficulties. Knowledge of coping resources provides a foundation for building confidence for the future and supports a growth-oriented approach.

Feminist counselors are likely to ask questions about the various ways in which the client has experienced empowerment and disempowerment. Gaining information about the impact of race, culture, social class, ethnicity, disability, sexual orientation, and gender on a person's life is important for understanding the impact of trauma as well as supporting successful coping. Abuses of power and experiences of oppression in a person's past may contribute to personal vulnerability as well as provide clues about how sexual violence myths may have an impact on survivors.

Revealing sexual violence to a stranger is difficult, and survivors may choose to disclose "safer" problems when they first enter counseling. Given the high frequency with which violence is related to psychological coping difficulties, feminist counselors are likely to ask all new clients whether they have experienced sexual violence. When appropriate, therapists may also use various trauma assessment questionnaires to gain a more complete sense of the types of symptoms that are disrupting the clients' equilibrium.[46] The feminist counselor will typically ask about any history of sexual violence within the context of a comprehensive social identity analysis.

Social identity analysis, the cornerstone of feminist assessment, can be defined as a variety of activities designed to explore a person's multiple identities related to gender, culture, race, religion, class, sexual orientation, and other personally relevant domains. The purpose of this assessment is to understand a client's life challenges and sources of empowerment or support, as well as their implications for change at personal, interpersonal, and institutional levels. One of the goals of these activities is to explore and raise consciousness about how a person's membership in these categories affects her or his life experiences and worldview. For example, the counselor explores the costs and benefits associated with these identities, as well as their implications for personal, interpersonal, and institutional change.[47,48] Knowledge of the person's cultural socialization and multiple identities reveals information about her or his experiences of disempowerment (e.g., being a member of a sexual or ethnic/racial minority group) or privilege (e.g., white or male status) and can be central to understanding the impact of sexual violence.[49]

Social identity assessment includes efforts to clarify the "rules" and expectations connected to various identities and how they affect the client's approach to the world and the challenges she or he faces. For example, women receive a wide variety of messages about what it means to be a woman, as well as what roles and behaviors are "appropriate." Families, friends, teachers, and other significant others convey a wide variety of "shoulds" about being a woman or man. Exploring these "shoulds," which are often subtle and unspoken, can provide insights about how women and men have been taught to cope with gender role expectations. As another example, women are often taught to be "nice" rather than assertive, to blame themselves for not fulfilling traditional gender roles adequately, or to question their realities when challenged by persons with greater power. These "rules" for behavior can interact with sexual violence myths and complicate healing from sexual violence experiences. Sexual violence can also illuminate or sensitize the survivor about how the culture supports sexual aggression or promotes dichotomized views of women as "virgins" or "whores."[50] Following sexual violence, survivors may be acutely aware of how gender socialization and other social identities are related to feelings of disempowerment associated with sexual violence as well as to other experiences of gender or racial discrimination. As they become sensitized to how sexual violence has reinforced other aspects of discrimination and social control, they may gain heightened access to strong feelings of anger. During feminist counseling, finding ways to channel this anger into productive healing and social change activities is a priority.

The gender role training of men can also contribute to coping difficulties and distortions. For example, men are encouraged to be powerful, controlling, and aggressive. These socialization messages and popular culture may lead some men to believe that paying for a date entitles them to sex. They may have learned to believe that a "no" from a woman means "maybe" or "yes." Although the focus of counseling is on healing for the survivor, there is value in exploring how a male gender-role conflicts and beliefs about power and dominance may have contributed to a victim's (either male or female) vulnerability. Gaining insight about these attitudes may also help reduce a person's self-blame and provide a foundation for feminist prevention training with men.

Stereotypes associated with diverse groups of women can be especially harmful and complicate healing. For example, Asian women are often placed into the polarized categories associated with the "China doll," which signifies subservience, compliance, and passivity, and the "dragon lady," which conveys a sexually opportunistic and cunning image.[51] For African American women, the Jezebel stereotype, which dates back to slavery eras, portrays Black women as hypersexual, promiscuous, and seductive. This image in combination with general rape myths contributes to invalidation and a lack of sensitivity to African American women's experiences.[52,53] Exploring and challenging the impact of these types of stereotypes may be crucial to social identity analysis and healing. The cultural, ethnic, and familial backgrounds of victims can also represent powerful sources of support and resilience. Assessing these strengths provides a foundation for building positive coping skills.

To summarize, social identity assessment is used to place sexual violence within a larger social context. It helps individuals (a) identify socialization, expectations, privileges, and oppressions related to multiple identities; (b) clarify the ways in which these messages and associated behaviors are reinforced or punished; (c) consider the costs and benefits of expectations attached to various social identities and gender roles; and (d) understand areas of resilience and strength associated with multiple social identities. This reflection phase is followed by decision making about challenging restrictions, and constructing new expectations and behaviors that are supportive and empowering. The final phase of gender and social identity analysis focuses on developing strategies for enacting changes.[54]

INTERVENTIONS IN FEMINIST COUNSELING

Prior to the emergence of feminist counseling approaches, most models of psychotherapy focused primarily on the importance of removing pain and helping clients adjust to existing realities, even if they were embedded in unjust circumstances. Although removing pain is a crucial step to healing, feminist counselors emphasize the value of transformative change for the individual as well as the culture. As noted by Mary Ballou and Carolyn West,[55] "The goals of feminist therapy are not about achieving a better, a quieter, a more compliant fit within a system that oppresses" (p. 275). Feminist therapists work with their clients to build personal resources to challenge the social attitudes and expectations that have contributed to their pain. Many of the specific interventions that feminist counselors use resemble those used by other therapists who do not refer to themselves as feminists. The tools used by the counselor depend, to a large degree, on the phase of recovery that is most relevant to the client. Distinctive to a feminist approach are its dual emphases on personal as well as social change and its philosophical assumption that equality is an important goal for all types of counseling issues. In other words, feminist counseling is concerned with all forms of social justice and seeks to eradicate multiple forms of oppression at personal and social levels.

Many clients seek counseling when they are feeling paralyzed by a variety of traumatic memories and reactions. In this case, one of the first goals of feminist therapists is to help their clients work through the disorienting symptoms that may limit their ability to function effectively. A variety of studies show that exposure to painful memories and symptoms is crucial for decreasing the intensity of traumatic memories, gaining new perspectives, decreasing anxiety, increasing mastery, and developing skills for reorganizing one's life and moving forward.[56,57] Interventions that help clients work through traumatic symptoms and memories focus on a variety of tasks including writing about trauma or visualizing trauma, challenging distorted thinking patterns about trauma, developing breathing and other skills for coping while processing painful memories, and reorganizing one's thinking about traumatic events. The feminist counselor is attentive to the timing and pacing of exposure to traumatic experiences and also helps the client develop self-nurturance and coping skills for dealing with occasions when disruptive memories or traumatic symptoms emerge outside of the safety of the counseling relationship. The goal of these techniques is to reestablish a client's sense of safety, trust, power, esteem, capacity for intimacy, and a sense of personal efficacy and competence, control, and meaning.

Self-care and self-nurturing skills are also important tools for this phase of work. Self-nurturance involves affirming one's value as a person, gaining awareness of personal goals and desires, considering new options, and transcending old roles. Self-nurturing activities often help the person experience a sense of pleasure and/or mastery and may include fantasy and goal-setting exercises, physical exercise, personal care, stress-management techniques, or classes that focus on building new skills. For sexual violence survivors, self-defense or martial arts training may also help increase a sense of bodily confidence and competence.[58,59]

As survivors explore the impact of sexual violence, social power differences, and socialization relevant to their social identities, they are likely to gain awareness of denied, buried, or distorted emotions. Survivors who have learned to use numbing, suppression, or denial to cope with pain may find that feelings of anger become more accessible and prominent. As a part of feminist counseling, clients learn to communicate their anger effectively so that it is not internalized or expressed haphazardly or indiscriminately. Instead, it is channeled in direct, constructive, assertive ways that decrease self-blame, redirect responsibility for violence on perpetrators, and facilitate personal efficacy and power.[60]

Sexual violence often contributes to one's sense of isolation and aloneness. Support groups and feminist group counseling are useful for decreasing feelings of isolation as well as counteracting negative and self-blaming thoughts. Participants realize that others have also survived sexual violence, and this commonality helps them place sexual violence within a more complete context. As members of a safe community, group members can facilitate trust, challenge each other, support each other's coping skills, and practice new skills. Group members may find that by supporting each other, they are also able to gain new perspectives on their own pain, thus helping them transcend personal circumstances. Support groups that make connections between sexual violence and the larger social context that condones victim blaming are likely to be especially helpful to recovery.[61]

Within feminist therapy, empowerment includes analyzing power structures in society, building awareness of how individuals are socialized to feel powerless, and discovering how clients can achieve power in personal, interpersonal, and institutional domains.[62] In light of these goals, feminist therapists are aware of the importance of linking personal empowerment and social change.

Many feminist therapists become involved in prevention, education, and social change activities related to sexual violence. As survivors develop greater confidence and feelings of personal power, feminist counselors may also encourage them to consider becoming involved in advocacy or social change roles. These activities may include participating in grassroots antiviolence community organizations, educational and prevention programs, local sexual assault coalitions, or online forums that combat violence.[63] One example of an influential social action program is INCITE!,[64] a multiracial, grassroots, feminist organization that has also published writings of activists. Too frequently, survivors are encouraged to see recovery as an individual experience alone. A feminist activist approach helps survivors envision and work toward a hopeful future for themselves and others.

CONCLUSION

Although this volume emphasizes recovery from sexual violence, it seems productive to conclude by highlighting the value of prevention and education activities. Although rape-supportive beliefs are deeply embedded within the culture, there is also evidence that well-structured, sustained, personally relevant, and well-timed interventions can lead to productive conversations about sexual violence and changed attitudes.[65] Educational interventions from the elementary school through college levels and in work settings can help potential victims become aware of circumstances associated with higher risk of sexual violence. More specifically, programs directed at college students can increase awareness of myths and facts about sexual assault as well as gender-role socialization relevant to sexual assault and can help individuals deal more effectively with risks related to sexual violence.[66] Feminist counselors and activists as well as survivors of sexual violence can play central roles in developing and supporting social change activities that educate potential victims, perpetrators, and those who provide services to victims/survivors.

Suggestions for Those Who Have Experienced Sexual Violence

1. Feeling safe and free of danger, both physically and psychologically, are crucial to achieving health. Surround yourself with people, activities, and environments that increase your sense of safety. This foundation is important for helping you explore and resolve the painful aspects of sexual violence. If you are in a relationship in which vio-

lence occurs, create a specific plan to ensure that you can get to safety when in crisis.

2. Coping with disorienting symptoms and impulses is a major challenge for survivors of sexual violence; these symptoms can surface at unexpected times. It is tempting to deny symptoms or to mask them through the use of alcohol or self-destructive behaviors. Instead, make a list of healthy coping options and develop a plan for implementing these healthy coping skills. The acronym CARESS can be used to organize adaptive options.[67] CA stands for communicate alternatively, and is especially useful when you feel like expressing or dulling pain in a self-harming or self-blaming manner. Methods for communicating alternatively may include writing a poem, creating a collage, or journaling. RE stands for releasing endorphins, and may include activities such as running, hiking, yoga, or even hugging a stuffed animal. SS stands for self-soothing, which can include a variety of self-nurturing and pleasurable activities such listening to soothing music, taking a warm shower, cooking a healthy and nutritious meal, or reading poetry.

3. Expressive writing is useful for regaining perspective after traumatic events, and many psychotherapists integrate writing activities with other activities. Typically, the first step involves writing about the factual aspects of the violence in as much detail as possible; during later stages of recovery, write down your thoughts, feelings, and as many sensory details as possible (e.g., sounds, smells, imagery). If, while writing, the intensity of emotions becomes difficult to manage, set aside the task and come back to it later. Before writing, make plans for implementing methods for coping with the intense feelings and thoughts that might emerge. Writing helps overcome avoidance forms of coping and can help defuse feelings of danger. Placing events, feelings, and thoughts on paper and "in the open" can help decrease rumination, brooding, and repetitive thinking patterns that reinforce depression and trauma symptoms. Writing allows you to break up overwhelming events into manageable parts and to reorganize your thoughts, feelings, and experience so that you can engage in greater closure and problem solving. It is often optimal to participate in writing and expression tasks under the guidance of a trusted counselor.

4. List some of the messages and myths about violence that you have seen in media or encountered from others. After listing the specific incident or myth, identify your feelings and personal reactions to the myth or stereotype. Now write an assertive challenge to the myth, validating your experience and clarifying how the myth is hurtful.

5. Create a list of your strengths and sources of resilience. When feeling paralyzed and unable to move forward, act "as if" you are feeling

healthy and whole, and choose to act on a strength. It is not essential to feel good in order to cope effectively. Behaving in a way that allows you to achieve a goal, even a small one, is likely to provide momentum and energy. Even small successes can help you get "unstuck" and serve as reminders of your potential. Feminist therapists emphasize resilience and growth as well as removing symptoms, and post-traumatic growth can be one outcome of surviving trauma.

6. Purchase a self-help guide that will assist your self-help recovery. One example is *The Rape Recovery Handbook* by Aphrodite Matsakis.[68]
7. Overcome feelings of isolation by staying engaged with people and trusted support systems. Joining a sexual assault survivors group within a local community or mental health service organization can facilitate insight about how the "personal is political." Support groups and sexual violence survivor groups can increase understanding that you are not alone. Within groups, members can listen and learn from others about coping while also giving back support and guidance to peers. Participating in a self-defense class or a program that focuses on physical strength and skills can also increase personal safety awareness and confidence in physical strength and resistance skills.
8. When ready, consider participating in some form of social change. Survivors of sexual violence have been major contributors to social activism projects that have increased social awareness of the culture of violence, supported prevention and education in schools and communities, and led to sexual violence advocacy services. Social activism can help survivors redirect anger in positive directions and contribute to more complete personal healing. Participation in social change activities may not be advisable during early phases of healing when feelings are raw, but can emerge and expand over time. A first step may involve becoming informed about sexual violence at local community or national levels and learning about existing organizations involved in combating sexual violence. Social change may encompass many types of activities such as providing material support or child care to victims/survivors, participating in victim advocate programs, cofacilitating a sexual assault education group, or providing leadership for community-wide programs. Self-monitoring of personal readiness and volunteering for smaller and then larger tasks helps to ensure that one's involvement will support personal growth and limit the likelihood of becoming overwhelmed.

REFERENCES

1. Klein, M.H. (1976). Feminist concepts of therapy outcome. *Psychotherapy: Theory, Research, and Practice, 13,* 89–95.

2. Hooks, B. (2000). *Feminism is for everybody.* Cambridge, MA: South End Press.
3. Rozee, P.D., & Koss, M.P. (2001). Rape: A century of resistance. *Psychology of Women Quarterly, 25,* 295–311.
4. Freud, S. (1925/1959). Some psychological consequences of the anatomical distinction between the sexes. In J. Strachey (Ed.), *The collected papers of Sigmund Freud* (Vol. 5) (pp. 186–197). New York: Basic Books.
5. Deutsch, H. (1945). *The psychology of women, Vol.2: Motherhood.* New York: Grune & Stratton.
6. Snell, J.E., Rosenwald, R.J., & Robey, A. (1964). The wifebeater's wife. *Archives of General Psychiatry, 11*(2), 107–112.
7. Chesler, P. (1972). *Women and madness.* New York: Doubleday.
8. Burgess, A.W., & Holmstrom. L.L. (1974). Rape trauma syndrome. *American Journal of Psychiatry, 131,* 981–986.
9. Walker, L. (1979). *The battered woman.* New York: Harper & Row.
10. American Psychiatric Association. (2000). *Diagnostic and statistical manual of mental disorders* (4th ed.). Washington, D.C.: American Psychiatric Association.
11. Franiuk, R., Seefelt, J.L., & Vandello, J.A. (2008). Prevalence of rape myths in headlines and their effects on attitudes toward rape. *Sex Roles, 58,* 790–801.
12. Grothues, C.A., & Marmion, S.L. (2006). Dismantling the myths about intimate violence against women. In P.K. Lundberg-Love & S.L. Marmion (Eds.), *"Intimate" violence against women: When spouses, partners, or lovers attack* (pp. 9–14). Westport, CT: Praeger.
13. Koss, M.P., Goodman, L.A., Browne, A., Fitzgerald, L.F., Keita, G.P., & Russo, N.F. (1994). *No safe haven: Male violence against women at home, at work, and in the community.* Washington, D.C.: American Psychological Association.
14. Ullman, S.E. (2010). *Talking about sexual assault: Society's response to survivors.* Washington, D.C.: American Psychological Association.
15. Campbell, R.C., Wasco, S.M., Ahrens, C.E., Sefl, T., & Barnes, H.E. (2001). Preventing the "second rape:" Rape survivors' experiences with community service providers. *Journal of Interpersonal Violence, 16,* 1239–1259.
16. Maier, S.L. (2008). "I have heard horrible stories . . .:" Rape victim advocates' perceptions of the revictimization of rape victims by the police and medical system. *Violence Against Women, 14,* 786–808.
17. Ullman, S.E. (2010). *Talking about sexual assault: Society's response to survivors.* Washington, D.C.: American Psychological Association.
18. Rozée, P.D. (1993). Forbidden or forgiven? Rape in cross-cultural perspective. *Psychology of Women Quarterly, 17,* 499–514.
19. Koss, M.P., Heise, L., & Russo, N.R. (1994). The global health burden of rape. *Psychology of Women Quarterly, 18,* 509–537.
20. Rozée, P.D. (1993). Forbidden or forgiven? Rape in cross-cultural perspective. *Psychology of Women Quarterly, 17,* 499–514.
21. Koss, M.P., Heise, L., & Russo, N.R. (1994). The global health burden of rape. *Psychology of Women Quarterly, 18,* 509–537.
22. Enns, C.Z. (2010). Locational feminisms and feminist social identity analysis. *Professional Psychology: Research and Practice.*
23. Ullman, S.E. (2010). *Talking about sexual assault: Society's response to survivors.* Washington, D.C.: American Psychological Association.

24. World Health Organization. (2005). *WHO multi-country study on women's health and domestic violence against women.* Geneva, Switzerland: World Health Organization.

25. Worell, J., & Remer, P. (2003). *Feminist perspectives in therapy: Empowering diverse women* (2nd ed.). New York: Wiley.

26. Worell, J., & Remer, P. (2003). *Feminist perspectives in therapy: Empowering diverse women* (2nd ed.). New York: Wiley.

27. Rothbaum, B.O., Foa, E.B., Riggs, D.S., Murdock, T., & Walsh, W. (1992). A prospective examination of post-traumatic stress disorder in rape victims. *Journal of Traumatic Stress, 5,* 455–475.

28. Elklit, A., & Christiansen, D.M. (2010). ASD and PTSD in rape victims. *Journal of Interpersonal Violence, 25,* 1470–1488.

29. Taft, C.T., Resick, P.A., Watkins, L.E., & Panuzio, J. (2009). An investigation of posttraumatic stress disorder and depressive symptomatology among female victims of interpersonal trauma. *Journal of Family Violence, 24,* 407–415.

30. Worell, J., & Remer, P. (2003). *Feminist perspectives in therapy: Empowering diverse women* (2nd ed.). New York: Wiley.

31. Najdowski, C.J., & Ullman, S.E. (2009). PTSD symptoms and self-rated recovery among adult sexual assault survivors: The effects of traumatic life events and psychosocial variables. *Psychology of Women Quarterly, 33,* 43–53.

32. Herman, J.L. (1992). *Trauma and recovery.* New York: Basic Books.

33. Worell, J., & Remer, P. (2003). *Feminist perspectives in therapy: Empowering diverse women* (2nd ed.). New York: Wiley.

34. Herman, J.L. (1992). *Trauma and recovery.* New York: Basic Books.

35. Ullman, S.E. (2010). *Talking about sexual assault: Society's response to survivors.* Washington, D.C.: American Psychological Association.

36. Ballou, M., & West, C. (2000). Feminist therapy approaches. In M. Biaggio & M. Hersen (Eds.), *Issues in the psychology of women* (pp. 273–297). New York: Kluwer Academic/Plenum.

37. Enns, C.Z. (2004). *Feminist theories and psychotherapies: Origins, themes, and diversity* (2nd ed.). New York: Haworth Press.

38. Brown, L.S. (1994). *Subversive dialogues: Theory in feminist therapy.* New York: Basic Books.

39. Brown, L.S. (2010). *Feminist therapy.* Washington, DC: American Psychological Association.

40. Enns, C.Z. (2004). *Feminist theories and psychotherapies: Origins, themes, and diversity* (2nd ed.). New York: Haworth Press.

41. Brown, L.S. (1994). *Subversive dialogues: Theory in feminist therapy.* New York: Basic Books.

42. Brown, L.S. (2010). *Feminist therapy.* Washington, D.C.: American Psychological Association.

43. Feminist Therapy Institute. (2000). *Feminist therapy code of ethics* [revised 1999]. San Francisco: Feminist Therapy Institute.

44. Feminist Therapy Institute. (2000). *Feminist therapy code of ethics* [revised 1999]. San Francisco: Feminist Therapy Institute.

45. Pope, K.S., & Brown, L.S. (1996). *Recovered memories of abuse: Assessment, therapy, forensics.* Washington, D.C.: American Psychological Association.

46. Enns, C.Z., Campbell, J., Courtoin, C.A., Gottlieb, M.C., Lese, K.P., Gilbert, M.S., & Forrest, L. (1998). Working with adult clients who may have experienced childhood abuse: Recommendations for assessment and practice. *Professional Psychology: Research and Practice, 29,* 245–256.
47. Brown, L.S. (2010). *Feminist therapy.* Washington, DC: American Psychological Association.
48. Enns, C.Z. (2010). Locational feminisms and feminist social identity analysis. *Professional Psychology: Research and Practice.*
49. Bryant-Davis, T. (2005). *Thriving in the wake of trauma: A multicultural guide.* Westport, CT: Praeger.
50. Lebowitz, L., & Roth, S. (1994). "I felt like a slut": The cultural context and women's response to being raped. *Journal of Traumatic Stress, 7,* 363–390.
51. Hall, C.I. (2009). Asian American women: The nail that sticks out is hammered down. In N. Tewari & A.N. Alvarez (Eds.), *Asian American psychology: Current perspectives* (pp. 193–209). New York: Psychology Press.
52. Townsend, T.G., Thomas, A.J., Neilands, T.B., & Jackson, T.R. (2010). I'm no Jezebel; I am young gifted, and black: Identity, sexuality, and black girls. *Psychology of Women Quarterly, 34,* I 273–285.
53. West, C.M. (1995). Mammy, Sapphire, and Jezebel: Historical images of Black women and their implications for psychotherapy. *Psychotherapy, 32,* 458–466.
54. Worell, J., & Remer, P. (2003). *Feminist perspectives in therapy: Empowering diverse women* (2nd. ed.). New York: Wiley.
55. Ballou, M., & West, C. (2000). Feminist therapy approaches. In M. Biaggio & M. Hersen (Eds.), *Issues in the psychology of women* (pp. 273–297). New York: Kluwer Academic/Plenum.
56. Cook, J.M., Schnurr, P.P., & Foa, E.B. (2004). Bridging the gap between post-traumatic stress disorder research and clinical practice: The example of exposure therapy. *Psychotherapy: Theory, Research, Practice, Training, 41,* 374–387.
57. Neville, H.A., & Heppner, M.J. (2002). Prevention and treatment of violence against women: An examination of sexual assault. In C.L. Juntunen & D.R. Atkinson (Eds.), *Counseling across the lifespan: Prevention and treatment* (pp. 261–277). Thousand Oaks, CA: Sage.
58. Brecklin, L.R. (2008). Evaluation outcomes of self-defense training for women: A review. *Aggression and Violent Behavior, 13,* 60–76.
59. Ullman, S.E. (2010). *Talking about sexual assault: Society's response to survivors.* Washington, D.C.: American Psychological Association.
60. Van Velsor, P., & Cox, D.L. (2001). Anger as a vehicle in the treatment of women who are sexual abuse survivors: Reattributing responsibility and accessing personal power. *Professional Psychology: Research and Practice, 32,* 618–625.
61. Ullman, S.E. (2010). *Talking about sexual assault: Society's response to survivors.* Washington, D.C.: American Psychological Association.
62. Hawxhurst, D.M., & Morrow, S.L. (1984). *Living our visions: Building feminist community.* Tempe, AZ: Fourth World.
63. Ullman, S.E. (2010). *Talking about sexual assault: Society's response to survivors.* Washington, D.C.: American Psychological Association.
64. INCITE! Women of Color Against Violence. (2006). *Color of violence: The INCITE! Anthology.* Cambridge, MA: South End Press.

65. Neville, H.A., & Heppner, M.J. (2002). Prevention and treatment of violence against women: An examination of sexual assault. In C.L. Juntunen & D.R. Atkinson (Eds.), *Counseling across the lifespan: Prevention and treatment* (pp. 261–277). Thousand Oaks, CA: Sage.
66. Anderson, L.A., & Whiston, S.C. (2005). Sexual assault education programs: A meta-analytic examination of their effectiveness. *Psychology of Women Quarterly, 29,* 374–388.
67. Ferentz, L., & Schwartz, R. (2002). Treating the self-harming client. *Psychotherapy Networker, 26*(5), 69–77.
68. Matsakis, A. (2003). *The rape recovery handbook: Step-by-step help for survivors of sexual assault.* Oakland, CA: New Harbinger.

13

Restoring Relationships: Group Interventions for Survivors of Sexual Traumas

Shannon M. Lynch

Trauma isolates; the group recreates a sense of belonging.
Trauma shames and stigmatizes; the group bears witness and affirms.
Trauma dehumanizes . . . the group restores humanity (p. 214).[1]

An act of sexual violence represents a clear betrayal of the recognition that we, when we are developmentally and psychologically ready, decide how and when to share our body with another. This is true in the case of childhood sexual abuse, adult rape, sexual assault, sexual harassment, sexual violence by a partner, sex trafficking, gang rape, and rape in the context of war. In each instance, at least one other individual has chosen to violate our basic assumption that we have the right to consent to sexual intimacy. When we are deprived of the right to consent (or dissent) via a perpetrator's use of manipulation, threat, physical violence, status as a caregiver, parent, or authority figure, or any exploitation of power, we experience a sense of loss of control and predictability over ourselves and our environment. Subsequently, many of us will develop feelings of shame and guilt as well as trauma-related distress. It is critical to understand that these reactions are in fact *normal* responses to extreme situations that compromise our understanding of who we are and what we can expect from others.

Common responses to sexual traumas in childhood and adulthood include substantial psychological distress such as post-traumatic stress disorder (PTSD), depression, anxiety, sexual confusion and risk taking, self-harming behaviors, and substance use.[2-3] While some individuals who experience a sexual trauma will recover without experiencing long-term psychological distress,[4-5] many individuals will struggle with trauma-related distress, feelings of shame, confusion about responsibility for the traumatic event, and difficulty trusting others or feeling safe. Furthermore, sexual traumas often result in an individual feeling isolated and alone. The survivor can be the carrier of a secret that is a heavy burden or unwelcomed disclosure. It is too easy to forget that sexual traumas, by definition, are interpersonal and require at least two people to occur.

The betrayal by the perpetrator or perpetrators, the feeling of being different and/or carrying the stigma of being a sexual trauma survivor, and the sense of powerlessness of an individual in the aftermath of a sexual trauma are most likely to be repaired in the context of positive, restorative connections with others. In other words, just as a sexual trauma represents betrayal by at least one other, recovery is facilitated by remembering or discovering, in interactions with others, that we are deserving of nurturing and caring relationships. Numerous studies have shown social support from others is a strong predictor of recovery from experiences of interpersonal violence.[6] Some individuals will find these connections without the structure of a psychotherapy group. For others, group therapy offers the opportunity to be safe with others, to relearn how and when to trust others and oneself, to work on regulating intense affect, to see oneself as effective and able to help others, and to develop and/or repair relationship skills.[7]

Irvin Yalom has written extensively about the theory of group therapy and why group treatment can be effective.[8] Yalom describes processes that occur in group therapy that provide opportunities for healing and gaining both a stronger sense of self and greater trust in others. First, Yalom identifies universality of experiences as a key component of a group experience. Talking about one's experiences and feelings with others allows group members to recognize what is similar about their experiences as well as common reactions (guilt or self-blame) to sexual traumas. Recognition of shared experiences can begin to degrade the sense of stigma and differentness associated with sexual trauma. A feeling of belonging to the group can allow individuals to begin to decrease the sense of secrecy and shame that often surrounds sexual trauma.[1]

Next, by seeing and hearing other survivors' stories in group, one is exposed to others' experiences of failure and success. Meeting with others and learning about their day-to-day coping often creates a sense of hope that distress will eventually lessen, that relationships can be safe, and that one can be successful in a variety of ways. Monitoring one's own progress is often challenging as we continually remind ourselves of ways we are either not successful or not good enough. Observing others' small victories offers a mirror that suggests the importance of recognizing and celebrating accomplishments, often first the accomplishments of others and then our own. Meeting with other survivors also offers a source of information. Group members can share information about functioning in general as well as resources within the community: ways of coping with triggers in public, which service providers work well with trauma survivors, what places feel safe and offer support, et cetera. Sharing knowledge about coping strategies and the community increases survivors' sense of control and ability to shape their future experiences.

Finally, the experience of offering others support and suggestions creates an opportunity for the survivor to recognize that she or he has something of value to share with the group. Acceptance of the supportive comments or information we offer results in a feeling of not only belonging but also having something to contribute. These experiences, multiplied over time, begin to counteract the sense of oneself as bad, unworthy, or undeserving of the support of others. Helping others increases our ability to see our own worth and deservingness.[8]

For a group to create a sense of safety, belonging, and hope, the environment of the group has to welcome and value all members. Sexual trauma survivors represent a diverse array of peoples of different cultures, spiritual beliefs, sexual orientations, socioeconomic status, ability and disability. Group facilitators and members are charged to create an environment that acknowledges and celebrates differences even as they strive to recognize shared or common experiences. Part of what a facilitator must strive for and a survivor must evaluate is whether each group member's perspective can be visible and respected in a particular group. Facilitators should express recognition that the impact of sexual traumas is heightened by the social context in which they occur. Many trauma survivors must cope with not only the trauma itself but also the meaning it holds for their identity as an individual and a member of a community. Individuals who belong to communities that experience discrimination and prejudice must take this sociopolitical reality into account as they work on creating a meaning for their own experience. Facilitators also must include recognition of the sociopolitical context of group members to create safe, respectful environments. It is critical that survivors evaluate the environment created by the group facilitator(s) and seek out a group where the facilitator explicitly strives to welcome and affirm everyone.

GROUP THERAPY FOR SEXUAL TRAUMA SURVIVORS

The research literature on group therapy is limited compared to the substantial research on the effectiveness of a variety of individual treatments for trauma survivors. In addition, the majority of the published literature in the area of sexual traumas is focused on female survivors of childhood sexual abuse (CSA) or adult rape. Discussion of group treatment interventions for survivors of other sexual traumas or for male survivors is very sparse. For female survivors of CSA, brief and long-term group treatments have been shown to be effective in reducing trauma-related distress, in particular symptoms of PTSD and depression.[9] Other studies have found decreases in shame, anxiety, and fear and increases in self-esteem after completion of group treatment.[7,10]

The variety of types of group interventions for sexual trauma survivors can be categorized as support groups; structured, skill-based groups; and semistructured and/or process-oriented groups. The length and goals of groups vary significantly. Groups may be open, inviting new members at any time, or closed, maintaining a consistent membership for the term of the group. These characteristics of a group are most often determined by the goals and orientation of the group facilitator(s). I will provide examples of groups in each of these categories shortly. First, it is critical to discuss key aspects of a group that should be present regardless of group type.

Qualities of Successful Therapeutic Groups

Sexual trauma survivors' basic sense of safety has been violated, often multiple times. A critical component of any trauma treatment therefore is the creation of a safe and respectful environment. Groups must have explicit rules as well as procedures for how to handle a situation when a rule is violated. While most therapy groups have an expectation of confidentiality, the belief that one can share one's experiences and know who is hearing them and that they will be held in confidence is particularly critical for the trauma survivor's ability to feel safe and trust others in group. Confidentiality rules should be clearly stated and discussed by the group in the first meeting.

Survivors often join groups to decrease their sense of isolation. However, groups will vary in the extent to which they limit relationships among group members outside of group meetings. First, once the group has ended, many group facilitators will encourage members to maintain contact with one another to the extent they wish to do so. However, some groups will specifically request no outside contact among group members while the group is actively meeting. Others will utilize group members as buddies to contact in times of high stress, while still others will encourage group members to develop supportive relationships with one another outside of group. The extent of group member contact outside of group while the group treatment is ongoing should be discussed and agreed to by all group members at the start of a group. Again, the most critical issue here is explicit communication about expectations and a sense of fairness for all involved. However, all groups should unambiguously ask group members to abstain from engaging in sexual relationships with one another for the duration of a group to avoid retraumatization of group members. We cannot predict the outcome of a relationship. Becoming intimately involved with a group member or a facilitator represents a risk of new hurt or betrayal for the individuals involved as well as divisiveness among group members as a whole if the relationship is unsuccessful. This threatens everyone's sense of safety in the group. In addition, becoming involved with a group member, or especially a facilitator, introduces questions about power and control that can negatively influence all group members, reminding them of their prior experiences of helplessness.

Next, an overarching goal in any group with survivors of sexual traumas should include empowerment of group members. Oftentimes facilitators will ask participants to discuss and establish rules for the group in the first or second meeting. Participation in identifying and defining the rules of a group intervention increases group members' sense of control and predictability. Another method of empowering group members is to involve them in setting the goals and tasks for the group. Group members may develop individual goals to pursue within the group or agree to goals for the group as a whole. It will depend upon the nature and time limitations of the group. If group members are not yet able to set specific goals, then to increase control and predictability, the facilitator should, at a minimum, communicate group goals and tasks.

Facilitators must also be prepared to address and manage conflict in the group. The safety of the group members and a respect for all members is vital to creating and maintaining therapeutic progress. An unpredictable group with unclear rules represents a high risk for retraumatization for group members. Groups may be semistructured or unstructured, but group members must be able to refer to clear rules, control their participation, anticipate that facilitators will address and contain conflict, and understand the rationale for the group and group processes.

Next, groups vary in the extent to which group members are expected to share specific details about their sexual traumas. Present-focused groups tend to emphasize the here and now and individuals' coping strategies and relationships and to discourage detailed descriptions of the abuse. In contrast, trauma-focused groups often include a focus on current coping and relationships but also discussion and detailed review of past traumatic experiences. Research comparing trauma- and present-focused treatment groups suggests both types of group treatment lead to decreases in interpersonal problems and/or trauma-related symptoms.[11-12] However, it is important to note that in some instances trauma-focused/exposure group treatments have led to higher dropout rates than the present-focused, problem-solving-focused groups.[12]

Participation in a present-focused versus trauma-focused group typically depends on the readiness of the survivor to share his or her story with others. Most facilitators will talk with group members prior to starting a new group to discuss the way the group is structured, goals for the group, and expectations for group members. Part of this conversation is often a screening process to determine whether the individual would benefit most from a highly structured, present-focused group or if he or she appears ready to engage in trauma-focused work. If a group facilitator does not ask questions about readiness to discuss traumatic experiences, it is essential that the survivor asks about who will be in the group and the expectations for sharing traumatic material.

Choosing a Group

Where you live and the extent of available resources will impact what choices you have regarding participation in group psychotherapy. If there is a trauma center or a variety of trauma experts working in your area, then there is a greater likelihood of being able to choose from among different types of groups. In more rural areas, the range of group interventions is likely to be more limited. Regardless of your location, learning about the variety of groups described in the literature can help you to identify the different types of services generally available and provide you with information that you can use to ask questions and to evaluate the kinds of groups offered in your own community.

Many practitioners will suggest participation in a group depending on your stage of recovery. Stage of recovery is a general way to describe where a survivor's energy is focused. Stages are not linear steps that, once accomplished, remain forever left behind. Instead, stages suggest a general location on the path of recovery. In stage one, the survivor is working on basic safety and restoring a sense of control over the self, and then the environment.[1] Individuals in this stage are often struggling with severe symptoms of distress, they may be engaging in self-harming or other risk-taking behaviors, or they may simply feel out of control. Groups for individuals in this stage are generally present-focused and time limited. They typically aim to provide education about symptoms and/or teach coping or affect regulation skills. In addition, many areas will have support groups aimed at helping individuals in this stage with safety planning and coping with current stressors and by providing information about resources. Practitioners often recommend that stage one groups have members with similar experiences to help facilitate a sense of belonging and trust.

Stage two recovery work is focused on remembrance, integration, and mourning.[1] Practitioners in the field disagree about exactly when an individual is ready to work on remembering and integrating specific details of sexual traumas. Most agree, however, that the individual should have skills that allow him or her to cope with intense emotions that can be evoked by a focus on remembering traumatic experiences. Individuals in this stage may still be struggling with trauma-related distress, but generally they have established a basic sense of safety, engage in self-care, and have some strategies for managing symptoms. Most stage two group facilitators will ask potential participants about current substance abuse, suicidal ideation or intent, self-harming behavior, current safety from revictimization, and co-occurring mental health problems. Many practitioners suggest that an individual who is actively using substances to cope, self-harming or considering self-injury, in an unsafe living situation, or seriously mentally ill (e.g., experiencing delusions) should not do trauma-focused or exposure work.

Stage two groups often include both present- and trauma-focused components. These groups may be structured, semistructured, or unstructured process-oriented groups. Once again, particularly in groups with substantial trauma focus and remembering, these groups often consist of individuals with more similar trauma experiences. Some practitioners believe that initial remembering or exposure work should take place in individual therapy, while others argue that for some populations, remembering in a supportive group situation (e.g., group for combat veterans) is more effective at reducing distress. In the end, this is generally the decision of the survivor and his/her assessment of his/her own readiness, in conjunction with a group facilitator, for the content of a trauma-focused group.

In stage three, recovery is essentially about reconnecting with others. At this point, sexual trauma survivors may choose to be in a more heterogeneous group; a group with individuals with a variety of experiences.[1] Groups at this stage tend to be interpersonal or psychodynamic, with a focus on understanding patterns in relationships with others, both within and outside of the group. These groups are often ongoing, with members remaining active for several months to a few years. The group leader in this type of group facilitates group members' discussions but does not tend to structure the group via the presentation of topics or educational materials. Participants in stage three groups challenge and confront one another with the explicit intent of helping one another to see what each individual contributes to their interactions with others and how their expectations of others shape the responses they receive.

SUPPORT GROUPS

Support groups are usually targeted at individuals in stage one of their recovery. They often are provided via community agencies such as domestic violence family services, battered women's shelters, rape crisis centers, or local organizations (e.g., Veterans of Foreign Wars). Support groups typically are organized with the primary goal of creating the opportunity to talk to others with similar experiences and share coping strategies as well as providing information about relevant community resources. Most support groups are present-focused, usually on helping participants with safety planning when applicable, and coping with current stressors. Group time is spent primarily on members checking in about current stressors and offering suggestions and support to one another. Many support groups are open, "drop-in" groups that invite individuals to attend as they are able. Most shelters and crisis centers provide intensive trainings for their volunteers and staff but do not necessarily have trained, licensed mental health professionals to facilitate the groups. Support groups offered by community or nonprofit organizations are often led by a survivor or survivors who have progressed in their recoveries and are committed to helping others with experiences similar to their own but who may not have any formal training as a counselor or mental health professional.

Many community agencies and organizations have information and brief descriptions online of the groups that they offer. There are also websites developed by national organizations or nonprofits that offer information for survivors and, in some cases, locations of support groups. Some are listed at the end of this book. In addition, there are a growing number of online support groups. Many appear to be forums for individuals who identify as survivors to talk with one another. These groups may offer an opportunity for connection to individuals who are seeking social interactions with others with similar experiences, but remember that in most cases, participants are not screened and posts may not be monitored.

Although support groups are among the most common type of group offered to survivors of interpersonal violence, there is very limited research on the effectiveness of support groups. Tutty and colleagues assessed outcomes for seventy-six battered women who attended support groups that meet weekly for ten to twelve weeks.[13] They found that the women reported increased self-esteem, belonging, support, and sense of control, and decreased stress. While there is little empirical research on support groups, they continue to be one of the most readily available forms of group interventions for trauma survivors. These groups are most often useful for individuals who are struggling to be safe and/or to cope with everyday stressors, who feel alone or unique in their experiences, and/or who are in need of information about area resources.

STRUCTURED GROUPS

Structured groups usually have a present focus and the goal of teaching a specific set of skills, such as stress management, relaxation training, emotion regulation, or assertiveness training. Generally, structured groups have a topic per meeting. Often members are provided with handouts that are reviewed and discussed by group members. Groups are usually structured with a brief check-in by group members (e.g., progress on identified goals since the last meeting or a brief update about how one is coping with current stressors), introduction of the topic, group member discussion (e.g., shared stories, role plays, etc.), and then a check-out (e.g., brief statement by each group member about a goal they intend to work on, a coping strategy they will practice, or an acknowledgment of feelings in response to the content of the session). These groups are usually time limited (e.g., three to six months in length). Many structured groups are open to new members for a few weeks and then closed for the duration of a group. However, structured groups can be open to new members throughout the group or closed, depending on the goals and needs of the group. These groups can be present- or trauma-focused. Present-focused groups typically work to decrease behaviors developed after the sexual trauma that result in avoiding rather than resolving problems. These groups are often offered for survivors of interpersonal violence in general unless the practitioner offering the group specifies that it is for survivors of sexual traumas. Many of these groups are also focused on stage one goals, such as increasing self-care, safety, and stabilization on a day-to-day basis.

One example of a structured, stage one group for trauma survivors is dialectical behavior therapy (DBT).[14] DBT is primarily focused on helping individuals develop better emotion regulation and tolerance for intense feelings. Feelings such as shame, grief, guilt, anxiety, and self-blame are very common in sexual trauma survivors and can be so intense that individuals feel out of control and day-to-day functioning is impaired. DBT is a therapy that can be provided in a group format to assist participants to learn distress tolerance, mindfulness (focusing on being aware and accepting rather than judging oneself), emotion regulation, and relationship skills. In a twelve-session DBT group adapted specifically for battered women, the thirty-one participants demonstrated improvements in depression, hopelessness, psychological distress, and social adjustment.[15] In addition, the majority of the group members (93%) reported being highly satisfied with their experience of the group.

There are also trauma-focused, structured groups. These groups often combine teaching coping skills with specific, focused remembering tasks or exposure to the traumatic events. These groups typically exclude individuals who are using substances, suicidal, or in unsafe living situations.[16] A number of groups combine coping and specific focus on traumatic experiences that have been demonstrated to be effective. For example, participants with histories of childhood sexual abuse and adult rapes have shown decreases in symptoms of PTSD and depression in cognitive processing groups.[17-18] Cognitive processing therapy (CPT) is a time-limited intervention (e.g., twelve sessions) that is based on reviewing the traumatic experience(s) and challenging negative or inaccurate thoughts (e.g., self-blame) associated with the trauma. Many times, we develop beliefs subsequent to a traumatic event that are based on our experience of that event (e.g., I cannot trust anyone, I was powerless to protect myself, or I deserve to be hurt by others) that we then apply to our general experiences.

CPT aims to identify maladaptive thoughts commonly developed after a traumatic experience, such as distorted beliefs about our safety, ability to trust others, self-efficacy or competence, and self-esteem, and to challenge these negative beliefs as they apply to one's life and abilities in general. A central, early component of CPT is writing out a detailed account of one's traumatic experiences, including all the sensory details and emotions related to the experience that one can recall. Next, the idea of "faulty thinking" is introduced, and group members learn about ways in which individuals often develop maladaptive beliefs subsequent to the sexual trauma in regard to safety, trust, power, esteem, and intimacy. Group members also learn about how prior positive beliefs can be disrupted by sexual traumas and prior negative beliefs can be confirmed by traumatic experiences. Then they listen to one another's accounts and point out maladaptive beliefs, challenging one another to have compassion for oneself and one's experiences.[18]

Dialectical behavior therapy and cognitive processing therapy are two examples of structured groups that have been tested and appear to be effective.[15,17-18] If you are interested in participating in a structured group, it is important to ask the facilitator about the nature of the group, to determine if it is present-focused or trauma-focused, how similar the members will be regarding their trauma histories, and what the facilitator knows about how effective the intervention is (e.g., whether it has been tested empirically). Most structured groups that have been assessed for effectiveness have treatment manuals with materials/handouts that the facilitator can share with participants. Many trauma treatments have not yet been empirically tested or have only been assessed with limited populations (e.g., female CSA survivors). Knowing what questions to ask about the structure and goals of the group, the focus and format, and the group leaders' qualifications will help you to determine if the group is a good match for you.

SEMISTRUCTURED GROUPS

Stage one semistructured or process groups typically include a combination of sharing coping strategies; validation of feelings and experiences; and opportunities to reframe ways of thinking about sexual traumas themselves, one's sense of self, and perceptions/expectations of others. Semistructured groups that are focused on stage one recovery will generally have a present focus and explicit tasks or aims for the group members as well as a predictable session structure: check-in, review of progress toward goals, and check-out. These groups differ from structured groups in that there is not usually an identified topic (or handouts) per session and the focus is not on decreasing specific symptoms or teaching specific skills, but rather group members are encouraged to use the group time to discuss their current experiences and to help one another in making progress toward their identified goals. The underlying aim of semistructured groups is to foster trust and cohesiveness among participants in order to change both how individuals see themselves and how they interact with others. Semistructured groups differ from support groups in that the group membership is usually more stable than a support group (e.g., closed), the group itself has a specific focus or task, participants are encouraged to have specific goals they are working on, and the group is more likely to be facilitated by a trained mental health professional.

An example is a semistructured, process group focused on stabilization such as the "Safety and Self Care" group described by Harney and Harvey.[19] This group is for individuals struggling with risk taking, self-harming urges, or self-destructive behaviors. Participants in this group set goals regarding safety and self-care and attend meetings for twelve to fifteen weeks to share progress on their goals as well as acknowledging and working on setbacks and difficulties. Facilitators help participants to set goals and identify incremental steps toward achieving their goals, and work with group members to maintain safety in the group.

Many stage two recovery groups are semistructured groups. These groups are often psychodynamic or interpersonal in orientation and focus on expression of emotion and identifying and understanding past and current patterns in relationships, thoughts, and feelings. Group members are encouraged to share common experiences and try new ways of interacting with one another. Reviews of studies of process-oriented groups for adult sexual abuse survivors suggest process groups are effective at decreasing symptoms of trauma-related distress and increasing social adjustment and relationship quality, with greater improvement in those groups that are semistructured rather than unstructured.[20]

The quality and nature of the therapy group will be determined in large part by the facilitator(s). It is critical that survivors ask about the qualifications of the facilitator(s), including their training to provide trauma-related or trauma-focused treatment. It is also important that facilitators are able to describe the group goals and rules clearly. Groups offered by practitioners who describe the treatment as behavioral or cognitive behavioral usually have a focus on symptom reduction and teaching new skills and/or ways of thinking about one's experiences. These are most likely to be structured groups. Practitioners who describe the group as interpersonal or psychodynamic will place more emphasis on the relationships among the group members and typically rely on group processes (increased sense of belonging, hope, and deservingness) as agents of change and recovery. They are more likely to offer semistructured or unstructured groups. Some practitioners may describe the interventions they offer as an integration of the approaches described above.

An additional orientation that facilitators may use is a feminist approach to trauma therapy. Group facilitators who identify as feminist will place an even greater emphasis on empowering the group members in their recovery, placing control of many tasks and decisions in the hands of group members (though still remaining active enough to maintain safety of the group). Oftentimes, feminist groups will explicitly acknowledge the ways in which the sociopolitical environment that we live in increases our risk for sexual victimization. For example, a feminist-identified facilitator is likely to explicitly encourage a discussion of the variety of ways in which gender oppression, or the devaluing of women and girls in society, as well as the narrow view of masculinity with which many men and boys are socialized, contribute to increased risk of sexual assaults. An additional component of feminist therapy often includes encouraging members to consider taking social action on behalf of themselves or others as part of their recovery.

RECOGNIZING THE DIVERSITY OF SURVIVORS

Though my description of group types has been general, it is likely you have noticed that the references to research have been focused on women, particularly battered women, female adult rape survivors, or female survivors of childhood sexual abuse. Literature about groups for adult male survivors or survivors of other types of sexual traumas is very sparse. In addition, much of the research on the effectiveness of groups described above excludes individuals who are experiencing multiple forms of psychological distress or struggling with substance abuse. Very little programming is available that was developed specifically for people of color or other minority group populations (e.g., gay/lesbian/bisexual individuals). Finally, there is a dearth of information regarding groups for the supporters of adult survivors (e.g., caregivers, partners, or others), who are also often deeply affected by what has happened to their loved one(s). The following information is based on select studies or articles describing interventions for specific populations. Again, this literature is limited, so many survivors of sexual traumas will be in the position of reading about groups that have been helpful to individuals who are like them in some ways, even if aspects of their experiences are very different.

Male Survivors

Literature on treatments specifically for male sexual trauma survivors is very limited. One recommendation is that male survivors participate, at least initially, in all-male groups given the pervasive silence about sexual traumas to males. Although male and female survivors of sexual traumas have many similar responses, men are more likely to react with greater confusion about how the sexual trauma affects their gender identity and/or sexual orientation, anger dysregulation, and shock that they could be the victim of a sexual attack.[10] Others suggest male survivors of childhood sexual abuse, in particular, struggle with shame and ambivalence about being sexual (which conflicts with societal messages about being male), emotional and sexual distance from others, and difficulties as adults in intimate relationships.[21]

Although there is comparatively little literature and research on male survivors of sexual traumas, there is growing recognition of males raping males in military organizations. In 1994, Congress amended a law requiring Veterans Affairs to provide services for sexual assault or harassment that occurred while on active duty to male as well as female soldiers. In response, some veterans' centers have begun offering groups for veterans who are male survivors of sexual traumas. Psychologists affiliated with a VA in Minnesota describe a process group for male veterans who were survivors of sexual assault while on duty or childhood sexual abuse that appears to have reduced participants' distress. They describe several stages of a long-term group therapy.[10]

During the first few months, group members worked on establishing trust and clarifying boundaries. For these men, part of getting to know one another was describing details of their military service to help them to recognize similarities and differences in their general experiences. At this time, group members were discouraged from describing their traumatic experiences in detail. Approximately three months into the group, group members began to discuss coping with current symptoms and to connect past traumatic events to current functioning. During this phase, they began to share more specific aspects of their experiences of sexual trauma with one another and to recognize similarities in their experiences. At approximately six months, the group began to work more on interpersonal goals and issues, including confronting and challenging one another, working on safely expressing anger and addressing conflict. In the third phase of the group (months seven through nine), members discussed gender identity and confusion about sexual orientation. In the final phase of the group, members focused on who was responsible for the sexual assaults and discussed the possibility of forgiving perpetrators. The authors/facilitators do not describe any specific outcomes of improvement that they measured for participants of the group. They do note, however, that the group was created in response to veterans' requests for a group for male sexual trauma survivors, and they offer their observation that the group participants seemed more able to recognize their individual strengths and contributions to relationships both within and outside of the group after several months of group treatment.[10]

A very different example of a group for male sexual trauma survivors is a short-term group treatment for gay male survivors of CSA who also were living with HIV/AIDS. Masten and colleagues describe a fifteen-week group that emphasizes building a safe and cohesive environment, teaching coping skills, and trauma exposure content.[22] Groups consisted of six to eight members for a total of forty-nine group participants in six groups. Individuals with cognitive impairments or severe depression were excluded. Group members began by sharing reasons for participating in the group, telling the story or stories of their sexual traumas, and identifying similarities in their experiences. Sessions five through eight focused on teaching members about models of coping and providing examples of alternative/adaptive coping skills. The final sessions focused on discussing expectations and perceptions in relationships and engaging in self-care (e.g., getting regular medical care, treatment adherence). Although these groups were structured by topic, the facilitators also emphasized building relationships among group members, encouraging members to share details of their traumatic experiences and to offer one another support throughout the sessions. This coping-focused, interpersonal group intervention demonstrated greater reduction in intrusive and avoidance symptoms of PTSD than a support group focused on trauma and HIV or a waitlisted comparison sample.[23] Group members were diverse: six identified as Caucasian, twenty-nine African American, eleven Latino, and three as multiethnic individuals. The coping groups were also offered and evaluated for heterosexual female survivors of CSA with HIV/AIDS and showed similar positive results. Very few heterosexual male CSA survivors with HIV/AIDS were referred, and thus there were not sufficient numbers to offer them a group.

The descriptions of the two groups for male survivors above give you an idea of the types of group interventions available and issues addressed in a group format. The availability of all-male groups is likely to be more limited in some geographic areas. There are websites that offer information specifically for male survivors, such as malesurvivor.org and aardvarc.org, both of which list resources/agencies providing services by state.

SURVIVORS OF SEXUAL TRAUMAS AND . . .

Many survivors of sexual traumas have serious concerns or difficulties in addition to substantial trauma-related distress. Individuals with symptoms of

PTSD also often struggle with depression, other forms of anxiety (e.g., panic attacks), self-harming behaviors, and substance abuse.[24-25] However, many groups for survivors of sexual traumas will exclude potential participants if they show evidence of severe depression, serious mental illness, suicidal ideation, and/or current substance use.

To address these clear gaps in treatment, some mental health professionals have worked to develop groups specifically for trauma survivors that recognize and attend to the complexity of their experiences. For example, Seeking Safety is a present-focused, structured cognitive-behavioral intervention developed to address co-occurring PTSD and substance use disorders (SUD).[26] Seeking Safety is a stage one trauma treatment that provides education about the consequences of trauma and links between trauma and substance use and teaches specific cognitive, interpersonal, and behavioral coping skills. This group explicitly does not include detailed discussion of past traumatic events. The group can range from twelve to twenty-five sessions. Seeking Safety has been employed with male and female survivors in a diverse array of settings (community and outpatient settings, inpatient settings, prisons, residential substance use facilities, etc.) and is effective at reducing symptoms of PTSD and SUD.[26-27] Seeking Safety is one example of an intervention for co-occurring PTSD and SUD with empirical support for its effectiveness, but there also are other group interventions aimed at helping individuals who are struggling with both symptoms of PTSD and substance abuse or dependence.[27]

Another group of individuals who frequently have been excluded from trauma-focused group interventions are survivors with chronic and/or severe mental illness. However, some groups have been developed to provide support and therapeutic interventions to individuals with these additional challenges. The trauma recovery and empowerment model (TREM) is a structured, twenty-four-session group intervention for females with severe mental disorders, including women with significant substance abuse problems.[28] TREM combines cognitive restructuring techniques, skills training, psychoeducation, limited exposure to traumatic memories, and peer support to foster recovery and improved functioning. TREM includes eleven areas of skill development: self-awareness, self-protection, self-soothing, emotion regulation, developing mutual relationships, accurate labeling of self and others' behaviors, sense of agency, problem solving, judgment and decision making, reliable parenting, and developing a sense of purpose and meaning. TREM is not the only group intervention designed for survivors with co-occurring serious mental illness. Other groups such as Women's Safety in Recovery,[29] which combines psychoeducation, problem solving, and skill building but prohibits explicit trauma disclosure, have been tested in various settings and have shown effectiveness at decreasing trauma-related distress. Trauma-related treatment for individuals with complex needs is a growing area of theory and research, but at this time, survivors and their advocates will have to use the information they have gathered from this source and others to determine what type of group best meets their needs.

GROUPS FOR PARTNERS/SUPPORT PERSONS

Sexual traumas also affect intimate others of survivors—caregivers, partners, and other important supporters. Very little is written about treatment interventions for support persons of adult trauma survivors. One area that has received limited attention is the topic of support groups for partners of sexual trauma survivors. Barcus described a group for male partners of female childhood sexual or physical abuse survivors that focused on offering support and educating partners about the effects of trauma on the individual and their family as well as teaching about the recovery process.[30] Generally, group interventions for partners, caregivers, and other supporters of survivors will combine support and validation of the challenges they face with information about the needs and struggles of trauma survivors as well as ways to assist survivors in their recovery. A safe and respectful environment also is critical for these supporters of survivors as well as confidentiality and clear expectations regarding group content.

CASE EXAMPLE

Nila was a nineteen-year-old African American woman who was in individual, trauma-focused treatment but decided to also seek out group therapy to help her to decrease her suicidal ideation and risk-taking behaviors and increase her ability to make healthy connections with others. Nila was sexually abused by her stepfather from the age of twelve until she left home at sixteen. Nila obtained her GED and was attending college classes, but her ability to succeed academically had been hampered by difficulties focusing in class, her feeling that she was different from everyone else, and suicidal ideation/attempts. Nila decided to participate in a stage one, process-oriented stabilization group for survivors of intimate interpersonal violence. She worked with the facilitators to identify the following goals: (1) to develop alternative coping strategies (decreasing risk taking and suicidal ideation), (2) to learn how to identify characteristics of healthy relationships, and (3) to decrease her sense of shame and responsibility for the abuse. She attended a weekly semistructured group where she reported on her progress toward achieving her goals, helped other group members to develop new coping strategies, identified barriers to carrying out her goals, and recognized common experiences and feelings held by many of the group members (e.g., the idea that she should have been able to stop/ prevent the abuse, worry that she "asked for" or provoked the sexual abuse, concern that speaking out divided the family, and the feeling that she is now "damaged goods"). After completing a three-month semistructured process group, Nila joined a sports team at her community college, began attending church again, reestablished contact with some family members, and secured a more stable living situation. She reported less frequent suicidal ideation as well as feeling like she felt she had "something to contribute" and deserved a chance to make a better life for herself.

CONCLUSION

At this time, general reviews of the research suggest that group interventions can be effective and beneficial for survivors of sexual traumas, including survivors with complex needs.[9] The majority of group interventions that have been evaluated have included adult, female sexual assault or childhood sexual abuse survivors. The literature about survivors of other forms of sexual trauma and/or male survivors is much more limited. This small body of literature does, however, also support participation in group treatment to decrease trauma-related distress, shame, and interpersonal difficulties, and to increase general functioning.

The groups described in this chapter are provided as examples to assist you to consider what type of treatment might be most useful to you and to evaluate what is currently known about the effectiveness of different treatment approaches. In many geographic areas, there will be limited options for group treatment. Sharing this material with providers in your area may assist them with learning about the variety of interventions that can be useful to sexual trauma survivors. Many times, the survivor will be put in the position of deciding whether a treatment will be helpful to him or her. It is my hope that by reading about what is known more generally about group treatment as well as the range of possible interventions, you as a survivor and consumer can make a more informed choice about what is most likely to help you on your path toward recovery.

The following questions have been formulated to help you consider whether you are ready for and would benefit from group work:

1. Are you ready to share your experiences, either in the here and now or past experiences, with others?
   - Individuals who rated group experiences positively indicated that they valued the opportunity to share experiences and feelings, improve self-understanding via role plays and other structured

activities, and feel accepted by others.[31] In contrast, group participants who rated groups poorly did not feel ready to hear others'
stories and felt overwhelmed by participating in group. While it
would be normal to experience both positive and negative feelings
about participating in a group, it is important that you consider
what you are ready to share and hear, so that you can identify the
type of group most appropriate for you.

2. How well do you tolerate intense feelings that you are experiencing?
What about others' expressions of intense feelings?
   - If it is very difficult for you to regulate your feelings or to tolerate
   others' expression of intense affect, you should consider a structured, present-focused group. If it is hard for you to have empathy
   for others' experiences and feelings, then it may be best to start with
   individual therapy.

3. How safe are you? Are you at risk of revictimization? Do you think
about engaging in self-harming behaviors? Are you actively using
substances?
   - Many treatment groups will not allow participants who are currently at risk of future assaults, self-harming, or abusing substances
   to cope. If you are struggling with one of these issues, most often
   a support group or present-focused, stage-one treatment group is
   your best option.

4. What have your past disclosure experiences been like? Are you ready
to talk about your experiences of sexual trauma with others?
   - Most of us have told someone what happened to us, and many of
   us have had negative experiences with disclosing our traumas to
   others in the past. Some of us have told no one. If you are considering participating in a group for trauma survivors, it is important
   to recognize you can tell your story in stages. Group should be a
   safe, respectful environment. However, starting by sharing discreet
   amounts of information and determining what that feels like and
   what the level of support is for you is an excellent way of engaging
   in self-care and feeling in control as you work toward your recovery.

5. Does the group you are considering have clear rules? What are the
goals of the group? What are the expectations regarding discussion of
traumatic experiences? How similar or different are group members?
   - It is critical that a group facilitator indicate general expectations for
   group content, how the group is structured, typical rules for this
   type of group, and who will be included in the group. Survivors
   early in recovery generally benefit from being in groups with others
   with similar experiences, groups that are more structured, and with
   a present focus.

REFERENCES

1. Herman, J.L. (1992). *Trauma and recovery: The aftermath of violence—from domestic abuse to political terror.* New York: Basic Books.
2. Beitchman, J.H., Zucker, K.J., Hood, J.E., DaCosta, G.A., Akman, D., & Cassavia, E. (1992). A review of the long-term effects of child sexual abuse. *Child Abuse & Neglect, 16*,101–118.
3. Koss, M.P., Bailey, J.A., Yuan, N.P., Herrera, V.M., Lichter, E.L. (2003). Depression and PTSD in survivors of male violence: Research and training initiatives to facilitate recovery. *Psychology of Women Quarterly, 27*(2), 130–142.
4. Resnick, H.S., Kilpatrick, D.G., Dansky, B.S., Saunders, B.E., & Best, C.L. (1993). Prevalence of civilian trauma and posttraumatic stress disorder in a representative national sample of women. *Journal of Consulting and Clinical Psychology, 61*(6), 984–991.
5. Whiffen, V.E., & MacInstosh, H.B. (2005). Mediators of the link between childhood sexual abuse and emotional distress: A critical review. *Trauma, Violence, & Abuse, 6*, 24–39.
6. Brewin, C.R., Andrews, B., & Valentine, J.D. (2000). Meta-analysis of risk factors for posttraumatic stress disorder in trauma-exposed adults. *Journal of Counseling and Clinical Psychology, 68*, 748–766.
7. Mendelsohn, M., Zachary, R.S., & Harney, P.A. (2007). Group therapy as an ecological bridge to new community for trauma survivors. *Journal of Aggression, Maltreatment & Trauma, 14*(1/2), 227–243.
8. Yalom, I.D. (1995). *The theory and practice of group psychotherapy* (4th ed.). New York: Basic Books.
9. Ford, J.D., Fallot, R.D., & Harris, M. (2009). Group therapy. In C. Courtious & J. Ford (Eds.) *Treating complex traumatic stress disorders: An evidence based guide* (pp. 415–440). New York: Guilford Press.
10. Leskela, J., Dieperink, M., & Kok, C.J. (2001). Group treatment with sexually assaulted male veterans: A year in review. *Group, 25*(4), 303–319.
11. Classen, C., Koopman, C., Nevill-Manning, K., & Spiegel, D. (2001). A preliminary report comparing trauma-focused and present-focused group therapy against waitlisted condition among childhood sexual abuse survivors with PTSD. *Journal of Aggression, Maltreatment, & Trauma, 4*, 265–288.
12. Schurr, P.P., Friedman, M.J., Foy, D.W., Shea, T., Hieh, F.Y., Lavori, P.W., et al. (2003). Randomized trial of trauma-focused group therapy for posttraumatic stress disorder. *Archives of General Psychiatry, 60*, 481–489.
13. Tutty, L.M., Bidgood, B.A., & Rothery, M.A. (1993). Support groups for battered women: Research on their efficacy. *Journal of Family Violence, 8*, 325–343.
14. Linehan, M. (1993). *Cognitive behavioral treatment of borderline personality disorder.* New York: Guilford.
15. Iverson, K.M., Shenk, C., & Fruzzetti, A.E. (2009). Dialectical behavior therapy for women victims of domestic abuse: A pilot study. *Professional Psychology: Research and Practice, 40*(3), 242–248.
16. Foy, D.W., Glynn, S.M., Schnurr, P.P., Jankowski, M.K., Wattenberg, M.S., Weiss, D.S., et al. (2000). Group therapy. In E.B. Foa, T.M. Keane, & M.J. Friedman (Eds.) *Effective treatments for PTSD* (pp. 155–175). New York: Guilford.

17. Chard, K. (2005). An evaluation of cognitive processing therapy for the treatment of posttraumatic stress disorder related to childhood sexual abuse. *Journal of Clinical and Consulting Psychology, 73,* 965–971.
18. Resick, P.A., & Schnicke, M.K. (1992). Cognitive processing therapy for sexual assault victims. *Journal of Consulting and Clinical Psychology, 60,* 748–756.
19. Harney, P.A., & Harvey, M. (1999). Group psychotherapy: An overview. In B.H. Young & D.D. Blake (Eds.), *Group treatments for posttraumatic stress disorder* (pp. 1–14). Philadelphia: Brunner-Hazel.
20. Callahan, K.L., Price, J.L., & Hilsenroth, M.J. (2004). A review of interpersonal-psychodynamic group psychotherapy outcomes for adult survivors of childhood sexual abuse. *International Journal of Group Psychotherapy, 54,* 491–519.
21. Gartner, R. (1999) Relational aftereffects in manhood of boyhood sexual abuse. *Journal of Contemporary Psychotherapy, 29*(4), 319–353.
22. Masten, J., Kochman, A., Hansen, N., & Sikkema, K.J. (2007) A short-term group treatment model for gay male survivors of childhood sexual abuse living with HIV/AIDS. *International Journal of Group Psychotherapy, 57*(4), 475–496.
23. Sikkema, K.J., Hansen, N.B., Kochman, A., Tarakeshwar, N, Neufeld, S., Meade, C.S., & Fox, A.M. (2007) Outcomes from a group intervention for coping with HIV/AIDS and childhood sexual abuse: reductions in traumatic stress. *AIDS and Behavior, 11*(1), 49–60.
24. Hedtke, K.A., Ruggiero, K.J., Fitzgerald, M.M, Zinzow, H.M., Saunders, B.E., Resnick, H.S., & Kilpatrick, D.G. (2008). A longitudinal investigation of interpersonal violence in relation to mental health and substance use. *Journal of Consulting & Clinical Psychology, 76*(4), 633–647.
25. Miller, M.W., Vogt, D.S., Mozley, D.G., Kaloupek, D.G., & Keene, T.M. (2006) PTSD and substance-related problems: The mediating roles of disconstraint and negative emotionality. *Journal of Abnormal Psychology, 115*(2), 369–379.
26. Najavits, L.M. (2002). *Seeking Safety: A treatment manual for PTSD and substance abuse.* New York: Guilford.
27. Najavits, L.M. (2009). Psychotherapies for trauma and substance abuse in women: review and policy implications. *Trauma, Violence & Abuse, 10*(3), 290–298.
28. Fallot, R.D., & Harris, M. (2002). The trauma recovery and empowerment model (TREM): Conceptual and practical issues in a group intervention for women. *Community Mental Health Journal, 38*(6), 475–485.
29. Talbot, N.L., Houghtalen, R.P., Duberstein, P.R., Cox, C., Giles, D.E., & Wynne, L.C. (1999). Effects of group treatment for women with a history of childhood sexual abuse. *Psychiatric Services, 50,* 686–692.
30. Barcus, R. (1997) Partners of survivors of abuse: A men's therapy group. *Psychotherapy, 34*(3), 316–323.
31. Palmer, S., Stalker, C., Gadbois, S., & Harper, K. (2004). What works for survivors of childhood abuse: Learning from participants in an inpatient treatment program. *American Journal of Orthopsychiatry, 74,* 112–121.

14

Mind-Body Practices for Recovery from Sexual Trauma

Patricia L. Gerbarg and Richard P. Brown

Nowhere is the link between mind and body more evident than in the experience of abuse. This connection gives us a unique opportunity to employ body-centered methods to heal emotional scars. While talk-based and cognitive therapies can be of great benefit, there are situations in which mind-body approaches, such as yoga, qigong, tai chi, breathing practices, and meditation can be extremely beneficial and sometimes necessary for full recovery.

Victims of abuse, especially children, are often unable to talk about what happened either because they are too young to have words to describe the experience or because the perpetrator has frightened them into permanent silence. When they reach adulthood, the prohibition against telling may still prevent them from talking about the assault, even to their therapist. Neuroimaging studies suggest that when a person with post-traumatic stress disorder (PTSD) is reminded of the traumatic event, there is a decrease in activity within the speech areas of the brain.[1] Moreover, the victim may need to avoid talking or thinking about the assault because just remembering can evoke painful or revolting physical sensations.

Mind-body practices provide a therapeutic approach using the body's own internal communication network, a system that does not require words. Learning how to use the body to speak to the mind circumvents the prohibition against talking and can be more effective than relying solely on verbal, cognitive, or intellectual approaches.

Dr. Susan Franzblau and colleagues[2] studied the effects of yogic breathing and testimony (disclosing the abuse to a nonjudgmental receptive listener) on forty women who reported intimate partner abuse. The women were randomly assigned to four groups: yogic breathing only; testimony only;

yogic breathing plus testimony; and no intervention. They were given two forty-five-minute sessions on two consecutive days. Testing revealed improvements in self-efficacy in the three intervention groups, but women who received both yogic breathing and testimony improved the most, including four out of five factors assessing self-control, security, fear, and confidence.

Dr. Sharon Sageman[3] described her work with seven women in spiritually oriented group therapy. All of the participants had severe, chronic mental illness and histories of abuse. The group expressed interest in working with a yoga teacher. Dr. Sageman arranged for them to be taught a basic breathing practice for thirty minutes at three of their group meetings. They learned to do a resistance breathing called *Ujjayi* in Sanskrit, also known as Victory Breath or Ocean Breath. Resistance to airflow is created by a slight tightening of muscles at the back of the throat, producing a soft sound like the sound of the sea or the inside of a seashell. The women learned to breathe at about five breaths per minute. Combining slow breathing with airway resistance further stimulates the vagus nerves and the relaxing, soothing part of the autonomic nervous system. The result is a state of calm alertness.[4] Dr. Sageman observed striking improvements in mood and interactiveness after the group did the yoga breathing. Relieving depression is particularly important because it can seriously interfere with engagement and recovery.

While mind-body programs have been recognized for their ability to relax the mind and body, and to relieve symptoms of anxiety, depression, and post-traumatic stress disorder (PTSD), their potential to induce deeper changes in trauma formations is not as well known.[5-12] We will start with the story of a woman who was sexually molested in childhood. Six levels of trauma healing will be explored. This will be followed by a discussion of abuse during mass disasters and genocide. Along the way, we will offer basic techniques the reader can start at home along with resources and recommendations for further healing and thriving.

SUSAN—"I CAN'T STOP CRYING AND I DON'T KNOW WHY."

Susan was repeatedly molested from the age of three until puberty by a middle-aged male cousin. He had frightened her into silence by convincing her that if she told about it, her family would throw her away. Although she suffered severe night terrors during childhood and anorexia during adolescence, no one suspected sexual abuse, she never spoke about it, and she never received treatment. Susan felt there was something defective about her buttocks (the focus of the molestation), and she worried that people could see what was wrong with her body. After two years of intensive psychotherapy, three times a week, she was finally able to tell her parents about the abuse.

On the outside Susan appeared well adjusted, an excellent student and an outstanding athlete. Although she had friends, her relationships were superficial. She developed an impenetrable façade, appearing poised and aloof while living in constant fear that someone would discover her secret. Susan never dated. She could not allow anyone—male or female—to become close to her. Any attention from men made her panic and freeze. She lavished her love on animals.

Susan started therapy with me (Dr. Gerbarg) at age twenty-five, saying, "I can't stop crying and I don't know why." She refused medication because to her it meant she was weak and defective. During eight years of intensive psychotherapy three times a week, she developed more self-confidence, overcame depression and many of her fears, formed deeper friendships with both women and men, and was able to tell her parents about the abuse. She stopped relentlessly criticizing and punishing herself, started her own business, and bought her dream house in the country. In many respects, she was happy, but she longed for an intimate relationship with a man, marriage, and children. Unfortunately, paralyzing fear of men still stopped her cold. At the age of thirty-three, she had not been on a single date. Week after week she expressed frustration, loneliness, and desire for a life partner. I suggested Susan try a yoga breathing course to help reduce anxiety, perhaps enough to enable her to start dating.

I recommended a yoga breathing course with an atmosphere of safety, caring, and understanding. During her first course, Susan told other participants about the abuse, and they responded supportively. This course included slow resistance breathing, brief rapid breathing, and cyclical breathing at varying rates. The first time Susan tried the breath practices she cried uncontrollably. Nevertheless, afterward she felt unusually calm and relaxed. The second time, she actually enjoyed it and wanted to do more. For the next eight months Susan practiced yoga breathing every day and attended group sessions twice a month. She repeated the breathing course. One month later during a group yoga breathing session, she had a healing experience:

> *"I felt a warm sensation in my uterus and genitals."* She reflected, *"I knew it was good for me, a healing sensation. And then it felt like an opening-up and I thought that it was just what I needed, that what had happened to me as a child, the molestation, would no longer have such an effect on my life."*

Two weeks later, Susan went on her first date. Although she felt some anxiety, she neither panicked nor froze. The relationship ended after three dates, but she promptly started seeing another man, Jason. As their relationship developed, Susan felt ready for her first sexual experience as an adult.

She had read many books about post-traumatic stress disorder and how difficult it can be for abused women to engage in sexual activities. After eight years of therapy, she felt mentally prepared for any reaction that might occur. Would it trigger a flashback? Would she panic or freeze or dissociate? She discussed her concerns with Jason, who was totally supportive. The first time they made love, Susan's sexual response was completely normal. She had no fear, no anxiety, no panic. She enjoyed sex with Jason, and her positive responses continued as they engaged in sex almost every day. Now Susan and Jason are together in her country house, where they plan to live happily ever after.

Although Susan made considerable progress in talk therapy, there were three problems that were not responding: (1) a distorted image of her body as defective; (2) defensive closing off of her genital area; and (3) panic and freeze reactions to men. How did yoga breathing change her body image, genital sensations, and fears of sexual intimacy?

Research on the effects of mind-body practices on trauma formations is preliminary. At this time we have more questions than answers, but we do have some viable theories based on neuroscience and physiology. We know that messages are constantly sent from the body to the brain carrying information about the internal state of the body. This process is called *interoception*. Much of this sensory information, including pain, pressure, temperature, air hunger, genital sensations, and information about respiration as well as all the internal body organs is carried by the vagus nerves, the main pathways of the parasympathetic nervous system, the calming, healing, recharging part of the nervous system.[13] This information goes to a part of the brain called the *interoceptive cortex*, where it becomes part of the body image and is interconnected with centers of emotional regulation, emotional reactions, decision-making, and behavior.[14] The physical sensations, reactions, and emotions associated with sexual abuse are processed in these networks and can become frozen in time, like a fly in amber, unchanged by subsequent experiences, for years. Such locked-in trauma formations are called *schemas*.[15]

It can be extremely difficult to access trauma schemas through verbal therapy alone. However, we can log on to the interoceptive network using mind-body practices to send therapeutic messages to penetrate schemas that may be resistant to verbal interventions. The fastest and most powerful way to do this is by changing the patterns of breathing. The pathways between the respiratory system and the brain are very strong and very rapid because breathing is our most vital function. When we change the pattern of the breath, tens of thousands of receptors throughout the lungs and respiratory passages change the messages being sent to the brain.[4] So, for example, by deliberately breathing very slowly the body can tell the brain that we are safe and no longer need to worry, be hypervigilant, or react with fear.[9] The ideal breath rate for balancing the stress response system and calming the mind is between 3.5 and 6 breaths per minute for most adults.[16-19] In Susan's case, yoga breathing began to help her feel calm and relaxed the first day she tried it. However, it took months of daily practice for it to penetrate and ultimately transform the trauma schema to restore a healthy body image with normal genital sensation and emotional reactivity.

SIX LEVELS OF HEALING WITH MIND-BODY PRACTICES

Level 1—Change Starts at the Cellular Level

Changing the mind-set of trauma involves changing the connections among brain cells (neurons) and thereby changing patterns of interaction among neural pathways where trauma memories are stored and PTSD symptoms are generated. *Plasticity* refers to this complex process of changing how the brain works. There are many ways to induce plasticity. Whenever we learn something new, somewhere in the brain, plasticity is occurring. The challenge in post-traumatic conditions is to access the problem areas, disrupt trauma-related connections between neurons, sprout new connections, and guide the course of reconnection toward healthy transformation.

Among the many elements that can influence this process of change are the following:

1. the intensity of input through the nerve networks and the repetition of input
2. the balance of excitatory and inhibitory (calming) neurotransmitters
3. the frequency, amplitude, and coherence of brain waves
4. the emotional state and the emotional meaning of input from other people and the environment
5. neurohormones such as oxytocin and prolactin—antistress, social bonding hormones that increase feelings of love and connectedness

Mind-body practices can disrupt trauma formations, stimulate neuroplasticity, and steer the system toward healthy recovery. Yoga breathing and movement stimulate interoceptive input to neural networks. We have already discussed ways that this interoceptive messaging can access and alter trauma formations (schema). We recommend daily practice because the repetition is necessary to bring about changes over time and to maintain improvements. Evidence suggests that yoga can reduce excitatory and increases inhibitory (calming) neurotransmitters toward a healthier, more stable balance.[20,21] Studies have shown that slow yoga breathing and resistance breathing can shift brain-wave frequencies toward more synchronous relaxed alpha rhythms associated with states of relaxation. They also increase coherence and synchrony, which further enhance plasticity and learning.[22,23]

Through yoga, an anxious, fearful, defensive person can become calm, unafraid, more trusting, and open. When in this more receptive state, they are better able to experience positive emotions (their own and those of others), to internalize positive messages, to learn from their therapy, and to incorporate all of this new information into their emotional and psychic reconstruction.

Although there have not yet been any studies of the effects of mind-body practices on levels of the bonding hormone, oxytocin, there is reason to think that it probably plays a role in the increased capacity for feelings of love, bonding, and connectedness many people describe when they engage in yoga. Also, the pathways of the parasympathetic system stimulated by yoga breathing are rich in oxytocin receptors. We hope to see studies measuring oxytocin levels in yoga practitioners someday.

Level 2—Tension Release

Mind-body practices release tension, relieve stress, and induce a calm state. This is crucial for trauma victims, who often hold a lot of tension in their bodies, causing muscle aches, back pain, shallow breathing, and headaches. Being in an acute or chronic state of stress and tension has negative effects on mood, physical health, relationships, and the ability to think clearly and make good decisions.

Level 3—Sense of Safety and Personal Boundaries

Trauma survivors need to lower anxiety and feel secure to engage in therapy and to develop trust in their therapist as well as other people they want to be close to. Yoga breathing, movement, and meditation engender feelings of safety and calmness. Movement practices help develop better awareness of the body and its boundaries. Mastery of physical postures with increasing strength and balance helps to build confidence.

Level 4—Restoring Balance in the Stress Response System

The sympathetic nervous system has both activation components (getting ready to fight or flee) and inhibition components (to hold us back when necessary for survival). Trauma and stress can cause either or both components to malfunction. The use of mind-body practices can strengthen both components and shift them back into proper balance. By correcting imbalances in the sympathetic nervous system as well as between the sympathetic and parasympathetic systems, mind-body practices reduce hyperarousal, hypervigilance, overreactivity, irritability, anger, impulsivity, and inappropriate fight, flight, or freeze reactions. This enables the survivor to respond more appropriately to people and situations based on the here-and-now reality rather than on impressions from the past.

Level 5—Self-Awareness and Reconnection with One's Body

During sexual trauma, victims are helpless, unable to stop the abuse or to run away. They describe feeling like they are going crazy, losing their mind, being destroyed, or exploding. Sometimes the only way out is to disconnect the mind from the body, which is being abused. Once this occurs, the victim may feel permanently disconnected, unable to experience the body as her own. This can lead to neglect of the body, fear of physical experiences, hatred of the body, self-inflicted injuries such as cutting or burning, and abnormal reactions to physical sensations. By focusing attention on the experience of gentle movements and breathing, yoga slowly reintroduces the survivor to her body as a source of comfort, pleasure, strength, and self-efficacy.

MIND-BODY PRACTICES FOR TRAUMA RECOVERY

Hundreds of mind-body practices for health and healing have evolved over the last 8,000 years in countries all over the world.[24] Although there is very little research on mind-body practices specifically for sexual trauma, a number of studies show that yoga, qigong, and tai chi can reduce the physical and emotional symptoms of PTSD, which in many ways overlap with symptoms related to sexual assault.[7,25-29]

We are going to focus on a simple set of practices that are easy to learn, safe for everyone, and that have been shown in clinical research to relieve symptoms related to stress, anxiety, trauma, and depression. In applying these techniques to victims of sexual trauma, the sensitivities of the individual must be anticipated and taken into consideration. Precautions must be taken to protect against overwhelming experiences such as flashbacks. Therapists should be knowledgeable in methods to assist victims who may be triggered into such distressing experiences despite the best precautions during any treatment, whether standard therapies or mind-body practices. While we offer basic practices that anyone can do at home, we recommend working with a certified yoga or qigong teacher who has experience with trauma victims for more advanced work. Establishing a safe environment is essential. The teaching and class atmosphere should be gentle, kind, gradual, supportive, noncompetitive, and nonjudgmental. Attention and awareness should be focused on the practices. The most effective programs include movement, breathing, and meditation. Here is a simple sequence to get you started.

MOVEMENT

Grounding helps restore the sense of being stable, centered, in the here and now. It is widely used at the beginning of yoga practices as well as to help abuse survivors stay in the present when they are being pulled into the past by trauma memories or flashbacks.

Grounding can begin in a comfortable standing position with feet shoulder-width apart. The chin should be slightly down and the knees kept soft. Gently shift your weight from side to side and back and forth to find your center of gravity. Come to rest with weight evenly balanced on both feet.

Become aware of your feet in contact with the floor. Notice how your body feels.

THE FOUR GOLDEN WHEELS BY MASTER ROBERT PENG

This is the first of the Four Golden Wheels of qigong. Letting your arms hang loosely at your sides, start to gently bounce up and down, keeping your feet on the floor and your knees loose. As you bounce, allow your arms to flop like wet noodles and let your head bob. Close your eyes if you are comfortable doing so. Continue gently bouncing for one, two, or three minutes. You may wish to enhance this practice by imagining a waterfall starting at the top of your head and flowing down through your body, flowing in steps with each bounce all the way down and out through the soles of your feet, washing away all negative emotions.

When you stop, notice the change in how you feel. This releases the first level of body tension. If you want to learn more about Four Golden Wheels from a course or videotape, you may visit www.RobertPeng.com.

BREATHING—BREATH AWARENESS, BELLY BREATHING, COHERENT BREATHING

Sit in a very comfortable chair or lie on your back on a bed or the floor with whatever pillows you need, under your legs or head, to feel relaxed. Close your eyes if you are comfortable doing so. Closing your mouth, breathe through your nose only.

Breath awareness. Become aware of your breathing. Feel the rise and fall of your belly and chest, the movement of your ribs. Next focus your attention on the feeling of the air as it moves in and out of your nose. Breathing deeply but without any straining, feel the air move through your nose and down into your lungs, then feel it move out again.

Belly breathing. As you take a deep breath in, relax your belly muscles so that your belly rises with each inhalation. Rather than actively pushing your belly out, just let the breath fill you up, causing it to rise naturally. Then let your belly come down naturally as you breathe out. Repeat this slowly several times. Take these deep belly breaths in and out two more times as you relax the muscles of your face and let your whole body relax.

Coherent Breathing. Focus your attention on the sensation of air moving in and out through your nose and airways to your lungs. If other thoughts enter your mind, just notice them and let them float through. Refocus your attention on the sensations of your breath. All breaths should be comfortable, not forced in any way.

Breathing through your nose with your eyes closed . . .
Taking your time, count slowly and silently in your mind: As you breathe in, count 1 . . . 2 . . .; as you breathe out, count 1 . . . 2 . . . for two breaths.
Taking your time, count slowly: As you breathe in, count 1 . . . 2 . . . 3; as you breathe out, count 1 . . . 2 . . . 3 for three breaths.
Taking your time, count slowly: As you breathe in, count 1 . . . 2 . . . 3 . . . 4; as you breathe out, count 1 . . . 2 . . . 3 . . . 4 for four breaths.
Taking your time, count a little more slowly: As you breathe in, count 1 . . . 2 . . . 3 . . . 4; as you breathe out, count 1 . . . 2 . . . 3 . . . 4 for four breaths.

Work on this until you are able to breathe at a rate between five and six breaths per minute. This is called Coherent Breathing. The best way to do this is to use the Two Bells chime track on Steven Elliot's *Respire-1* CD available at www.coherence.com, or download the chime track onto an MP3 player. Listening to the chime track, just breathe in with one tone and breathe out with the next. You won't have to count and you can relax even more.

Start with five to ten minutes of coherent breathing once or twice a day and gradually increase up to twenty minutes at a time. Once you master Coherent Breathing, you can go right into it without having to slow your breath in stages. Whenever you feel stressed or anxious, use Coherent Breathing to stop worrying and relax. If you have difficulty falling asleep, just get into bed, turn on the chime track, turn out the light, and breathe yourself to sleep.

After two months of practicing with your eyes closed, you may also do Coherent Breathing with your eyes open. Just play the chime recording and breathe along with it as you putter around the house, commute on the train, or take a walk. You can even breathe coherently while working on the computer, doing paperwork, taking tests, or any other anxiety-provoking activity. No one will know how slowly you breathe or how you manage to stay so calm when all around you people are stressing out.

MEDITATION

Meditation allows the effects of movement and breathing to be integrated or stored in the mind. In this way, meditation takes the healing even deeper. This is a simple body-scan meditation. It can be used by itself or as preparation for other meditation practices.

Keeping your eyes closed, relax your eyelids, your eyebrows, and your forehead. Relax your cheeks, jaw, chin, and mouth. Then relax the muscles of your shoulders, arms, and hands. Relax all the muscles of your back, starting at the top of your spine and going all the way down your back. Relax the muscles of your chest, belly, and pelvis. Relax your legs starting at the top and going down to your calves and feet. Relax all the muscles of your body from your head to your feet.

POSITIVE AFFIRMATIONS

Now that you feel relaxed, you may give yourself a positive message, either one of your own or one you have read and found to be especially meaningful for you. Let this positive message sink deep into your mind.

FINISHING

Roll over onto your right side. Lie still, curled up and cozy. Use a blanket if you feel cool. Just rest for a while.

Before you open your eyes, notice how your mind and body are feeling. Then slowly and gently open your eyes.

For those of you who want to learn more movement and breathing practices, we suggest taking classes such as our Breath~Body~Mind workshops, using our new book and CD set, *The Breathing Cure*, or finding instructional videotapes. Master Robert Peng offers Elixir Light Qigong classes and his DVDs are available at www.robertpeng.com. Many women enjoy Amy Weintraub's program, LifeForce Yoga. Her courses and DVDs can be found at www.yogafordepression.com. Heather Mason trains yoga therapists in her Yoga for the Mind sequence and teaches trauma-sensitive yoga; see www.yogaforthemind.info. See the resources section at the end of this chapter for information on finding programs and teachers in your area.

YOGA POSTURES FOR EMPOWERMENT AS TAUGHT BY AMY WEINTRAUB

Yoga postures can help develop a sense of empowerment. Here is a sequence of yoga postures that Amy finds helpful in working with sexual abuse survivors[30]: Five-Pointed Star, Victory Goddess, Victory Goddess with Lotus, and Warrior Pose. Amy uses sounds to enhance the effects of movement. The *a* sound is pronounced like the *a* in the word *calm*. As you make each sound, feel the vibrations resonate within your body, providing more interoceptive stimulation to the healing parts of your nervous system.

Before you begin, think of an image that represents strength to you, perhaps an image from nature. Then choose an intention for your practice this day. For example, your intention could be self-healing or any other goal for your personal development. When repeating or holding poses, do only what is comfortable for you.

Five-Pointed Star

Stand straight with feet about twenty-four inches apart and turned slightly outward. Raise arms to shoulder level, held straight out on each side. The head, hands, and feet create the five points of the star. Bring into your mind an image for strength. With your feet grounded firmly in the earth, radiate strength out through your fingertips and up through the crown of your head. Take five full breaths through the nose, and then hold the last breath with your image for strength in your mind. Using your imagination, move the image for strength from your mind into your heart. From the Five-Pointed Star, move into Victory Goddess.

Victory Goddess

Exhale forcefully while making this sound loudly, "di-ri-hah!" as you bend your knees into a partially squatting position with your tailbone tucked while bending your elbows with arms and hands pointing upward. Inhale through your nose as you rise back up into Five-Pointed Star. Repeat this squatting and rising sequence five to ten times. On your final round rise to Five-Pointed Star and hold the breath as you see your image for strength. Exhale with "di-ri-hah!" moving back into Victory Goddess. Hold the Victory Goddess pose with your body while you hold your image for strength in your mind and heart, and breathe slowly and deliberately for five more breaths. Say to yourself, "I am that." Relax standing for a moment, feeling your feet on the earth.

Victory Goddess with Lotus

Inhale to Five-Pointed Star one more time, holding the breath for five counts, and think of your intention. Exhale into Victory Goddess with Lotus by bringing arms to your sides with elbows bent and hands moving toward the center of your chest. Bringing the base of the palms, the pinkies, and thumbs together near your heart, form a lotus cup. Hold your intention close to your heart and nourish it with this sound softly: "yyyyyam."

Warrior Pose

Raise arms above your head, bringing palms together as you step your left foot forward and bend your front knee, squaring your hips toward the front. Take five deep breaths as you hold the pose. You may wish to repeat the word "rrrrram" to energize your solar plexus, the seat of identity and self-esteem. Repeat on the right side. When you finish, close your eyes and stand straight and tall with your arms at your sides and your palms open and facing forward. Feel your own healing energy vibrating through your arms, your legs, the palms of your hands, awakening your spiritual warrior.

MIND-BODY PROGRAMS FOR MASS DISASTERS, WAR, AND GENOCIDE

During mass disasters such as war and genocide, women and children suffer extreme physical and sexual abuse complicated by witnessing the murder of loved ones, loss of community, displacement into refugee camps or foreign countries, and the stress of an ongoing life of poverty, deprivation, and grief. Sexual abuse may involve permanent internal damage or external mutilation.

After peace is established, some countries, such as Kosovo, have managed to provide large-scale public mental health services that incorporate mind-body programs. Dr. James Gordon and colleagues[26] of the Center for Mind-Body Medicine found that mind-body practices significantly reduce symptoms of post-traumatic stress disorder and depression in postwar Kosovo. However, there have been no published studies of mind-body practices that focus specifically on sexual trauma related to genocide. It is extremely difficult to do treatment studies soon after natural or man-made disasters, particularly in remote areas and in countries lacking resources and infrastructure.

In one yoga study for relief of trauma in survivors of the 2004 Southeast Asian tsunami, we (Dr. Brown and Dr. Gerbarg) worked with Teresa Descilo, traumatologist and director of the Trauma Center of Miami. We collaborated with the National Association for Mental Health and Neurosciences of India and the International Association for Human Values.[25] Symptoms of PTSD and depression were measured before and after an eight-hour yoga breathing and movement program created by Sri Sri Ravi Shankar. The program included Ocean Breath (*Ujjayi*), brief rapid breathing (*Bhastrika*), and cyclical breathing (*Sudarshan Kriya*). Within one week of doing this program, scores for PTSD fell 60%, while depression scores dropped 90%. The benefits were maintained throughout the six-month follow-up period.

Starting in 2007, working with the nonprofit Serving Those Who Serve (www.stws.org), we have been using a two-day, twelve-hour workshop, called Breath~Body~Mind, to relieve symptoms of anxiety, depression, and PTSD in people affected by the September 11 World Trade Center attacks in New York City. Two open studies in collaboration with Dr. Martin Katzmann and Dr. Monica Vermani found significant reductions in measures of anxiety, worry, depression, and PTSD among those who completed our workshop.[31,32,33]

Many African nations, ravaged by war, are unable to provide mental health care to vast areas, leaving tens of thousands of survivors without treatment. Moreover, thousands of sex slaves captured during wars are still being held and abused. Among the numerous organizations working with survivors of genocide and sexual abuse in Africa, Global Grassroots and Christian Solidarity International have focused on assisting women survivors. Global Grassroots integrates mind-body practices, consciousness training, and nonprofit start-up skills to help village women become social change leaders within their communities. Christian Solidarity International raises money to purchase freedom for enslaved women and return as many as possible to their homelands.

Gretchen Wallace, president of Global Grassroots, and Ellen Ratner of Talk Radio news service (working with Christian Solidarity International, www.csi-int.org) asked us (Dr. Brown and Dr. Gerbarg) to create a mind-body program that they could implement in disaster areas. We had to take into account the strengths, limitations, and coping methods of each culture. For example, among African survivors, most women cope by not thinking about the past and by suppressing their feelings, because the pain from the past is so overwhelming that it can render them unable to function. Therefore, the program had to be gentle enough to reduce stress without opening the floodgates to painful memories and unbearable emotions. Also, we had observed that rapid or forceful breath practices sometimes trigger panic attacks or flashbacks. Consequently, we only used slow breathing techniques.

Based on our research and experience, we developed the following guidelines for the disaster relief program:

1. portable, inexpensive, requiring no equipment and no electricity
2. easy to teach and learn in one short session (no more than two hours)
3. effective in providing immediate relief the first time it is practiced
4. effective with less than ten minutes of daily practice and increasing benefits the more it is used
5. safe for everyone, causing no adverse physical or emotional reactions regardless of age or health status
6. containing no religious words or elements that could offend or frighten people of different cultures
7. containing no physical movements that could make abuse victims feel unsafe
8. sustainable in the community by training of local leaders

By selecting four simple qigong movements (derived from the Four Golden Wheels of Master Robert Peng) and Coherent Breathing, we created a mind-body intervention that fulfilled our guidelines.

Having taken several of our Breath~Body~Mind courses, Ellen Ratner was able to teach Coherent Breathing to Sudanese survivors of war, abduction, and slavery. She reported that they responded well with rapid relief of stress symptoms. The women continued doing the Coherent Breathing regularly on their own with a village matron keeping time with a chime bowl. A program evaluation of nineteen Sudanese women documented that those who did the Breath~Body~Mind practices for twenty minutes a day five days a week for eighteen weeks had a mean improvement of 71% in PTSD and 66% in mood on test measures.[33]

Gretchen Wallace taught the qigong and Coherent Breathing to Haitian women two weeks after the January 12, 2010, earthquake. She observed immediate improvements in anxiety and physical discomforts. Women being trained in the Global Grassroots Academy for Conscious Change in Rwanda also responded well. Now Global Grassroots is incorporating these practices into all of their disaster relief and women's empowerment programs.

When Gretchen teaches a group of disaster survivors, she first explains that stress and trauma can cause the symptoms the women are experiencing, such as fear, anxiety, shaking, inability to sleep, fatigue, and physical pains. This explanation provides relief because many survivors mistakenly interpret their symptoms to mean that they are crazy. Naturally, they feel reassured to find out that they are not. Next, she invites them to learn practices to calm the stress reactions and restore balance to their nervous system. She leads them through four qigong movements (Four Golden Wheels) standing up. Then, the women sit or lie down for breath practices. First they learn to inhale slowly, letting their bellies rise, just as we described above. Then, listening to a small handheld bell, they breathe in with one ring and out with the next. Within ten minutes, most of the women feel relaxed, and some fall asleep. They wake up feeling better and notice that some of their aches and pains are gone. The women can do the practices on their own, but they particularly enjoy meeting to breathe together as a group.

SELF-HEALING THE MIND-BODY WAY

Because breathing is automatic, we tend to take it for granted, not realizing that within our own bodies we have a profound healing potential. Anyone who has suffered abuse or trauma of any kind can use breathing and movement practices to cope with immediate symptoms, to enhance recovery, and to continue to thrive despite the inevitable stresses life brings. We believe that these programs should be an integral part of any therapeutic plan.

Understanding the scientific basis for the effects of mind-body practices and reading about the success stories of other survivors may help to convince our doubting minds that this is something worth trying. We can only give you a small sampling of the many techniques and programs available. The next steps, actually starting some simple practices, and finding a teacher or therapist to help you get the most out of the techniques will make a real difference in your life. We hope that the resources listed below will help you take those steps.

RESOURCES

The Breathing Cure, Richard P. Brown, M.D., and Patricia L. Gerbarg, M.D., Shambhala Publications (in press).

www.haveahealthymind.com. Dr. Patricia Gerbarg and Dr. Richard P. Brown provide information, courses, updates, and a free newsletter on complementary and alternative treatments.

Organizations

The following organizations can provide information on how to find yoga teachers, courses, and resources in your area.

International Association of Yoga Therapists, www.iayt.org
International Yoga Teachers' Association, www.iayt.org.au
Yoga Alliance, www.yogaalliance.org
The Center for Mind-Body Medicine, www.cmbm.org

International Association for Human Values, www.iahv.org
Mind and Life Institute, www.mindandlife.org.

Yoga Websites, CDs, and DVDs

Coherent Breathing, www.coherence.com. Offers *Respire-1* CD with tracks for pacing at five breaths per minute.

Yoga for Depression, www.yogafordepression.com. Amy Weintraub's Life Force Yogaâ site offers videotape programs at all levels, courses, newsletter.

Yoga for the Mind, www.yogaforthemind.info. Heather Mason offers classes, private consultations, a CD set of breathing practices, and a You-Tube video on how to do ocean breath (*Ujjayi*): http://www.youtube.com/watch?v=PqR_HSDXuEk.

Elixir Light Yoga, www.robertpeng.com. Master Robert Peng provides qigong teachings, courses, videotapes.

Kripalu Yoga Center, http://www.kripalu.org, yoga courses in Massachusetts

Yoga Journals

International Journal of Yoga Therapy, www.iayt.org/site/publications/journal.php

The Yoga Journal, www.yogajournal.com

Yoga Magazine, www.yogamag.netsubs.shtml

Acknowledgments: The authors wish to thank Amy Weintraub, Gretchen Wallace, Ellen Ratner, Dr. Sharon Sageman, and Master Robert Peng for their support in the preparation of this chapter.

REFERENCES

1. Rauch, S.L., van der Kolk, B.A., Fisler, R.E., Alpert, N.M., & Orr S.P., et. al. (1996). A symptom provocation study of posttraumatic stress disorder using positron emission tomography and script-driven imagery. *Archives of General Psychiatry*, 53(5), 380–387.

2. Franzblau, D.H., Smith, M., Echevarria, S., & VanCantford, T.E. (2006). Take a breath, break the silence: The effects of yogic breathing and testimony about battering on feelings of self-efficacy in battered women. *International Journal of Yoga Therapy*. 16, 49–57.

3. Sageman, S. (2004). Breaking through the despair: Spiritually oriented group therapy as a means of healing women with severe mental illness. *Journal of the American Academy of Psychoanalysis and Dynamic Psychiatry*, 32(1), 125–141.

4. Brown, R.P., & Gerbarg, P.L. (2005). Sudarshan Kriya yoga breathing in the treatment of stress, anxiety, and depression part I: Neurophysiological model. *Journal of Alternative and Complementary and Medicine, 11,* 189–201.
5. Becker, I. (2000). Uses of yoga in psychiatry and medicine. In P.R. Muskin (Ed.), *Complementary and alternative medicine and psychiatry* (pp. 107–145). Washington, D.C.: American Psychiatric Press, Inc.
6. Benson, H. (1996). *Timeless healing: The power and biology of belief* (pp. 222–234). New York: Scribner.
7. Brown, R.P., & Gerbarg, P.L. (2005). Sudarshan Kriya yoga breathing in the treatment of stress, anxiety, and depression part I: Neurophysiological model. *Journal of Alternative and Complementary and Medicine, 11,* 711–717.
8. Brown, R.P., & Gerbarg, P.L. (2009). Yoga breathing, meditation, and longevity. In C. Bushness, E. Olivo & N. Theise (Eds.), *Longevity, Regeneration, and optimal health, integrating Eastern and Western perspectives* (1172, pp. 54–62). *Annals of the New York Academy of Sciences.*
9. Gerbarg, P.L. (2008). Yoga and neuro-psychoanalysis. In F.S. Anderson (Ed.), *Bodies in treatment: The unspoken dimension* (pp. 127–150). Hillsdale, NJ: The Analytic Press, Inc.
10. Katzman, M., Vermani, M., & Gerbarg, P.L., et al. (2009). Art of living course (SKY) as adjunctive treatment in GAD. Albuquerque, NM: Anxiety Disorders Association of America.
11. Shapiro, D., Cook, I.A., & Davydov, D.M., et al. (2007). Yoga as a complementary treatment of depression: Effects of traits and moods on treatment outcome. http://ecam.oxfordjournals.org//cgi/reprint/nell14v1
12. van der Kolk, B.A. (2006). Evidence based clinical implications of neuroscience research in PTSD. *Annals of the New York Academy of Sciences. 1071,* 277–293.
13. Porges, S.W. (2001). The polyvagal theory: Phylogenetic substrates of a social nervous system. *International Journal of Psychophysiology, 42*(2), 123–146.
14. Craig, A.D. (2003). Interoception: The sense of the physiological condition of the body. *Current Opinion Neurobiology, 13*(4), 500–505.
15. Bucci, W. (2001). Pathways of emotional communication. *Psychoanalytic Inquiry, 20,* 40–70.
16. Bernardi, L., Porta, C., Gabutti, A., Spicuzza, L., & Sleight, P. (2001). Modulatory effects of respiration. *Autonomic Neuroscience, 90*(1–2), 47–56.
17. Brown, R.P., Gerbarg, P.L., & Muskin, P.R. (2009). *How to use herbs, nutrients, and yoga in mental health care* (pp. 71–139). New York: W.W. Norton.
18. Karavidas, M.K., Lehrer, P.M., Vaschillo, E., Vaschillo, B., & Marin, H., et. al. (2007). Preliminary results of an open label study of heart rate variability biofeedback for the treatment of major depression. *Applied Psychophysiology and Biofeedback, 32*(1). 19–30.
19. Vascillo, E.G., Vascillo, B., & Lehrer, P.M. (2006). Characteristics of resonance in heart rate variability stimulated by biofeedback. *Applied Psychophysiology and Biofeedback, 31*(2), 129–194.
20. Streeter, C.C., Jensen, J.E., Perlmutter, R.M., Cabral, H.J., & Tian, H., et al. (2007). Yoga Asana sessions increase brain GABA levels: A pilot study. *Journal of Alternative and Complementary and Medicine, 13*(4), 419–426.

21. Streeter, C.C., Whitfield, T.H., Owen, L., Rein, T., & Karri, S.K., et al. (2010). Effects of yoga versus walking on mood, anxiety, and brain GABA Levels: A randomized controlled MRS study. *Journal of Alternative and Complementary and Medicine,* *16*(11), 1145–1152.

22. Bhatia, M.A., Kumar, N., Kumar, R.M., (2003). Pandy Kochupillai V. electrophysiologic evaluation of Sudarshan Kriya: An EEG, BAER, P300 study. *Indian Journal of Physiology and Pharmacolpgy, 47,* 157–163.

23. Larsen, S., Yee, W., Gerbarg, P.L., Brown, R.P., Gunkelman, J., & Sherlin, L. (2006). Neurophysiological markers of Sudarshan Kriya Yoga practices: A pilot study (pp. 36–48). Proceedings World Conference Expanding Paradigms: Science, Consciousness and Spirituality. 24–25 February 2006. New Delhi, India, All India Institute of Medical Sciences.

24. Feuerstein, G. (1998). *The yoga tradition: Its history, literature, philosophy, and practice.* Prescott, AZ: Hohm Press.

25. Descilo, T., Vedamurtachar, A., Gerbarg, P.L,, Nagaraja, D., & Gangadhar, B.N.G. (2010). Effects of a yoga-breath intervention alone and in combination with an exposure therapy for PTSD and depression in survivors of the 2004 Southeast Asia tsunami. *Acta Psychiatrica Scandcandinavica, 121*(4), 289–300.

26. Gordon. J.S., Staples, J.K., Blyta, A., Bytyqi, M., & Wilson, A.T. (2008). Treatment of posttraumatic stress disorder in postwar Kosovar adolescents using mind-body skills groups: A randomized controlled trial. *Journal of Clinical Psychiatry, 69*(9), 1469–1476.

27. Grodin, M.A., Piwowarczyk, L., Fulker, D., Bazazi, A.R., & Saper, R.B. (2008). Treating survivors of torture and refugee trauma: A preliminary case series using Qigong and T'ai Chi (pp. 801–106). *Journal of Alternative and Complementary and Medicine, 14*(7).

28. Telles, S., Naveen, K.V., & Dash, M. (2007) Yoga reduces symptoms of distress in Tsunami survivors in Andaman Islands. *Evidence Based Complementary and Alternative Medicine, 4,* 503–509.

29. Telles, S., Singh, N., Joshi, M., & Balkrishna, A. (2010). Post-traumatic stress symptoms and heart rate variability in Bihar flood survivors following yoga: A randomized controlled study. *BioMed Central Psychiatry, 10,* 18–28.

30. Weintraub, A. (2004). *Yoga for depression.* New York: Broadway Books of Random House, Inc.

31. Brown, R.P., Gerbarg, P.L., Vermani, M., & Katzman. (2010). First trial of breathing, movement, and meditation PTSD, depression, and anxiety related to September 11th New York City World Trade Center Attacks. American Psychiatric Association, New Orleans, LA, May 22, 2010.

32. Brown, R.P., Gerbarg, P.L., Vermani, M., & Katzman. (2010). Second trial of breathing, movement, and meditation PTSD, depression, and anxiety related to September 11th New York City World Trade Center Attacks. American Psychiatric Association, New Orleans, LA, May 22, 2010.

33. Gerbarg, P.L., & Wallace, G. (in press). Mass disasters and mind-body solutions. *International Journal of Yoga Therapy.*

15

An Integration of Narrative Therapy and Positive Psychology with Sexual Abuse Survivors

Z. Seda Sahin and Melissa L. McVicker

The impact of sexual abuse may vary, depending on the individual's perception of the experienced abuse. The experienced trauma can influence beliefs about oneself, life experiences, and relationships, often creating abuse-dominated stories laden with generalizations of helplessness or sense of lost agency. The use of narrative therapy in aiding sexual abuse recovery may not only support survivors in exposing the stories around the abusive experience, but encourage the creation of new, personal meanings and preferred stories of strengths, competence, and resilience. In addition, integrating positive psychology with narrative therapy can build on the individual's resources and strengths in overcoming adversity and building on discourses of hopefulness and healing.

SEXUAL ABUSE

The impact of sexual abuse can be influenced by many factors, including the survivor's perception of the abuse and causal attributions around the experience. Experiences of trauma can inform or challenge individuals' beliefs about themselves, their life experiences, and even their relationships. The narratives that are developed around significant life events can include causal explanations and evaluations of losses and changes.[1] The perception of the experience of sexual abuse, and the meanings attributed to the experience, may change over time or as a result of other life events and experience of relationships.[2] Often the themes or meanings given to specific traumatic experiences need to be narrated for the individual's recovery or resolution, not only to facilitate the expression of these narratives but also to place them in perspective for the individual.[1]

SURVIVOR NARRATIVES

While sexual abuse experiences may be ignored, minimized, or even denied, feminists and systems theorists have challenged these responses—insisting that the voices of survivors be heard and acknowledged.[3,4] However, while the development of the survivor narrative can encourage people to speak out about abusive sexual experiences, it can also lead to survivor blaming and be potentially stigmatizing for the individual who experienced such experiences.[4,5,6] As such, victim stories have begun to be replaced by survivor narratives in the last twenty years.[4,7] Replacing a story of victimization with one of being a survivor may allow a focus on strength, courage, and resilience of those who had overcome adversity. In addition, survivor narratives portray an individual who has overcome adversity and been transformed in the process.[4] This narrative offers survivors a sense of power that may be absent from victim stories and can offer hope of healing and recovery to those that have experienced sexual abuse.[4]

However, narratives, whether victim or survivor stories, still may connect an individual's identity to the abusive experiences, which may be rejected by the individual or seen as different types of stigmatizing identities.[7] In addition, narratives, such as those of transcendence, support a social constructionist approach, which challenges both the victim and survivor narratives.[4] Therefore, for the purpose of this chapter, narrative therapy will be introduced as a tool to encourage the creation of preferred stories of strengths and resilience in sexual abuse recovery.

NARRATIVE THERAPY

Don't we all write stories about life—stories about how we have experiences with other people, places, sounds, and smells? While we live in our own worlds, do we not sometimes forget that there are other realities? We give meaning to the world, and that meaning becomes the reality. So are there multiple realities? Whose reality is the real reality? How much of our reality is shaped by our society, our family, and our relationships?

Imagine two people sitting on a bench, looking at the lake in front of them. Let's say that each of them comes and sits there for a half an hour. Both of them look at the same image but experience something very different. They narrate their experiences in a different way. Here are two excerpts from their minds:

It was boring sitting there. Crickets annoy me, too. The lake was a fake one anyway; just filling spaces with water does not make it real. I do not understand why people have to imitate everything. Why can't people just be satisfied with what they have? I would rather sit on my comfortable couch at home and read my book. It is really sunny today; even this breeze is not helping. In addition, the sun is burning my skin. I should have grabbed the sunscreen before I left. It is becoming more like a habit of forgetting things these days. Why can't I remember anything? God, how am I going to finish all those tasks at work? I can't wait to retire.

Here is the second experience:

Sometimes a half an hour helps me to refresh myself. I sometimes get sucked into the craziness of the world, but it is good to take a break. I love this breeze. It makes me feel like I am part of something, like I am sharing this piece of wind that is coming from the other side of the world. It is really easy to forget to appreciate life these days. I am trying to make it a habit to remind myself to be grateful and recognize the beauty of this world, how everything is connected and how magnificent every piece of life is. I am amazed by how we even see this world. I mean literally, don't you get shocked about the incredible mechanisms that allow us to see the light and transform the light into images in our brains? I thank God every day for that.

Is it not the same image that these two people are looking at? Why do they narrate their experiences so differently?

Narrative therapy argues that our worlds are constructed by how we give meaning to our experience; therefore, there are multiple explanations for any event, experience, or memory. Narrative therapy approach adopts a worldview that an individual has a multistoried life. It is a social constructionist therapeutic model that argues that we cannot have direct knowledge of the world, and we can only know life through experience. White and Epston (1990) state that "persons organize and give meaning to their experience through the storying of experience, and in the performance of these stories they express selected aspects of their lived experience. It then follows that these stories are constitutive—shaping lives and relationships" (p. 12).

Narrative therapists allow the individual to deconstruct his/her problem-dominated stories. Problem-saturated story has a focus that does not allow the individual to tell any alternative story.[8] During therapy, narrative therapists highlight the life events that were formerly untold and create space through reauthoring.[9] Monk et al. explain reauthoring as "developing an alternative story in therapy" (1997, p. 305).

In order to develop alternative stories, problem-saturated stories need to be altered. Problem-saturated/dominated descriptions are narratives that focus on the negative aspects of their life explanations. The dominant story can be reauthored, and an alternative story can be created through externalization and finding unique outcomes. White and Epston (1990) describe this process:

> The identification of the unique outcomes can be facilitated by the externaliza-
> tion of the dominant "problem-saturated" description or story of a person's
> life and relationships. The externalization of the problem-saturated story can
> be initiated by encouraging the externalization of the problem, and then by the
> mapping of the problem's influence in the person's life and relationships. This
> is begun by asking persons about how the problem has been affecting their
> lives and their relationships. By achieving this separation from the problem-
> saturated description of life, from this habitual reading of the dominant story,
> persons are more able to identify unique outcomes. (pg. 16)

By viewing the problems as existing outside them, the individuals are empowered through narrative therapy.[10,11] In this therapeutic process both the therapist and the individual contribute and are responsible for the construction of the reality. Externalization distances the individual from the problems and creates space for him or her to reflect on the influence of the problems.[9] Through this process, the individuals are encouraged to find unique outcomes, representing the untold stories in their lives. In this new space that has been created by acknowledging these unique outcomes, individuals have more power to come up with alternative solutions and to regain their sense of self-agency. The reauthoring process allows the clients to discover their hidden strengths and use their skills to create a storyline that is more in line with them.

Narrative therapists map the influence of the problem on the individual's life and relationships by asking about the effect of the problem. These are questions that can help the clients discuss the psychological, physical, and behavioral aspects of the influence of the problem on their lives.[11] This step is called mapping the influence of the individual with the problem. It includes asking questions related to how the individual has been trying to cope with the problem, amplifying the recognition of strengths, and nurtur-ing the alternative story. During this process, unique outcomes are identi-fied that enable new meanings. Figure 15.1 provides a visual representation of this process.

THE USE OF NARRATIVE
THERAPY IN SEXUAL VIOLENCE RECOVERY

From a narrative therapy perspective, knowledge is understood as being socially constructed, with individuals creating a personal narrative about themselves and their interactions with others—describing and understand-ing their experiences while being influenced by the dominant discourses of

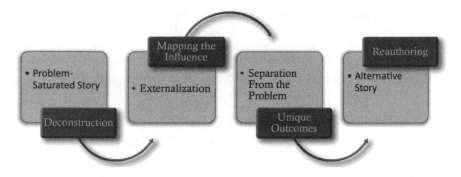

society.[12,14] Stories around sexuality and sexual experiences may be particularly sensitive to social influences, as social context and changes in norms may influence the meaning attributed to such concepts and experiences.

In addition, reality is not seen as something that is objective or permanent, but is viewed as being constructed by the exchange and interaction between the contributors. Narrative therapy expands the possibilities of this reality, allowing the creation of new constructions and meanings around abusive experiences.[15]

DOMINANT STORIES OF ABUSE

The experience of the abuse, specifically if the individual feels responsible for the abusive experience, continues to victimize the survivor by becoming the dominant story for the individual.[16] Narratives that may emerge in therapy could include those of silence (a form of denial or coping); ongoing suffering; transformation or survivorhood; or transcendence.[4] Characteristic of those who experience sexual abuse, the individual may feel powerless to resolve the problem (or to modify the dominant story), especially as the abusive symptoms and effects continue to take away the individual's sense of control.[15] Individuals who identify themselves as victims or as being responsible for the abuse are at risk of developing abuse-dominated narratives.[17]

Furthermore, abuse-dominated narratives can also involve disqualifying stories, in which a person is unable to recognize experiences or events that reflect talents, accomplishments, positive values, or competence of the individual.[12] Disempowering stories may also occur when the individual's sexual abuse experience is denied by others, blamed on the individual who experience the abuse, or defined as not abusive. If one of these beliefs is accepted, the individual may have difficulty trusting one's own experience of the abuse, thus possibly maintaining the strength of the dominant story of being responsible for the abusive experience.[17]

Narratives that overlook strengths and positive experiences, focusing instead on the negative aspects of a person's life, are problem-dominated narratives.[12] These narratives can often surface in therapy with sexual abuse survivors, offering an opening for therapists to address them.

DEVELOPING ALTERNATIVE STORIES

Narrative therapy considers both the therapist and client as contributors, each responsible for the construction of reality. However, a narrative approach emphasizes the client (in this case, the survivor) as the expert on his or her experiences, emphasizing the strengths, resources, and self-perception of the individual.[9] The therapist assumes a nonexpert stance (a "not-knowing position"), not intending to solve the survivor's problems or repair the survivor from abuse, but rather supporting the client to modify and explore stories and meanings.[15] This not-knowing position encourages the development of the client's sense of competence and empowerment, promoting an atmosphere in which the client is considered the expert on the abusive experiences.[12,18]

In the process of narrative therapy, the client and the therapist expose the dominant discourses around the experience of abuse—exploring such aspects as what supports the problem or who benefits from the problem.[9] The mapping of the problem not only exposes the dominant stories around the abuse, but in this way, creates space for new stories to develop. Furthermore, the therapist and client can map the negative influences of the abuse through relative influence questioning, establishing that the person is not the problem, but rather the person has a relationship with the problem.[9] In addition, the therapist and client can map the times when the client, or others, have refused to give in to the effect of the abuse, such as refusing to maintain the secrecy or accept blame for the abuse having occurred.[9,14]

Through this collaboration, questions are asked to increase the understanding and awareness of the resources and strengths of the client. The conversation generated between the client and therapist can open up opportunities to discuss and identify times when the client has been successful in controlling the effects of the abuse, with the therapist building on the strengths and resources of the client in doing so. In this way, preferred stories, and a preferred way of living, can be facilitated through organizing and examining the client's experiences and successes.[10] Narrative therapy can assist the sexual abuse survivor in recognizing the personal power to recognize and create new stories.[15] In addition, through the use of narrative

techniques, the client and therapist can modify narratives that are ineffec-
tive or unhelpful for the client, opening up the abuse-dominated stories.[19]

Without having to directly challenge the dominant story, a narrative approach guides the individual to focus on indications of alternative stories
already occurring. The client is supported in broadening the possibility of
new, preferred stories through deconstructing the dominant story of being a
victim.[15] Through developing different, more functional, narratives around
the sexual abuse, individuals can be assisted in making meaning of their
experiences, which do not necessarily have to focus on the traumatic events
the individual experiences.[20]

Narrative therapy can encourage the client to explore the possibility of
moving on in life in a preferred way, empowering the client to not focus
on the abuse as the problem (which cannot be undone) but rather to view
the problem as existing outside him- or herself.[10,11] Narrative therapy has
demonstrated the effectiveness of externalizing conversations in generating
individuals' sense of responsibility for behavior.[9] Through externalizing the
problem (and seeing the self as separated from the problem), the client
then has the responsibility for the interactions with it and can see more
possible ways to change their situation.[14] Importantly, sexual abuse (as the
problem) should not be externalized; it is the attitudes, beliefs, and effects
of the violence that are externalized, such as the imposition of isolation or
secrecy on individuals who were abused.[11]

Through reauthoring conversations, the individual develops and tells
his/her story but also can begin to incorporate some of the neglected, or
subjugated, events or experiences not present in the dominant stories—referred to as "exceptions" or "unique outcomes."[14] Reauthoring conversations begin with identifying these unique outcomes, which may include
experiences in which the client refused to be defined by the abusive experience; made the decision to disclose the abuse; resisted fear in telling about
the experience; or acted in a way to protect someone else from harm.[12,13]
Through identifying a unique outcome, the client is able to realize the control he or she has over the effect of the problem, and in this way, the power
to change it.[12]

CONSIDERATION OF CLIENT
VALUES, RESOURCES, AND STRENGTHS

Treatment for sexual abuse survivors often encourages the individual's
movement from "victim" to "survivor," supporting a nonobjectified status.[15] This process facilitates the sexual abuse survivor regaining control
over his or her life and defining the self by a reality that is self-determined—
developing self-affirmation and a sense of competence.[15,19] In addition,

when working with an individual who has experienced trauma, the therapist should be attuned to the client's responses to the traumatic events, as responses are often based on what the individual gives value to in life.[12,13] Therapists should not only hear what the individual feels is important to share about the experienced trauma, but also should notice opportunities to recognize responses to trauma, specifically identifying what the client has continued to value despite what he or she has experienced.[13] Through the practice of double listening, the therapist can listen to the story of the trauma experience but also attune to indicators of the client's ability to find, and maintain, values in spite of the trauma.[13] Furthermore, combined with positive psychology, narrative therapy allows a more preferred, perhaps even optimistic, way of storying the client's past, present, and future experiences.

INTEGRATING POSITIVE PSYCHOLOGY

To help the sexual abuse survivor to realize their abilities, talents, and competencies, the positive psychology approach can be integrated with narrative therapy. The client's skills and knowledge are the resources that can be built on and use while creating the alternative stories.

Positive psychology is the science of positive subjective experience, which studies concepts such as well-being, contentment, hope, optimism, flow, and happiness.[21] Positive psychology examines the circumstances that strengthen the performance of individuals, families, and groups, reinforcing the good things in life as well as repairing the worst. It also focuses on what makes life fulfilling as well as on helping the distressed.[22] In the last ten years, research about positive psychology interventions started to underscore the efficacy of this field. A meta-analysis of fifty-one positive psychology interventions indicated that these interventions significantly enhance well-being and decrease depressive symptoms.[23] Positive psychology relies on empirical research, which distinguishes it from the positive thinking movement.[24]

Building positive emotions with sexual abuse survivors is a goal that should be pursued in therapy, as desensitization work with the survivors is not enough to build back their strengths. Individuals who have experienced sexual abuse may also have a poor self-image, lower self-esteem, relationship difficulties, and other characteristics that can affect their sense of self and their interactions with others.[25,26,27] Helping clients who have experienced sexual abuse to construct positive emotions could support them in communicating differently with themselves and with others.

According to Fredrickson (1998), negative emotions constrict the individual's "thought-action tendencies." This is an adaptive function, considered as a response to dangerous circumstances. When faced with risky situations, we need to make decisions quickly to stay alive. This narrowing process for giving automatic responses such as fight, flight, or freeze is not true for the positive emotions. Thus, this researcher suggests a different interpretation of positive emotions' function as broadening the "thought-action" range for the individual.[30] By experiencing positive emotions, the individual does not get hooked to the evolutionarily appropriate limited responses. Instead of being limited, he or she actually experiences the expansion of new, different, inventive routes of reactions. Fredrickson (1998) discusses four different positive emotions (joy, interest, contentment, and love) to show how these emotions enable the individual to make creative, novel, and explorative decisions that broaden their "thought-action" possibilities. This process also builds individuals' personal coping skills and reserves.

Fredrickson (1998) also reviewed the research of Isen (1987) and his colleagues (1984) and states that "these and other findings have led Isen to conclude that positive affect leads people to see relatedness and interconnections among thoughts and ideas and to material in a more integrated and flexible fashion.[28,29] Expansion of thinking and solving problems also broadens the possibility of taking action and makes the individual more flexible. Positive emotions also build physical, intellectual, and social resources, which increase survival.

Promoting positive feelings enables the individual to develop psychologically and physically.[31] This process facilitates growth and broadens the response repertoires, which can be beneficial for the sexual abuse survivors in their recovery. Thus, therapists should underline the importance of cultivating positive emotions to help to cope with life stressors and to improve life satisfaction. Positive emotions not only indicate but also produce well-being.[30] The well-being is also accompanied by widening of cognitive and social resource–building abilities.

Positive psychology concentrates on three main areas: the study of positive subjective experiences, the study of positive individual traits, and the study of institutions that allow positive subjective experiences and positive traits.[22] The study of character strengths and virtues is an effort to understand positive individual traits. Peterson and Seligman (2004) state that a person's character can be fostered, but psychology needs empirical ways to achieve this. To answer the question of "how can we measure good character among youth?" Peterson and Seligman developed a categorization called VIA (Values in Action) Classification of Strengths. This scientific effort focuses on what people's strengths are and how to categorize them. Interventions related to character strengths and virtues can be a different avenue for therapists to increase individuals' life satisfaction and life meaning. Narrative therapy highlights the importance of strengths and assets of individuals and helps the survivors to construct a more positive perception of themselves.[9] Cultivating character strengths might be another avenue to enable sexual abuse survivors to build their alternative stories. Let us describe character strengths and give an example about the application with a sexual abuse survivor.

CHARACTER STRENGTHS

Character strengths began to be classified to help create common vocabulary in positive psychology in regard to defining positive traits. According to Peterson and Seligman (2004), virtues are the characteristics that are valued by moral philosophers, religious thinkers, psychologists, psychiatrists, and other youth development researchers. The researchers identified six virtues: (a) wisdom and knowledge, (b) courage, (c) humanity, (d) justice, (e) temperance, and (f) transcendence. These six categories of virtues seem to be consistent across culture and history.[32] Virtues are defined by twenty-four character strengths, which include creativity, curiosity, love of learning, open-mindedness, perspective, bravery, persistence, integrity, zest, kindness, love, social intelligence, citizenship, fairness, leadership, forgiveness, humility, prudence, self-regulation, appreciation of beauty and excellence, gratitude, hope, humor, and spirituality.

According to Park and Peterson (2006),[33] character is "a multidimensional construct comprised of a family of positive traits manifest in an individual's thoughts, emotions, and behaviors" (p. 891). Thus, a quantitative measure plays an important role in assessing and helping to enhance character strengths. These character strengths are measured by a free Internet-based questionnaire called the VIA Survey of Character, which was created by Dr. Christopher Peterson, and the VIA Survey for Youth, which is for ages ten through seventeen and was authored by Dr. Nansook Park. VIA Survey has acceptable internal consistency and test-retest reliability and has been taken more than 1.5 million times.[34]

The next and final section is devoted to representing our integration of narrative therapy and positive psychology with sexual abuse survivors and self-help recommendations used in a case study.

CASE STUDY

Lily was a fifteen-year-old teenager who was brought to therapy by her mother for help getting through the residual effects of trauma. She looked more mature than her age group, had a lot of makeup on, and dressed provocatively. Lily's mother, Emma, was a lawyer, and her father worked for the government. She had two younger siblings, Russ (ten) and Jim (seven).

Lily had gone to therapy for a year, but due to her therapist leaving town, she was transferred to me (ZSS). According to her mother, Lily's previous experience in therapy was not very successful; she continued lying and was very distant from her family. Lily was very quiet in the initial session. Her mother did most of the talking and informed me about what Lily has gone through. Lily was sexually abused from ages twelve to fourteen by Lily's father's friend, who was also their neighbor. The abuser was arrested and sentenced to prison. Emma struggled with much guilt and shame at the same time. She disclosed that she was also raped when she was a teenager. After learning about the assault, Emma became overly protective and was not allowing Lily to have a personal life, which frustrated Lily extremely. While Emma was explaining how learning about her daughter being molested affected her, Lily was staring at the floor and had no emotional response to what was being shared in the session.

I saw Lily alone the rest of the initial session and tried to get more information about the assaults. Lily started sharing her "problem-saturated" description of her story in the first session. In the next couple of sessions, through externalization and finding unique outcomes, I tried to alter this problem-dominated story and create an alternative story. To start the externalization process, I started by asking Lily how this abuse affected her.

Seda: From what I am hearing from you, I understand that you would like to get some help with how to deal with these traumatic events. Can you tell me more about how this abuse had an effect on you?

Lily: I don't trust people now, and I don't care if I have friends or not.

Seda: So the abuse that you have experienced made you not trust people and not worry about if you have close friends or not. How else have these traumas played a role in your life?

Lily: I can get any boy in the school I want. I don't care if they like me or not but when we go to the bathroom, I can make them happy and get attention from them.

Seda: It sounds like the abuse has affected your sexuality and how you relate to the opposite sex. How did these traumas affect other aspects of your life or your relationships?

Lily: It definitely made my mom stricter. She does not let me hang out with friends or stay over at any friends' houses. She checks my cell phone and does not let me go on the Internet. So it really affected how she treats me. It was not this bad before.

Seda: Has your father been affected by your traumas?

Lily: I think it made him feel very guilty. Since it was his friend who made me touch him, I think he feels that all this is his fault.

Here I realized that Lily was having a hard time externalizing the abuse and putting a name to it. She was also having a hard time naming her feelings when I asked about the effects, and it seemed that she was very numb about how these abusive experiences affected her. She was very withdrawn and mistrustful of adults.

Problem-saturated stories have become like her identity, and it was hard for her to see any alternative stories being created. At this point, I decided to ask her to take the character strengths questionnaire online. Previous research shows that integrating character-strengths assessment and recovery work with veterans has been a successful avenue for specifying and promoting the goals of recovery.[35] Therefore, we suggest that it would be beneficial for the therapists to integrate the character-strengths work while working with sexual abuse survivors in the narrative therapy approach.

Lily came the following week with the results of the questionnaire. The top five character strengths of the VIA inventory are called the signature strengths. Here is how we started talking about them and integrating them with narrative therapy.

Seda: So how has taking this test been for you? What do you think about the results?

Lily: It was pretty cool. I like taking tests online. It's fun.

Seda: What have you learned from the results? What were your top five strengths? We will call them "the signature strengths," okay?

Lily: Okay. I had love of learning, bravery, curiosity, humor, and kindness as my top five.

Seda: That's great. Do you think that your friends would use similar words to describe you if I asked them to talk about you?

Lily: I guess so, I love reading books, and they always say I am funny, so I guess they would agree.

Seda: Well, for the next five weeks what I would like you to do is to practice using these top five strengths in different ways.

Lily: What do you mean in different ways?

Seda: That is a great question. The reason that you have these signature strengths as your top five is because you use them more than the other strengths. So it doesn't mean that you don't have the strengths that are in the bottom, you just don't use them as your signature strengths. I would like you to try using your signature strengths in different ways than you usually do. To help you to do this I am going to give you a print-out, which is going to give you some ideas as well . . .

Here, the purpose is trying to step away from the problem-saturated story of her life and explore some untold aspects of her. Research has shown that identifying character strengths and using them in new ways had long-term positive effects on happiness.[36] Here is the link to the 340 Ways to Use VIA Character Strengths exercise.[37]

With the help of using character strengths, it was easier to identify unique outcomes and clearer for Lily to see that she had so many strengths, which would assist her with forming her alternative story. I shared with her research about trauma survivors following the national crisis on September 11. We talked about how these individuals demonstrated an increase of gratitude, hope, kindness, leadership, love, spirituality, and teamwork after the attack.[38]

Adding character-strengths perspective to the existing narrative therapy approach also can reduce negative family interactions. Since both authors are family therapists, we propose to use character-strengths work in the family context. The following is an excerpt from the sixth session with Lily, where I invited her mother, Emma, her father, Greg, and her brothers, Jim and Russ, for a session.

Seda: I bet you are all wondering why I brought all of you guys here. Today I planned a different and fun activity for all of us. It is pretty simple. We will take turns pulling a piece of paper from this bag. Each paper has words written on it, and we are going to read them out loud. There will be explanations of the words, which are actually the strengths that we use in our lives. So, when we read the strength and the explanation, I will ask each one of you who uses this strength the most in the family. I think it will be pretty fun. Shall we start? Okay, why don't you go first, Jim, and pick a piece from the bag.

Jim: "Curiosity: Taking an interest in all ongoing experiences, finding all subjects and topics fascinating, exploring, and discovering."

Seda: So, who do you think uses their curiosity strength most in this family, Jim?

Jim: I guess Russ is very interested in video games. He always wants to find new games and learns them very quickly and teaches me.

Seda: That is a great example, Jim. Thank you very much. Does anyone have any other ideas about who uses their curiosity strength in the family?

Greg: I think Emma is pretty curious about cooking and trying new recipes, which I really like (laughs), and Lily has an interest in mascaras. I think she has tried every one of the brands in the market (laughs).

Seda: Thank you very much, Greg. How about you choose the next strength?

Greg: "Open-mindedness: Thinking things through and examining them from all sides; *not* jumping to conclusions; being able to change one's mind in light of evidence; weighing all evidence fairly."

Emma: I think most of us do not use this strength much. Everybody here thinks they know it all, and nobody changes their minds no matter how much we argue.

Seda: That is a very good point, Emma. Thank you very much for bringing that up. Actually, we all have all of these strengths, but what makes us different is the amount we use them. I hear that you are saying you do not use your open-mindedness strength as much as the other strengths you have. Is that correct?

Emma: Yeah, we jump to conclusions about what the other thinks and stop listening to them.

Greg: I agree with Emma. I think that is something we need to work on.

Seda: That is a great goal as a family—to focus on the strengths that you do not use as much as the other ones. We can come back to this and decide how you can work on the strengths that you want to cultivate more. How about you choose another one, Lily?

Lily: "Humor: Liking to laugh and tease; bringing smiles to other people; seeing the light side; making (not necessarily telling) jokes." Oh, this is totally dad. He teases us all the time. And I think Russ is picking up on it and sometimes can be pretty funny.

Jim: I know, he told me a joke the other day, and when I told it in school, the boys really liked it a lot.

Seda: I can see that as a family, you use humor a lot and there is a very playful approach to life. After we finish picking from the bag, we can talk about how we can use the strengths that we already use more. In addition, at the end of the session, I am going to give you homework, which will be to use one of your own strengths during the next week.

During the family session, Lily was very engaged, enjoyed herself, and saw that her family was very supportive. Recruiting other family members in the creation of an alternative story by using character strengths has been very successful in our practices.

In another session, Lily shared with me about being anxious and not being able to relax. An intervention that can be used in therapy sessions with sexual abuse survivors is teaching mindfulness meditation to let them to take charge of their breathing. Research shows significant positive changes in the brain and immune system as a result of eight weeks of mindfulness meditation training.[39] In this randomized, controlled study, results indicated that "meditation can produce increases in relative left-sided anterior activation that are associated with reductions in anxiety and negative affect and increases in positive affect" (pg. 569). In a three-year follow-up study, scientists showed that mindfulness meditation has constructive long-term effects on individuals, such as improvements in symptoms of anxiety and decreases in depressive symptoms.[40]

MINDFULNESS MEDITATION EXERCISE

Here is a beginner's mindfulness meditation exercise that we teach our clients; we ask them to continue doing the exercise at home as well. We do this exercise in the session with them to show them how to apply it.

I would like you to sit in a comfortable position and place your hands on your lap. Please close your eyes fully or partially, however you like, and take a couple of deep breaths to relax.

- Now I'd like you to bring your attention to your breathing and just to your breathing. Turn your attention to how your belly and chest are filling with air . . . where the air is traveling.
- I'd like to you to think about how a bottle is filled, starting from bottom to top, and how it gets emptied, from top to bottom. This is how you are going to try breathing.
- Start with the expansion of your belly with every in-breath and then moving to your chest. With every out-breath the contraction starts from your chest and then moves to your belly.
- Now try inhaling and exhaling, paying attention to your breath. It might feel a little different than your typical breathing pattern, which will take some time for you to adjust.
- Pay attention to your breathing. Different thoughts will arise and distract you from paying attention to just your breathing. This is very normal. What I want you to do is just gently bring your attention to your breathing. This is our exercise. Exercise bringing the attention to breathing.
- Your mind might start wandering away; just gently bring your attention back to your breathing.
- I'm going to do this with you for the next ten minutes, breathing in and out. My mind will wander away, and I'll be trying to bring my attention back to my breathing. At the end of ten minutes, I will ask you open your eyes when you are ready.

Lily said that she felt relaxed after doing the meditation, and I advised her to practice this two times each day. In the following sessions, we continued to deconstruct her problem-saturated story by emphasizing her strengths and creating a survivor narrative. Focusing on strengths has allowed her to find unique outcomes more easily and reauthor her alternative story.

CONCLUSION

When individuals experience trauma, a shift to their perception of themselves and the world is likely. It is an extensive therapy process to view oneself as a survivor rather than a victim. A narrative therapy approach allows individuals to rewrite their experiences by enabling them to create a new personal narrative, outside being a "victim of abuse." Integrating character-strengths work allows the individuals to look at what is working in their lives and what they are good at. Using narrative therapy, clients can deconstruct their problem-saturated story through externalization and mapping the influence of the problem. When individuals can separate from the problems, they can explore unique outcomes and reauthor their alternative story. Incorporating character-strengths investigation and cultivation into the narrative therapy process can make the results more efficient and supportive of clients. In conclusion, combining narrative therapy with positive psychology can allow individuals to externalize their problems and internalize their strengths.

RECOMMENDATIONS

As previously mentioned in this chapter, the mindfulness breathing exercise and completion of the strengths inventory can be useful in managing the sexual abuse symptoms and exploring aspects of the self unrelated to the abusive experience. In addition, the integration of the narrative component with the character strengths can be practiced and supported by creating a "strengths scrapbook." Survivors can build a scrapbook album depicting the times and experiences in which they used their strengths, including images, words, and drawings to capture their stories. Through this activity, the survivors can identify their values that have continued despite what they have experienced, as well as acknowledge the positive traits and qualities in themselves over time and in experiences not related to the abuse. The pages then become artifacts of the recovery process, documenting the alternative stories and highlighting the demonstrated strengths of the survivor. In this way, the survivor's journey can be visualized and complemented by the created pages, signifying successes and progress in recovery and hence, further empowering survivors.

REFERENCES

1. Krause, E., DeRosa, R., & Roth, S. (2002). Gender, trauma themes, and PTSD: Narratives of male and female survivors. *Gender and PTSD* (pp. 349–381). New York: Guilford Press. Retrieved from PsycINFO database.
2. Leahy, T., Pretty, G., & Tenenbaum, G. (2003). Childhood sexual abuse narratives in clinically and nonclinically distressed adult victims. *Professional Psychology: Research and Practice, 34,* 657–665.
3. Breckenridge, J. (1999). Subjugation and silences: The role of the professions in silencing victims of sexual and domestic violence. In J. Breckenridge & L. Laing

(Eds.), *Challenging silences: Innovative responses to sexual and domestic violence* (pp. 6–30). St. Leonard's, Australia: Allen & Unwin.

4. Hunter, S.V. (2010). Evolving narratives about childhood sexual abuse: Challenging the dominance of the victim and survivor paradigm. *The Australian and New Zealand Journal of Family Therapy*, 31, pp. 176–190.

5. Dunn, J. (2005). 'Victims' and 'survivors': Emerging vocabularies of motive for 'battered women who stay.' *Sociological Inquiry*, 75(1), 1–30. Freedman, J. & Combs, G. (1996). Narrative therapy: The social construction of preferred realities. New York: W.W. Norton & Company.

6. Jenkins, P. (1998). *Moral panic: Changing concepts of the child molester in modern America.* New Haven, CT: Yale University Press.

7. Phillips, A., & Daniluk, J.C. (2004). Beyond 'Survivor': How childhood sexual abuse informs the identity of adult women at the end of the therapeutic process. *Journal of Counseling & Development*, 82(2), 177–184.

8. Monk, G., Winslade, J., Crocket, K., & Epston, D. (Eds.). (1997). *Narrative therapy in practice: The archeology of hope.* San Francisco: Jossey-Bass.

9. Freedman, J., & Combs, G. (1996). *Narrative therapy: The social construction of preferred realities.* New York: W.W. Norton & Company.

10. McKenzie, A. (2005). Narrative-oriented therapy with children who have experience sexual abuse. *Envision: The Manitoba Journal of Child Welfare*, 4, 17–29.

11. White, M., & Epston, D. (1990). Narrative means to therapeutic ends. New York: Norton.

12. Brooks, G. (2010). Creating a narrative therapy workbook for children who have experienced extra-familial sexual abuse and their parents. *Dissertation Abstracts International*, 70, Retrieved from PsycINFO database.

13. White, M. (2006). Working with people who are suffering the consequences of multiple trauma: A narrative perspective. In D. Denborough. (Ed.) *Narrative responses to traumatic experiences* (pp. 25–85). Adelaide, S. Australia: Dulwich Centre Publications.

14. White, M. (2007). *Maps of narrative practice.* New York: W.W. Norton & Company Inc.

15. Baird, F. (1996). A narrative context for conversations with adult survivors of childhood sexual abuse. *Progress-Family Systems Research and Therapy*, 5, 51–71.

16. Reavey, P., & Warner, S. (2001). Curing women: child sexual abuse, therapy, and the construction of femininity. *International Journal of Critical Psychology*, 3, 49–72.

17. Adams-Westcott, J., & Dobbins, C. (1997). Listening with your "Heart's Ears" and other ways young people can escape the effects of sexual abuse. In C. Smith & D. Nylund (Eds.), *Narrative therapies with children and adolescents* (pp. 195–220). New York: The Guilford Press.

18. Durrant, M., & White, C. (1990). *Ideas for therapy with sexual abuse.* Adelaide: Dulwich Centre Publications.

19. Sahin, Z.S., & McVicker, M. (2009). The use of optimism in narrative therapy with sexual abuse victims. *Journal of European Psychology Students*, 1, 1–6.

20. White, M. (1989). Negative explanation, restraint, and double description: A template for family therapy. In M. White (Ed.), *Selected papers* (pp. 85–100). Adelaide: Dulwich Centre Publications.

21. Seligman, M.E.P., & Csikszentmihayli, M. (2000). Positive psychology: An introduction. *American Psychologist, 55,* 5–14. doi:10.1037//0003-066X.55.1.5
22. Seligman, M.E.P. (2002). *Authentic happiness.* New York: Free Press.
23. Sin, N.L., & Lyubomirsky, S. (2009). Enhancing well-being and alleviating depressive symptoms with positive psychology interventions: A practice friendly meta-analysis. *Journal of Clinical Psychology: In Session, 45,* 467–487. doi:10.1002/jclp.20593
24. Peterson, C., & M.E.P. Seligman. (2004). *Character strengths and virtues: A classification and handbook.* Washington, D.C.: American Psychological Association.
25. Kendall-Tackett, K.A., Williams, L.M., & Finkelhor, D. (1993). Impact of sexual abuse on children: A review and synthesis of recent empirical studies. *Psychological Bulletin, 113,* 164–180.
26. Swenson, C.C., & Hanson, R.F. (1998). Sexual abuse of children: assessment, research, and treatment. In J.R. Lutzker (Ed.), *Handbook of child abuse research and treatment. Issues in clinical child psychology* (pp. 475–499). New York: Plenum Press.
27. Zurbriggen, E.L., & Freyd, J.J. (2004). The link between childhood sexual abuse and risky sexual behavior: The role of dissociative tendencies, information-processing effects, and consensual sex decision mechanisms. In L.J. Koenig, L.S. Doll, A. O'Leary, & W. Pequegnat (Eds.) *From Child Sexual Abuse to Adult Sexual Risk: Trauma, Revictimization, and Intervention* (pp. 135–158). Washington, D.C.: American Psychological Association.
28. Isen, A.M., & Daubman, K.A. (1984). The influence of affect on categorization. *Journal of Personality and Social Psychology, 47,* 1206–1217.
29. Isen, A.M., Daubman, K.A., & Nowicki, G.P. (1987). Positive affect facilitates creative problem solving. *Journal of Personality and Social Psychology, 52,* 1122–1131.
30. Fredrickson, B.L. (1998). What good are positive emotions? *Review of General Psychology: Special Issue: New Directions in Research on Emotion, 2,* 300–319.
31. Fredrickson, B.L. (2004). The broaden and build theory of positive emotions. *Philosophical Transactions of the Royal Society of London, 359,* 1367–1377. doi:10.1098/rstb.2004.1512
32. Dahlsgaard, K., Davis, D., Peterson, C., & Seligman, M.E.P. (2003). *Do character strengths really matter? A prospective longitudinal study of signature character strengths and adolescent development.* Poster presented at the 2003 Biennial Meeting of the Society for Research in Child Development, April 10, Tampa, FL.
33. Park, N., & Peterson, C. (2006). Moral competence and character strengths among adolescents: The development validation of the Values in Action Inventory of Strengths for Youth. *Journal of Adolescence, 29,* 891–909. doi:10.1016/j.adolescence.2006.04.011
34. VIA Strengths Inventory. (2010). Retrieved September 28, 2010 from http://www.viacharacter.org/Surveys/SurveyCenter.aspxfgfg
35. Resnick, S.G., & Rosenheck, R.A. (2006). Recovery and positive psychology: Parallel themes and potential synergies. *Psychiatric Services, 57,* 120–122. doi:10.1176/appi.ps.57.1.120

36. Seligman, M.E.P., Steen, T.A., Park, N., & Peterson, C. (2005). Positive psychology progress: Empirical validation of interventions. *American Psychologist, 60,* 410–421. doi:10.1037/0003-066X.60.5.410

37. Rashid, T., & Anjum, A. (2010). 340 ways to use VIA character strengths. Retrieved September 28, 2010 from http://education.ucsb.edu/janeconoley/ed197/documents/WaystouseSignStrengthsFilms.pdf

38. Peterson, C., & Seligman, M.E.P. (2003). Character strengths before and after September 11. *Psychological Science, 14,* 381–384. doi: 10.1111/1467-9280.24482

39. Davidson, R.J., Kabat-Zinn, J., Schumacher, J., Rosenkranz, M., Muller, D., Santorelli, S., et al. (2003). Alterations in brain and immune function produced by mindfulness meditation. *Psychosomatic Medicine, 65(4),* 564–570.

40. Miller, J.J., Fletcher, K., & Kabat-Zinn., J. (1995). Three-year follow-up and clinical implications of a mindfulness meditation-based stress reduction intervention in the treatment of anxiety disorders. *General Hospital Psychiatry, 17(3),* 192–200.

16

A Psychodynamic Approach to Recovery from Sexual Assault

Pratyusha Tummala-Narra

The long-term implications for sexual assault, such as risk of anxiety, depression, suicidal ideation, eating disorders, substance abuse, and sexual dysfunction, have been documented by researchers and clinicians working with survivors.[1,2,3] The internal life of survivors is often marked with feelings of shame, self-blame, and powerlessness, all of which contribute to challenges in self-care and establishing safe and fulfilling relationships.[2] Sexual violence further involves stress that is rooted in social injustice and requires attention on individual, community, and societal levels. Despite these challenges, survivors find ways to cope with the extraordinary demands of the aftermath of sexual violence.

As traumatic experiences such as childhood sexual abuse, incest, and adulthood rape have highly complex and individualized effects on survivors' lives, various approaches to recovery need to be considered in attending to the unique needs of survivors. This chapter will address a psychodynamic approach to recovery from sexual violence that is based on contemporary theory and practice integrating individual, relational, and sociocultural contexts of survivors. Psychodynamic theory with its close relationship with psychoanalysis expands on particular aspects of traumatic experience, such as the relationship between external traumatic events and internal processes related to these experiences. The ways in which sexual violence overwhelms the sense of self and the relationship between the individual and his/her environment (family, community) will be explored through a psychodynamic lens, informed by trauma theory and research. A clinical case example will be discussed to illustrate the contributions of psychodynamic theory to an understanding of traumatic experience, resilience, and recovery. First, I will provide a brief overview of psychodynamic psychotherapy followed by a discussion of specific aspects of psychodynamic psychotherapy related to recovery from sexual trauma, including attachment and relationships, affect and memory, real and symbolic features of trauma, and the social context of trauma.

OVERVIEW OF PSYCHODYNAMIC PSYCHOTHERAPY

Psychodynamic psychotherapy includes treatments based on psychoanalytic concepts. In a recent review of the efficacy of psychodynamic psychotherapy, Shedler[4] highlighted empirical evidence supporting psychodynamic psychotherapy for clients coping with a range of psychological concerns. While psychodynamic therapies vary to some degree with respect to specific foci, some common features of these approaches include an attention to affect and expression of emotion, exploration of attempts to avoid distressing thoughts and feelings, identification of recurring themes and patterns, discussion of past experience as it may influence present challenges, focus on interpersonal relations, focus on the therapy relationship, and exploration of fantasy or symbolic life.[4] Psychodynamic psychotherapy emphasizes moving beyond relieving immediate crisis or symptoms and helping the client additionally through self-reflection or introspection within a safe therapeutic relationship. As such, the process of psychodynamic psychotherapy may be either short-term, lasting several weeks, or long-term, lasting several months or years.

With respect to trauma, various short-term and long-term models of psychodynamic treatment for post-traumatic stress disorder have been developed.[5,6] For example, Krupnick[6] developed a twelve-session treatment approach for a single event of trauma that focuses on the traumatic experience and related intrapersonal (e.g., self-concept) and interpersonal (e.g., typical ways of relating with others). Long-term models of psychodynamic psychotherapy usually address complex post-traumatic stress disorder or complex PTSD,[2] which is experienced in cases of chronic, repeated trauma. These models emphasize the relationship between the therapist and client to help the client better understand his/her interpersonal patterns and their connection to childhood relationships with significant people, such as caregivers.[7] The role of developmental stress, such as life transitions, losses, and separations, as it intersects with traumatic experience is a focus of psychodynamic approaches to trauma.

Much of traumatic and nontraumatic stress, in a psychodynamic perspective, is conceptualized as located in the individual's unconscious, and the concept of bringing unconscious material to conscious awareness in a safe therapeutic space is thought to be central to effectively and accurately discovering connections between past events (traumatic and nontraumatic) and present day-to-day struggles. Psychodynamic psychotherapy is further concerned with defenses or ways of dealing with painful and/or conflictual needs, feelings, wishes, or impulses that often become compromised under traumatic conditions. This approach focuses on helping a survivor develop the meaning of the trauma itself and how it may fit with his/her sense of self. Finally, psychodynamic psychotherapy is concerned with the ways in which traumatic events interact with an individual's broader personality and development.[7]

Trauma theory, such as that developed by Judith Herman,[2] involves psychodynamic ideas such as the use of defense mechanisms, such as repression and dissociation, in coping with traumatic experience. However, Herman[2] emphasizes the feminist concepts of empowerment and reconnection as central parts of the recovery process, which is conceptualized as involving three stages, including the establishment of safety, remembering and mourning traumatic events, and reconnection or the establishment of intimacy in safe relationships. The idea that the survivor be the "author" of his/her own recovery is central to the recovery process.[2] In the sections that follow, I will describe in more detail some central aspects of recovery from sexual trauma from a trauma-informed, psychodynamic perspective.

SEXUAL ASSAULT AND RELATIONAL LIFE

Sexual violence in childhood and adulthood contributes to significant challenges in survivors' ability to establish safe, trusting relationships. Childhood sexual abuse, including incest, is especially fraught with betrayal and boundary violations that have lasting impact on the child's attachment with significant people in his/her life such that the child comes to expect into adulthood that relationships will be abusive. Psychodynamic theorists, such as Davies and Frawley,[8] similar to feminist trauma theorists, value the importance of validating the survivor's traumatic experience. It is often the case that the therapist is either the only person or among the few people with whom the survivor has discussed his/her sexual trauma. A trauma-informed, psychodynamic approach entails bearing witness to the survivor's narrative of traumatic experience.

A focus on developmental issues related to traumatic experience is especially helpful in clarifying how early attachments and traumatic experience shape one's identity. The adverse effects of traumatic experience on attachment are well documented. Studies in developmental psychopathology have found not only that insecure attachment resulting from trauma and severe neglect is connected with difficulties in regulating emotions, attention, and self-control, but also that insecure attachment is a relatively stable problem for individuals, particularly in the face of ongoing negative life events.[9,10,11]

Fonagy and Bateman[9] suggest that trauma in early or late childhood causes disruption in one's capacity to understand and differentiate one's own experiences as well as those of others. They point out that a child who is sexually violated may identify with the aggressor or perpetrator in order to gain or maintain a sense of control over the abuser and abusive conditions. In this case, the child internalizes the "intent of the aggressor in an alien (dissociated) part of the self," (p. 5), and while this internalization is an adaptation to the trauma, it can contribute to feelings of self-hatred and self-blame. Psychodynamic theorists, focusing primarily on childhood sexual abuse, further conceptualize dissociation in traumatic experience to be unavoidable as a survivor attempts to integrate contradictory images of the self and abusive adult. Dissociation in this sense can be a positive adaptation when an individual is experiencing trauma as he/she copes with overwhelming feelings of terror and helplessness, and may later continue to persist as an individual copes with new traumatic and nontraumatic stress. New experiences, both positive and negative, intersect with old images of self and other, consciously and unconsciously, to form self-concept in the present day.[12,13] Internalizing aspects of the abuser and the abuse are thought to be rooted in the experience of powerlessness and loss of hope, both of which are central parts of traumatic experience.[14] In other words, internalization is a way to maintain connection in the face of loss of personal control and safety. Even in situations when a maltreated child defies the abuser, he/she may internalize negative attitudes of the abuser, such as feeling like he/she is a bad person, characterizing a traumatic bond that may be resistant to change.[2,14] Marjorie, a thirty-five-year old survivor of childhood sexual abuse by an uncle, stated in a psychotherapy session, "I just avoid him (uncle) most of the time, but when I saw him at my sister's wedding, it felt like his opinion matters to me. I used to look up to him. I hate him, and I want him to leave me alone." Deidre, a twenty-seven-year-old survivor of rape in adulthood, stated, "I still think that sometimes that I let this guy do this (rape) to me, like he saw something about me that was vulnerable. I'm not a strong person, and maybe he could see that about me." These struggles with emotionally separating oneself from the abuser and the abuse characteristic of traumatic bond are especially difficult in the case of sexual abuse in childhood, which involves distortion and over-stimulation of bodily sensations without boundaries between the abusive adult or older child, and the child who is violated; the confusion of loving and hostile feelings; the betrayal of trust; and the secrecy imposed by the abuser.[13,15]

In addition to internalization of negative attitudes, sexual violation contributes to confusion about sexuality. Trauma research has indicated an association between trauma and sexual risk behaviors.[1,16] For example, women of diverse ethnic backgrounds (White, African American, Hispanic) who experienced sexual trauma were at greater risk to use substances at the time of sexual intercourse with partners, and to have two or more sexual partners at the same time.[17,18] Additionally, sexual violation can contribute to confusion concerning sexual orientation and identity, even though the experience of sexual violation does not determine sexual orientation. While both men and women who have been sexually abused may experience post-traumatic symptoms, such as flashbacks, loss of trust, depression, feelings of shame, dissociation, addictive behaviors, and boundary violations, sexual abuse may have different meanings for boys and girls.[19] For example, men tend to underreport experiences of sexual violation and may experience sexual trauma as undermining or challenging a sense of gender identity and sexual orientation. James, a twenty-five-year-old gay survivor of childhood sexual abuse by a male "friend" of the family, stated in a psychotherapy session, "I don't think that I'm gay because of what happened to me, but I think that he (abuser) might have figured out that I'm gay. Maybe this is why he kept pursuing me and just spending so much time with me. I've realized that I'm like him in that I try too hard to pursue other men now." My client's experience of being chosen for this abuse is common to both female and male survivors. James's struggle with being "too pushy" at times in finding a sexual partner in his adult life reflects his struggles with his early experience with his abuser. For male survivors, the difficulty with negotiating differences between sex, love, affection, and abuse may be pronounced as they cope with traditional expectations of masculinity.[19]

One of the most salient consequences of sexual violation on relationships involves the degree to which external validation and supports are available to a survivor. Smith[14] has described the intense emotional aloneness that characterizes traumatic experience, which can exacerbate difficulty in revisiting or talking about the trauma. Psychodynamic therapy approaches the experience of emotional isolation through the survivor's connection with the empathic presence of the therapist.[15] Just as the survivor's interactions with the abuser hold significant meanings for the survivor's relational life, the experience of neglect or parental absence in the case of childhood sexual trauma can be equally important. For example, when a survivor of childhood sexual abuse is not protected by the other parent or caregivers or when an adult survivor of sexual assault is told by a family member or a friend that the assault was provoked by the survivor, the capacity to establish trust and self-esteem is compromised. A nonprotecting bystander who does not bear witness to the survivor's experience or trauma contributes to ongoing emotional costs to the survivor.[20] A survivor may feel distrustful and become hypervigilant to his/her surroundings or maintaining safety in relationships. This may be true in the case of psychotherapy, as well. The lack of safety in relating to others can be reexperienced in psychotherapy, as the therapist may be experienced unconsciously by a survivor as an abuser, victim, rescuer, or nonprotective bystander at varying times in the course of psychotherapeutic work. This type of traumatic transference is worked through and discussed with the survivor, as healing from trauma requires that sexual violence be revisited through talking.[2,21] The role of the therapist as bearing witness to the trauma story and holding hope for the survivor is a central part of the healing from the relational challenges implicated in sexual trauma.

SEXUAL ASSAULT, AFFECT, AND MEMORY

Sexual assault occurring in childhood and adulthood contributes to important changes in one's emotional functioning. Children need emotional signals to be accurately mirrored by their caregivers to develop a positive, coherent sense of self. Recent research in neuroscience indicates that the experience of early childhood abuse and neglect has adverse effects on the nonverbal right hemisphere of the brain, which is involved with regulation of emotions and dissociation.[22] When traumatic experience is invalidated by parents in the case of sexual abuse in childhood, or by significant others in the case of sexual violence in adulthood, the survivor's self-perceptions and his/her ability to identify and label emotions are compromised.[9] When a safe emotional environment is unavailable, an individual's sense of self or ego is overwhelmed with the cruelty of abuse, and self states or fragmented aspects of the self can form as a way of coping with unbearable emotional pain.[8,23,24] These self states are thought to function independently and can remain disconnected from each other even when the abuser is no longer a threat to the survivor. The survivor then faces difficulty with feeling his/her experience as "multidimensional, layered, conflictual, and contextual,"[23] and may find that he/she cannot access internalized anger, sadness, or shame.

In the case of childhood sexual abuse by a caregiver, the need to stay connected with the abusive parent perpetuates these dissociative processes, in which affect or emotional experience is disconnected from conscious-level experience. Trauma experts[2,15] have pointed out how child survivors of sexual abuse experience internal splitting as they face separate realities, including the reality of abuse and the minimization or denial of the child's experience by the abuser and/or family environment. In such cases, affect, memory, meaning, and fantasy remain dissociated from conscious awareness and remembered only as isolated parts of the trauma. Dissociation is experienced by children and adults who suffer sexual trauma and tends to persist in cases of chronic or repeated abuse, particularly when the experience is not discussed or validated.[2,15,25] One of the most pronounced ways in which dissociation is evidenced in survivors is the disconnection between cognition and affect, where a survivor becomes numb or talks about the abuse in a way that is only factual.

Psychoanalytic scholars have written about the concept of "unformulated experience,"[26] or the way in which dissociated, traumatic material remains closed to elaboration and symbolization, such that this aspect of the experience is not connected with verbal language.[27] As separate self states are formed in the case of sexual violence, memories of abuse may resurface unconsciously as nightmares or flashbacks, somatic or physical distress, and through reenactments or repetitions of abusive or destructive relational patterns.[2,8] Traumatic experience expressed and remembered through physical distress may be particularly salient in the experience of survivors whose cultural backgrounds may emphasize the expression of psychological distress through physical symptoms, such as headaches and gastrointestinal problems, rather than verbal expression of distress.[28]

An example of the way that trauma is remembered behaviorally is evident in the case of a survivor who engages in risky sexual behavior, perhaps as a way to regain control and mastery over past abusive experience, only to experience fear, sadness, and aloneness. The recovery from sexual trauma necessitates that a survivor discloses his/her story gradually in psychotherapy, and while revisiting the traumatic past, address feelings of shame, guilt, loss of control, and conflicts related to one's own aggressive thoughts and impulses. Psychodynamic approaches to recovery emphasize the unique meanings of the trauma to the survivor, and related affective and memory processes that are shaped through past and ongoing interpersonal contexts. As such, the survivor faces his/her ambivalence, confusion, and doubt about the traumatic memories and works toward a more coherent, meaningful narrative of his/her traumatic experience and its place in present-day life.

THE REAL AND SYMBOLIC ASPECTS OF TRAUMA

Psychodynamic approaches to recovery from sexual assault address the ways in which external realities of sexual violence are experienced by an individual in the context of his/her unique developmental and interpersonal contexts. This intersection of external events and internal life, as evidenced in psychodynamic concepts such as internalization of traumatic experience, is the basis for attending to the real and symbolic features of trauma. Maureen, a forty-six-year-old survivor of sexual violence by her former husband, expressed in a psychotherapy session, "I hated it when he would drink. This pretty much meant that he was going to rape me. I was scared that he would kill me. He just saw me as a thing to control, like a nobody. I think I felt like this even before I got married to him, but he just made it worse. I guess I didn't accomplish what he did professionally. I thought I was nobody for a long time." Maureen's statement concerning the meaning of her husband's aggression against her speaks to not only the actual sexual violence, threat to her life, and related dissociation from the rape, but also the symbolic meaning of her traumatic experience, which involved feelings of worthlessness or like a "nobody," a feeling she described as a familiar one that dates back to her life prior to marriage. The ways in which this external traumatic event is processed in the context of her life preceding her marriage (childhood, adolescence, early adulthood) and following her divorce is a focus of psychodynamic psychotherapy.

Maureen's internalization of feeling like a "nobody" is an aspect of her trauma that has implications for her personality. Mathews and Chu[15] highlighted the way in which actual trauma and the memory of trauma are composed of external and internal elements. One example of this intersection of the external and internal aspects of trauma occurs when an adult survivor of childhood sexual abuse remembers being threatened by an abusive parent, and at the same time remembers his/her own imagined or fantasied feelings of terror, guilt, or rage. A fantasy of feeling guilty or responsible for the abuse is then met with the terrible reality of abuse. These interactions between the abuse and beliefs about the self in relation to the abuser become components of personality functioning, as evidenced in vulnerability to fragmentation, dissociation, feelings of self-blame, helplessness, problems in forming and maintaining supportive relationships, limited range of defenses and positive ways of coping with stress, and difficulty with authenticity and positive life change in adulthood.[15]

Psychodynamic approaches conceptualize psychological distress, including that resulting from trauma, as involving a narrative of the self and the external world as evolving.[2,29] How trauma is experienced for a survivor changes with time, as new experiences influence self-image and interactions with others. Additionally, the therapeutic relationship contributes to these evolving narratives, as trauma may be understood and experienced differently by a survivor as he/she works through enactments within the therapy that reflect aspects of the traumatic experience. For example, Malcolm, a thirty-eight-year-old survivor of rape in his early twenties, stated, "I want to start trusting you (the therapist), but it still feels like if I start talking about more details, then you might see me as weak or something." At this point in his treatment, Malcolm acknowledged the importance of trusting me, which he was unable to do early in our work, as he worried that trusting me would signify weakness or vulnerability.

Over the course of several months, he was able to share with me his concerns about trust more explicitly and how this difficulty fits with the actual rape. In the second year of psychotherapy, he expressed in one session, "I've told you what happened to me (the rape). You seem like you can handle it. I've always been a strong person, independent. This feels different in here to talk about this stuff. Maybe this is being strong . . . I don't know." Malcolm's statement indicates a movement toward a possibly different narrative of his internal experience of the actual traumatic experience and specifically his self-image as someone who is still strong and independent even when he feels vulnerable. Psychoanalysts such as Davies and Frawley[8] have also suggested that different self states or ego states experienced by the survivor should be explored in psychotherapy as a way of ongoing elaboration of narrative of trauma and of the self. In other words, psychodynamic therapy involves the therapist and client to explore fully the various aspects of the self that have been shaped by the traumatic experience, how constructions of the self may change with context and time, and eventually how an individual makes meaning of his/her trauma and develops new safe and fulfilling relationships.

ATTENDING TO SOCIOCULTURAL CONTEXT

In recent years, psychodynamic approaches have increasingly considered the role of sociocultural context to be a critical element of understanding the effects of traumatic experience on survivors of trauma. Traumatic experience and expression of distress are influenced by cultural beliefs, sociocultural histories, and community of reference. A survivor of sexual assault who has been raised with a cultural value on modesty of clothing style may experience a sense of guilt and wonder whether or not she had somehow provoked the assault. In another instance, a survivor of sexual abuse who strongly identifies with a religious belief that denounces premarital sex may feel that she is damaged or dirty. In a different example, a survivor for whom it is more culturally compatible or congruent to express psychological distress through physical symptoms may find it challenging to talk about the sexual trauma in psychotherapy. Sociocultural context further involves the issue of language. For bilingual or multilingual survivors, memories may be processed in the first or native language, contributing to varying experiences of sexual trauma in each language. Some of my clients who are bilingual have expressed that it is easier to talk about their childhood sexual abuse in English rather than a native language, as the abuser was someone who spoke the native language and the abuse "occurred" in the native language. For other clients, the reverse is more compatible with their experience, when it is important to talk about the traumatic experience in the native language. In some cases, speaking in one's own native language can facilitate a more immediate connection to and accessibility to a wider range of feelings associated with the traumatic experience. These variations in sociocultural context hold important meanings for the ways in which social roles and identifications shape aspects of self-experience in the case of sexual trauma.[30,31]

Social structures such as racial hierarchies evident in many societies, including the United States, further engender experiences of good and bad self states, involving feelings of devaluation and shame imposed by dominant society to members of racial and ethnic minority groups.[30,32] Racial identity and ethnic identity have important implications for survivors' constructions of sexual violence, and their identifications with and relationships with their communities of reference. Daniel[33] has written about the negative impact of racial and sexual trauma directed against African American women. She highlighted the problem of negotiating identity in the context of historical and ongoing racial injustice and sexualization of African American women by dominant society. In such instances, survivors of sexual violence cope with multiple burdens imposed by social context, contributing to silence and invisibility of traumatic stress.[31,34] The invisibility of traumatic stress experienced by many ethnic minorities contributes to the perpetuation of stereotypes and racially driven trauma perpetrated by abusers from both within and outside the survivor's racial and/or ethnic group.

The experience of homophobia in conjunction with sexual trauma is further reflective of how social context can influence traumatic experience. Gay, lesbian, and bisexual (GLB) survivors of sexual violence remain largely neglected in the research literature. Russell, Jones, Barclay, and Anderson[35] pointed out that GLB survivors are often blamed for their abuse by others, contributing to feelings of powerlessness, shame, and fear. The lack of acceptance and homophobic reactions of significant people in a survivor's life can engender confusion about sexual, gender, and social identity and complicate the coming-out process.[35] Different forms of oppression such as racism, homophobia, sexism, and poverty compound the effects of sexual violence and are sometimes used to shift blame to the survivor.[36] Psychodynamic approaches to sexual assault consider the ways in which a survivor makes meaning of his/her social context as it shapes and informs his/her experience of trauma, and how social difference between therapist and client may influence the therapeutic relationship.[31,37]

RECOVERY AS COMPLEX AND MULTIDIMENSIONAL

Recovery from sexual trauma, from a psychodynamic perspective, is conceptualized as complex, involving multiple dimensions of exploration. A trauma-informed psychodynamic perspective focuses on the ways in which sexual trauma interfaces with internalized aspects of the trauma to give meaning to one's experience of the self, and therefore addresses conscious and unconscious dimensions of trauma. Similar to trauma theory, psychodynamic theory conceptualizes recovery from trauma as involving validation of the survivor's experience, integration of self-identity, improvement in affect tolerance, impulse control, organization of defenses and coping, and supportive interpersonal relationships.[2,38,39] Additionally, the role of bearing witness and sharing power in the therapy relationship is a central goal of trauma-informed psychodynamic psychotherapy.[40]

The recovery process from a psychodynamic perspective is thought to be "structured and paced"[15] such that traumatic experience is discussed in the context of a safe therapeutic space. The initial stages of therapy involve the development of safety and trust, and the pace of therapy is largely directed by the client. Many survivors who enter psychotherapy are coping with significant difficulties with trust, and through developing a safe and consistent relationship with a therapist, develop an increasing capacity to trust others and recognize and tolerate their own feelings of anger toward others and themselves. During the early phase, the therapist validates the survivor's intense emotional suffering connected with the traumatic event and facilitates the survivor's attempts to tolerate and accept these painful feelings. A major goal of this initial stage of recovery involves improving one's self-care and safety in areas such as substance abuse, self-injury, and high-risk or dangerous situations where a survivor could be victimized. Safety and self-care are achieved through a growing awareness of the impact of trauma on one's life, mobilizing resources to increase day-to-day functioning, developing strategies to express one's feelings more effectively, and encouraging one's connections to others who are supportive.[2,15]

As a survivor develops adequate safety in his/her life, therapeutic work increasingly involves a more in-depth discussion of traumatic history, at a pace that is tolerable and therapeutic. As this exploration can be experienced as retraumatizing, it is critical that safety and supports are well enough established for this work to proceed in an effective way. An important aspect of this phase of treatment is the exploration of the details of the trauma and what may be fantasy connected with and produced in the context of trauma. Mathews and Chu[15] suggest that the middle stage of psychodynamic psychotherapy entails a period of mourning of both the sexual trauma as well as what was lost as a result of the sexual trauma, such as the wish for a loving parent or a trusted significant other. Additionally, this phase of recovery involves remembering and reconstructing traumatic experiences into a more coherent narrative than what previously was remembered by the survivor. Traumatic memories that were previously dissociated may emerge in the context of the interaction between the therapist and the client, in which the therapist may be experienced unconsciously by the survivor as a loving parent or friend and at other times as an aggressor or perpetrator. The therapist may also develop a wide range of feelings, such as anger, helplessness, and sadness, as the survivor discusses traumatic experiences. It is by working through the transference and countertransference that traumatic memories and reconstruction of these memories gradually inform the survivor's present experience and understanding of the traumatic event(s). This process of remembering and reconstruction typically involves grief and mourning in which a survivor may experience intense feelings of loss connected to the trauma, as he/she begins to make sense of what has happened in his/her life.[2,8,15]

The final stages of trauma recovery involve the consolidation of new insights, practicing new skills, developing new relationships, and transforming identity.[2,15] In this phase, a survivor actively seeks to confront and engage with his/her fears and seeks positive, mutual relationships with others. For example, a survivor of rape may work more actively to experience sexual pleasure with a partner, something that he/she felt was impossible or difficult to attain following the rape. In other cases, survivors are engaged with social action as a form of empowerment and healing. One recent example of this type of engagement involves the survivors of sexual abuse by priests who have spoken out about their experiences of sexual trauma and its impact on their lives. A survivor's public expression of these experiences can help to transform the stifling and sometimes debilitating silence of sexual trauma for the survivor and other survivors and raise societal awareness of sexual violence directed against children and adolescents. While recovery from trauma has been described in the language of stages or phases, it is clear that recovery does not follow a linear path and that each phase may be revisited throughout one's life, particularly during important life transitions.

Psychodynamic perspectives further consider the centrality of resilience in the trauma recovery process. While this approach is deeply concerned with the losses incurred in sexual trauma, it also attends to how a survivor has coped with and adapted to unbearable circumstances and betrayal. This approach honors survivors' ability to not only survive the trauma but also to create stability in various aspects of their lives. Most of my clients who are survivors of sexual assault have mobilized their internal strengths and capacities and external resources to achieve success in important areas of their lives, such as academic achievement and raising children in a safe environment. Lily, a forty-year-old survivor of rape, stated, "I don't think anyone now could guess that I was raped. I know I come off strong because I'm a leader at work. I wonder sometimes, though, if someone can tell." Lily's comment speaks to the complex nature of trauma, resilience, and recovery, in which parts of her experience are separated from each other. Nonetheless, her ability to transform her traumatic experience is evident.

Resilience in the face of sexual trauma can be conceptualized as multidimensional, including individual, family, and community levels.[39] While individualistic notions of resilience tend to focus on an individual's personality traits or achievement as characterizing resilience, collective resilience is defined through positive connections with family members and larger communities.[31] Engaging in groups for the purpose of social action and change compose other ways of mobilizing one's supports and resilience. Herman,[41] in a study of restorative justice among victims of violent crime, found that the role of community support is critical in helping a survivor who chooses to take legal action against the perpetrator, as the survivor's anger toward the perpetrator is often stigmatized in the legal system and more generally in society. The wish for communities to take a stand against the offense was clearly voiced among the participants in Herman's study.[41]

Psychotherapy can be one critical means through which a survivor accesses his/her resilience, as the therapeutic space is one in which the survivor feels empowered and gains a sense of agency in his/her own life. A trauma-informed psychodynamic approach to recovery considers the importance of addressing sexual violence on multiple levels, all of which may help a survivor to engage with unique and multiple layers of traumatic experience. This approach seeks to facilitate the ability of the survivor to voice his/her own narrative and aims to help the survivor to gain insights that he/she will integrate with new relationships and a transformed sense of self. Such work requires attention to both what is lost and sustained in the traumatic experience. The following case example illustrates the way that a trauma-informed, psychodynamic approach to recovery from sexual assault contributes to the changes that I have mentioned.

CASE EXAMPLE

Lorna is a thirty-two-year-old single, second-generation Chinese American woman, who sought psychotherapy to cope with increasing anxiety in her relationships with her family and her boyfriend. I worked with Lorna for three years in weekly individual psychotherapy. When I first met Lorna, she was enrolled in a graduate program in a finance-related discipline. Lorna had seen a therapist in her third year of college when she had experienced recurrent nightmares about being locked in a room by her paternal aunt. While working with a female therapist for four months in college, she disclosed to her therapist that she had been sexually abused by her paternal aunt, who was in charge of taking care of her periodically throughout her childhood (ages five through nine). Lorna had not told anyone other than her best friend in college that she had been abused in childhood. After learning that her therapist was relocating, she decided to end psychotherapy, although she reported feeling helped by her therapist. Approximately five years later, she was raped by a former boyfriend whom she had dated for a year. The rape occurred after he had followed her home after a party at a mutual friend's home. Lorna expressed that she had ended the relationship because she felt "emotionally and financially controlled" by him. After the rape, she called a friend who helped her access medical care. Lorna decided to not press charges against her former boyfriend. Other than speaking with her physician about the rape, she has not discussed it with anyone in depth.

Lorna was born and raised in a poor, urban neighborhood in the United States. Her parents immigrated to the United States prior to her birth and worked in a family business owned by her father's older brother. Lorna has a younger brother who apparently did not suffer any sexual abuse, although she recalls that both she and her brother were often left alone to care for themselves for long periods of time. Her parents worked long hours and had minimal financial resources to access child care. Lorna's paternal aunt was one of their relatives who was apparently available to take care of her and her brother while her parents were working. Her aunt sexually molested her and threatened to hurt her, her brother, and her parents if Lorna ever revealed the abuse to anyone. The abuse continued until she was nine years old, after her paternal aunt and uncle divorced and relocated to different parts of the country. Lorna remembered that she did not sleep or eat well throughout her childhood and adolescence. When she was an adolescent, her parents tried to establish a closer relationship with her and her brother as they attained financial stability. However, she remembers feeling lonely and tended to withdraw from them when they tried to become more involved in her life.

Lorna enjoyed attending school, as she felt that this gave her a "break" from her home life. She excelled academically and studied dance for several years. At the same time, she experienced difficulty with fitting in socially with the other children at school. She described herself as shy and feeling as though she was different because of her Chinese background. While school felt like a place of respite in some ways, Lorna continued to feel lonely. In college, she developed a few close friendships and attempted to create an identity that was separate from her parents and from other Chinese Americans. After graduating from college, Lorna worked in a bank for several years and then decided to pursue a graduate degree. During her years of working at the bank, she began to use marijuana regularly to cope with her feelings of loneliness, depression, and anxiety. The substance use increased in frequency after she had been raped. She eventually decided to seek help from a therapist to address her long-standing distress, after one of her professors noticed her anxiety in interacting with others.

When I first met Lorna, she talked about her difficulty in talking openly about the sexual abuse and the rape. She was unsure of whether or not talking about the sexual trauma would be helpful to her. Our initial work focused on establishing her personal sense of safety, as she joined Narcotics

Anonymous to help address her ongoing substance use. Lorna and I also worked on breathing and relaxation exercises to help her cope with her immediate feelings of anxiety. As our work progressed, we talked increasingly about the ways in which she coped with her traumatic experiences, including her tendency to avoid painful memories by disconnecting herself through substance use. Over the next several months, Lorna spoke more about her family life, and eventually details of her sexual abuse and rape. She tended to focus primarily on her feelings of shame and self-blame concerning the sexual abuse and often wondered why she was chosen by her aunt to be abused. She was not able to imagine the possibility of telling her parents about what had happened to her, as she continued to feel distant from her family and worried that they would blame her for the abuse. At the same time, Lorna hoped for a closer relationship with her parents, particularly since her relationship with her boyfriend had deepened. She was also concerned about telling her boyfriend about her sexual trauma both in childhood and adulthood. While exploring details of her trauma in therapy, Lorna stated, "I always wanted to hide what had happened to me, maybe so that I wouldn't have to believe that everything actually happened. Now, it feels like I can't escape it. It keeps creeping up no matter how much I want it to go away."

Lorna further struggled with her Chinese American identity, as she associated intensely negative feelings about her heritage with her abusive aunt, whom she remembered as a "traditional Chinese woman," at least in the perception of others in the family. She also had mixed feelings about speaking in Chinese, as she simultaneously wished to distance herself from her painful traumatic memories and connect with positive aspects of being of Chinese heritage. When her boyfriend who is White, European American, urged her to teach him more about Chinese culture, Lorna reacted with ambivalence even though she appreciated his efforts to build intimacy with her. As their relationship deepened, Lorna became increasingly anxious about her intimacy with him and worried that he may leave her if he learned about her sexual trauma. In a session during the second year of psychotherapy, she stated, "I don't know how I'm going to talk about the rape with him. I think he would think the sexual abuse was weird but not my fault. It might not be the same with the rape. He might think I did something to provoke this." I asked her if these concerns were more reflective of her own view of herself, and not only her concerns about her boyfriend's perspective. Lorna responded, "I feel like this could be me—someone who is responsible in some way. Maybe I could have stopped it. I don't want to think about losing him (boyfriend). He is the first person I feel safe with." We continued to discuss the ways in which Lorna was both traumatized by her aunt and her former boyfriend, how she had internally constructed her trauma, and its implications for her image of herself and for what was possible for her in the future.

As Lorna's work progressed further, she began to talk with her closest female friends about her sexual trauma and her concerns about her relationship with her boyfriend and was no longer using marijuana. She also began to explore friendships with a few Chinese American peers and to attend cultural events, such as Chinese music and dance programs. During this time, she also wondered about her attachment to me. She stated, "I'm feeling like I rely on you a lot more than what I thought when I first started seeing you." She talked about her concern that we would end the treatment before she felt ready. We discussed the ways in which our relationship at times felt as though she had little power, and we agreed that our work would end when she decided that she was ready to end it, and when we had adequate time to talk about ending the work. We also talked about the ways in which she may have experienced having a female therapist who is of a South Asian background, particularly when considering her abuse by a female caregiver. The issue of power in our relationship was critical to Lorna's feelings of safety and to addressing her anxiety, substance use, and loneliness, all of which were directly related to her sexual trauma.

CONCLUDING COMMENTS

Lorna's case illustrates some basic foundations of trauma-informed, psychodynamic psychotherapy as a path to recovery from sexual violence, including attending to the horrible realities of her sexual abuse and rape, her coping with these experiences, her ongoing concerns about safety, her internal constructions about the abuse and about herself, her resilience, and her relational life both within and outside of psychotherapy. While Lorna's recovery extends beyond our work together, my hope was that she is able to integrate her new insights to her life in an ongoing way. She decided to end treatment as she relocated out of the area to begin her career. Lorna stated in our last sessions that she would resume psychotherapy with another therapist when she felt that she could benefit from this work again in the future. Lorna's recovery, as with many other survivors of sexual trauma, is one that will involve continued negotiation of her traumatic past and internal struggles throughout life transitions, as she moves toward a more coherent sense of self and a more satisfying relational life.

While a psychodynamic path to recovery typically entails a survivor's engagement with psychotherapeutic treatment, aspects of this perspective can be integrated with other forms of healing from trauma. In particular, the psychodynamic focus on safety in relationships, coping and defenses used in the face of trauma, emotions and memory, internal constructions and meanings of traumatic experience, social context, and individual strengths are all relevant to healing from sexual trauma. Each of these aspects of trauma is especially important to explore in recovery, in light of the complex and multidimensional nature of sexual trauma.

STRATEGIES FOR SELF-CARE

1. Increasing safety
   A. Identify and record in a journal people, places, and situations that are emotionally and physically safe.
   B. Attend to your physical needs, such as eating a balanced diet, exercising, and getting adequate sleep.
   C. Read literature informing you about the effects of trauma on the individual and/or his/her family.
   D. Identify and engage in activities that decrease stress. These activities might include physical exercise (walking, jogging, yoga), dance, listening to music, playing a musical instrument, painting, watching a movie or a show that is a comedy, meeting with a supportive friend or family member.
   E. Identify triggers (people and surroundings) that increase stress. What is a typical way that you would manage this stress? Write down in a journal or tell a supportive person in your life how you may try to use a positive coping strategy to deal with this stress.
2. Coping with traumatic memories
   A. Write down in a journal memories of the traumatic event. If and when you feel that you want to read what you have written, read your journal.
   B. Talk about your memories in a pace that is comfortable for you with a trusted friend or family member.
   C. Allow yourself the time and space to think about the memories. You may choose to schedule a specific amount of time in the day or evening to reflect on the memories, so that you feel more in control of your memories.
   D. Practice relaxation strategies, such as yoga, meditation, quiet reflection, and breathing.
3. Forming positive connections
   A. Identify and write in a journal what you hope for in your future.
   B. Identify your major goals in a relationship with a significant other. What is it that you hope for in a relationship with a family member or a romantic partner? What are your expectations? Write your thoughts in a journal or talk with a trusted friend or family member.

C. Continue engaging in activities that relieve stress as you take new risks in building new, positive relationships.

D. Discuss your concerns about your relationships with someone whom you trust.

E. Explore ways in which you may connect with broader social action. One example is to volunteer your time in an effort to promote safe and healthy relationships.

REFERENCES

1. Harvey, M.R., & Harney, P.A. (1997). Addressing the aftermath of interpersonal violence: The case for long-term care. *Psychoanalytic Inquiry, 17,* 29–44.
2. Herman, J.L. (1997). *Trauma and recovery.* New York: Basic Books.
3. van der Kolk, B.A. (1997). The psychobiology of posttraumatic stress disorder. *Journal of Clinical Psychiatry, 58(Suppl 9),* 16–24.
4. Shedler, J. (2010). The efficacy of psychodynamic psychotherapy. *American Psychologist, 65*(2), 98–109.
5. Boulanger, G. (2002). The cost of survival: Psychoanalysis and adult onset trauma. *Contemporary Psychoanalysis, 38,* 17–44.
6. Krupnick, J.L. (2002). Brief psychodynamic treatment of PTSD. *Journal of Clinical Psychology, 58,* 919–932.
7. Schottenbauer, M.A., Glass, C.R., Arnkoff, D.B., & Gray, S.H. (2008). Contributions of psychodynamic approaches to treatment of PTSD and trauma: A review of the empirical treatment and psychopathology literature. *Psychiatry, 71*(1), 13–34.
8. Davies, J.M., & Frawley, M.G. (1994). *Treating the adult survivor of childhood sexual abuse: A psychoanalytic perspective.* New York: Basic Books.
9. Fonagy, P., & Bateman, A. (2008). The development of borderline personality disorder: A mentalizing model. *Journal of Personality Disorders, 22*(1), 4–21.
10. Lyons-Ruth, K., & Jacobovitz, D. (1999). Attachment disorganization: Unresolved loss, relational violence and lapses in behavioral and attentional strategies. In J. Cassidy & P.R. Shaver (Eds.), *Handbook of attachment theory and research,* pp. 520–554. New York: Guilford.
11. Weinfield, N., Sroufe, L.A., & Egeland, B. (2000). Attachment from infancy to early adulthood in a high risk sample: Continuity, discontinuity and their correlates. *Child Development, 71,* 695–702.
12. Davies, J.M. (1996). Linking the "pre-analytic" with the postclassical: Integration, dissociation, and the multiplicity of the unconscious process. *Contemporary Psychoanalysis, 32,* 553–576.
13. Silverman, D.K. (2007). A despairing, repetitive scream for the loss of the body electric. *Psychoanalytic Inquiry, 27*(2), 155–165.
14. Smith, J. (2004). Reexamining psychotherapeutic action through the lens of trauma. *Journal of American Academy of Psychoanalysis, 32,* 613–631.
15. Mathews, J.A., & Chu, J.A. (1997). Psychodynamic therapy for patients with early childhood trauma. In P.S. Appelbaum, L.A. Uyehara, & M.R. Elin, (Eds.),

Trauma and memory: Clinical and legal controversies, pp. 316–343. New York: Oxford University Press.

16. Munroe, C.D., Kibler, J.L., Ma, M., Dollar, K.M., & Coleman, M. (2010). The relationship between posttraumatic stress symptoms and sexual risk: Examining potential mechanisms. *Psychological Trauma: Theory, Research, Practice, and Policy*, 2(1), 49–53.

17. Brener, N.D., McMahon, P.M., Warren, C.W., & Douglas, K.T. (1999). Forced sexual intercourse and associated health-risk behaviors among female college students in the United States. *Journal of Consulting and Clinical Psychology*, 67, 252–259.

18. Shibusawa, T., Gilbert, L., El-Bassel, N., & Engstrom, M. (2004). HIV-risk among mid-life and older minority women in a methadone treatment program. *The Gerontologist*, 44, 291.

19. Gartner, R.B. (1997). Considerations in the psychoanalytic treatment of men who were sexually abused as children. *Psychoanalytic Psychology*, 14, 13–41.

20. Lord, S.A. (2008). Therapeutic work with trauma, revictimization, and perpetration: Bearing witness, offering hope, embracing despair. *Psychoanalytic Social Work*, 15(2), 110–131.

21. Pearlman, L.A., & Courtois, C.A. (2005). Clinical applications of the attachment framework: Relational treatment of complex trauma. *Journal of Traumatic Stress*, 18(5), 449–459.

22. Schore, A.N. (2002). Advances in neuropsychoanalysis, attachment theory, and trauma research: Implications for self psychology. *Psychoanalytic Inquiry*, 22, 433–484.

23. Black, M.J. (2007). Enhancing the therapeutic experience: A relational commentary on Judith Pickles' case. *Psychoanalytic Inquiry*, 27(1), 66–86.

24. Lachmann, F.M., & Beebe, B. (1997). Trauma, interpretation, and self-state transformations. *Psychoanalysis and Contemporary Thought*, 20, 269–291.

25. Nemiroff, H., Schindler, R., & Schreiber, A. (2000). An interpersonal psychoanalytic approach to treating adult survivors of childhood sexual abuse. *Contemporary Psychoanalysis*, 36, 665–684.

26. Stern, D.B. (1983). Unformulated experience. *Contemporary Psychoanalysis*, 19, 71–99.

27. Bromberg, P.M. (1996). Standing in the spaces: The multiplicity of self and the psychoanalytic relationship. *Contemporary Psychoanalysis*, 32, 509–535.

28. Tummala-Narra, P. (2001). Asian trauma survivors: Identity, loss, and recovery. *Journal of Applied Psychoanalytic Studies*, 3(3), 243–258.

29. Sarnat, J. (1997). Working in the space between psychoanalytic and trauma oriented approaches to stories of abuse. *Gender and Psychoanalysis*, 2, 79–102.

30. Bodnar, S. (2004). Remember where you come from: Dissociative process in multicultural individuals. *Psychoanalytic Dialogues*, 14, 581–603.

31. Tummala-Narra, P. (2007). Conceptualizing trauma and resilience across diverse contexts: A multicultural perspective. *Journal of Aggression, Maltreatment, and Trauma*, 14(1/2), 33–53.

32. Boyd-Franklin, N. (1989). *Black families in therapy: A multisystems approach*. New York: Guilford.

33. Daniel, J.H. (2000). The courage to hear: African American women's memories of racial trauma. In L.C. Jackson & B. Greene (Eds.), *Psychotherapy with African American women: Innovations in psychodynamic perspective and practice*, pp. 126–144. New York: Guilford.

34. Bryant-Davis, T., Chung, H., & Tillman, S. (2009). From the margins to the center: Ethnic minority women and the mental health effects of sexual assault. *Trauma, Violence, & Abuse, 10*(4), 330–357.

35. Russell, J.D., Jones, R.A., Barclay, K., & Anderson, M. (2008). Managing transference and countertransference in the treatment of gay, lesbian and bisexual survivors of childhood sexual abuse. *Journal of Gay and Lesbian Mental Health, 12*(3), 227–243.

36. Tummala-Narra, P. (2005). Addressing political and racial terror in psychotherapy. *American Journal of Orthopsychiatry, 75*(1), 19–26.

37. Altman, N. (2010). The analyst in the inner city. New York: Routledge.

38. Alpert, J.L. (1994). Analytic reconstruction in the treatment of an incest survivor. *Psychoanalytic Review, 81,* 217–235.

39. Harvey, M.R. (2007). Toward an ecological understanding of resilience in trauma survivors: Implications for theory, research, and practice. *Journal of Aggression, Maltreatment & Trauma, 14*(1-2), 9–32.

40. Pickles, J. (2007). Alone together: The case of Judy and Ann. *Psychoanalytic Inquiry, 27*(2), 106–124.

41. Herman, J.L. (2005). Justice from the victim's perspective. *Violence Against Women, 11*(5), 571–602.

17

Psychoeducation to Reduce Distress and Promote Adaptive Coping among Adult Women Following Sexual Assault

Joanne L. Davis, Heidi S. Resnick, and Rachael M. Swopes

According to a national survey, approximately 18% of American women will experience an attempted or completed rape in their lifetime.[1] The course of recovery following a sexual assault may vary across individuals as a function of different factors including individual, event-related variables, pre- and postassault stressors, social support, and prior learning history.[2] Some people may experience few symptoms until days, weeks, or months after the assault. Some people may naturally heal from a trauma and not ever experience more than transient adverse reactions, while others may develop symptoms of psychological disorders.[3] However, when someone experiences a traumatic event and resulting symptoms, she may wonder "Is this normal?" "Will I get better?" "Do I need to get some help?" or "Am I alone?" She may believe that life will never be the same again or not know what to expect in terms of recovery, or if recovery is even a possibility. The survivor may wonder if there is anyone out there who can help her through this difficult situation.

Psychoeducation provided after a traumatic event can help answer these and other questions for the survivor, as well as her friends and family. Psychoeducation also can provide information about adaptive coping strategies that can be utilized to minimize some of the naturally occurring posttraumatic distress.[4] According to Phoenix, such strategies can also be used to avoid maladaptive strategies such as substance use that might lead to increased symptoms or adverse long-term consequences.[4] While psychoeducation has the potential to provide benefits to survivors of sexual violence, limited research has examined the efficacy of psychoeducation alone to impact short- and long-term outcomes in terms of symptoms and functionality following sexual violence. Our chapter focuses primarily on the use of psychoeducation as a component of secondary intervention approaches in which information is delivered relatively soon after a highly stressful event (e.g., assault) has occurred. In addition, our primary focus is on effects of sexual violence occurring to adult women. It should be noted, however, that psychoeducation content describing possible reactions following a traumatic event, the theories behind development and maintenance of such reactions, and strategies for successful coping and related rationale are also integral components of traditional (e.g., tertiary interventions) treatment for post-traumatic stress disorder (PTSD) and other psychological disorders,[5,6] as well as included within multiple-session early interventions that also include additional treatment strategies such as imaginal and in-vivo exposure to trauma-related cues.[7,8]

WHAT IS PSYCHOEDUCATION?

Psychoeducation is considered delivery of information aimed at preventing or reducing problems following exposure to a potentially traumatic event and that may be used with individuals prior to exposure to an event or as secondary intervention to prevent or reduce problems that may develop after an event has occurred.[9] The content may include information about psychological or behavioral reactions that may occur, as well as coping strategies that may be helpful. As noted by Wesseley and colleagues, information may be provided in different ways, and these might include written materials, direct verbal communication, or other media such as video, audio, or web-based delivery.[9] These methods may vary from purely informational, or passive, approaches to more active therapist-led interventions.[10] For example, one might hand out pamphlets or brochures. The Internet is now an easily accessible way to distribute large amounts of information. Help lines and call centers may be able to provide information to someone in crisis, and widespread media outlets such as television or radio are efficient ways to disseminate information. Self-help books attempt to provide step-by-step guidance through a crisis. In addition, some counselors are trained to provide psychoeducation either as stand-alone services or as part of larger interventions. Psychoeducation provides information but may also include additional components, such as teaching cognitive behavioral tasks.[10] It is important that content and delivery modes be evaluated in terms of possible efficacy and effectiveness of information delivery. Additional information will be provided later in this chapter regarding extant knowledge about efficacy of these various techniques.

IMPORTANT ELEMENTS OF PSYCHOEDUCATION

Phoenix discussed several key content areas that are often included in psychoeducation programs for trauma survivors.[4] First, information may be presented on the body's natural responses to stressful situations. This information can help normalize reactions that the individual may be experiencing, as well as provide information regarding what to expect in the future. Second, information may be discussed regarding trauma history and previous attempts at coping with stressful events. Third, general information related to the traumatic event or common reactions that may follow exposure may be presented. Fourth, the survivor may be taught new skills for coping with negative reactions (e.g, relaxation exercises, deep breathing, and ways to manage stress). Of course, this type of skills training is also part of various treatment approaches (e.g., cognitive-behavioral therapy), and as previously discussed, the literature is not always clear regarding what falls under the broad umbrella of psychoeducation.

Another important element to include is information identifying which reactions to trauma may benefit from more formal help seeking. Teaching an individual when to ask for help can be invaluable, as many people do not seek help following a traumatic event.[11] They may be afraid that they will be stigmatized for admitting that they were the victims of a trauma or that they need help. People may believe that they can handle it on their own, or they might believe that no treatments are available to help them with their symptoms. Educating survivors on the range of treatments available for common post-traumatic symptoms, such as PTSD, depression, or increased anxiety or substance use, might empower them to seek help. Psychoeducational materials could provide referrals to local clinicians or agencies along with specific information regarding available resources in the community. While many elements of post-trauma recovery are similar across types of traumatic events, the following provides information specific to sexual violence.

PSYCHOEDUCATION SPECIFIC TO SEXUAL VIOLENCE

Whether provided as a stand-alone intervention or part of a broader treatment intervention, a number of areas of information may be helpful to discuss with survivors, and potentially family members and friends, including facts about sexual violence, common immediate and long-term effects, positive coping skills, and times of high risk for relapse.

FACTS ABOUT SEXUAL VIOLENCE

Survivors of sexual violence may often feel that they are alone in their experience because they are not aware of how many other women have had similar experiences. It may be helpful for survivors to know that, unfortunately, sexual violence is far too common in our society. In addition to forcible rapes that include physical force or threat and that may include injuries related to assault, another type of rape occurs when a woman is incapacitated due to alcohol or drug use (incapacitated rape, or IR) and incapable of consent or control of the situation or when a drug is administered without knowledge or permission of the victim (drug or alcohol facilitated rape, or DAFR).[12] Kilpatrick and colleagues found that 14.6% of women in a general population sample reported a lifetime history of forcible rape while 5% reported a history of DAFR/IR.[12] Kilpatrick and colleagues also studied the prevalence of these types of rape within a college sample of women and found that 6.4% reported a lifetime history of forcible rape and 6.4% reported a lifetime history of DAFR/IR.[12]

Sexual violence that entails unwanted sexual contact or attempted sexual assault, whether due to force or threat or incapacitation of the victim, is not the fault of the victim. Unfortunately, however, victims of sexual violence often blame themselves for the assault.[13] It is important that the survivor receive the message from friends, families, and professionals that regardless of what she did or did not do during the assault, it is not her fault. People do what they need to do during an assault to survive it—sometimes this may be attempting to fight the attacker off, sometimes this may be acquiescing to the perpetrator's demands. Whatever the survivor did may have helped her live through the experience.

COMMON EFFECTS: IMMEDIATE AND LONG TERM

People respond to sexual assaults in a number of ways. Some feel acute distress, while others may feel little distress at first or may be in a state of shock or feel numb, then experience more difficulties later on, sometimes even years after the event. Still others report experiencing few difficulties at all.[2;14] Recovery may also seem like a "one step forward, three steps back" kind of process at times, which can be very frustrating and may increase feelings of hopelessness and distress. Some individuals may be at higher risk for experiencing significant distress following a sexual assault. For example, research finds that individuals who have a previous history of trauma, which is not uncommon among victims of rape,[15] may experience a cumulative impact of these events and experience more symptomatology than someone without a previous history.[16;17] Individuals whose lives were threatened or who perceived life threat may also be at greater risk for significant distress.[18]

Most individuals who report experiences of sexual violence to police, rape crisis, or other authorities appear to experience initial symptoms of PTSD,[19] although not everyone will meet criteria for the disorder. PTSD includes three categories of symptoms including reexperiencing symptoms (e.g., flashbacks, nightmares, intrusive thoughts), avoidance symptoms (e.g,. not talking or thinking about the assault as well as avoiding people, places, and situations that remind them of the assault), and hyperarousal symptoms (e.g., always feeling on guard, difficulty falling or staying asleep).[20]

At first, these symptoms may be helpful—indeed acute responses of physiological arousal, hypervigilance, and so on, may have been what helped survivors to make it through the experience. They become problematic, however, when they keep occurring, after the danger is gone. Also, survivors may begin to be afraid of and react to things, people, and situations that are similar to the assault but were not present during the assault. For example, rape victims may grow to fear men who look like the perpetrator, then perhaps most men. When survivors fear an increasing number of people, places, or things, they are likely to experience physiological and psychological responses to these stimuli and begin to avoid them. Not only will this restrict a person's life considerably, but it will keep the survivor at a high state of arousal, which may wear her down psychologically and physically.[17]

Other consequences after a sexual assault may include feeling confused, angry, sad, anxious, and afraid, having panic attacks, interpersonal problems, self-destructive and impulsive behaviors, dissociative symptoms, somatic complaints, feelings of shame, despair, and hopelessness, and social withdrawal.[23] Experiencing a sexual assault can also change how we think about ourselves, other people, and the world.[21] This may happen particularly in the areas of powerlessness, esteem, safety, intimacy, and trust.[22] In fact, these areas have been called "stuck points"[25] and may be related to significant negative emotions and behaviors during wake time and may also show up in bad dreams and nightmares.

COPING SKILLS

As noted above, psychoeducation also may involve information on coping skills. Although this may overlap with more in-depth therapeutic interventions, many coping skills do not require the assistance of a mental health professional. If survivors have not had an occasion to develop such skills in the past, however, the assistance of a mental health professional may be useful. Coping strategies generally fall into one of two categories—adaptive or maladaptive. Adaptive strategies include those that will draw on the survivor's natural strengths and help her to feel mentally and physically better. In the days and weeks following the sexual assault, self-care is very important, especially making sure that basic needs are being met, particularly for those areas comprising three primary indices of health: healthy eating, exercising, and sleeping well.

Many resources are available to help survivors cope with the experience of sexual violence. Maintaining a routine as much as possible including attending school, work, and social activities is important. While survivors may feel like isolating and withdrawing from others, it is important to utilize those social supports and activities that have helped in the past. These natural resources often include social supports that the individual typically turns to in times of stress: family, friends, community, and spiritual connections. While survivors may not wish to disclose everything about their experience to everyone, it may be important for them to let some people know that they are going through some hard times and need extra support.

If survivors do choose to disclose their experiences, they will likely come across a variety of responses. People often do not know how to respond to disclosures of sexual violence and reactions may range from support and love to anger at the perpetrator and desire for revenge to disbelief. Negative reactions to sexual violence disclosures are not uncommon.[23] There are numerous reasons why people have negative reactions, and even those who are generally supportive may have a difficult time coping with and understanding this event.[16] While there is little information on why others may react negatively, we do know that negative responses may be related to increased symptoms for the survivor and self-blame.[16] If survivors are struggling with sexual violence and have had difficulty with others' responses, it may be helpful for them to attend a support group of sexual violence survivors.

Many survivors benefit from engaging in activities to help themselves feel mentally and physically stronger. Some activities include working out at a gym or at home, taking a martial arts class, and learning other means of self-defense. Another way for survivors to feel empowered is to identify those situations or places that are not actually dangerous, but in which they feel afraid and try to face those head-on. This is generally called *exposure* and involves gradually facing fears until the situation no longer produces feelings of anxiety. Exposure is a key component of many of the best treatments available for PTSD, and some people will feel more comfortable trying this technique with the assistance of a mental health professional.

Many also find healing and empowerment from giving their time, money, or attention to others who have been through similar experiences.

Generally, survivors would not do this until they have experienced significant healing and recovery from their own experiences. There are a number of ways to give back, including volunteering for agencies that target sexual violence, becoming a sexual assault advocate, working to raise awareness of the issue, and helping community efforts to fight crime in general.

Other potential coping strategies include finding ways of reducing one's overall level of physiological and psychological arousal, becoming more relaxed and calm. Yoga, meditation, or progressive muscle relaxation may be helpful in learning new strategies for achieving relaxation in this stressful time. Bookstores often sell audio versions of relaxation scripts that survivors can listen to and follow along with when feeling distressed. It is important to keep in mind, however, that while many of the strategies mentioned above may be helpful, there is limited evidence to indicate that they will lead to long-term recovery on their own. Recovery will likely take engaging in a number of these strategies, the support of others, and possibly the help of a mental health professional who specializes in treating survivors of traumatic events.

Following a highly stressful or traumatic event, people may also engage in maladaptive coping strategies, especially if they have not learned adaptive coping strategies. Maladaptive strategies include drinking alcohol, using illicit drugs or misusing licit drugs, smoking, isolating from others, over- or undereating, and over- or undersleeping. Some of these strategies may be comforting and provide short-term relief from or avoidance of distress but are unlikely to be helpful in the long term and may actually be quite harmful. In general, attempts to escape from or avoid talking about or working through the assault for extended periods of time are associated with greater, not lesser distress.[24] Thus, psychoeducation can address these pitfalls and provide information about strategies to counteract such behaviors.

When to seek additional help. Knowledge can be very empowering, and understanding the facts about sexual violence and its aftermath, engaging in coping strategies that are based on empirically supported cognitive behavioral approaches, seeking help and support from friends and family, and taking care of themselves may be sufficient for some people to alleviate some distress and/or promote adaptive coping following an assault. For others, this may not be sufficient, and further help may be needed. Typically individuals choose to seek professional help when they are having a hard time doing things they used to do, including attending school, working, and engaging in social activities. While it is not unusual for these "normal" activities to be interrupted in the immediate aftermath of sexual violence, if the survivor continues to experience difficulties a few weeks following the event, she may want to talk to a mental health professional. Even if the survivor has made significant progress, there may be times when she may experience an increase in her distress level. New experiences of significant life stressors or additional traumatic events, anniversaries of the sexual assault, or encountering trauma-related stimuli may lead to increased distress.

This book describes a number of treatment options that exist for individuals who may be struggling to cope with the sexual assault on their own and want to seek professional help. Many of these treatments have been tested by researchers. The treatments have varying levels of study and support. A number of manuals are also available for use by practitioners and some for use by survivors themselves and are identified at the end of the chapter. Most approaches will include psychoeducation as well as in-depth intervention content.

EVIDENCE FOR USE OF PSYCHOEDUCATION

A recent (2008) series of articles in volume 71, issue 4, of the journal *Psychiatry* raised key issues about psychoeducation, including how to define it, limitations of existing data about its efficacy, and recommended future research questions and approaches. As noted by Wesseley and colleagues, research is needed to determine which types of information might be helpful, harmful, or have no appreciable impact.[9] They suggested that a potential negative consequence of psychoeducation is that symptoms might be prescribed or suggested when they otherwise might not be problematic and that psychoeducation might interfere with other naturalistic approaches to recovery such as use of existing social support networks.

Potential benefits of psychoeducation and risks of not providing information that might be helpful were also discussed,[5;6;25] as was the need for theoretical underpinnings, broader conceptualization of what might be included,[26] and questions of what might constitute sufficient and ecologically valid approaches.[27] The need for evaluation of psychoeducation was consistently recognized, and suggested factors to be controlled for or further studied included content, context of information delivery, targeted population (e.g., all exposed or those with risk factors that might include symptoms predictive of later problems, prior history of victimization), timing relative to event, duration, and depth of focus. The suggestion by Wesseley and colleagues to tailor content in ways that are designed to foster resilience was consistently noted as an optimal approach.[9]

Three studies cited by Wesseley et al.[9] evaluated the use of psychoeducation booklets given to individuals who had experienced a variety of traumatic events that led to injury[28;29] or automobile accident victims[30] who sought emergency hospital treatment. These studies, as well as a fourth study that included education alone as a condition compared with debriefing and assessment only in a mixed group of violent crime victims,[31] are reviewed here. Psychoeducation content in all cases appeared to include information about symptoms and possible help available. Content beyond that was difficult to determine across studies without more information. The content in the booklet used in the Scholes et al.[31] study may have been most comprehensive and was briefly described as including information about cognitive behavioral strategies to prevent or reduce symptoms associated with traumatic events.

The time of delivery of content across studies ranged from an average of three weeks postevent,[33] at least two weeks but within one month,[31] approximately one month,[32] or six to eight weeks postevent.[30] Participants in two of the studies were prescreened as either having symptoms indicative of acute stress disorder and increased risk of subsequent PTSD[31] or meeting symptom criterion score after an initial three-week assessment period.[32]

Results of two studies indicated significant reductions in symptoms of PTSD, depression, and/or other anxiety across time, with no differences as a function of psychoeducation as compared to assessment only or debriefing[33] or similarly high risk control.[31] Results of Ehlers et al.[32] were that attending multiple sessions of cognitive behavioral therapy was associated with significant reduction in PTSD, depression, anxiety, and disability compared to assessment only or self-help booklet. They also found that the self-help booklet did not appear to be more helpful than assessment only and was associated with poorer end state functioning and lower prevalence of asking for treatment. Findings from the Turpin et al.[30] study indicated reduced symptoms over time and few differences associated with psychoeducation. They reported that those in the control group were less depressed at follow-up and that there was a nonsignificant trend for higher reduction of PTSD cases in the control group as well. The authors raise the issue of potential lack of representativeness of recruited participants (approximately 10% of those who were eligible to participate). Those assigned to treatment and control groups did not differ on baseline measures of functioning; however, the extremely low recruitment rates in some studies call into question representativeness and make it difficult to evaluate utility of information that may be targeted broadly to the population seen in specific settings.

A limitation of the studies reviewed above is the lack of information about potential utility of psychoeducation delivered much sooner after an event has occurred. If information might usefully prevent or reduce symptoms of PTSD or other problems such as potential for alcohol or drug use as an avoidant coping strategy, it would be important to evaluate such strategies at earlier time points following a potentially traumatic event. As suggested by Kilpatrick, Cougle, and Resnick,[27] research that evaluates specific psychoeducation content in the early aftermath of traumatic events is warranted to answer questions about the utility of specific content of information as a preventive intervention. Such data would be useful in terms of evaluating types of informational messages, if any, in the shorter-term aftermath of specific stressor events. It is also important to consider the representativeness of samples included in such studies, whether or not they are selected based on additional risk characteristics.

EVALUATION OF PSYCHOEDUCATION IMPLEMENTED FOLLOWING RAPE OR OTHER SEXUAL ASSAULT

Psychoeducation alone or as part of multiple-session treatment has been evaluated within studies of early post-sexual-assault interventions designed to reduce acute distress and prevent or reduce longer-term problems such as PTSD. Mixed findings have been observed related to psychosocial early interventions that include psychoeducation as one component among cognitive behavioral approaches delivered within one month after a sexual assault. For example, Kilpatrick and Veronen found symptom improvement among victims of rape who received four to six hours of an early cognitive behavioral skills–based intervention between six and twenty-one days postassault, but improvement was not greater than that seen in the control group.[32] Foa and colleagues found that a brief multisession cognitive behavioral intervention delivered within one month postassault (including rape) was associated with reduced prevalence of PTSD post-treatment but not at a follow-up at 5.5 months postassault.[33] A subsequent study found reduced symptoms of PTSD and general anxiety associated with cognitive-behavioral treatment relative to supportive counseling at three months postassault but not at longer-term follow-up.[34] Foa and colleagues noted that finding may be consistent with cognitive behavioral intervention affecting earlier recovery postassault.[35]

With regard to interventions that may be more consistent with psychoeducation delivered apart from additional intervention components directed by a therapist, Resnick, Acierno, and colleagues developed a psychoeducational cognitive-behavioral intervention delivered in a video format titled *Prevention of Post-Rape Stress*.[35] The video comprises two major components: 1) *Medical Exam Preparation*, which includes information about the medical exam, supportive messages from health care providers and rape crisis advocates, and a woman modeling positive coping (not blaming self, positive statements about care seeking) during the exam; and 2) *Steps to Recovery*, including description of reactions that may occur during (e.g., panic or other physiological, cognitive, or behavioral reactions) or in the days and weeks after an assault, modeling of coping strategies in the aftermath of assault that are based on cognitive-behavioral approaches including in-vivo graduated exposure, behavioral activation, identification of cues or situations that may be associated with drug or alcohol use, and promotion of activities and contexts that do not involve substance use. A learning theory model of possible later reactions to reminders of assault is presented to promote a sense of understanding of how reactions may be maintained over time and to provide a rationale for in-vivo exposure exercises and strategies to counter potential avoidance behaviors including use of drugs or alcohol.

Extant studies of the *Prevention of Post-Rape Stress* intervention have been conducted with samples of those consecutively seeking post-rape medical care, without screening to identify individuals at additional high risk based on initial symptom profile. It should be noted, however, that over 90% of such patients may report symptoms sufficient to meet PTSD criteria at two weeks post-rape,[22] and as such they may be considered fairly high risk across the board. Preliminary data reported by Resnick and colleagues indicated that women who were shown the video were less distressed immediately following the medical exam, controlling for pre-exam self-reported distress.[37] Results indicated differences between women who had experienced prior sexual violence and women who had no previous history of sexual violence. Specifically, women who had experienced previous sexual violence showed positive effects of the treatment video in that they endorsed reduced frequency of PTSD and depression symptoms at a six-week follow-up. At the six-week follow-up, women in the video condition with no history of sexual violence had a higher PTSD symptom frequency count, but this effect was no longer statistically significant by the six-month follow-up.[20] A second report of findings with a larger sample of 268 participants found that among women and adolescents who reported recent preassault marijuana use, those who were in the intervention condition reported significantly lower frequency of marijuana use at each assessment point through six months postassault than preassault marijuana users who received standard care alone.[36]

Current research is ongoing to evaluate potential effects of the two-part *Prevention of Post-Rape Stress* intervention (NIDA, R01DA023099; PI Heidi Resnick and Patricia Frazier). Another study is currently evaluating the *Steps to Recovery* component only. While previous research examined the use of the full intervention shown prior to the sexual assault exam, a study currently under way is evaluating implementation of only the *Steps to Recovery* component of the video shown immediately *after* the sexual assault exam has been completed (OCAST HR-08-017, PI Joanne L. Davis). There are several potential advantages to such an approach, including shortening the amount of time needed to deliver the intervention by almost half and allowing for further refinement and focus on potential key psychoeducation elements. The advantageousness of this approach, of course, also hinges on demonstration that the shorter *Steps to Recovery* component delivered postexam is efficacious in terms of reduced distress at the medical exam time frame and/or reduced frequency of psychological reactions and targeted behaviors at later follow-up assessments.

Despite potential limitations in terms of longer-term effects (six months postassault) with regard to PTSD and depression symptoms, and limited extant research in general, whether psychoeducation delivered at early points or in specific contexts such as postassault medical care is beneficial in terms of prevention, early reduction of symptoms, or as a means of increasing knowledge about and accessing more in-depth services if needed, remain questions of interest with broader implications. Sexual assault victims who seek immediate postassault medical care are a high-risk group in terms of PTSD and other potential problems such as substance abuse. The medical exam is conceptualized as a potential stressful experience, and there may be benefit to providing information about adaptive coping skills, understanding of potential reactions, and supportive information. The focus at the medical exam is on compassionate and professional care as well as gathering forensic evidence in cases in which a criminal case is being investigated. Thus, complementary information about psychological reactions and ways to achieve a successful recovery may be feasible to incorporate if accepted by medical personnel and patients alike. If such content is helpful for some women in the medical exam context and in the initial weeks postassault (particularly women who may be most vulnerable in the aftermath of assault), the benefits of including it may outweigh the risks. The data from one study indicate that there may also be longer-term positive effects in terms of some behavioral outcomes.[38]

In addition, based on the extant literature, it would be expected that inclusion of additional, more in-depth content and multiple delivery or access opportunities would enhance efficacy and perhaps be associated with longer-term effects. It is possible that early psychoeducation may be beneficial as part of a more stepped approach in which booster content and integration with subsequent additional sessions or content is delivered. Such an approach was used by Zatzick et al., who implemented a motivational interviewing treatment targeting alcohol abuse at a hospital trauma unit for accident or assault victims who were positive for alcohol use and who were randomly assigned to treatment.[43] Booster sessions and case management were conducted over the course of follow-up, and empirically supported treatment for PTSD was offered for those who met criteria at three months postinjury. Those assigned to treatment were less symptomatic on measures of PTSD and less likely to meet criteria for alcohol abuse than those receiving standard care at long-term follow-up. Additional research is needed to evaluate whether psychoeducation is beneficial, optimal timing of delivery, coordination with other treatment components, and specific populations and contexts in which it might be helpful or potentially harmful. Future research might usefully explore whether psychoeducation at an early posttreatment time point would enhance efficacy of components delivered subsequently.

HOW DOES IT WORK?

This section is somewhat limited, given the few studies that find support for early, brief psychoeducation designed to promote recovery and to prevent or reduce PTSD symptoms or other problems that may occur following sexual assault. Theoretically, the research reviewed in the preceding section (with regard to psychoeducation integrated within multiple-session cognitive-behavioral therapy or as a more stand-alone approach) is conceptualized within behavioral and cognitive frameworks, and the psychoeducation content reflects an emphasis on nonavoidance of realistically safe cues, and other positive coping strategies such as engaging social support, maintaining positive activities, and not using drugs or alcohol to cope with distress. As such, the content included may be consistent with recommendations for promoting resilience, rather than symptom prescription, by fostering adaptive coping. The findings reported by Resnick et al.[20] indicated a significant moderating effect of prior history of rape on reported psychological distress outcomes. It was hypothesized that women with a prior history of assault, who were also at risk of more severe problems following a new assault, might have more of a range in terms of functioning such that the intervention could be helpful. It was also suggested that they might better understand the content of the intervention, and it may have been more salient given their prior history of assault and/or subsequent reactions including PTSD. Further examination of prior assault history or other factors that may relate to positive or negative effects of psychoeducation are critical to explore in additional research and have implications for future use of such interventions as broad based or restricted to groups that are high risk or most likely to benefit.

Given the potential for negative experiences or negative perceptions related to medical or legal service interactions by some sexual assault victims,[37] content promoting a supportive response on the part of health care and other service providers as well as content addressing blame attributions may positively impact the experience of women or adolescents at the time of the medical exam and/or help to promote cognitive interpretations about the incident that would be consistent with adaptive perspectives of perceived blame and/or control. Other possible factors include potential reduction of acute distress that may then affect strength of conditioned cues or avoidance behaviors.[7]

As noted by Resnick et al.,[38] there is empirical support for use of brief intervention strategies for substance abuse targeting both drug and alcohol abuse.[38,39, 40,41] Such brief interventions include individualized assessment and targeted feedback or strategies. The psychoeducation intervention reported in Resnick et al. was broad based, and thus content was not tailored based on individual history or attitudes regarding problem use or behavior change.[38] Information was presented that "some" women or girls may use more alcohol or drugs after an assault. Specific brief content was included that was designed to promote identification of situations that may be high risk for use of drugs or alcohol and engagement in activities in which drug use was not a component. In addition, discussion of avoidance of painful emotions via use of drugs or alcohol was included with disadvantages noted (potential for prolonged recovery period and risk for safety). It is possible that content directly related to potential disadvantages of drug use and strategies for coping or activities that do not involve drug use was helpful. In addition, content related to acceptance of emotional reactions such as sadness as painful but not dangerous may also decrease avoidance.

As suggested by Ruzek[28] and emphasized by Feldner and colleagues,[7] research that includes development and clarification of theoretical rationale underlying proposed intervention and careful measurement of potential effects is needed. Thus, research should move beyond assessment of symptoms over time. As they noted, measurement strategies should include evaluation of change in variables that are proposed as critical or important and that are targeted by intervention content. Examples may include knowledge change based on content delivered, changes in physiological arousal, use of social support, as well as changes in beliefs and/or changes in behaviors that are specifically addressed and that may mediate observed differences in functioning or quality of life. Measures of positive functioning as well as distress would also be consistent with evaluation of psychoeducation content designed to promote resilience.

SOURCES AND TOOLS

The information above may be helpful for the survivor to understand in order to move forward and continue on their road to recovery. Often, simply "knowing" this information is not enough—many people need to talk about what they are going through, read about the issue, or talk to others who have gone through similar experiences. Luckily, there are many resources that survivors can access for information on sexual assault and recovering from sexual assault. Survivors may want to speak to a mental health practitioner. A *psychologist, psychotherapist,* or *counselor* is someone with training in helping people with many different types of problems and issues. An important consideration for sexual assault survivors who may be interested in seeking help from a mental health practitioner is whether or not to find someone who has specialized training in issues of trauma and victimization. While many mental health practitioners have skills and knowledge that can be helpful, not all are familiar with the specific struggles facing survivors of sexual assault. Survivors may request the name and contact information for trauma specialists in their area from their primary care physicians, spiritual leader, the local mental health association, or state licensing boards for psychologists, social workers, and counselors. There are also databases established by professional organizations that list professionals and their stated areas of expertise by location (e.g., the American Psychological Association: www.apa.org; the Association for Behavioral and Cognitive Therapies: www.abct.org).

Many communities also have *rape crisis centers* that can provide a wealth of information and resources and may also provide counseling services. One service often provided is an advocate to accompany the survivor to the initial forensic exam and subsequent court appearances (if appropriate) and to provide important information about sexual assault. Many communities also have specially trained nurses to conduct the postassault forensic medical exams, sexual assault nurse examiners, who may also be a source to receive psychoeducation about sexual assault. Unfortunately, little information is currently available to determine the efficacy of information provided in this way. The few studies that have compared services as usual with services as usual plus a psychoeducational video–based intervention suggest that there may be an advantage to including the video intervention.

Medical personnel who conduct post-rape medical exams or mental health practitioners who see sexual assault survivors soon after the assault or at later points in time may consider providing handouts or pamphlets during the initial visit. They may also consider showing the brief video developed by Dr. Resnick, Dr. Acierno, and colleagues as a means of providing information and as a starting point for discussing other assault-related issues that the survivors may be struggling with. It is recommended that the efficacy of this video be evaluated by programs that use it and that they understand that research to evaluate its efficacy is ongoing. Current studies are under way to evaluate whether findings from the prior studies are replicated. In general the use of video to deliver psychoeducation content may have benefits over self-help booklet content since it does allow modeling of behaviors by individuals who might be relatable. It is possible that learning may be enhanced with the added component of being able to visualize implementation of skills. There is some support for use of video modeling as an efficacious tool to increase patient self-care behaviors as well as to educate and/or reduce anxiety or distress related to medical procedures.[42] As part of a Substance Abuse and Mental Health Services and Administration grant project (PI, Benjamin Saunders), the video has been made available for training and education purposes, as it is still undergoing evaluation. Additional potential use of the video is for training with medical professionals and rape crisis advocates. Thus, this information might be helpful for such professionals or volunteer advocates to get a better understanding of possible psychological reactions postassault, behavioral conceptualizations of reactions, and behavioral strategies that may promote adaptive coping and reduce distress and problematic coping strategies. The video is available for programs or researchers to view at www.musc.edu/saprevention. The site also includes a collateral brochure and instruction manual for the video, which are available for download.

A number of websites exist that provide information and psychoeducational resources related to experiencing traumatic events including sexual assault. It is important to note that all websites are not created equal and may not be reviewed for accuracy or based on scientifically derived information. The National Crime Victims Research and Treatment Center [NCVC] in Charleston, South Carolina, has been an important leader in research and clinical developments in the area of traumatic experiences broadly. The website of the NCVC includes a number of resources for clinicians and the public, including a four-page handout describing common reactions to experiencing a sexual assault [*Victim Reaction to Sexual Assault*; http://academicdepartments.musc.edu/ncvc/resources_prof/reports_prof.htm]. The International Society for Traumatic Stress Studies [www.istss.org] also has a number of resources available for practitioners and the lay public.

Numerous support groups exist for survivors of sexual assault. These may be conducted through or in affiliation with rape crisis centers. There also may be support groups run by independent practitioners or survivors themselves. While the nature of support groups varies from group to group, they generally consist of a group of same-gendered individuals who have all experienced some form of sexual assault. Many survivors take comfort in knowing that they are not alone and in the support they receive from some group members. Others may not be comfortable sharing their story within a group context or hearing other people's stories.

A number of self-help books or books about rape and sexual assault may also be of help for some survivors. Again, the quality of these is likely to vary considerably. It may be helpful to get some recommendations from a mental health practitioner for specific books. A number of treatment options exist for individuals who may be struggling to cope with the sexual assault on their own and want to seek professional help. Many of these treatments have been tested by researchers. The treatments have varying levels of study and support. A number of manuals are also available for use by practitioners and some for use by survivors themselves (e.g. *Treating Post-Trauma Nightmares: A Cognitive Behavioral Approach* [Davis, 2009]; *Prolonged Exposure Therapy for PTSD: Emotional Processing of Traumatic Experiences Therapist Guide (Treatments That Work)* [Foa, Hembree, & Rothbaum, 2007]; *Reclaiming Your Life from a Traumatic Experience: A Prolonged Exposure Treatment Program Workbook (Treatments That Work)* [Rothbaum, Foa, & Hembree]; *Cognitive Processing Therapy for Rape Victims: A Treatment Manual* [Resick & Schnike, 1993]; *Cognitive-Behavioral Therapy for PTSD: A Case*

Formulation Approach [Zayfert & Becker, 2008]). Most approaches will include psychoeducation as well as in-depth intervention content.

CASE EXAMPLE

Evyn was brought to the emergency room by her sister after disclosing that she had been raped the previous evening in a parking garage at the airport. A sexual assault advocate met them in the waiting room. The advocate provided Evyn basic information about the process and purpose of the forensic exam as they waited for the sexual assault nurse examiner [SANE] to arrive. Evyn was visibly distressed and nervous but appeared to relax a bit as she was able to ask questions of the advocate. Evyn's sister asked about her options for legal action; Evyn turned away during this discussion and stated she did not want to talk about whether she planned to report the assault or not. The advocate provided a brochure to Evyn's sister that outlined the different legal options and procedures that Evyn would need to consider. The SANE nurse arrived and reiterated the information about the exam provided by the advocate. Following the exam, the SANE nurse showed a video to Evyn, her sister, and the advocate that described some common symptoms that some rape victims experience and various ways of coping with those symptoms. A month following the assault, Evyn was struggling with returning to work. In particular, she had trouble parking in the parking garage next to her office building, instead parking several blocks away and subsequently being frequently late for meetings. She discussed her distress about getting in trouble at work for being late with her sister. Evyn remembered part of the video describing how a woman had taught herself to not sleep with all the lights on in the house. She and her sister described how they might do something similar to help Evyn face her fear of the parking garage. They decided on a plan, which included calling the rape crisis center to talk to a counselor about their ideas.

AUTHOR NOTES

Research and manuscript preparation supported by:

1. National Institute on Drug Abuse grant no. R01 DA11158, titled "Prevention of Post Rape Psychopathology and Drug Abuse" (Heidi Resnick, PI);
2. National Institute on Drug Abuse grant no R01DA023099, titled "Prevention of Postrape Drug Abuse: Replication Study" (Heidi Resnick, PI);

3. Substance Abuse and Mental Health Services Administration, Grant No. 1-UD1-SM56070, titled "Service Systems Models Intervention Development and Evaluation Center" (Benjamin Saunders, PI);

4. Oklahoma Center for the Advancement of Science and Technology, Grant No. HR-08-017, titled "Mitigating the Effects of Sexual Assault" (Joanne Davis, PI);

5. We wish to acknowledge the contributions of Dr. Monica Fitzgerald to the development of the www.musc.edu/saprevention website and downloadable brochure materials.

REFERENCES

1. Tjaden, P., & Thoennes, N. (2000). Prevalence and consequences of male-to-female and female-to-male partner violence as measured by the National Violence Against Women Survey. *Violence Against Women, 6,* 142–161.
2. Brewin, C., Andrews, B., & Valentine, J. (2000). Meta-analysis of risk factors for posttraumatic stress disorder in trauma-exposed adults. *Journal of Consulting and Clinical Psychology, 68*(5), 748–766.
3. Bonanno, G.A. (2005). Resilience in the fact of potential trauma. *Current Directions in Psychological Science, 14,* 135–138.
4. Phoenix, B.J. (2007). Psychoeducation for survivors of trauma. *Perspectives in Psychiatric Care, 43,* 123–131.
5. Southwick, S., Friedman, M., & Krystal, J. (2008). Does psychoeducation help prevent post traumatic psychological stress disorder? In reply. *Psychiatry, 71,* 303–321.
6. Creamer, M., & O'Donnell, M. (2008). The pros and cons of psychoeducation following trauma: Too early to judge? *Psychiatry, 71,* 319–321.
7. Feldner, M.T., Monson, C.M., & Friedman, M.J. (2007). A critical analysis of approaches of targeted PTSD prevention: Current status and theoretically derived future directions. *Behavior Modification, 31,* 80–116.
8. Litz, B.T., Gray, M.J., Bryant, R.A., & Adler, A.B. (2002). Early intervention for trauma: Current status and future directions. *Clinical Psychology: Science and Practice, 9,* 112–134.
9. Wesseley, S., Bryant, R.A., Greenberg, N., Earnshaw, M., Sharpley, J., & Hughes, J.H. (2008). Does psychoeducation help prevent post traumatic psychological distress? *Psychiatry, 71,* 287–302.
10. Donker, T., Griffiths, K.M., Cuijpers, P., & Christensen, H. (2009). Psychoeducation for depression, anxiety, and psychological distress: a meta-analysis. *BMC Medicine, 7,* 79–87.
11. Sayer, N., Clothier, B., Spoont, M., & Nelson, D. (2007). Use of mental health treatment among veterans filing claims for posttraumatic stress disorder. *Journal of Traumatic Stress, 20*(1), 15–25.
12. Kilpatrick, D.G., Resnick, H.S., Ruggiero, K.J., Conoscenti, L.M., & McCauley, J. (2007). Drug-facilitated, incapacitated, and forcible rape: A national study. Final report submitted to the National Institute of Justice.

13. Roth. S., & Lebowitz, L. (1988). The experience of sexual trauma. *Journal of Traumatic Stress, 1,* 79–107.

14. Davis, J.L. (2009). *Treating post-trauma nightmares: A cognitive behavioral approach.* New York: Springer Publishing Company.

15. Nishith, P., Mechanic, M., & Resick, P.A. (2000). Prior interpersonal trauma: The contribution to current PTSD symptoms in female rape victims. *Journal of Abnormal Psychology, 109,* 20–25.

16. Koss, M.P., Figueredo, A.J., & Prince, R.J. (2002). A cognitive mediational model of rape's mental, physical, and social health impact: Preliminary specification and evaluation in cross-sectional data. *Journal of Consulting and Clinical Psychology, 70,* 926–941.

17. Resnick, H., Acierno, R., Waldrop, W.E., King, L., King, D., Danielson, C., Ruggiero, K.J., Kilpatrick, D.G. (2007a). Randomized controlled evaluation of an early intervention to prevent post-rape psychopathology. *Behaviour Research and Therapy, 45,* 2432–2447.

18. Resnick, H.S., Kilpatrick, D.G., Best, C.L., & Kramer, T.L. (1993). Vulnerability-stress factors in development of posttraumatic stress disorder. *The Journal of Nervous and Mental Disease, 180,* 424–430.

19. Rothbaum, B.O., E.B. Foa, D. Riggs, et al. (1992). A prospective examination of post-traumatic stress disorder in rape victims. *Journal of Traumatic Stress 5,* 455–475.

20. American Psychiatric Association. (2000). *Diagnostic and statistical manual of mental disorders* (4th ed.). Washington, D.C.: Author.

21. McCann, I.L., Sakheim, D.K., & Abrahamson, D.J. (1988). Trauma and its victimization: A model of psychological adaptation. *Counseling Psychologist, 16,* 531–594.

22. Resick, P.A., & Schnicke, M.K. (1993). *Cognitive processing therapy for rape victims: A treatment manual.* Newbury Park, CA: Sage.

23. Athrens, C.E. (2006). Being silenced: The impact of negative social reactions on the disclosure of rape. *American Journal of Community Psychology, 38*(3–4), 263–274. doi: 10.1007/s10464-006-9069-9.

24. Littleton, H., Horsley, S., John, S., & Nelson, D.V. (2007). Trauma coping strategies and psychological distress: A meta-analysis. *Journal of Traumatic Stress, 20,* 977–988.

25. Kilpatrick, D.G., Cougle, J.R., & Resnick, H.S. (2008). Reports of the death of psychoeducation as a preventative treatment for posttraumatic psychological distress are exaggerated. *Psychiatry, 71,* 322–328.

26. Ruzek, J.I. (2008). Wanted: A theory of post-trauma information delivery. *Psychiatry, 71,* 332–338.

27. Hobfoll, S., Walter, K., & Horsey, K. (2008). Dose and fit are vital to intervention success. *Psychiatry: Interpersonal and Biological Processes, 71*(4), 308–318. doi:10.1521/psyc.2008.71.4.308

28. Turpin, G., Downs, M., & Mason, S. (2005). Effectiveness of providing self-help information following acute traumatic injury: Randomised controlled trial. *British Journal of Psychiatry, 187,* 76–82.

29. Scholes, C., Turpin, G., & Mason, S. (2007). A randomised controlled trial to assess the effectiveness of providing self-help information to people with symp-

toms of acute stress disorder following a traumatic injury. *Behaviour Research and Therapy, 45,* 2527–2536.

30. Ehlers, A., Clark, D.M., Hackmann, A., McManus, F., Fennell, M., Herbert, C., & Mayou, R. (2003). A randomized controlled trial of cognitive therapy, a self-help booklet, and repeated assessments of early interventions for posttraumatic stress disorder. *Archives of General Psychiatry, 60,* 1024–1032.

31. Rose, S., Brewin, C. R., Andrews, B., & Kirk, M. (1999). A randomized controlled trial of individual psychological debriefing for victims of violent crime. *Psychological Medicine, 29,* 793–799.

32. Kilpatrick, D.G., & Veronen, L.J. (1984). Treatment for rape-related problems: Crisis intervention is not enough. In L. Cohen, W. Claiborn, & G. Specter (Eds.), *Crisis Intervention* (2nd ed.): Community-clinical psychology series. New York: Human Services Press.

33. Foa, E.B., Hearst-Ikeda, D., & Perry, K.J. (1995). Evaluation of a brief cognitive-behavioral program for the prevention of chronic PTSD in recent assault victims. *Journal of Consulting and Clinical Psychology, 63,* 948–955.

34. Foa, E., Zoellner, L., & Feeny, N. (2006). An evaluation of three brief programs for facilitating recovery after assault. *Journal of Traumatic Stress, 19*(1), 29–43. doi:10.1002/jts.20096.

35. Resnick, H., Acierno, R., Kilpatrick, D.G., Holmes, M. (2005). Description of an early intervention to prevent substance abuse and psychopathology in recent rape victims. *Behavior Modification, 29,* 156–188.

36. Resnick, H.S., Acierno, R., Amstadter, A.B., Self-Brown, S., Kilpatrick, D.G. (2007b). An acute post-sexual assault intervention to prevent drug abuse: Updated findings. *Addictive Behaviors, 32,* 2032–2045.

37. Campbell, R., Wasco, S.M., Ahrens, C.E., Sefl, T., & Barnes, H.E. (2001). Preventing the "second rape." Rape survivors' experiences with community service providers. *Journal of Interpersonal Violence, 16,* 1239–1259.

38. Moyer, A., Finney, J.W., Swearingen, C.E., & Vergun, P. (2002). Brief interventions for alcohol problems: A meta-analytic review of controlled investigations in treatment-seeking and non-treatment-seeking populations. *Addiction, 97,* 279–292.

39. Stephens, R., Roffman, R.A., & Curtin, L. (2000). Comparison of extended versus brief treatments for marijuana use. *Journal of Consulting and Clinical Psychology, 68,* 898–908.

40. Monti, P., & Spirito, A. (1999). Brief intervention for harm reduction with alcohol-positive older adolescents in a hospital. *Journal of Consulting & Clinical Psychology, 67*(6), 989. Retrieved from Academic Search Complete database.

41. Zatzick, D., Roy-Byrne, P., Russo, J., Rivara, F., Droesch, R., Wagner, A., et al. (2004). A randomized effectiveness trial of stepped collaborative care for acutely injured trauma survivors. *Archives of General Psychiatry, 61,* 498–506.

42. Krouse, H.J. (2001). Video modeling to educate patients. *Journal of Advanced Nursing, 33,* 748–757

18

The Benefits of Self-Defense Training for Sexual Assault Survivors

Leanne R. Brecklin

INTRODUCTION

Between 13% and 20% of adult women experience rape in their lifetime, according to data from both community and college student samples.[1,2,3,4] Rape has been linked with several negative consequences including post-traumatic stress disorder (PTSD), depression, anxiety, fear, suicidal ideation, alcohol/substance abuse, poorer physical health, lower self-esteem, and sexual dysfunction.[5,6] Efforts to reduce these negative effects and prevent repeat sexual victimization need to be made a priority, given that prior victimization is such a strong predictor of future victimization.[7,8,9,10,11,12,13] According to a recent literature review, two of three sexually victimized women will experience sexual revictimization.[14] Traditional rape risk reduction programs (without self-defense training) targeting college women have typically been unsuccessful at reducing the revictimization of sexual assault survivors,[15,16] even when specifically targeting women with victimization histories.[15]

Self-defense training is an additional option that sexual assault survivors may seek out in the hopes of reducing their risk of revictimization. Even though it is always the offender who is to blame for committing sexual assault, it is still key to educate women about how they can effectively respond to and hopefully avoid potential assaults. Self-defense training prepares women both mentally and physically for potential assaults[17] by providing them with opportunities to learn, observe, and practice physical, social, and cognitive skills through the use of role-plays, discussion, and simulation exercises.[18,19,20] This training gives women access to a new set of assertive and combative responses to various forms of intimidation and threat along the continuum of sexual violence.[21,22]

ARE SELF-DEFENSE TECHNIQUES EFFECTIVE?

Are the techniques taught in self-defense classes actually effective at reducing the sexual victimization of women? Prior research studies suggest that participation in self-defense training may be related to rape avoidance for participants.[23,24,25] In addition, several empirical studies of the role of victim resistance strategies in rape incidents have demonstrated that victims' use of forceful physical resistance (e.g., hitting, kicking, biting), nonforceful physical resistance (e.g., fleeing, hiding, blocking blows), and forceful verbal resistance (e.g., screaming, yelling at, or threatening offender) are typically related to avoiding completed rape and unrelated to physical injury. On the other hand, nonforceful verbal resistance (e.g., pleading, begging, or reasoning with the offender) has been found to be related to greater severity of sexual abuse but not related to physical injury. For a more in-depth review on resistance strategies and rape outcomes, see Ullman's (2007) article.[26] In sum, more physical and assertive responses seem to be related to less severe sexual assaults.

Based on the above research, it appears that the techniques taught most often in self-defense training (e.g., hitting, kicking, yelling) are related to rape avoidance, implying that participation in self-defense training may reduce women's severity of sexual victimization and may be a fruitful avenue for the prevention of revictimization of sexual assault survivors. Prior research has demonstrated that previously victimized women are less likely to report that they would use verbal assertiveness and physical defense strategies (strategies related to rape avoidance) and more likely to use indirect methods of resistance in response to an assault compared with nonvictimized women.[27,28,29,30,31] In addition, Gidycz, Van Wynsberghe, and Edwards (2008) discovered that women with sexual victimization histories were more likely to either be immobile or use nonforceful verbal resistance when actually faced with another assault compared to women without a victimization history.[32]

Thus, it would appear that sexual assault survivors would benefit from participation in self-defense training where they could learn not only self-defense skills but also about the skills' effectiveness in reducing victimization severity. Evaluations have demonstrated that training participants do increase their self-defense skills and perceive themselves to be more physically competent after course completion (see Brecklin, 2008 for a review of women's self-defense training evaluations).[33] With training, perhaps sexual assault survivors would be able as well as more willing to effectively fight back and avoid revictimization. Teaching survivors effective resistance strategies is especially important in light of research showing that women who intend to use assertive resistance strategies actually do use these strategies when faced with an attack.[32] Based on this result, Gidycz and colleagues (2008) suggested that women need to be knowledgeable about effective resistance strategies while at the same time practicing and planning to use them in a potential assault situation.[32] In addition, victims who feel future rapes are avoidable report fewer psychological symptoms and disruptions in their beliefs,[34] a feeling that could be affected by participation in self-defense training.

CHARACTERISTICS OF SEXUAL ASSAULT SURVIVORS

Because victimization can shatter women's assumptions of personal invulnerability and positive views of themselves,[35] sexual assault victims frequently suffer long-lasting fear, anxiety, and helplessness in addition to lower levels of assertive communication, self-esteem, perceived control, and self-efficacy.[5,6,36,37,38,39] All of these detrimental attributes have been shown to be positively affected by self-defense training participation in several evaluation studies (see Brecklin, 2008 for a review).[33] Increasing survivors' assertiveness skills is especially important in light of a prospective study showing that low assertiveness specific to situations with men and prior victimization were consistent predictors of future sexual victimization in a sample of 274 college women.[9] In addition, studies have shown that successful rape resisters were more assertive, confident, perceived more control over their lives, and showed more initiative, persistence, and leadership compared with women who were raped,[40,41,42] demonstrating that psychological changes due to participation in self-defense training may have substantial implications for subsequent rape avoidance.

Not only are there differences between sexual assault victims and nonvictims in psychological outcomes, revictimized women experience more distress, depression, PTSD, and feelings of shame and powerlessness than women with only one victimization.[14] Furthermore, research shows that women with a history of child sexual abuse and current PTSD who were revictimized in the previous six months described themselves as overly responsible, socially avoidant, and nonassertive compared with nonrevictimized women.[43] Vanzile-Tamsen, Testa, and Livingston (2005), using a sample of 318 community women, found that women sexually victimized in both childhood and adulthood were less likely to say they would use direct verbal resistance if faced with another attack compared to nonvictims and women victimized in a single life phase.[44] In addition, women without a sexual assault history intended to use the highest level of sexual refusal assertiveness, while revictimized women demonstrated the lowest level. Lower assertiveness was then related to a lower likelihood of using direct resistance against an attack. Based on results from their experimental study, Wilson, Calhoun, and Bernat (1999) suggested that women with multiple victimization experiences may show delays in recognizing and responding to cues of sexual assault.[45] Women with multiple victimization incidents may particularly benefit from participation in self-defense training.

CHARACTERISTICS OF SURVIVORS WHO PARTICIPATE IN SELF-DEFENSE TRAINING

Little research has been conducted on why certain women choose to take self-defense training after assault experiences. According to DeWelde (2003-b), one of the main reasons why recently victimized women reported enrolling in feminist self-defense training was so that they could be better prepared in case they were faced with another assault.[46] Various studies have shown that the majority of self-defense training participants (44%–90%) have been physically or sexually abused in their lifetime.[38,46,47,48,49,50,51,52,53] A prior study using a sample of 3,187 female college students found that women who took self-defense/assertiveness training were more likely to have suffered adult sexual victimization as well as both child sexual and physical abuse than women without training.[54] Furthermore, Follansbee (1982) found that almost one-third (30%) of women taking self-defense were victims of rape compared with only 12% of subjects from a general studies course.[17] However, one study of women found that this relationship was only true for the offense of attempted rape,[50] and three other studies found no significant differences in sexual assault history between women with and without self-defense[55,56] and martial arts training.[57]

A study of 1,623 sexual assault survivors showed that victims who took self-defense/assertiveness training after their assaults were more likely to have experienced completed rape with more offender aggression than did victims without training.[58] Therefore, it is possible that more severe assaults may lead to self-defense training enrollment. Because another study demonstrated that greater sexual victimization severity in the past increased the chances of future victimization,[8] it may be especially important for women with severe assault histories to participate in self-defense training as a way of reducing revictimization.

Brecklin and Ullman (2004) also discovered that victims with postassault training were more likely to have used forceful physical resistance (e.g., hitting), nonforceful physical resistance (e.g., fleeing), and forceful verbal resistance (e.g., yelling) during their assaults than victims without training.[58] This finding can possibly be explained by the higher levels of offender aggression in the assaults experienced by training participants, because victims typically match their degree/type of resistance to offender level of aggression.[32,59,60,61,62,63] Even though victims with postassault training were more likely to use resistance, they were actually less likely to report that their resistance was effective compared to nonparticipants.[58] Women may choose to enroll in postassault training because their past resistance was unsuccessful at preventing the rape. If rape survivors enrolled in postassault self-defense training more frequently, it is possible that the cycle of revictimization could be broken for at least some women. For example, Bart and O'Brien (1985) reported that one rape survivor learned judo after her sexual assault and subsequently was able to avoid a second attack.[23]

THERAPEUTIC BENEFITS OF SELF-DEFENSE TRAINING FOR ASSAULT SURVIVORS

Women's self-defense tactics are meant to be practical, simple, and effective in common situations so that all women can learn them regardless of age, size, previous experiences, or physical strength.[64,65,66,67,68] Many different types of self-defense training are available to women, including brief single-session classes, twelve-hour Rape Aggression Defense courses, twenty-two half-hour padded attacker courses (e.g., Model Mugging), semester-long college courses, and multiyear martial arts training degree programs. These courses also vary in philosophical foundation. However, for most women, self-defense courses with a feminist philosophy are recommended,[18,69] as they demonstrate how gender socialization inhibits women from fighting back against assault and teach participants that they have the right to act in their own defense.[18,70,71,72]

In addition, female instructors of courses can serve as models of strong, confident, and capable women to their students.[18,68,69,71,72,73,74] However, male instructors can also be useful, especially as mock offenders in self-defense classes with simulated attacks, which dramatically increase the perceived reality of the attack situations and allow female participants to successfully defend themselves against powerful attackers.[75] Evaluations have shown that participants in programs with simulated assaults and padded attackers have stronger self-defense skills[49] and moderately higher self-defense self-efficacy[76] than participants in programs without these simulations.

Similarly, researchers have strongly advocated women-only self-defense classes,[18,71] as they provide a more supportive environment where women can be more open about their past experiences and fears of sexual assault. After women-only self-defense courses, participants have commented on the importance of the group environment for encouragement, emotional support, bonding, and sisterhood both in semistructured interviews[48] and qualitative questionnaires.[38,77] This emotional support may be particularly important for sexual assault survivors, which will be discussed more in a later section of this chapter.

According to Stevenson (2006), "A self-defense class is not only an opportunity to learn a practical, physical skill; it is an opportunity for connection and healing" (p. 213).[75] Self-defense training can have several positive benefits for sexual assault survivors. Two prior studies reported that, before enrollment in self-defense training, women with assault histories had lower self-efficacy, felt more vulnerable to assault, and perceived less personal control over their lives than women without an assault history.[38,78] Victims and nonvictims no longer differed on these traits immediately after the training[38,78] and at a six-month follow-up.[78] Ozer and Bandura (1990) argued that self-defense classes might be able to override preexisting adverse effects of abuse and instill enhanced perceptions of control in survivors.[78] Moreover, McCaughey (1998) stated that child sexual abuse survivors in her self-defense classes had to overcome their tendencies toward helplessness.[74]

In addition, Shim (1998) discovered a significant increase in the physical self-efficacy of participants, regardless of assault history, after participation in Model Mugging.[52] Qualitative statements from the survivors of physical and sexual abuse show that Model Mugging participation helped to increase their self-awareness, assertiveness, confidence in ability to handle potential assaults, and appreciation for their physical and emotional strength.[52] Furthermore, another study's multivariate results demonstrated that women who took self-defense/assertiveness training after their assaults exhibited less current anxiety than nonparticipants.[58] As a psychiatric nurse who previously experienced victimization, Ellensweig (1997) reported the following about her participation in Model Mugging: "I experienced a letting go of a feared event. I now could and would defend myself in a similar situation. This experience had a positive effect on my self-esteem, self-reliance, and self-assurance" (p. 44).[79]

A seventy-two-year-old Caucasian woman who participated in the Rape Aggression Defense course reported similar positive changes, according to my post-training interview with her. She had been victimized in the past and stated, "I lived in fear, there was buried fear for years and years and years, and I was able to deal with a great deal of that. Today I still have fear, but it's a manageable fear and I feel like I can take care of myself." She also spoke of increased confidence as a result of the self-defense course. When asked about any changes within herself as a result of participating in Rape Aggression Defense, she declared,

A lot more confident, I feel a lot more confident about myself. When one is attacked, I lost a part of myself. A lot of that was buried deep within me. And,

there were years that I could hardly talk above a whisper and being empowered
of learning to use my voice gave me so much confidence . . . it was like that
inner spirit of mine began to blossom again and to be able to say I am okay. I
am just like anyone else. I cannot speak too highly of how empowering it was
for me, an old lady (laugh) . . . . . And, I know that it helped me back in many
areas of my life. It doesn't matter when you get it back, you get it back.

Clearly, this self-defense course benefited her in many ways.

Peretz (1991) conducted an evaluation of a self-defense training program
and a psychotherapy group, each targeting women who had experienced
rape at least three months prior to the study.[19] She randomly assigned rape
survivors to three groups of twenty-four each: self-defense, psychotherapy,
and wait-list control, and both treatment strategies lasted for eight 1 1/2-
hour sessions. Peretz (1991) found that both treatment groups significantly
reduced their levels of psychological distress, fear, and vulnerability compared with a wait-list control group at an immediate post-test.[19] She argued
that the two treatments were effective because they both discussed issues
of control, vulnerability, trust, and the impact of rape myths, and provided
support and validation for survivors' experiences.

Gidycz et al. (2006) evaluated a sexual assault risk reduction program
(including 2 1/2 hours on self-defense) for college women.[37] The authors
randomly assigned participants to either a treatment (N = 234) or wait
list control group (N = 266). Six months after the program, participants
exhibited significantly more protective behaviors than the control group.
The program participants also reported several instances of actual use
of self-defense techniques taught in the course since program completion. Unfortunately, the program was not successful in reducing women's
sexual victimization at a three- or six-month follow-up. Because the study
also found that treatment group participants demonstrated more accurate
knowledge on sexual assault and were more likely to report sexual victimizations on a survey after the program than the control group, Gidycz and
colleagues (2006) maintained that this may have affected results pertaining
to program effects on victimization.[37] Women in the treatment group may
be labeling experiences as rapes that they wouldn't have prior to the program and may be more likely to report them in a research study. In another
evaluation of a slightly revised version of this sexual assault risk reduction
program with 300 college women, Orchowski, Gidycz, and Raffle (2008)
found that the incidence of rape was lower among program participants
over the two-month follow-up than the control group.[80] The program
participants also used more self-protective behaviors and assertive sexual
communication compared to the control group.

Brecklin and Ullman (2004) found that survivors with postassault training felt less responsible for their previous assaults than victims without
training.[58] Similarly, in an evaluation of a sexual assault risk reduction

program including a self-defense component, the women who were sexually victimized after participating in the program were less likely to feel responsible for their assault and were more likely to place responsibility on the attacker compared to the victimized control group participants.[37] This is consistent with self-defense evaluations that found that sexual assault survivors who took self-defense came to understand that they were not to blame for the incident.[38,81] Research has shown that decreasing behavioral self-blame is important for sexual assault victims' recovery.[82] Furthermore, using structural equation modeling with 415 college women who experienced some form of sexual victimization by a male acquaintance, Nurius, Norris, Macy, and Huang (2004) found that reduced self-blame predicted more assertive responses and less diplomatic responses and immobility during victimization.[83]

Based on her participant observation of a feminist self-defense course, DeWelde (2003-a) reported that some survivors were able to determine where their loss of control in past victimization experiences occurred.[84] Furthermore, in another study, a female martial artist stated that martial arts helped her not to be a victim anymore.[57] Similarly, according to women enrolled in Model Mugging, several abused women felt the training helped them to become angry about the victimization,[48,52] which is important because past research has shown that women who reported feeling more anger during their attacks were more likely to avoid rape.[23,42,85] This may in part be explained by the fact that feelings of anger are often related to more physically assertive responses to sexual assault.[60,83]

A common thread noted in several self-defense evaluations was the importance of the group dynamic in facilitating the survivors' healing process.[19,52] DeWelde (2003-a) used participant observation in a self-defense course and discovered that many of the women shared their personal victimization experiences with the rest of the class.[84] In fact, the female instructor shared her own experience with violent crime at the start of the course, which may have encouraged the students to do the same. Discovering this commonality of victimization experiences can help survivors to combat isolation and stigma and to confront challenges presented by the course.[75] According to a Model Mugging participant,

> Every woman that takes that class, there's some importance for them to take this class, because they've been violated, because they are afraid of being violated. And that's the bottom line . . . We were all real unified in that goal . . . to learn how to defend ourselves (p. 408).[73]

In addition, several Model Mugging participants reported that the group process was therapeutic and provided them with support and a sense of belonging.[48,52] Many of the fifty-nine Model Mugging graduates in Fraser and Russell's (2000) study stated that the self-defense group was their primary source of emotional support for their intense feelings developed during the course.[73]

Some sexual assault survivors choose to act out past assault experiences in self-defense classes so that they can fight back against the offender and be victorious.[38,73] It is "important for women to see how the same bodies that they believed once betrayed them can now be transformed to help keep them safe" (p. 115).[86] This helps victims to overcome their fears, reclaim the power that their offenders took away, and increases their determination to fight back in the future.[22,87] According to a Model Mugging participant who acted out a past victimization in a mock simulation, "I realized how powerful it was when I looked down and I saw several people crying . . . it was an incredible validation for how I had been feeling and what I had been experiencing" (p. 412).[73] Fraser and Russell (2000) discussed how the group allowed women to face experiences they couldn't alone.[73] As explained by the following participant, "The emotions stirred up . . . were such that no one person could contend with it. So you had to have this clump . . . You're limited if you contain within yourself, limited in a way that you are not with a group" (p. 410).[73] During the mock attack simulations, the female participants cheer each other on, which also encourages the women to keep fighting even when faced with emotionally difficult scenarios.

On the other hand, simulated assault scenarios in self-defense training may remind female participants of repressed traumas,[48] which may make the training more emotionally difficult. One-quarter of participants in a mastery-modeling self-defense program remembered an assault during training; however, their statements demonstrated that the supportive environment helped them to explore these memories and led to healing.[38] At the same time, women who participate in training may expand their definition of victimization, resulting in more women recognizing themselves as survivors.[84] In another study, a female Model Mugging participant reported disliking the class because the assault scenarios triggered bad memories, while another participant felt too overwhelmed by reminders of past abuse to complete her survey packet.[77] According to Anderson (1998), most self-defense courses are not structured to help women with abuse histories to process their intense memories.[81] Perhaps therapy or referral programs are needed for sexual assault survivors enrolled in training with simulated assaults. Courses combining self-defense training and therapy are discussed next.

SELF-DEFENSE TRAINING
AND THERAPY FOR ASSAULT SURVIVORS

Traditional psychotherapy can be effective in treating the long-term symptoms resulting from either child sexual abuse or adult sexual assault, but this form of treatment often fails to address the physical aspects of healing and the prevention of revictimization.[81] Victims of sexual abuse have stated that healing through martial arts training is qualitatively different than healing from traditional therapy, mainly due to the physical component of martial arts.[88] Fifty-eight percent of the assault survivors enrolled in self-defense training in Lidsker's (1991) evaluation were also in therapy, and all of these women said that the self-defense training was complementary to their therapy.[38] Several of the participants noted that their therapy helped them to deal with the emotions brought up by their participation in self-defense training.[38] The combination of self-defense training and therapy may offer both treatment for the long-term symptoms of abuse and opportunities for survivors' empowerment.

In her dissertation, Daniels (2001) created a template for a treatment program for female child sexual abuse survivors incorporating self-defense training and traditional group therapy techniques; however, this program had not been implemented.[87] She argued that therapy would allow the abuse survivors to discuss any feelings and reactions surfacing from their self-defense training. Because several evaluations have noted the importance of group interactions and discussion for assault survivors,[19,52,89] it is believed that group therapy (when composed only of female sexual assault survivors) would be more effective than individual therapy. These group therapy sessions could offer survivors support, normalization for their experiences and reactions, and a safe place to explore their feelings about their abuse histories as well as the self-defense training.[19] These groups may even form their own support networks; for example, rape survivors enrolled in Peretz's (1991) group psychotherapy continued to meet weekly on their own after the sessions ended.[19]

Anderson (1998) conducted an evaluation of an eight-week program with both self-defense training (one hour each week) and group psychotherapy (1 1/2 hours each week) for eight female survivors of childhood incest recruited through newspaper ads and mental health professionals.[81] Whenever possible, the topic of the group therapy was coordinated with the self-defense topic for that week. Program participants were asked to describe their experiences in two-hour focus group sessions one month after the program (N = 8) and individual interviews immediately (N = 8) and one year after the program (N = 5). Participants found the experience to be both empowering and healing. The combination of self-defense and therapy deepened the experience for all eight participants, with therapy helping them to process their emotional reactions to the self-defense training. One survivor commented on the importance of the order of the sessions; participating in therapy right after the self-defense gave her time to calm down.[81]

All of the women commented on the supportive group environment and participant bonding, and in fact, one year after the program, several members were still in touch with each other.[81] For many participants, telling the story of their victimization to the group was cathartic, and they also mentioned the importance of a female-only setting. Several of the survivors commented that they saw other group members as role models and that watching other survivors perform the self-defense techniques was helpful. The eight participants also appreciated learning that their experiences were not unique and that others were facing similar problems, feelings, and symptoms. Seven of the participants specifically stated that the sessions advanced their healing.

Furthermore, survivors reported increases in self-confidence, self-care, assertiveness, perceived control, self-efficacy, and feelings of anger due to the sessions. The participants commented on an increased physicality and connection with their bodies, and many women saw themselves as more capable of defending themselves and believed now that they had the right to do so after the training sessions. The opportunity to physically fight back against attackers helped them work through some of their traumas.[81] Some participants mentioned that hitting the punching bag helped them to release their anger.[81]

Schuiteman (1990) used participant observation and post-treatment interviews to examine a course combining self-defense training and therapy for sixteen sexual assault survivors (two classes of eight).[68] The first class (pilot study) included eight two-hour sessions, with one hour each of self-defense and unstructured group therapy. Using the pilot study's results, she improved on the second class, by expanding each class session an extra half-hour, adding four extra sessions, and adding structure to the group therapy sessions (e.g., themes). After the class, participants reduced their helplessness and increased their confidence to defend themselves and their ability to set boundaries.[68] Similar to Anderson (1998),[81] the physicality of the self-defense training was an important component of the healing process, helping them to feel more in touch with their bodies and to integrate their mind, body, and spirit. Several participants mentioned that self-defense helped them to feel empowered. Expressing anger was an emotionally freeing experience for many of the women. As in Anderson's (1998) study,[81] participants remarked on the sense of community and trust in the group, due to the commonality of experience, and they also mentioned that the other class members and instructors served as role models.[68]

David, Simpson, and Cotton (2006) created a pilot therapeutic self-defense course "for women veterans who were sexually traumatized and who had PTSD" (p. 557).[90] Of the twelve women in the pilot group, ten participated in the research study. The program lasted twelve weeks for a total of thirty-six hours and was led by three psychologists and two martial artists. In each session, the first hour included sexual assault facts and role-plays involving assertive behavior, while the second hour focused on the actual self-defense training. In the final hour of each session, group debriefing took place, with an emphasis on supportive psychotherapy. All twelve program participants successfully completed the program.

Results demonstrated that the participants were less fearful of assault immediately after the program compared to their pretest levels, but this reduction was not maintained at the three- or six-month follow-ups. The women's perception of general assault risk did not change as a result of the program, but they demonstrated significant improvement in identifying risky situations at immediate and three-month post-tests. In addition, the participants exhibited less PTSD symptom severity at the three- and six-month follow-ups (but not immediately after the program), primarily due to decreased avoidance and hyperarousal symptoms. The female veterans also exhibited less depression and increases in interpersonal, self-defense, and activity self-efficacy immediately, three months, and six months after the program. David et al. (2006) concluded that a therapeutic self-defense course was a viable treatment for sexual assault survivors.[90]

In a case study of a participant in the program described above,[90] "Phyllis," a Caucasian woman in her late sixties, initially had some skepticism about completing the program at her age.[91] At first, she had difficulty with some of the self-defense moves, as they "were highly triggering for her as they reminded her of past traumas. She worked hard on grounding, breathing, and concentrating throughout these lessons, and ultimately, was able to execute all moves effectively without panicking." (p. 117).[91] She successfully finished the program, gained confidence, and found the training empowering. Upon graduating from the self-defense course, "Phyllis" proclaimed, "I feel I can go places, do things, live again. I got my life back" (p. 117).[91] It is likely that without the therapeutic component of this self-defense program, "Phyllis" wouldn't have successfully completed the course.

Similarly, in both Anderson's (1998)[81] and Schuiteman's (1990)[68] evaluations, participants said that they would not have been able to complete a regular self-defense class, as they would have been too overwhelmed by the realism of practice situations. All of the participants in Anderson's (1998) study remarked that the self-defense training brought back memories of their abuse but did help them learn how to defend themselves.[81] However, one participant limited her involvement in the self-defense training due to her memories. Schuiteman (1990) discussed her dilemma in balancing the use of realistic simulated assault scenarios while still trying to help the survivors' healing process.[68] Overall, the combination of self-defense training and therapy provided abuse survivors with a safe place to process their feelings.

Sexual assault survivors may enroll in training as a way to exercise control over future assaults and work through some of the trauma. Based on past research, it appears that self-defense training is effective in decreasing sexual assault survivors' feelings of vulnerability, anxiety, and use of avoidance behaviors, while at the same time increasing their self-efficacy, assertiveness, and perceived control over their environment.[19,38,52,58,78] Because the risk of revictimization is higher shortly after the initial assault,[14] it may be beneficial for sexual assault victims to enroll in self-defense training soon after an attack. Unfortunately, many survivors may not feel psychologically ready to take a self-defense course so soon after the assault.[87] In fact, in two qualitative evaluations of programs combining self-defense training and therapy for assault survivors, several women remarked that they wouldn't have been able to take a regular self-defense course, as they needed help processing their feelings and dealing with the realism of the assault scenarios.[68,81] According to past studies, women who take self-defense training after sexual assaults typically experienced more brutal attacks and have more severe victimization histories than women without training.[54,58] Due to their more severe victimization histories, these survivors might benefit more from programs combining self-defense training and therapy, which may increase their capacity to successfully defend themselves and simultaneously ameliorate their psychological distress. As Stevenson (2006) stated, self-defense training should not replace other forms of psychotherapy but rather should be used as a complement.[75] Ellensweig (1997) suggested that "psychiatric nurses can use ("Model Mugging") as a resource along with psychotherapy to increase a client's sense of self-esteem and self-defense skill level" (p. 42).[79]

Efforts to expand the combined offerings of group therapy and self-defense training to female sexual abuse survivors should be a priority of the anti-rape movement. A sample of sixty-seven female veterans with physical or sexual assault histories receiving outpatient mental health services thought self-defense would be a suitable addition to their treatment, and 91% stated that taking self-defense would increase their ability to defend themselves against future attacks.[92] Because sexual assault survivors often turn to rape crisis centers for counseling, these centers might be the ideal setting for this undertaking. In addition, some states' victim assistance programs reimburse victims for self-defense training,[46] a reimbursement that should be offered by more states, given the therapeutic benefits of this training for assault survivors.

SELF-DEFENSE TRAINING RECOMMENDATIONS FOR SURVIVORS

Sexual assault survivors interested in enrollment in self-defense training should look around their communities for course opportunities; rape crisis centers, therapy groups, colleges, and friends may be able to provide suggestions. If a survivor is reluctant to enroll in a self-defense course alone, they should consider taking the course with a friend or family member who can offer extra support and comfort. In addition, concurrent therapy may help survivors to deal with any emotional stress brought up by training participation. Sexual assault survivors should only enroll in training when they feel emotionally ready. Survivors should also try to assess whether a particular self-defense course is a good fit for them prior to enrollment, which will also help them to know what to expect and how to prepare themselves. According to Stevenson (2006), some questions that should be asked prior to selecting the right self-defense course include, "Do the members participate in role-plays while in an adrenalized state?" "What type of helping relationship is established between the members?" and "How does the first class differ from the last class?" (p. 213–214).[75] Self-defense programs that include practical techniques and hands-on repetitive training are recommended, in particular those that offer multiple mock simulations for feedback and eventual perfection of skills,[93] but as stated earlier, these may be more difficult for sexual assault survivors to cope with. However, these mock simulations, by offering participants the chance themselves and to see other women successfully fighting off attackers, instills in participants that they too can be victorious. In addition, women should practice moves outside of (and after) the course, and some programs like Rape Aggression Defense offer free refresher training sessions across the United States after initial completion of the course.

CONCLUSION

More research clarifying why prior sexual victimization is such a strong predictor of future victimization is imperative, as this would help practitioners design more effective treatment and prevention programs for these women. Self-defense training may be one avenue for preventing repeat sexual assault victimization; however, more research is needed on how the effectiveness of self-defense training might differ by prior sexual victimization history.[20] In addition, the therapeutic benefits of self-defense training for survivors may depend on the type or severity of past abuse, time since the assault, or current social support systems, all variables that should be examined in future research. Very few longitudinal studies on the effectiveness of self-defense programs for sexual assault survivors exist, which clearly should be a priority for future research, along with larger sample sizes and longer follow-up times. In addition, because the majority of participants in past studies were Caucasian, more research needs to be done on the effectiveness of self-defense training with more diverse samples of survivors.

As shown in this chapter, self-defense training offers a variety of benefits and may be therapeutic for rape survivors. For example, according to a female Rape Aggression Defense participant I interviewed about program benefits, "Life is just more joyful. I feel confident, I feel like I could whip the world." A combination of therapy and self-defense training may offer sexual assault survivors additional psychological healing as well as strategies to prevent revictimization.[68,81,87] Furthermore, self-defense can provide much-needed emotional support and validation for sexual assault survivors,[19,20,52,73] especially if combined with traditional group psychotherapy.[68,81,87,88] In summary, self-defense training holds promise for sexual assault risk reduction in women and improved mental health, but sexual assault survivors may require more intensive interventions to reduce their risk of revictimization than women without sexual assault histories.

REFERENCES

1. Brener, N.D., McMahon, P.M., Warren, C.W., & Douglas, K.A. (1999). Forced sexual intercourse and associated health-risk behaviors among female college students in the United States. *Journal of Consulting and Clinical Psychology, 67,* 252–259.
2. Kilpatrick, D.G., Edmunds, C.N., & Seymour, A.K. (1992). *Rape in America: A report to the nation.* Arlington, VA: National Victim Center.
3. Koss, M.P. (1993). Detecting the scope of rape: A review of prevalence research methods. *Journal of Interpersonal Violence, 8,* 198–222.
4. Tjaden, P., & Thoennes, N. (2000). *Full report of the prevalence, incidence, and consequences of violence against women: Findings from the National Violence Against Women Survey.* Washington, D.C.: U.S. Department of Justice.
5. Koss, M.P., Heise, L., & Russo, N.F. (1994). The global health burden of rape. *Psychology of Women Quarterly, 18,* 509–537.
6. Resick, P.A. (1993). The psychological impact of rape. *Journal of Interpersonal Violence, 8,* 223–255.
7. Fisher, B.S., Cullen, F.T., & Turner, M.G. (2000). *The sexual victimization of college women.* Washington, D.C.: U.S. Department of Justice.
8. Gidycz, C.A., Hanson, K., & Layman, M.J. (1995). A prospective analysis of the relationships among sexual assault experiences: An extension of previous findings. *Psychology of Women Quarterly, 19,* 5–29.
9. Greene, D.M., & Navarro, R.L. (1998). Situation-specific assertiveness in the epidemiology of sexual victimization among university women: A prospective path analysis. *Psychology of Women Quarterly, 22,* 589–604.
10. Koss, M.P., & Dinero, T.E. (1989). Discriminant analysis of risk factors for sexual victimization among a national sample of college women. *Journal of Consulting and Clinical Psychology, 57,* 242–250.
11. Messman, T.L., & Long, P.J. (1996). Child sexual abuse and its relationship to revictimization in adult women: A review. *Clinical Psychology Review, 16,* 397–420.

12. Messman-Moore, T.L., & Long, P.J. (2000). Child sexual abuse and revictimization in the form of adult sexual abuse, adult physical abuse, and adult psychological maltreatment. *Journal of Interpersonal Violence, 15,* 489–502.

13. Roodman, A.A., & Clum, G.A. (2001). Revictimization rates and method variance: A meta-analysis. *Clinical Psychology Review, 21,* 183–204.

14. Classen, C.C., Palesh, O.G., & Aggarwal, R. (2005). Sexual revictimization: A review of the empirical literature. *Trauma, Violence, & Abuse, 6,* 103–129.

15. Breitenbecher, K.H., & Gidycz, C.A. (1998). An empirical evaluation of a program designed to reduce the risk of multiple sexual victimization. *Journal of Interpersonal Violence, 13,* 472–488.

16. Hanson, K.A., & Gidycz, C.A. (1993). Evaluation of a sexual assault prevention program. *Journal of Consulting and Clinical Psychology, 61,* 1046–1052.

17. Follansbee, P.A. (1982). *Effects of a self-defense program on women's psychological health and well-being.* Southern Illinois University: Doctoral dissertation.

18. Cummings, N. (1992). Self-defense training for college women. *Journal of American College Health, 40,* 183–188.

19. Peretz, M.E. (1991). *The effects of psychotherapy and self-defense training on recovery of survivors of acquaintance and stranger rape.* California School of Professional Psychology: Doctoral dissertation.

20. Thompson, M.E. (1991). Self-defense against sexual coercion: Theory, research, and practice. In E. Grauerholz & M.A. Koralewski (Eds.), *Sexual coercion: A sourcebook on its nature, causes, and prevention* (pp. 111–121). Lexington, MA: Lexington Books.

21. Kelly, L. (1988). *Surviving sexual violence.* Minneapolis, MN: University of Minnesota Press.

22. McCaughey, M. (1997). *Real knockouts: The physical feminism of women's self-defense.* New York: New York University Press.

23. Bart, P.B., & O'Brien, P.H. (1985). *Stopping rape: Successful survival strategies.* New York: Pergamon Press.

24. Brecklin, L.R., & Ullman, S.E. (2005). Self-defense/assertiveness training and women's responses to sexual attacks. *Journal of Interpersonal Violence, 20,* 738–762.

25. Peri, C. (1991). Below the belt. *Women in the Martial Arts, Newsletter of the National Women's Martial Arts Federation, March,* 6–14.

26. Ullman, S.E. (2007). A 10-year update of "Review and critique of empirical studies of rape avoidance." *Criminal Justice and Behavior, 34,* 411–429.

27. Corbin, W.R., Bernat, J.A., Calhoun, K.S., McNair, L.D., & Seals, K.L. (2001). The role of alcohol expectancies and alcohol consumption among sexually victimized and nonvictimized college women. *Journal of Interpersonal Violence, 16,* 297–311.

28. Mallon, S.D.K. (2000). Conceptualization of acquaintance rape and resistance strategies within a constructivist self-development theory framework. University of Connecticut: Doctoral dissertation.

29. Norris, J., Nurius, P.S., & Dimeff, L.A. (1996). Through her eyes: Factors affecting women's perceptions of and resistance to acquaintance sexual aggression threat. *Psychology of Women Quarterly, 20,* 123–145.

30. Nurius, P.S., Norris, J., Dimeff, L.A., & Graham, T.L. (1996). Expectations regarding acquaintance sexual aggression among sorority and fraternity members. *Sex Roles, 35,* 427–444.

31. Stoner, S.A., Norris, J., George, W.H., Davis, K.C., Masters, N.T., & Hessler, D.M. (2007). Effects of alcohol intoxication and victimization history on women's sexual assault resistance intentions: The role of secondary cognitive appraisals. *Psychology of Women Quarterly, 31,* 344–356.

32. Gidycz, C.A., Van Wynsberghe, A., & Edwards, K.M. (2008). Prediction of women's utilization of resistance strategies in a sexual assault situation: A prospective study. *Journal of Interpersonal Violence, 23,* 571–588.

33. Brecklin, L.R. (2008). Evaluation outcomes of self-defense training for women: A review. *Aggression & Violent Behavior, 13,* 60–76.

34. Frazier, P.A. (2000). The role of attributions and perceived control in recovery from rape. *Journal of Personal and Interpersonal Loss, 5,* 203–226.

35. Janoff-Bulman, R., & Frieze, I.H. (1983). A theoretical perspective for understanding reactions to victimization. *Journal of Social Issues, 39,* 1–17.

36. Calhoun, K.S., Atkeson, B.M., & Resick, P.A. (1982). A longitudinal examination of fear reactions in victims of rape. *Journal of Counseling Psychology, 29,* 655–661.

37. Gidycz, C.A., Rich, C.L., Orchowski, L., King, C., & Miller, A.K. (2006). The evaluation of a sexual assault self-defense and risk-reduction program for college women: A prospective study. *Psychology of Women Quarterly, 30,* 173–186.

38. Lidsker, J. (1991). *Women and self-defense training: A study of psychological changes experienced by participants in relation to assault history.* Pacific Graduate School of Psychology: Doctoral dissertation.

39. Myers, M.B., Templer, D.I., & Brown, R. (1984). Coping ability of women who become victims of rape. *Journal of Consulting and Clinical Psychology, 52,* 73–78.

40. Amick, A.E., & Calhoun, K.S. (1987). Resistance to sexual aggression: Personality, attitudinal, and situational factors. *Archives of Sexual Behavior, 16,* 153–163.

41. Burnett, R.C., Templer, D.I., & Barker, P.C. (1985). Personality variables and circumstances of sexual assault predictive of a woman's resistance. *Archives of Sexual Behavior, 14,* 183–188.

42. Selkin, J. (1978). Protecting personal space: Victim and resister reactions to assaultive rape. *Journal of Community Psychology, 6,* 263–268.

43. Classen, C., Field, N.P., Koopman, C., Nevill-Manning, K., & Spiegel, D. (2001). Interpersonal problems and their relationship to sexual revictimization among women sexually abused in childhood. *Journal of Interpersonal Violence, 16,* 495–509.

44. VanZile-Tamsen, C., Testa, M., & Livingston, J.A. (2005). The impact of sexual assault history and relationship context on appraisal of and responses to acquaintance sexual assault risk. *Journal of Interpersonal Violence, 20,* 813–832.

45. Wilson, A.E., Calhoun, K.S., & Bernat, J.A. (1999). Risk recognition and trauma-related symptoms among sexually revictimized women. *Journal of Consulting and Clinical Psychology, 67,* 705–710.

46. DeWelde, K. (2003-b). White women beware!: Whiteness, fear of crime, and self-defense. *Race, Gender, & Class, 10,* 75–91.

47. Frost, H.L. (1991). *"Model Mugging": A way to reduce women's victimization.* University of Kansas: Doctoral dissertation.

48. Gaddis, J.W. (1990). *Women's empowerment through Model Mugging: Breaking the cycle of social violence.* University of California: Doctoral dissertation.

49. Henderson, M.C. (1997). *Women's self-defense training: An applied analysis of self-efficacy theory.* Loyola University of Chicago: Doctoral dissertation.
50. Huddleston, S. (1991). Prior victimization experiences and subsequent self-protective behavior as evidenced by personal choice of physical activity courses. *Psychology: A Journal of Human Behavior, 28,* 47–51.
51. Michener, S.O. (1996). *An analysis of Rape Aggression Defense as a method of self-empowerment for women.* Walden University: Doctoral dissertation.
52. Shim, D.J. (1998). *Self-defense training, physical self-efficacy, body image, and avoidant behavior in women.* Boston University: Doctoral dissertation.
53. Smith, D.R. (1983). *A program evaluation: The effects of women's self-defense training upon efficacy expectancies, behaviors, and personality variables.* Michigan State University: Doctoral dissertation.
54. Brecklin, L.R. (2004). Self-defense/assertiveness training, women's victimization history, and psychological characteristics. *Violence Against Women, 10,* 479–497.
55. Cox, D.S. (1999). *An analysis of two forms of self-defense training and their impact on women's sense of personal safety self-efficacy.* Old Dominion University: Doctoral dissertation.
56. Hollander, J.A. (2010). Why do women take self-defense classes? *Violence Against Women, 16,* 459–478.
57. Sedlacek, D.L. (2000). *Gender role adherence, martial arts training, self-defense myths, and expectancies regarding attack: Implications for sexual assault prevention.* Cleveland State University: Doctoral dissertation.
58. Brecklin, L.R., & Ullman, S.E. (2004). Correlates of post-assault self-defense/assertiveness training participation for sexual assault survivors. *Psychology of Women Quarterly, 28,* 147–158.
59. Murnen, S.K., Perot, A., & Byrne, D. (1989). Coping with unwanted sexual activity: Normative responses, situational determinants, and individual differences. *Journal of Sex Research, 26,* 85–106.
60. Nurius, P.S., Norris, J., Young, D.S., Graham, T.L., & Gaylord, J. (2000). Interpreting and defensively responding to threat: Examining appraisals and coping with acquaintance sexual aggression. *Violence and Victims, 15,* 187–208.
61. Siegel, J.M., Sorenson, S.B., Golding, J.M., Burnam, M.A., & Stein, J.A. (1989). Resistance to sexual assault: Who resists and what happens? *American Journal of Public Health, 79,* 27–31.
62. Ullman, S.E. (1998). Does offender violence escalate when rape victims fight back? *Journal of Interpersonal Violence, 13,* 179–192.
63. Ullman, S.E., & Knight, R.A. (1992). Fighting back: Women's resistance to rape. *Journal of Interpersonal Violence, 7,* 31–43.
64. Burton, N. (1999). *Tools not rules: Cultivating practices of resistance to and prevention of sexualized violence.* University of Toronto: Doctoral dissertation.
65. McDaniel, P. (1993). Self-defense training and women's fear of crime. *Women's Studies International Forum, 16,* 37–45.
66. Quinsey, V.L., Marion, G., Upfold, D., & Popple, K.T. (1986). Issues in teaching physical methods of resisting rape. *Sexual Coercion and Assault, 1,* 125–130.
67. Rentschler, C.A. (1999). Women's self-defense: Physical education for everyday life. *Women's Studies Quarterly, 1,* 152–161.

68. Schuiteman, J.A. (1990). *Self-defense training and its contributions to the healing process for survivors of sexual assault.* Michigan State University: Doctoral dissertation.
69. Kidder, L.H., Boell, J.L., & Moyer, M.M. (1983). Rights consciousness and victimization prevention: Personal defense and assertiveness training. *Journal of Social Issues, 39,* 155–170.
70. Hollander, J.A. (2004). "I can take care of myself": The impact of self-defense training on women's lives. *Violence Against Women, 10,* 205–235.
71. Searles, P., & Berger, R.J. (1987). The feminist self-defense movement: A case study. *Gender and Society, 1,* 61–84.
72. Searles, P., & Follansbee, P. (1984). Self-defense for women: Translating theory into practice. *Frontiers, 8,* 65–70.
73. Fraser, K.L., & Russell, G.M. (2000). The role of the group in acquiring self-defense skills: Results of a qualitative study. *Small Group Research, 31,* 397–423.
74. McCaughey, M. (1998). The fighting spirit: Women's self-defense training and the discourse of sexed embodiment. *Gender and Society, 12,* 277–300.
75. Stevenson, S. (2006). Group work gets physical: Self-defense class and social work. *Social Work with Groups, 29,* 195–215.
76. Michener, T.D. (1997). *An analysis of the effectiveness of Rape Aggression Defense presented with and without simulated assaults.* Walden University: Doctoral dissertation.
77. Rowe, N.P. (1993). *Self-defense training: An empowerment process for women.* California Institute of Integral Studies: Doctoral dissertation.
78. Ozer, E.M., & Bandura, A. (1990). Mechanisms governing empowerment effects: A self-efficacy analysis. *Journal of Personality and Social Psychology, 58,* 472–486.
79. Ellensweig, D. (1997). "Never again" Model Mugging: A therapeutic resource for the psychiatric nurse. *Journal of Psychosocial Nursing, 35,* 41–44.
80. Orchowski, L.M., Gidycz, C.A., & Raffle, H. (2008). Evaluation of a sexual assault risk reduction and self-defense program: A prospective analysis of a revised protocol. *Psychology of Women Quarterly, 32,* 204–218.
81. Anderson, K.M. (1998). *Healing the fighting spirit: Combining self-defense training and group therapy for women who have experienced incest.* University of Minnesota: Doctoral dissertation.
82. Koss, M.P., & Figueredo, A.J. (2004). Change in cognitive mediators of rape's impact on psychosocial health across 2 years of recovery. *Journal of Consulting and Clinical Psychology, 72,* 1063–1072.
83. Nurius, P.S., Norris, J., Macy, R.J., & Huang, B. (2004). Women's situational coping with acquaintance sexual assault: Applying an appraisal-based model. *Violence Against Women, 10,* 450–478.
84. DeWelde, K. (2003-a). Getting physical: Subverting gender through self-defense. *Journal of Contemporary Ethnography, 32,* 247–278.
85. Queen's Bench Foundation. (1976). *Rape prevention and resistance.* San Francisco, CA: Author.
86. Harris, M. (1998). *Trauma recovery and empowerment: A clinician's guide for working with women in groups.* New York: Free Press.

87. Daniels, K.M. (2001). A program incorporating self-defense training and group therapy in the treatment of adult child sexual abuse survivors. University of Hartford: Doctoral dissertation.

88. Guthrie, S.R. (1995). Liberating the Amazon: Feminism and the martial arts. *Women and Therapy, 16,* 107–119.

89. Marx, B.P., Calhoun, K.S., Wilson, A.E., & Meyerson, L.A. (2001). Sexual revictimization prevention: An outcome evaluation. *Journal of Consulting and Clinical Psychology, 69,* 25–32.

90. David, W.S., Simpson, T.L., & Cotton, A.J. (2006). Taking charge: A pilot curriculum of self-defense and personal safety training for female veterans with PTSD because of military sexual trauma. *Journal of Interpersonal Violence, 21,* 555–565.

91. Westrup, D., Weitlauf, J., & Keller, J. (2005). I got my life back! Making a case for self-defense training for older women with PTSD. *Clinical Gerontologist, 28,* 113–118.

92. David, W.S., Cotton, A.J., Simpson, T.L., & Weitlauf, J.C. (2004). Making a case for personal safety: Perceptions of vulnerability and desire for self-defense training among female veterans. *Journal of Interpersonal Violence, 19,* 991–1001.

93. Angleman, A.J., Shinzato, Y., Van Hasselt, V.B., & Russo, S.A. (2009). Traditional martial arts versus modern self-defense training for women: Some comments. *Aggression and Violent Behavior, 14,* 89–93.

19

Social Support and Resilience in the Aftermath of Sexual Assault: Suggestions across Life Course, Gender, and Racial Groups

Tamara G. J. Leech and Marci Littlefield

Social support plays a central role in breaking the connection between sexual abuse and trauma symptoms. To illustrate this role, various scholars have argued that the existence and severity of negative outcomes among abuse survivors result from two different webs of events. The first web is concerned with the stressors among survivors, where the severity, frequency, duration, and timing of sexual abuse determine the intensity of the resultant psychological and social stress.[1-3] The second, and more important, web shows how this stress can be buffered if the survivor has social support, positively appraises the abuse, and develops active coping mechanisms.[3-6]

The stress-buffering potential of the second web of influence is particularly important because it can empower survivors and the people who care about them. Social support, in the form of both emotional support and tangible support, can directly lead to positive outcomes among survivors. Emotional support constitutes showing care or concern, and tangible support represents the provision of information or resources to help survivors navigate their situation. Both of these types of support have the potential to sway survivors toward positive appraisals and active rather than avoidant coping, thus indirectly buffering the effect of initial abuse.[4] When all of these considerations are combined, the role of social support can be depicted by figure 1. This model makes it clear that the amount of social support itself is partially dependent on the severity of abuse exposure and the age of onset of abuse.[7-9] Nonetheless, social support primarily serves as a safeguard in the nexus between sexual abuse and quality-of-life issues.

For this reason, Prati[10] discusses social support as an important precursor to both post-traumatic general growth (e.g. an alteration of priorities,

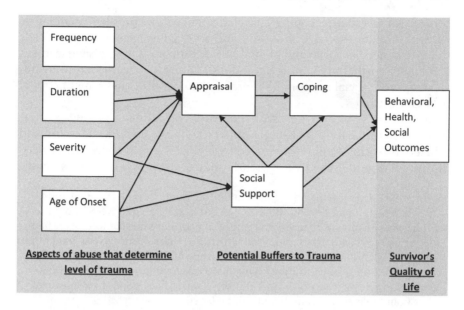

spiritual development, etc.) and personal growth (in the form of adaptation and coping). A variety of empirical investigations establish social support as a significant factor in the progression from sexual abuse victimization to positive psychological adjustment.[11] For example, at the most basic level, family connectedness is associated with half the odds of suicide attempts among sexual abuse survivors.[12] Furthermore, social support from family and/or others erases the association between sexual assault and outcomes like loss of self, loss of childhood,[11] depression, low self-concept,[2] and post-traumatic stress disorder.[13] In this way, social support empowers the survivor and those close to him/her to positively affect their outcomes. Consequently, it also empowers professionals to assist survivors because it is related to two factors that can be modified through clinical intervention: appraisals and coping.

Appraisals refer to an individual's understanding of an event (especially concerning the *cause* of the event). There is strong evidence that internal causal appraisals (i.e., self-blame) of sexual abuse are associated with negative symptoms and behavioral outcomes, including post-traumatic stress disorder (PTSD).[14-16] Additionally, negative appraisals are connected to coping strategies that lead to undesirable outcomes.[4] Thus, when social support leads to more positive appraisals, it can decrease the odds of negative outcomes associated with both appraisal and coping.

Two styles of coping are primarily associated with sexual abuse. The first, engagement (or active) coping, involves problem solving, expressing emotions, cognitive restructuring, and so on. The second, disengagement coping (or avoidance coping), is characterized by problem avoidance, wishful thinking, social withdrawal, and so on. Engagement coping leads to more beneficial social and mental health outcomes than disengagement coping.[13,17] Furthermore, a large amount of research suggests that individuals with more social support are more likely to exhibit engagement coping behaviors.[4,5,17]

In Domitrz's *Voices of Courage*,[18] one survivor, Shirley, provides a short description of the forty-fourth year of her life: the year when she found and utilized the social support she needed to deal with sexual abuse experienced during childhood.[18] Her writing is indicative of the power of social support:

> Forty-four—I discovered where my childhood went. I discovered that my father is a pedophile. Beyond difficult. But supportive people were in my life. Gone were Shame, Depression and Anger. Everything I needed to recover had been put in my path. I was told, "You are only as sick as your secrets." And out they poured. A turning point: I gave up the hope of a different childhood. Why do we hold on to such things? I have discovered what nourishes me. I have learned to release that which does not serve my highest good. I have learned that I can be open and honest and still be loved.

Shirley's experience reinforces research indicating that the general path between social support and positive outcomes is both direct and indirect. Yet the specific aspects of this process of recovery largely depend on survivors' social situations. For example, boys and men survivors who report seeking out emotional support are actually *less* likely to engage in positive coping behaviors.[6] In the next sections, we investigate this and other subgroup-specific relationships between social support and paths of recovery. We first turn to life course considerations and show that the social networks that are most salient to everyone in that particular stage—parents/family during childhood, peers and schools during adolescence, friends and intimate partners during adulthood, and social services during late adulthood—also have the greatest effect on sexual abuse survivors' outcomes. We then move on to discuss gender and the ways that social support systems are altered yet can be responsive to masculinity issues. We end with a brief consideration of the way in which racial and ethnic context modifies the effect of different sources of social support.

LIFE COURSE CONSIDERATIONS

Childhood

Research indicates that between 12% and 35% of girls and 4% and 9% of boys are sexually abused during childhood.[1] There is no officially recognized disorder specific to the aftereffects of childhood abuse, but aggressive behavior, social isolation, anxiety, depression, and inappropriate sexualized behaviors are some of the most commonly reported symptoms. Many of these items are similar to symptoms of PTSD, and it is estimated that around 40% of sexually abused children exhibit PTSD symptoms.[1]

Seventy to eighty percent of these children disclose the abuse before they are adults, but typically less than half of cases are acted upon.[19] Parents and family members are the most likely recipients of these disclosures,[19,20] despite some children's fears that sharing the information with others might break up the family or lead to the loss of a parent.[6] Actually, a substantial amount of research shows that disclosure and the associated support from family protects childhood sexual assault survivors from various negative psychological responses.[1,2,20-22] Although various other factors—including cognitive variables, family stability, and neighborhood characteristics[2,23]— interact to ultimately determine children's outcomes, parental support may be the key factor associated with positive outcomes.

Various studies show that the large majority of mothers are supportive following a child's disclosure of sexual abuse.[6] However, these studies differ in their definition of "support." In general, parental support encapsulates four factors: (a) believing the allegations; (b) providing emotional support (e.g., showing the child that the parent wants to hear about their problems, cares about their feelings, etc.);[2] (c) seeking out professional services such as therapy; and (d) acting against the perpetrator.[21] The first three types of support are especially important, as they can defend against the potentially negative responses of the child's personal involvement in the fourth form: taking action against the perpetrator.[2,20] Again, despite these high standards of support, most mothers are found to be supportive of their children, even if that support is inconsistent.[6,24]

Parents' ambivalence toward their children's experience should not be confused with lack of support. Ambivalence is recognized as "a phenomenon that occurs when one is conflicted, either consciously or unconsciously, in attitude or thought."[24] It is a normative expression of internal conflict that—at some point—manifests among nearly all parents. For example, many parents who value spending time with their children need "adult time" on occasion. In a similar way, ambivalent parents of sexual abuse survivors might have moments when they fail to provide emotional support, doubt their child's allegations, fail to enforce action against the perpetrator, or miss a therapy session. As long as these thoughts or feelings are recognized and addressed in a safe manner (e.g., discussed with other adults, do not lead to contexts that place the child in further danger, etc.), ambivalence does not constitute neglect.

A possible explanation for this ambivalence may be that the mothers' level of support is often influenced by their social situation at the time when the abuse is disclosed. Because of psychological and social constraints, mothers tend to offer less support if they are financially dependent on the perpetrator, live in the same house as the perpetrator, when the abuse involves penetration, or if the abuse is not confirmed by other sources.[2] It is understandable, then, that levels of support would vary if and when these social factors change; for example, if the mother becomes gainfully employed or if another survivor reveals abuse from the same perpetrator. More typically, overall inconsistency takes the shape of gradually increasing support, strengthening as parents have more time to psychologically digest their child's reports.[20,21] Given government agencies' oversimplified conception of "guardian support" as present or lacking,[6] it is important to recognize this convincing empirical evidence that nonoffending parents can be both ambivalent and supportive.[24]

Also related to ambivalence is the common feeling of incompetence among parents. Many parents and their children feel that parents are emotionally overwhelmed by information about the abuse or just do not have the training and knowledge to help their children.[8] There have been efforts (called filial therapy) to train parents as therapists,[8] but placing parents in the role of therapist may not relieve their anxiety about dealing with their children's experiences.[25] Instead, professional intervention that trains parents in supportive responses[26] and/or includes parents in their child's therapy sessions[8,27] seems to increase parental supportiveness.

However, the strongest and most influential parental support seems to originate from parent and child attachment. Bowlby[28] argues that the bond formed between a parent and child in the first several years of a child's life determines his/her level of security and affects his/her future social ties and relationships. Securely attached children have a caregiver (and in the long term other friends and family) to whom they can turn for care and protection.[22] Thus, secure attachment can facilitate resilience following abuse in several ways. For example, securely attached children are more likely to disclose sexual abuse.[20] This disclosure is likely to be directed toward a parent, but securely attached children are also more likely to develop social skills that lead to strong peer friendships and positive relationships with nonfamilial adults (especially within the school setting).[22] Finally, strong attachment to parents may even lead to more successful therapy, as parents may be able to help children feel secure and safe before, during, and/or after sessions.[8]

In this way, attachment is a powerful form of social support for child survivors of sexual abuse. However, all is not lost if a child does not form attachment to his/her parents in the early years of life. Positive, supportive relationships with nonfamilial adults[29] or nonabusing siblings[23] are also associated with resilience. Similarly, living in a stable situation—regardless of whether that is with biological parents or a foster family—increases an abused child's odds of resilience threefold.[23] In the end, despite the extensive documentation of the importance of parental (or more precisely, maternal) social support, the key factor that seems to buffer negative outcomes among child sexual abuse survivors is support from a consistent caregiver.

Adolescence

Whereas the literature on childhood sexual abuse is dominated by research on maternal support, the resilience perspective is salient in scholarship on adolescent sexual abuse. In general, the concept of resilience describes positive adaptation among adolescents who are faced with significant hardships,[30] such as sexual abuse. Originally, resilience was thought of as a personality characteristic, but more recent scholarship has shown that it is better described as a continual developmental process that is affected by the adolescent's personality, his/her family, and his/her social environment.[30] Three types of resilience are generally acknowledged: performing better than expected, adapting well when faced with challenging circumstances, and recovering after experiencing trauma.[31] The third type of resilience is most applicable to survivors of sexual abuse. Although their levels of resilience may grow and wane over time,[23] adolescent survivors of sexual abuse report that they view their recovery process as an ongoing progression that is often spurred by a "second chance" provided by someone in their support network.[32]

Compared to other teens, adolescent sexual abuse survivors have higher rates of mental health and behavioral problems such as anxiety, post-traumatic stress disorder, and substance abuse.[30] However, if adolescents have access to social support, traumatic experiences like sexual abuse can also spur emotional growth.[33] Actually, research shows that, although they have higher rates of problematic outcomes, the majority of adolescent survivors of sexual abuse are resilient. In one study, over half of the adolescents had no psychiatric disorder, two-thirds had no alcohol or drug dependence, and more than 80% had never participated in violent behavior.[23]

Parents and other caregivers may play a significant role in placing adolescents on the path toward resilience,[12] but the evidence is not as clear cut or consistent as that regarding the influence of parental support on child survivors.[30] In line with the ecology of the life course, supportive relationships with other social contacts seem to be particularly important for adolescents. Teen sexual abuse survivors with strong connections to school personnel tend to have lower levels of stress or mental health problems.[30] These survivors report less negative trauma effects if they receive support from friends and/or professionals.[6] Finally, strong associations with and support from church or religious organizations are also likely to be a vehicle toward resilient growth.[10,30] In general, adolescent sexual abuse survivors have the opportunity and likelihood to follow a developmental path toward resilience if they become involved in various socially supportive relationships outside the family.

Adulthood

In the United States, it is estimated that approximately 1.5 million women fall victim to sexual abuse by an intimate partner each year.[17] In addition to these women, many other women begin to deal with sexual abuse from earlier in their lifetime, as many disclosures of child sexual abuse occur in adulthood, not childhood.[6] These women who delay disclosure are at increased risk of revictimization by the same or different perpetrators.[32] This issue of revictimization is important, as more frequent and intrusive abuse is more likely to result in negative outcomes.[19] Regardless of whether or not the victimization is repeated, adult survivors have to deal with issues that do not apply to other groups such as a decline in work productivity and/or increased economic pressures due to health care costs.[17] Due to the direct trauma from abuse, as well as these increased economic pressures, adult survivors of sexual abuse are especially likely to suffer from depression and suicidal behavior.[19]

However, as in all life stages, the effects of trauma can be buffered by social support. For adult survivors of sexual abuse, both emotional support (perceived availability of others to participate in social activities) and tangible/instrumental support (availability of material resources) are related to more positive outcomes among survivors, with emotional support being particularly important during the early crisis stages.[10,17] Some adult survivors of sexual abuse have reported feeling distressed or anxious because of having no one to confide in and are especially relieved when someone— even a professional—validates their choices and feelings.[19] Complementarily, tangible support seems to empower adults to take criminal action against their perpetrator.[17]

Adult survivors of sexual abuse are distinct from children or adolescents in that the reciprocity of supportive relationships becomes significant. For these survivors, "communal mastery"—shared connections that lead to a sense of self-competence—is of principal import.[32,34] Adults are more likely to disclose abuse to friends than to family, and a positive response from these friends seems to be less important than a shared sense of experience (Ullman, 2003).

Various adult survivors of sexual abuse report that helping others through community involvement or peer groups played an important role in their paths toward resilience.[32] Women who have been subjected to sexual abuse have more access to resources and/or are empowered to change their situation if they are part of a strong community of peers.[17]

Yet this community of peers, especially if it consists of other survivors, also provides the opportunity for advocacy efforts that can build survivors' self-esteem.[6] Thus, it may be particularly important for adult survivors of sexual abuse to actively engage in peer relationships that require and/or establish a sense of community.

In addition to these community ties, relationships with intimate partners are essential to the adult experience of sexual abuse. The effect of intimate partner relationships is obvious when one partner serves as the abuser. In these cases, the survivor may find it difficult to leave the situation because of financial dependence, fear, and/or love.[20] However, the relationship between a nonabusive partner and survivor particularly shapes the relationship between social support and outcomes. Often, the intimate partner fails to provide social support by responding negatively to instances of disclosure—e.g. displaying sexual intrigue, replicating dynamics of the sexual abuse, or pressing sexual interaction.[35] In this and other ways, disclosure of sexual abuse leads to more relationship stress than social support, and there is evidence that subsequent breakups serve as triggers for negative behaviors among sexual abuse survivors.[19]

Other studies show that a positive response to disclosure from a romantic partner is one of the key determinants of positive adult health.[9] These positive responses may be most impactful if they take on the form of communal experience as discussed above. For example, reactions could take the form of sharing previous struggles with addiction, disclosing family members' experiences with abuse, or relating to the experience through their own professional training. Regardless of the method, this support from romantic partners plays a pivotal role in the healing process of adult survivors.[32,3]

Seniors

Elder mistreatment can be divided into six categories: sexual abuse, physical abuse, psychological abuse, financial exploitation, neglect, and violation of rights. Despite the fact that many of these forms of abuse overlap, sexual assault is the least common form.[36] Various sources estimate that around 6% of the senior population falls victim to elder sexual abuse, the large majority being women.[37-39] Romantic partners are unlikely to be the perpetrator of these assaults (less than one-third of the abuse is committed by these individuals),[37] perhaps because seniors' physical and social situation places them at risk from various assailants. Declining health, financial struggles, and housing situations make seniors vulnerable to abuse from individuals outside of intimate partner relationships.[40]

Declining physical condition also amplifies the consequences of sexual assaults, as they have more severe physical ramifications for elderly survivors than other age groups.[41] Depression and shame/guilt is also amplified within this population, perhaps because of the cultural and social standards of the time in which they grew up.[37] Of course, mistreatment and these additional, negative outcomes are less likely to occur among seniors who are involved in systems of social support.[42] Low social support triples the likelihood of victimization among the elderly. Social and physical isolation can also contribute to the continuation of abuse, as survivors may be reluctant to leave an abusive caregiver if they perceive no other available support.[38,43] These social factors can exasperate existing limitations—for example, physical disabilities, mental limitations, residence in unsafe neighborhoods—on seniors' ability to take actions to end sexual abuse.[40,43,44]

In all, studies indicate that elder sexual abuse relies heavily on the disempowerment that results from the social isolation of seniors in U.S. society. Sexual abuse from marital partners may be influenced by the historic sense of male privilege and wives as sexual property that dominated cultural beliefs at the time of seniors' unions,[43] but this is probably not dominant because of the previously noted low rate of abuse originating from the spouse. Instead, it is more helpful to recognize the deterioration of elders' social networks—due to mortality, retirement, relocation, and so on—that leads to disempowerment directly and also indirectly by contributing to cognitive and functional decline.[39] Along these same lines, the seniors' location within social networks and cultural depictions may also weaken survivors' voices. Given that sexual abuse is often misunderstood by professionals and laypeople alike as an act of sexual desire (instead of as a weapon of violence to establish power) and our culture does not consider seniors as sexual or sexually attractive, senior sexual abuse is likely to go unrecognized and untreated.[39,44]

The cultural myth that seniors are unlikely to be victims of sex crimes makes their family members and other informal support groups unlikely to recognize abuse when it occurs.[37,44] Furthermore, this misunderstanding extends to medical professionals—often the only other consistent social connection for many elderly individuals—who may not think to look for signs of abuse nor recognize their responsibility to report the abuse in the same way they would for child abuse.[37,39,40] Given that seniors may have definitions of abuse that do not match present-day standards[37] and that they may be conflicted about reporting victimization if they have a dual role as victim and caregiver (in the case of being victimized by individuals who were previously their dependents),[43] the most prevalent and most empowering form of social support is likely to come from senior services professionals.

Senior service providers are the professionals most likely to recognize the fact that—due to growing up in a time where there was no permission to discuss sexuality or sexual activity—elders may feel more shame and guilt than any other group of sexual assault survivors.[40,44] Given that our society has moved toward institutionalized support of the elderly in the form of nursing homes, assisted living facilities, Social Security, and so on, these individuals are most likely to have consistent, meaningful social interactions with senior sexual assault survivors.[39] They are, therefore, in the position to provide the most meaningful and effective social support for senior survivors.

At the same time, the tangible resources that they provide as part of their agencies' mission serve as an additional source of social support that buffers the trauma associated with sexual assault. Addressing transportation problems, assisting with hearing or vision issues, and fixing problems with the built environment (e.g., lighting, door lock, and window issues) can serve to decrease fear and anxiety after an assault.[40] Providing opportunities for community interaction as well as initiating public awareness campaigns can alleviate associated distress and increase the likelihood of reporting/recognizing sexual assault.[37,42] In sum, due to the social and cultural situations of seniors in our society, adult service providers may be the most likely and most effective sources of social support.

Hence, it is important to recognize the various sources of adult services for sexual assault survivors. Adult protective services (APS) is perhaps the most commonly recognized and easily accessible service, but it came to focus on sexual assault late and is underfunded relative to child protective services.[37,39] Today APS can provide various, tangible forms of social support from securing housing to serving as a client advocate. In addition to APS, several national agencies, including the National Center for Elder Abuse, Clearinghouse for Abuse Neglect of the Elderly, and the National Clearinghouse on Abuse in Late Life, can provide information and materials necessary for outreach campaigns. These elder-focused agencies may be more helpful in providing social support specific to the senior context than the typical social services agencies geared toward sexual abuse. (Women's shelters have staff with expertise in domestic and intimate partner abuse, but shelters specifically for abused elders are rare and therefore may lack specialized resources and accessibility.[37,39]) The rape crisis movement has yet to fully incorporate seniors' unique situation as adults who may not have the agency to fully adhere to professionals' or organizations' recommendations and requirements.[44]

On a final note, if we are going to rely on senior service providers for the tangible and emotional support of sexual abuse survivors, the potential deleterious effects on this population should be recognized and addressed. Familial caregivers of victimized seniors have been known to display anxiety and depression,[36] and professional caregivers are not immune to these effects. APS agents, social workers, and nurses can fall victim to "compassion fatigue" if faced with being the only form of social support for many survivors of these crimes.[45] Although all individuals providing social support to survivors run this risk, the nature of these occupations means that these agents are more likely to support more individuals simultaneously and/or deal with these issues more often than other, informal sources of support. If they are not integrated into their own system of social support, they can fall victim to the same negative outcomes of many sexual assault survivors—PTSD, depression, anxiety, and so on.[45] If this occurs, it not only leads to a new set of negative outcomes among an additional population; it also erodes the primary source of social support that can buffer traumatic effects of sexual abuse on senior survivors.

GENDER CONSIDERATIONS

Men as Survivors

Women and girls are 7.5 times more likely to be sexually abused or assaulted over their lifetime than men or boys, and therefore much of the information discussed to this point has focused on the experience of women.[19,44,46] However, recently scholars have established the existence and importance of sexual assault among men and boys. Much of this literature focuses on men's victimization in prison or in childhood sexual assault,[47] but this focus does not capture the experience of all male survivors. According to official statistics for 2006, 26% of the rapes/sexual assaults reported to police involve a male survivor.[47] In the United States, one out of every seven boys can expect to be sexually assaulted by the age of 18;[6] furthermore, one study found that in one year, 3,635 adult men sought professional help for sexual assault.[47] These statistics indicate that male survivors of sexual assault are neither rare nor abnormal.

The long-term implications of experiencing sexual abuse are generally similar for men and women, but they show some important marked differences. There is consensus that men share the risk of mental health problems (e.g., low self-esteem, decreased self-worth, emotional maladjustment) with women survivors.[13,48] Yet perhaps due to influence on their masculine identity and the experience of severe guilt, men are more likely to use avoidance coping such as substance abuse and to exhibit aggressive behaviors.[13,49] Of particular concern is suicidal behavior. Due to many of these gender-specific responses, men survivors of sexual abuse are more likely to successfully commit suicide (although suicidal behavior is more common among women survivors of sexual abuse).[12,19,47] These differences in coping and the associated outcomes lead to a greater probability of resilience among women.[23] Nonetheless, there is strong evidence that young men survivors who receive social support can enter into a positive emotional growth path.

The first step toward this path involves disclosing the abuse. Disclosure is simply the process of attempting to convey the experience of abuse to another person;[49] yet research shows that this process is anything but simple. The process of disclosing sexual assault involves a difficult choice: go without social support in order to avoid possible negative reactions and additional distress, *or* tolerate some negative reactions in a continued effort to find that support.[6,35] Similar to so many other aspects of surviving sexual abuse, disclosure should not be considered a one-time event, but a complex, continual process of reaching out for support.

Our societies' gender norms make it difficult for both men and women to disclose abuse. Women and girls who attempt to disclose abuse may run the risk of being labeled a tease or be accused of playing games. Thus, disclosure may not be *more* difficult for men than women, but men face unique barriers applied due to gendered social messages. First, masculine socialization leads to expectations of enjoying sexual experiences, acceptance of precocious activity as "initiation," and a demand for stoicism and strength; all of which make it more difficult for men and boys to disclose their abusive experiences.[46,49] Second, for some of these same reasons, men are less likely to be supportive if they are the recipient of disclosure.[6,23] Men's socialization teaches them to devalue relationships and intimacy,[49] so this limits the possibility of disclosing or being supportive of disclosure. Third, these cultural issues mean that men risk being labeled homosexual or being accused as the perpetrator to a greater extent than women survivors.[49] Fourth, and finally, because of men's physical strength and the cultural myth that they should be able to protect themselves, they may be accused of not trying to avoid the victimization.[23,47,48] The effects of all of these aspects of gender socialization may be even further enhanced within the senior population, as these cultural beliefs and standards were even stronger during their childhood.[44] For all of these reasons, boys and men may be reluctant to disclose abuse and start the process of obtaining social support.

Few victims are likely to report a sexual assault, but men are 1.5 times less likely than women.[50] It becomes increasingly disheartening, then, when men report feeling abandoned or judged by members of the medical profession. Male sexual abuse survivors state that they are met with disbelief from some medical professionals, reprimands from others, and are discouraged from reporting the abuse by still others.[47] At the same time, these boys and men may be unable to turn to parents or family members to adjust for this lack of support. Boys who experience sexual abuse are likely to come from dysfunctional households and/or family relationships where they feel unsafe and isolated.[46,48] Depending on the cultural beliefs about male roles and responsibilities, the family members may discourage boys and young men from discussing these issues and even punish them when they do.[49] These experiences with physicians and family members contribute to a sense of isolation among male survivors.[47,48]

Other social connections, then, become markedly important for male survivors of sexual abuse. To compensate for these familial relationships, recovery is often facilitated by the initiation of "safe" relationships where the survivor feels empowered.[46] Sometimes these relationships are with children or pets because they are nonthreatening. More often, men survivors are greatly (and positively) affected by gentle, caring adults. These relationships are often with individuals who have maternal characteristics and can even be characterized by seemingly mundane behaviors (e.g., providing chicken soup or brushing a child off after he falls).[46]

While individual relationships may help men survivors feel secure, belonging to a group allows these survivors to address their feelings of isolation. Sharing and interacting with other individuals who are survivors of sexual abuse provides men survivors a sense of belonging and connectedness to a community.[48] However, these connections do not have to be specific to sexual abuse. Men who survive sexual abuse can also develop positive, influential relationships with survivors of other violent or traumatic events.[46] In these situations, men might find a way to rectify their masculinity with their past experience because men are socialized to be providers and protectors.[43] Thus, if men are able to (eventually) take the role of counselor or sponsor, for example, they are especially likely to benefit emotionally and mentally from the situation.[46]

RACE AND ETHNICITY CONSIDERATIONS

The available information regarding racial and ethnic differences in exposure to sexual abuse is inconsistent, leading some scholarly reviews to determine that no particular race is at increased risk of sexual abuse,[51,52] while others suggest otherwise. For example, one study finds that white women are most likely to be the victim of forcible rape at very young ages,[51] but African American women experience forcible rape at a rate of 50% higher than white and Latina women.[53] This type of nuanced difference is common in the literature on sexual abuse according to race and ethnicity, providing very detailed depictions of sexual abuse events by race and ethnicity. Thus, the literature indicates that young black girls are more likely to be subjected to abuse by family members and perpetrators of the same race.[54] White women are more likely to experience noncontact abuse in public and prolonged contact abuse.[55,56] Asian and Hispanic women are more likely to experience abuse at older ages.[57]

Scholars suggest that some of these differences are related to ethnic variations regarding the definition of sexual abuse and also are influenced by whether researchers take socioeconomic status into consideration.[58] Regardless of these differences, survivors of all races encounter physical and psychological coercion as part of the experience of sexual abuse,[56] and this commonality in experience leads to few differences in response to abuse incidents.[51] Yet the differences that do exist have important implications for the role of social support. Research has progressed substantially from initial studies finding that "non-white" survivors have higher rates of depression and negative behaviors, and lower rates of self-esteem[59] to disentangle the effects of minority status from race and ethnicity. As a result, we have come to understand that all survivors of sexual abuse run the risk of these outcomes, but symptoms seem to vary according to cultural context:

- Asian survivors are less likely to externalize (exhibit developmentally inappropriate sexual behavior and anger), and instead tend to internalize (have suicidal thoughts and attempt suicide) more often than other groups.[57,60]
- The magnitude of severe abuse (e.g., penetration, victimization by a stranger, etc.) is consistently greater for Latinas (specifically Mexican women) than any other group and is more likely to be manifested in depression and behavioral problems.[2,55,61]
- For African American survivors, sexual abuse is less likely to result in psychological problems (e.g., depression and PTSD) than are other forms of abuse such as physical or emotional abuse from an intimate partner.[61] Instead, black sexual abuse survivors are more likely to experience problems with sexual functioning, to engage in high-risk sexual practices, and to participate in problem drinking behavior.[51,62,63]

These specific manifestations of the abuse experience highlight the need to take into account the culture-specific norms, values, attitudes, expectations, and customs of each group before potential sources of social support can be properly identified.[65]

For this reason, the sociopolitical and cultural context experienced by ethnic minority women is an important factor in understanding domestic violence and sexual assault victimization. As was previously discussed, the highest levels of social support are unattainable if the abuse is not disclosed. Therefore, the risk factors associated with abuse among minority women and the internal and exterior barriers to help-seeking behavior are especially important for social support.[58]

The external barriers can be best understood in the sociopolitical environment, which places all minority groups in a historical context of oppression and makes minority women more vulnerable to negative reactions to their abuse experience. Scholars suggest that the history of racial oppression is unique for minority women for a number of reasons. Their bodies have been systematically and routinely objectified and devalued,[66] and the interaction of multiple oppressions of race, ethnicity, and class make them more vulnerable to more lethal forms of violence and greater severity of violence than other groups of women.[58]

Their structural circumstances also place greater limitations on their abilities to disclose sexual abuse. For example, African American girls are more likely to have a stepfather (or stepfather figure) in the home, and stepfathers have been associated with greater risk of victimization and a lower likelihood of maternal support.[56,67] Similarly, traditional Asian family roles dictate an unquestioning respect for elders and men, which may help to explain high rates of abuse by male relatives and lower rates of reporting the abuse to authorities.[60]

Furthermore, when they become adults, evidence suggests that minority women are more likely to have their children removed from the home, and some even experience discriminatory treatment during the intervention.[68] Scholars have also noted that Asian American women are discouraged from disclosing, hold negative attitudes toward seeking help from formal services, and are more likely than white women to believe that women are responsible for preventing sexual assault.[58] If early in the acculturation process, distrust of the government and limited English language skills and education must also be taken into consideration;[69] and these issues tend to extend to other ethnic groups such as Native American tribes and immigrant Latinas.[58] Thus, the ways that disclosing sexual abuse is contextualized for minority girls and women is important in addressing the availability of social support mechanisms.

Yet these constraints and the experience of oppression are not completely owned by women. One influential study reports that men survivors' sources and extent of social support are also shaped by their racial and ethnic context.[70] Specifically, the study finds that parents of young men often worry that sexual abuse will compound the amount of discrimination facing their child. Fathers of various ethnicities support their male child survivor by encouraging them to re-create their masculinity through athleticism, emotional detachment, and heterosexual behavior. Yet, African American and Puerto Rican parents emphasize this re-creation of masculinity more than any other group and see their sons' racial authenticity as inseparable from their masculinity.[70]

As a result, parents of these young men take action—initiating play dates, joining clubs, even moving residences—to increase same-race interaction between their sons and other boys.[70] These efforts at providing social support are evidence of a larger phenomenon. Latino and African American communities are similar in that that both rely on informal support networks in response to family crisis and their cultural norms foster a strong sense of communalism and familism.[69] While white, adult survivors are likely to utilize friends and authority figures for support,[51] their Latina peers are likely to seek maternal support, and their African American peers are more likely to reach out to extended family members.[57] Because of the previously discussed social, political, and cultural contexts, members of these ethnic groups are more likely to use informal sources of social support even though they may be aware of formal sources. Informal sources of support are by far the most helpful and protective factors for African American trauma survivors.[58,62]

In contrast, formal sources of support may be most helpful for Asian American survivors of sexual abuse. Even when experiencing emotional distress, members of Asian cultures tend to underutilize mental health services because mental illness is seen as less legitimate than physical illness. For this reason, mental health services are underutilized, but not physical health services.[60] Thus, medical doctors may be an important source of social support for Asian American survivors of sexual abuse.

For all minority groups it is important to utilize culturally sensitive methods and programs, which will take into account their unique experiences and worldviews. Whether minority groups distrust formal social services or have a preference for medical doctors, each community has unique needs when seeking social support to deal with sexual violence. Furthermore, it should be recognized that survivors in every culture have developed systems of social support to buffer the effects of sexual victimization. One study finds that the large majority of adult sexual abuse survivors report high levels of nonpartner social support (76% of white, 77% of African American, 71% of Latina, and 79% of other races).[71] Efforts to improve the quality of that support should recognize these existing assets and develop culturally relevant programs to enhance these formal or informal resources.

CONCLUSION

Social support can serve as a powerful buffer between the experience of sexual abuse and negative emotional, psychological, and behavioral outcomes. Providers of social support help to shape survivors' appraisals of the experience as well as their coping strategies. Various survivors report that these individuals' and/or groups' actions can represent an important juncture that leads survivors toward resilience trajectories. Thus, all sources of social support—whether emotional or tangible—are potentially beneficial, yet the potency of specific types of sources depends on the survivor's social characteristics.

The previous review reveals that the survivor's gender, ethnic/racial background, and location in the life course help to determine the salience of certain sources and types of support. It is important for the survivor, as well as their potential sources of support, to recognize these cultural-specific considerations and use them to guide help-seeking and help-providing efforts. It is equally important for interventionists and policy makers to be aware of these cultural-specific sources so they can bolster, augment, and/ or further develop existing assets.

To recap, we provide the following brief overview of sources of social support that are most salient to subpopulations.

Children: Child survivors of sexual abuse respond most positively when they are in a prolonged, caring relationship with a primary caregiver. Most of the literature focuses on mothers, but there is strong evidence that any stable, caring adult who provides both expressive and instrumental support can have a strong positive effect.

Adolescents: Adolescence represents the first time in the life course when the power of the familial social setting is rivaled by other social groups. For adolescent survivors of sexual abuse, support from community members—schools, churches, and so on—may be as important as support from family members.

Adults: Adult survivors are most heavily influenced by support from their peers and nonabusive romantic partners. Communal mastery—shared connections that lead to a sense of self-efficacy—seems to be the defining characteristic of these relationships, as adult survivors (compared to children or adolescents) benefit from the associated feeling of self-competence and empowerment.

Seniors: In U.S. society, we have developed institutions—Social Security, Medicare, nursing homes, and so on—that serve to formalize the care of seniors. As a result, formal forms of social support are particularly important for seniors who experience sexual abuse. It is very important, then, to support senior service providers so they do not succumb to compassion fatigue.

Men: Boys and men who survive sexual abuse benefit greatly from *nonthreatening* sources of social support, especially if these sources help them to tackle a daunting hurdle for this group: disclosure. The essential element seems to be social relations that do not challenge their physical or masculine power (e.g., relationships with children, pets, and caring adults).

Race/ethnicity: Different worldviews and access to resources serve to influence the forms of support that minority survivors are likely to recognize, appreciate, and benefit from. For example, Latino and African American sexual abuse survivors find informal support to be particularly beneficial (for Latinos, this tends to originate with mothers, but for African Americans it involves the extended family). Yet the cultured worldview of many Asian Americans makes formal support—especially from medical doctors—more desirable and influential.

Thus, anyone attempting to provide social support to sexual abuse survivors—whether a family member, friend, or practitioner—should take the survivor's social location into consideration. Of course, these categories are not mutually exclusive, and many survivors may simultaneously fall into several categories. This fact should be seen as a benefit, increasing the number of potential sources of support for any individual survivor.

If there is one consistent finding across all of these subpopulations, it is that more social support will increase the already large percentage of survivors who report positive life outcomes following their experience of sexual abuse.

Survivors of sexual abuse can draw strength from this fact. Sexual abuse is painful and can be quite challenging; however, if you are in this situation, you have choices:

1. Understand sexual violence is sex obtained without the other person's consent. There is no justification for violence.
2. Choose to disclose your abuse. You are not being disloyal to anyone if you report abuse. It is common to feel anxious about the possibility of a negative response, but the value of potentially positive responses is tremendous.
3. Seek assistance from at least one member of a support system. Social support can provide an outlet for expressing emotions and can educate you in different coping mechanisms. Even untrained friends and family members may be able to provide the support that you need.
4. Do not hesitate to utilize formal support services. Formal support services may be obtained from a variety of locations: local hospitals, clinics, schools, shelters, places of worship, and so on. Approach a professional you trust and he or she may be able to provide or direct you to appropriate sources of support.
5. Consider joining a support group. These groups improve self-esteem, help you feel empowered, provide a supportive environment, and encourage relationships with others in similar situations. These groups also foster an environment of respect and freedom of expression and allow you to learn new strategies for dealing with issues.

REFERENCES

1. Bernard-Bonnin, A., Hébert, M., Daignault, I., & Allard-Dansereau, C. (2008). Disclosure of sexual abuse, and personal and familial factors as predictors of post-traumatic stress disorder symptoms in school-aged girls. *Paediatrics & Child Health, 13*(6), 479–486.
2. Reyes, C. (2008). Exploring the relations among the nature of the abuse, perceived parental support, and child's self-concept and trauma symptoms among sexually abused children. *Journal of Child Sexual Abuse, 17*(1), 51–70.
3. Spaccarelli, S. (1994). Stress, appraisal, and coping in child sexual abuse: A theoretical and empirical review. *Psychological Bulletin, 116*, 340–362.
4. Bal, S., Crombez, G., De Bourdeaudhuij, I., & Van Oost, P. (2009). Symptomatology in adolescents following initial disclosure of sexual abuse: The roles of crisis support, appraisals and coping. *Child Abuse & Neglect, 33*, 717–727.

5. Folkman, S., Lazarus, R., Dunkel-Schetter, C., DeLongis, A., & Gruen, R. (1986). Dynamics of a stressful encounter: Cognitive appraisal, coping, and encounter outcomes. *Journal of Personality and Social Psychology, 50*(5), 992–1003.

6. Ullman, S. (2003). Social reactions to child sexual abuse disclosures: A critical review. *Journal of Child Sexual Abuse, 12*(1), 89–121.

7. Fassler, I., Amodeo, M., Griffin, M., Clay, C., & Ellis, M. (2005). Predicting long-term outcomes for women sexually abused in childhood: Contribution of abuse severity versus family environment. *Child Abuse & Neglect, 29*(3), 269–284.

8. Hill, A. (2009). Factors influencing the degree and pattern of parental involvement in play therapy for sexually abused children. *Journal of Child Sexual Abuse, 18*(4), 455–474.

9. Jonzon, E., & Lindblad, F. (2005). Adult female victims of child sexual abuse: Multitype maltreatment and disclosure characteristics related to subjective health. *Journal of Interpersonal Violence, 20*(6), 651–666.

10. Prati, G., & Pietrantoni, L. (2009). Optimism, social support, and coping strategies as factors contributing to posttraumatic growth: A meta-analysis. *Journal of Loss and Trauma, 14*(5), 364–388.

11. Murthi, M., & Espelage, D. (2005). Childhood sexual abuse, social support, and psychological outcomes: A loss framework. *Child Abuse & Neglect, 29*(11), 1215–1231.

12. Eisenberg, M., Ackard, D., & Resnick, M. (2007). Protective factors and suicide risk in adolescents with a history of sexual abuse. *The Journal of Pediatrics, 151*(5), 482–487.

13. O'Leary, P. (2009). Men who were sexually abused in childhood: Coping strategies and comparisons in psychological functioning. *Child Abuse & Neglect, 33*(7), 471–479.

14. Barker-Collo, S., Melnyk, W., & McDonald-Miszczak, L. (2000). A cognitive-behavioral model of post-traumatic stress for sexually abused females. *Journal of Interpersonal Violence, 15*(4), 375–392.

15. Dunmore, E., Clark, D., & Ehlers, A. (2001). A prospective investigation of the role of cognitive factors in persistent posttraumatic stress disorder (PTSD) after physical or sexual assault. *Behaviour Research and Therapy, 39*(9), 1063–1084.

16. Kilpatrick, D., Resnick, H., Ruggiero, K., Conoscenti, L., & McCauley, J. (2007). Drug-facilitated, incapacitated, and forcible rape: A national study. Charleston, SC: National Crime Victims Research and Treatment Center, Medical University of South Carolina.

17. Taft, C., Resick, P., Panuzio, J., Vogt, D., & Mechanic, M. (2007). Examining the correlates of engagement and disengagement coping among help-seeking battered women. *Violence and Victims, 22*(1), 3–17.

18. Domitrz, M. (2005). *Voices of Courage: Inspiration From Survivors of Sexual Assault.* Greenfield, WI: Awareness Publications.

19. Curtis, C. (2006). Sexual abuse and subsequent suicidal behaviour: Exacerbating factors and implications for recovery. *Journal of Child Sexual Abuse, 15*(2), 1–21.

20. Malloy, L., & Lyon, T. (2006). Caregiver support and child sexual abuse: Why does it matter? *Journal of Child Sexual Abuse, 15*(4), 97–103.

21. Cyr, M., Wright, J., Toupin, J., Oxman-Martinez, J., McDuff, P., & Thériault, C. (2003). Predictors of maternal support: The point of view of adolescent victims of sexual abuse and their mothers. *Journal of Child Sexual Abuse, 12*(1), 39–65.

22. Korol, S. (2008). Familial and social support as protective factors against the development of dissociative identity disorder. *Journal of Trauma & Dissociation, 9*(2), 249–267.

23. DuMont, K., Widom, C., & Czaja, S. (2007). Predictors of resilience in abused and neglected children grown-up: The role of individual and neighborhood characteristics. *Child Abuse & Neglect, 31*(3), 255–274.

24. Bolen, R., & Lamb, L. (2007). Can nonoffending mothers of sexually abused children be both ambivalent and supportive? *Child Maltreatment, 12*(2), 191–197.

25. Costas, M., & Landreth, G. (1999). Filial therapy with nonoffending parents of children who have been sexually abused. *International Journal of Play Therapy, 8*(1), 43–66.

26. Jinich, S., & Litrownik, A. (1999). Coping with sexual abuse: Development and evaluation of a videotape intervention for nonoffending parents. *Child Abuse & Neglect, 23*(2), 175–190.

27. Cohen, J., Deblinger, E., Mannarino, A., & Steer, R. (2004). A multisite, randomized controlled trial for children with abuse-related PTSD symptoms. *Journal of the American Academy of Child and Adolescent Psychiatry, 43*(4), 393–402.

28. Bowlby, J. (1988). *A Secure Base*. London: Routledge.

29. Wolff, S. (1995). The concept of resilience. *Australasian Psychiatry, 29*(4), 565–574.

30. Edmond, T., Auslander, W., Elze, D., & Bowland, S. (2006). Signs of resilience in sexually abused adolescent girls in the foster care system. *Journal of Child Sexual Abuse, 15*(1), 1–28.

31. Masten, A. (2001). Ordinary magic: Resilience processes in development. *American Psychologist, 56*(3), 227–238.

32. Banyard, V., & Williams, L. (2007). Women's voices on recovery: A multimethod study of the complexity of recovery from child sexual abuse. *Child Abuse & Neglect, 31*(3), 275–290.

33. Tarakeshwar, N., Hansen, N., Kochman, A., Fox, A., & Sikkema, K. (2006). Resiliency among individuals with childhood sexual abuse and HIV: Perspectives on addressing sexual trauma. *Journal of Traumatic Stress, 19*(4), 449–460.

34. Hobfoll, S., Jackson, A., Hobfoll, I., Pierce, C., & Young, S. (2002). The impact of communal-mastery versus self-mastery on emotional outcomes during stressful conditions: A prospective study of Native American women. *American Journal of Community Psychology, 30*(6), 853–871.

35. Del Castillo, D., & O'Dougherty Wright, M. (2009). The perils and possibilities in disclosing childhood sexual abuse to a romantic partner. *Journal of Child Sexual Abuse, 18*(4), 386–404.

36. Shields, L., Hunsaker, D., & Hunsaker 3rd, J. (2004). Abuse and neglect: A ten-year review of mortality and morbidity in our elders in a large metropolitan area. *Journal of Forensic Sciences, 49*(1), 122.

37. Brandl, B., & Cook-Daniels, L. (2002). Domestic abuse in later life. *Applied Research Forum*, at www.vawnet.org.

38. Dietz, T., & Wright, J. (2005). Victimization of the elderly homeless. *Care Management Journals, 6*(1), 15–21.

39. Dyer, C., Heisler, C., Hill, C., & Kim, L. (2005). Community approaches to elder abuse. *Clinics in Geriatric Medicine, 21*(2), 429–447.

40. Simmelink, K. (1996). Lessons learned from three elderly sexual assault survivors. *Journal of Emergency Nursing, 22*(6), 619–621.

41. Muram, D., Miller, K., & Cutler, A. (1992). Sexual assault of the elderly victim. *Journal of Interpersonal Violence, 7*(1), 70–76.

42. Acierno, R., Hernandez, M., Amstadter, A., Resnick, H., Steve, K., Muzzy, W., et al. (2010). Prevalence and correlates of emotional, physical, sexual, and financial abuse and potential neglect in the United States: The national elder mistreatment study. *American Journal of Public Health, 100*(2), 292–297.

43. Ramsey-Klawsnik, H. (2004). Elder sexual abuse within the family. *Journal of Elder Abuse & Neglect, 15*(1), 43–58.

44. Vierthaler, K. (2008). Best practices for working with rape crisis centers to address elder sexual abuse. *Journal of Elder Abuse & Neglect, 20*(4), 306–322.

45. Bourassa, D.B. (2009). Compassion Fatigue and the Adult Protective Services Social Worker. *Journal of Gerontological Social Work, 52*(3), 215–229.

46. Kia-Keating, M., Sorsoli, L., & Grossman, F.K. Relational challenges and recovery processes in male survivors of childhood sexual abuse. *Journal of Interpersonal Violence, 25*(4), 666–683.

47. Willis, D. (2009). Male-on-male rape of an adult man: A case review and implications for interventions. *Journal of the American Psychiatric Nurses Association, 14*(6), 454–461.

48. Ray, S. L. (2001). Male survivors' perspectives of incest/sexual abuse. *Perspectives in Psychiatric Care, 37*(2), 49–59.

49. Sorsoli, L., Kia-Keating, M., & Grossman, F.K. (2008). "I keep that hush-hush": Male survivors of sexual abuse and the challenges of disclosure. *Journal of Counseling Psychology, 55*(3), 333–345.

50. Pino, N., & Meier, R. (1999). Gender differences in rape reporting. *Sex Roles, 40*(11), 979–990.

51. Wyatt, G. (1990). The aftermath of child sexual abuse of African American and White American women: The victim's experience. *Journal of Family Violence, 5*(1), 61–81.

52. Putnam, F. (2003). Ten-year research update review: Child sexual abuse. *Journal of American Academy of Child & Adolescent Psychiatry, 42*(3), 269–278.

53. Kilpatrick, D., Saunders, B., Amick-McMullan, A., Best, C., Veronen, L., & Resnick, H. (1989). Victim and crime factors associated with the development of crime-related post-traumatic stress disorder. *Behavior Therapy, 20*(2), 199–214.

54. Wyatt, G., Axelrod, J., Chin, D., Carmona, J., & Loeb, T. (2000). Examining patterns of vulnerability to domestic violence among African American women. *Violence Against Women, 6*(5), 495–514.

55. Mennen, F. (1995). The relationship of race/ethnicity to symptoms in childhood sexual abuse. *Child Abuse & Neglect, 19*(1), 115–124.

56. Wyatt, G. (1985). The sexual abuse of Afro-American and White-American women in childhood. *Child Abuse & Neglect, 9*(4), 507–519.

57. Rao, K., DiClemente, R., & Ponton, L. (1992). Child sexual abuse of Asians compared with other populations. *Journal of Amer Academy of Child & Adolescent Psychiatry, 31*(5), 880–886.
58. Bryant-Davis, T., Chung, H., & Tillman, S. (2009). From the margins to the center. *Trauma, Violence & Abuse: A Review Journal, 10*(4), 330–357.
59. Morrow, K., & Sorell, G. (1989). Factors affecting self-esteem, depression, and negative behaviors in sexually abused female adolescents. *Journal of Marriage and the Family, 51*(3), 677–686.
60. Futa, K., Hsu, E., & Hansen, D. (2001). Child sexual abuse in Asian American families: An examination of cultural factors that influence prevalence, identification, and treatment. *Clinical Psychology Science and Practice, 8*(2), 189–209.
61. Roosa, M., Reinholtz, C., & Angelini, P. (1999). The relation of child sexual abuse and depression in young women: Comparison across four ethnic groups. *Journal of Abnormal Child Psychology, 27*(1), 65–76.
62. Fowler, D., & Hill, H. (2004). Social support and spirituality as culturally relevant factors in coping among African American women survivors of partner abuse. *Violence Against Women, 10*(11), 1267–1282.
63. Jasinski, J., Williams, L., & Siegel, J. (2000). Childhood physical and sexual abuse as risk factors for heavy drinking among African-American women: A prospective study. *Child Abuse & Neglect, 24*(8), 1061–1071.
64. Wingood, G., & DiClemente, R. (1998). Partner influences and gender-related factors associated with noncondom use among young adult African American women. *American Journal of Community Psychology, 26*(1), 29–51.
65. Gillum, T. (2008). The benefits of a culturally specific intimate partner violence intervention for African American survivors. *Violence Against Women, 14*(8), 917–943.
66. Franklin, A., Boyd-Franklin, N., & Kelly, S. (2006). Racism and invisibility. *Journal of Emotional Abuse, 6*(2), 9–30.
67. Turner, H., Finkelhor, D., & Ormrod, R. (2006). The effect of lifetime victimization on the mental health of children and adolescents. *Social Science & Medicine, 62*(1), 13–27.
68. Bent-Goodley, T. (2009). A black experience based approach to gender-based violence. *Social Work, 54*(3), 262–269.
69. Domitrz, M. (2005). *Voices of Courage: Inspiration from Survivors of Sexual Assault.* Greenfield, WI: Awareness Publications.
70. McGuffey, C. (2008). "Saving masculinity:" Gender reaffirmation, sexuality, race, and parental responses to male child sexual abuse. *Social Problems, 55*(2), 216–237.
71. Carlson, B., McNutt, L., Choi, D., & Rose, I. (2002). Intimate partner abuse and mental health: The role of social support and other protective factors. *Violence Against Women, 8*(6), 720–745.

20

Spirituality/Religion as a Healing Pathway for Survivors of Sexual Violence

Sannisha Dale and Jessica Henderson Daniel

INTRODUCTION

Many survivors of sexual violence face a journey of negative psychological consequences.[1] However, depending on factors existing before, during, and after the trauma, many survivors experience healing. Two factors that have provided a pathway to healing for some survivors of sexual violence are spirituality and religion. This chapter discusses the role of spirituality and religion in the healing process. Definitions for spirituality and religion and distinctions between the two concepts will be provided in section one. Section two will present a review of the literature on spirituality/religiosity as coping strategies that promote healing. In section three we will acknowledge the recent emerging literature that explores the reciprocal impact of sexual abuse on spirituality as well as negative forms of spiritual coping. Additionally, we note the implications for mental health interventions, describe a case example of a survivor whose use of spirituality was central to her recovery, and summarize the major points made throughout the chapter. Finally we will conclude with a few exercises for survivors who would like to connect with their spirituality as a part of their recovery.

SPIRITUALITY VERSUS RELIGION

Spirituality and religion have been defined as similar yet separate multidimensional concepts in psychology. Spilka highlighted three conceptualizations of spirituality: (1) a form of spirituality that is God-oriented with thoughts and practices rooted in theologies; (2) a world-oriented spirituality that emphasizes the individual's relationship with ecology or nature; and (3) a humanistic spirituality highlighting human potential and achievement.[2] LaPierre noted that a spiritual experience may have several components including a search for meaning and ultimate truth, sense of community, and personal transformation.[3] Similarly religion assists individuals in finding meaning and community as well as addressing their ultimate concerns. However, religion is often viewed as an institution that encourages certain behaviors and practices based on doctrines, creeds, and values.[4,5] A person's religious experience might be organized (e.g., attending church services) or nonorganized (e.g., praying at home).[6] Although many psychologists distinguish between religiosity and spirituality, some argue that the separation might be artificial[7] and insignificant since the majority of Americans maintain active religious beliefs and practices[8] and consider religiosity and spirituality to be interchangeable.[7] In the U.S. population estimates of the distribution of groups related to faith are 82.3% Christian, 11.2% agnostic, 1.8% Jewish, 1.6% Muslim, and 0.9% Buddhist.[9]

HEALING PATHWAY

Several research studies have highlighted spirituality/religiosity as a coping strategy that promotes healing in general and specifically among victims of sexual violence. As stated in prior chapters, sexual violence results in short-term and long-term consequences for many of its victims. Valentine and Feinauer interviewed twenty-two women with childhood sexual abuse histories who in adulthood were able to maintain stable relationships, successful careers, and healthy personalities.[10] These women reported that spirituality/religiosity contributed to their recovery from sexual abuse in several ways. First, through their religion and church they found a supportive network of people with whom they were able to interact. Second, it gave them faith, which helped them to find meaning and purpose. Third, they gained the understanding that they could survive the hard times and God would help to make things better. Fourth, spirituality/religiosity gave them the insight that they were of worth despite the adversity they were experiencing.

Chandy, Blum, and Resick found that among adolescent girls who were victims of childhood sexual assault, those who viewed themselves as religious/spiritual were less at risk for psychological or interpersonal problems.[11] Similarly in a sample of 653 men and women it was found that victims of childhood sexual abuse who engaged in more religious practices reported fewer symptoms of depression and higher self-esteem.[12] Among twenty-five men sexually abused in childhood, some men reported using spirituality to make meaning of the abuse and also entering professions to help others.[13] Bryant-Davis (2005) conducted a retrospective study among seventy African American adult survivors of childhood violence (25% of whom survived childhood sexual abuse) to explore the use of various coping strategies.[14] Her findings were that both males and females in the sample utilized spirituality as a coping strategy in the form of beliefs, prayer, and attending pastoral counseling. In general spirituality/religiosity has been recognized as an important coping strategy in the African American community.[15]

In a naturalistic study on the experiences of fourteen women healing from childhood sexual abuse, some participants described that they found support in "relationships with God, church, religion, angels and nature."[16] In interviews with ten women who survived childhood sexual abuse, Bogar and Hulse-Killacky found that spirituality was a common aspect of their recovery from the abuse.[17]

Knapik, Martsolf, and Draucker developed a theoretical framework to explain how survivors of sexual violence utilize spirituality to respond to the abuse on their path to recovery based on interviews with twenty-seven women and twenty-three men.[18] The framework consists of the core category of the Being Delivered and categories of Spiritual Connection, Spiritual Journey, and Spiritual Transformation. Being Delivered captures the participants' experience of being set free or rescued from the aftermath of the sexual violence by a spiritual power. Spiritual Connection reflects the participants' description of a connection or attempt to connect with a higher power via activities such as prayer or worship. Having a strong spiritual connection laid the foundation for some participants to begin on a Spiritual Journey on which they are strengthened and supported; develop a greater sense of awareness and insight from a divine perspective; and/or experience trials and tribulations from God that help them grow stronger. A few participants' spiritual journey led them to Spiritual Transformation as they began to view their sexual violence in a spiritually meaningful way and experienced a deep sense of divine intervention in their lives. Knapik et al. quoted one of their participants to illustrate spiritual transformation.[18]

> It was a healing process. You know, sometimes, you don't know you're hurting. Sometimes you don't know you are a wounded person, but what is that scripture "a new being in Christ, he's a new creature, the old things have passed away and behold all things become new." And that's basically the truth, I had a new way of doing things, a new way. (p. 345)

RECIPROCAL IMPACT OF SEXUAL ABUSE ON SPIRITUALITY

Although studies described previously have found spirituality/religiosity to contribute to healing for victims of sexual violence, the negative impact of sexual abuse on spirituality/religiosity must also be acknowledged. Among a sample of 150 college students Reinert and Edwards[19] found that verbal, physical, and sexual abuse during childhood correlated with views of God as controlling, distant, and unloving. Similarly in a sample of 150 Mormon women who were sexually abused during childhood, abuse was associated with lower spiritual well-being as well as viewing God as more punitive and distant.[20] The severity and frequency of sexual abuse have also been associated with lower spiritual well-being.[21,22]

One can also imagine how damaging sexual abuse committed by members/leaders of the church might be to the spirituality of the victim. Isely et al. conducted interviews with nine men who were sexually abused by members of the Catholic clergy, and the men reported feelings of guilt, confusion, and anger.[23] Studies have found individuals are more likely to disclose childhood sexual abuse when the perpetrator is a stranger and not a family member[24,25] and take longer to disclose when it is a member of their family.[26] The extent to which the church represents a pseudofamily to its members may further complicate the challenges to disclosure[27,28] by victims of sexual violence within the church. For instance, in the Black community churches play important supportive roles such as caring for children after school.[29] Recently a lawsuit was filed against a bishop of the New Birth Missionary Baptist Church, a predominantly Black congregation in Georgia, by two young men who claimed that they were sexually abused by a bishop who gave them gifts such as expensive cars and free hotel stays.[30] There were also allegations that officials of the church knew of the sexual acts but concealed them. Besides having their crimes concealed, some convicted sex offenders may seek restoration in churches and be embraced and forgiven by some church members.[31] These occurrences may further exacerbate the anger and confusion of victims toward the church and religion as well as place other members at risk.

Given the fact that sexual violence may negatively impact the survivors' religiosity/spirituality, reconstructing or maintaining a sense of spirituality may be significant and beneficial. For instance, Gall et al. found that victims of long-term abuse viewed God as less benevolent, but participants who reported a more positive relationship with God reported fewer symptoms of depression, anger, and anxiety.[32] Elliot reported similar findings among 2,964 professional women (918 CSA).[33] Among those from conservative Christian backgrounds, abuse survivors were less likely to participate in organized religion in adulthood; however fewer post-traumatic stress symptoms were reported among those who practiced organized religion as adults.

NEGATIVE SPIRITUAL COPING STRATEGIES

While the distinction between positive and negative spiritual/religious coping strategies is not always made by researchers, it is important. Pargament et al. explored positive and negative religious strategies among individuals coping with the Oklahoma City bombing, college students dealing with major life stressors, and patients coping with medical illnesses.[34] He found that positive religious coping consisted of religious forgiveness, seeking spiritual support, collaborating with God to solve problems, spiritual connection, searching for purification through religious activities, and religiously viewing the stressor as potentially benevolent. Negative spiritual coping strategies included spiritual discontent, viewing the stressor as a punishment from God because of their sins, dissatisfaction with religious leaders and members, appraising the stressor as the devil's doing, and reappraisal of God's powers. Gall examined the role of spiritual coping in addressing current life stressors for adult survivors of child sexual abuse, and in doing so he distinguished between negative and positive spiritual coping strategies.[35] Negative spiritual coping includes anger, detachment, and personal discontent in the relationship with the higher being or church community. Examples of positive forms of spiritual coping are reliance on the security and comfort of a higher being, and during stressful events seeking support from the higher being. Gall's study found that negative spiritual coping (e.g., discontent) predicted greater depressive mood while positive spiritual coping (e.g., seeking God's support) was related to lower levels of depression.[35]

IMPLICATIONS FOR MENTAL HEALTH PROVIDERS

Given that spirituality/religiosity may help survivors as they strive to heal from sexual violence, mental health providers may consider incorporating discussions about spirituality/religion into the therapeutic process based on the client's interest. However, in broaching the subject of religion/spirituality therapists cannot assume that spirituality/religion will be eagerly welcomed by the survivor, because as stated above, sexual trauma can be related to negative views of religion (e.g., God as distant and unloving). Likewise not all forms of spiritual coping are positive, and therefore if a client utilizes spirituality as a coping strategy, the therapist is advised to gain an understanding of how the client conceptualizes spirituality in their life. As with all values, it is critical that the therapist be aware of their own spiritual/religious or nonspiritual ideologies and be mindful not to use these beliefs to guide their decision in whether they explore spirituality as a coping strategy if the client wishes to do so.

CASE EXAMPLE

A nineteen-year-old African American female presented for therapy with complaints of nightmares, disrupted sleep, flashbacks, and hypervigilance.

She wanted to learn ways to alleviate her symptoms, but initially she was reluctant to disclose or revisit the traumatic events that caused her symptoms. After two months of increasing her trust in the therapist and the process the client shared that her virginity was stolen and she had been violently raped by a family friend as her male cousin looked on and yelled at her to stop resisting. The client reported that after the assault she was in disbelief, especially because of her relationship with the perpetrators. Prior to the rape the client was raised in a Christian home and had been a frequent churchgoer. When she disclosed the trauma to a female relative, who was a devout Christian and sibling to the brother who looked on, she was told that she should get baptized and give her life over to the Lord. The client expressed outrage at the emphasis that was placed on her doing something to heal and the lack of discourse about the perpetrators. For months the client felt isolated and alone in her struggle. She distanced herself from church members and stopped attending church because she feared that their reaction would be similar to that of her female relative who centered the conversation on the client trying to get better and dismissing the role of the perpetrators. Following her sharing of the trauma in therapy, sessions were spent addressing themes of anger, trust, and spirituality. The client questioned the idea of a "just God" because although she called on him for help during the assault and the aftermath, she felt that her prayers went unanswered. The therapist acknowledged and empathized with the client's shattered view of God and members of her religious community. The therapist also suggested an activity in which the client could choose a story of suffering and healing from her religious doctrines and share it with the therapist in the following session, in which they would discuss the themes of the story and how the person healed. Forgiveness was a significant theme in the first story, and the client was adamant that she was not ready to either forgive or forget. The therapist again validated her emotions and reassured her that healing was a process that she could take at her own pace. After a few months of sharing and discussing stories of suffering and healing in Christianity the client explained that she was still disappointed that God did not prevent the rape from occurring, but she believed He helped her to survive and make it to where she is today. She also believed that God could help her on her journey as she moved forward. The client expressed that she missed praying, listening to gospel, and attending church. The therapist helped her explore her desire to engage in those activities as well as her ambivalence. For instance the client shared that she wanted to pray, but she feared that God would sense her remaining anger toward him and she had never expressed negative emotions toward God in prayer before. Through exploration of the issues that arose around spirituality for this client she gradually returned to praying, listening to gospel, and attending church, all of which contributed to her healing.

CHAPTER SUMMARY

Sexual violence is widespread and can result in short-term (e.g., fear) and long-term consequences (e.g., post-traumatic stress disorder, substance abuse) for many of its victims. Spirituality/religion is a coping mechanism that provides a pathway to healing for some survivors of sexual violence. Throughout this chapter we (a) compared the definitions for spirituality and religion; (b) reviewed research studies that support spirituality/religiosity as coping strategies that promote healing; and (c) acknowledged the recent emerging literature that explores the reciprocal impact of sexual abuse on spirituality as well as negative forms of spiritual coping. Lastly, based on the presented information, we noted a few implications for mental health providers.

Further research is needed for practitioners to have a more nuanced awareness and understanding of spirituality/religiosity. The exploration of the intersection of spirituality/religiosity with variables such as race/ethnicity, gender, sexual orientation, disability status, immigrant status, socioeconomic status, and development (emotional, cognitive, and social) may provide additional insights for both researchers and practitioners regarding spirituality/religiosity and other coping mechanisms as strategies for coping with and healing from sexual violence.

EXERCISES FOR SURVIVORS TO CONSIDER

For survivors who are interested in utilizing spiritual/religious coping strategies as they heal from sexual abuse, several activities might be beneficial. Defining what spirituality/religiosity means in their personal life is the first step. Some individuals might adhere to specific doctrines and practices as recommended by a religious denomination, but for others spirituality might entail believing in a higher power and engaging in explorations of nature and meditation. Once survivors have began to clarify the meaning of spirituality in their lives, engaging in applicable activities such as prayer, meditation, relaxation exercises, and so on, might be helpful. Other activities include reading spiritual/religious writings about healing and growth and listening to related music. Many spiritual/religious activities can be done in solitude or with groups. Private activities may help a survivor to strengthen their personal sense of spirituality, while attending groups (e.g., church ceremonies, meditation groups, and prayer groups) also offers a community of members who can be a source of support. In seeking support from members/leaders of spiritual/religious groups survivors may wish to disclose their sexual abuse history; however, survivors must be careful in seeking out members/leaders who are non-victim-blaming and nonjudgmental. If a survivor is engaging in therapy and desires to have their spiritual/religious thoughts and practices integrated in the treatment, survivors should broach the topic with the therapist. Some therapists are trained and comfortable addressing issues around spirituality, while others are not. Those who are not trained may be able to provide referrals to counselors who are. Healing after sexual abuse is a challenging journey, and spirituality/religion can be a source of strength along the way.

REFERENCES

1. Resick, P.A. (1993): The psychological impact of rape. *Journal of Interpersonal Violence, 8*, 223–255.
2. Spilka, B. (1993, August). Spirituality: Problems and directions in operationalizing a fuzzy concept. Paper presented at the meeting of the American Psychological Association. Toronto, Ontario.
3. Lapierre, L.L. (1994). A model for describing spirituality. *Journal of Religion and Health, 33*, 153–161.
4. Marty, M.E., Applyby, R.S., Eds. (1991). *Fundamentalisms observed.* Chicago: University of Chicago Press.
5. King, D.G. (1990). Religion and health relationships: A review. *Journal of Religion and Health, 29*(2), 101–112.
6. Strawbridge, W.J., Shema, S.J., Cohen, R.D., Roberts, R.E., & Kaplan, G.A. (1998). Religiosity buffers effects of some stressors on depression but exacerbates others. *Journal of Gerontology, 53B*(3), S118–S126.
7. Hill, P.C., & Pargament, K.I. (2003). Advances in the conceptualization of and measurement of religion and spirituality: Implications for physical and mental health research. *American Psychologist, 58*, 64–74.
8. Gallup, G., Jr. (1994). *The Gallup Poll: Public opinion 1993.* Wilmington, DE: Scholarly Resources.
9. Association of Religion Data Archives. (2010). United States: Religious Adherents. Retrieved from http://www.thearda.com/internationalData/countries/Country_234_2.asp
10. Valentine, L., & Feinauer, L.L. (1993). Resilience factors associated with female survivors of childhood sexual abuse. *The American Journal of Family Therapy, 21*, 216–224.
11. Chandy, J.M., Blum, R.W., & Resnick, M.D. 1996. Female adolescents with a history of sexual abuse. Risk outcome and protective factors. *Journal of Interpersonal Violence, 11*, 503–518.
12. Doxey, C., Jensen, L., & Jensen, J. (1997). The influence of religion on victims of childhood sexual abuse. *International Journal for the Psychology of Religion, 7*, 179–186.
13. Etherington, K. (1995). Adult male survivors of childhood sexual abuse. *Counseling Psychology Quarterly, 8*, 233–242.
14. Bryant-Davis, T. (2005). Coping strategies of African American adult survivors of childhood violence. *Professional Psychology: Research and Practice, 36*, 409–414.

15. Joseph, M. (1998). The effect of strong religious beliefs on coping with stress. *Stress Medicine, 14,* 219–224.
16. Glaister, J.A., & E. Abel. 2001. Experiences of women healing from childhood sexual abuse. *Archives of Psychiatric Nursing, 15*(4), 188–94.
17. Bogar, C.B., & Hulse-Killacky, D. (2006). Resiliency determinants and resiliency processes among female adult survivors of childhood sexual abuse. *Journal of Counseling and Development, 84,* 318–327.
18. Knapik, G.P., Martsolf, D.S., & Draucker, C.B. (2008). Being delivered: Spirituality in survivors of sexual violence. *Issues in Mental Health Nursing, 29*(4), 335–350.
19. Reinert, D.F., & Edwards, C.E. (2009). Attachment theory, childhood maltreatment, and religiosity. *Psychology of Religion and Spirituality, 1,* 25–34.
20. Pritt, A.F. (1998). Spiritual correlates of reported sexual abuse among Mormon women. *Journal for the Scientific Study of Religion, 37,* 273–285.
21. Feinauer, L., Middleton, K.C., & Hilton, G.H. (2003). Existential well-being as a factor in the adjustment of adults sexually abused as children. *The American Journal of Family Therapy, 31,* 201–213.
22. Weber, L.J., & Cummings, A.L. (2003). Relationships among spirituality, social support, and childhood maltreatment in university students. *Counseling and Values, 47,* 82–95.
23. Isely, P.J., Isely, P., Freiburger, J., & McMackin, R. (2008). In their own voices: A qualitative study of men abused as children by Catholic clergy. *Journal of Child Sexual Abuse, 17,* 201–215.
24. Hanson, R.F., Resnick, H.S., Saunders, B.E., Kilpatrick, D.G., & Best, C. (1999). Factors related to the reporting of childhood rape. *Child Abuse & Neglect, 23,* 559–569.
25. Smith, D., Letourneau, E.J., Saunders, B.E., Kilpatrick, D.G., Resnick, H.S., & Best, C.L. (2000). Delay in disclosure of childhood rape: Results from a national survey.*Child Abuse & Neglect, 24,* 273–287.
26. Ussher, J.M., & Dewberry, C. (1995). The nature and long-term effects of childhood sexual abuse: A survey of women survivors in Britain. *British Journal of Clinical Psychology, 34,* 177–192.
27. London, K., Bruck, M., Ceci, S.J., & Shuman, D.W. (2005). Disclosure of child sexual abuse: What does the research tell us about the ways that children tell? *Psychology, Public Policy, and Law, 11*(1), 194–226.
28. Sorsoli, L., Kia-Keating, M., & Grossman, F.K. (2008). "I keep that hush-hush": Male survivors of sexual abuse and the challenges of disclosure. *Journal of Counseling Psychology, 55*(3), 333–345.
29. McAdoo, H., & Crawford, V. (1991). The Black church and family support programs. *Prevention in Human Services, 9*(1), 193–203.
30. Brown, R. (2010, September 21). Lawsuits accuse megachurch leader of sexual misconduct. *The New York Times.* Retrieved from http://www.nytimes.com/2010/09/22/us/22church.html
31. Yantzi, Mark. (1998). *Sexual offending and restoration.* Pennsylvania: Herald Press.
32. Gall, T.L., Basque, V., Damasceno-Scott, M., & Vardy, G. (2007). Spirituality and the current adjustment of adult survivors of childhood sexual abuse. *Journal for the Scientific Study of Religion, 46,* 101–117.

33. Elliott, D.M., Mok, D.S., & Briere, J. (2004). Adult sexual assault: prevalence, symptomatology, and sex differences in the general population. *Journal of Traumatic Stress, 17*(3), 203–211.

34. Pargament, K.I., Smith, B.W., Koenig, H.G., & Perez, L. (1998). Patterns of positive and negative religious coping with major life stressors. *Journal for the Scientific Study of Religion, 37*(4), 710–724.

35. Gall, T.L. (2006). Spirituality and coping with life stress among adult survivors of childhood sexual abuse. *Child Abuse and Neglect, 30,* 826–844.

21

Writing Your Way to Peace and Power: Empowerment Journaling as a Pathway to Healing and Growth

Shelly P. Harrell

Release your pain.
Express yourself.
Free your mind.
Find your voice.
Speak your truth.
Connect to your spirit.
Tell your story.
Process your experiences.
Gain understanding.
Make your action plan.
Focus your energies.
Bear witness to your own transformation.
Let your creativity break through.

These are pathways to healing, empowerment, and transformative growth that I have observed among men and women who have experienced sexual violence. Writing is a vehicle that can be used to travel these pathways. Sexual violence can create internal unrest and lessen the feeling of personal power. This chapter will introduce you to a journaling method and offer strategies that can become important tools for the journey to peace, power, and transformation. Survivors of sexual violence often struggle with issues of shame and guilt. Trusting other people, feelings of safety and security, and self-esteem are frequently threatened by experiences of sexual violence. Withdrawing from or avoiding relationships and shutting down emotionally, or increased conflict in relationships and trouble controlling one's emotions are other common consequences. Sometimes these factors prevent the survivor from disclosing the experience or sharing what they have gone through in the aftermath.[1-3] Unfortunately, this way of coping can prolong the time it takes to fully emerge from living in the shadow of sexual violence. Journaling allows you to process your experiences, thoughts, and feelings so that you can emerge strengthened with increased clarity and positive feelings about yourself and your purpose.[4-7] Through a process that can happen in your own time, with your own voice, in your own way, writing can forge a path to come into the light. *Empowerment journaling* is offered here as an approach to writing that focuses on methods that can help you find your peace and claim your power.

Psychologists have done decades of research providing strong evidence that writing helps to decrease distress over time, improve physical health and immune system functioning, increase working memory, and enhance positive well-being.[8-13] The research supports what everyday people have known for centuries—that writing heals, empowers, and transforms. From keeping a daily diary, to documenting a trip in a travel log, to reflecting on happenings in the world, to telling one's life story, to expressing feelings through lyrics and poetry, to composing a love letter, writing has always served important personal, social, and cultural functions. Writing is a powerful opportunity for personal expression that emphasizes freedom, choice, and self-determination. Writing interventions have been used by therapists in the form of journaling, poetry, and structured "homework" exercises. Writing is used in education to teach critical thinking and reflective practice and encourage self-evaluation. Writing is an active, creative process that happens at the intersection of internal processes, external experience, and the culture and context in which experience occurs. Journaling is a vehicle for self-expression that differentiates itself from other forms of expressive arts therapies because the act of writing, which requires language and cognitive functions, provides an opportunity to integrate thinking and emotional processes in a holistic process. Lepore and Smyth suggest that writing has a powerful role "to positively shape, or reshape, human experiences, in the context or aftermath of stressful life experiences" (p. 3).[14]

So how does writing help? Writing helps by opening an opportunity for you to clear your mind and release built-up feelings. Writing helps by providing a place to express yourself and speak your truth freely, without interruption or judgment. Writing helps by integrating your thoughts and your emotions so that you can feel whole. Writing helps by setting aside time to organize your thoughts, set goals, and figure out how you are going to achieve them. Writing helps by allowing you to actively process something that can lead to insights, revelations, and new understandings. Writing helps by giving you space for your creative self to break through. Writing helps by documenting your journey so that you can see how far you have come. Writing helps by providing a safe space where you are in control. Research studies are increasingly adding knowledge that is giving us better clues on the multiple mechanisms involved in the pathway between writing about something personal and the beneficial outcomes that studies consistently find. These include catharsis, exposure, emotional regulation, self-affirmation, narrative coherence, meaning making, benefit finding, broaden-and-build theory of positive emotions, insight and reflexivity, self-understanding, experiential learning, identity stabilization, and the integration of emotional and cognitive processes.[14-22] For readers interested in the theoretical and empirical foundations for writing as an effective element of the healing process, I particularly encourage you to explore work by James Pennebaker, Gillie Bolton, Stephen Lepore, and Joshua Smyth.[8-9,12-14,18-19]

A JOURNAL ENTRY YOU CAN DO RIGHT NOW
Visualize and Mobilize
Purpose: To provide a space to identify your wants and needs and begin making steps toward fulfilling them.

What is something that you would like to see manifest in your life? 1. Write it down. *Example: "I want a car so I don't have to take the bus to work anymore."* Close your eyes and transport yourself to your life with the change you want. Visualize it. 2. Now write a description of a snippet of a day in your life with this change. *Example: "I wake up in the morning and . . .."* 3. Finally, make a list of three things you can start doing right now that will move you toward the change. *Example: "1. Save $100 out of every paycheck; 2. Research cars and prices; 3. Identify cars within my budget to test drive."* Activation of the behaviors you identified in the third step may require assistance or further planning. Moreover, the specifics of what you want may change as you get more information or as your priorities shift. Flexibility in the target outcome is important. The healing process is the use of writing to increase the intentionality of your behavior and to direct cognitive and emotional energy toward mobilizing yourself to action that reflects your values.

Incorporating writing into your healing process can be done in several ways. Writing can be guided by a therapist or counselor as part of treatment. Writing can be used as an adjunct to therapy through workbooks[17] or writing groups.[18] Most commonly, however, writing is a self-guided activity. Many, many journaling and writing strategies have been developed.[7,18-19, 23-24] Journal therapists and writing coaches agree that there is no single "best" way to journal. There is only the best way for you. The following three examples provide illustrations of how these clients found their way to journaling.

Kayla: "But I don't like to write"

Kayla was thirty-two years old when I met her. She had been sexually abused by her uncle from age nine until she ran away to live with her boyfriend when she was seventeen. By the time she was twenty-five she had been beaten, thrown down steps, strangled, and raped by this boyfriend too many times to mention. After a brief period of homelessness, she was hired by an elderly woman as a live-in caregiver. She hasn't been in an intimate relationship since then and has steadily gained weight over the years, reaching her highest weight of 314 pounds when I started working with her.

"That's not going to work for me," Kayla stated emphatically.

I responded, "How do you know?"

"Because I don't like to write, it gives me a headache."

"Okay. I hear you. Do you have a notes function or notepad in your phone?"

"Yeah."

"How about if you just type in a note with just one word each day that describes something about how you are feeling or something that happened. If you sat on the couch all day watching TV you could write *bored* or *couch* or *TV*.

"That seems stupid."

"It may *feel* stupid too. But what will it hurt to try it?" I smiled.

"Alright. Whatever." Kayla smiled back.

"Let's start right now. Take your phone out and type in just ONE word that describes something about how you are feeling or what you are thinking now."

Kayla typed the word *nothing*. For three weeks she either input the word *nothing* or didn't input anything at all. Then one day she typed the word *mad*. And she typed *mad* every day for a week, sometimes more than once a day. The last input she made in her phone was the word *mad* . . . twenty-seven times with no spaces. She then sent me a text and said she was ready to write. Kayla's been writing ever since. She told me writing still gives her a headache . . . but that it's the good kind of headache.

Freddie: "It happened so long ago, what's the big deal?"

A friend told Freddie about me. He didn't want to come to therapy; he just wanted to "ask a few questions." I told him that I could do a single consultation and evaluation session. Twenty-six years old, married, with a one-year-old son and a successful restaurant business, he shared with me that when he was seven years old, his swimming teacher at summer camp had molested him. He found out that the man had died recently, and since then he had not been able to get what happened out of his mind. His "just a few questions" started off with wanting to know if there were exercises he could do to get certain thoughts out of his mind and what the formal criteria were for being considered a homosexual. Although experiencing distressing symptoms, Freddie did not meet criteria for any major mental illness and said that he didn't have the time or money to come to therapy regularly "unless he had to." Since he was a veteran, I told him about a strategy that some VA hospitals were doing with veterans that involved writing and asked him if he wanted to try it. We went over a handout together, and he was willing to give it a try. Writing served as a stepping-stone to subsequent psychotherapy for Freddie who, a couple of years later, pursued therapy with a colleague to whom I had referred him.

Julie, Kim, and Gail: The Scarlet Letter Club

Sharing and connecting with others who have had similar experiences is an important pathway to healing and empowerment.[18] A few years ago I had the opportunity to advise the start-up of a journaling group for three college women who were close friends. Julie, my client, had recently experienced date rape and described the reactions when she disclosed it to her two best friends. Kim shared that she had never been raped but remembered her teenage cousin making her sit on his lap and look at pornography on the Internet with him while he "rocked" back and forth. Gail disclosed an experience during high school of partially stripping at a party, exposing her breasts in video chats, and the fear she felt when she began being "cyberstalked" by boys who became obsessed with her. Though they had different experiences, these young women found commonality in their feelings of shame, guilt, and fears that a "normal" man would not want them if he found out about their experiences. They felt like they were somehow "marked" and damaged. Julie joked about them forming a "Scarlet Letter" club, and the journaling group evolved from there.

EMPOWERMENT JOURNALING

"One writes out of one thing only—one's own experience."

—James Baldwin

What does the term *empowerment* mean? Empowerment can be defined at many different levels of analysis including internal, behavioral, interpersonal, and community. At all levels it refers to a process where people gain mastery over their own situation.[20] The emphasis of the journaling approach presented here is to first enhance empowerment at the internal, psychological level of analysis. It is my experience that this can then extend to the actions one takes, the quality of relationships, and involvement in addressing issues (such as sexual violence) in one's community or society as a whole. The central purpose of empowerment journaling is to utilize writing as a method of self-expression to help you gain greater awareness, knowledge, and compassionate understanding of yourself, including your thoughts and feelings, your needs, and your life experiences. Just as knowledge is power, self-knowledge is self-empowering. The experience of sexual violence involves someone imposing their will on you without regard for your feelings or needs. It is an act where the intention is to take away your power and dominion over your own body. For many survivors, the lasting effects of sexual violence are rooted in the ways that the experience increases separation from a sense of empowerment over one's self and life circumstances. Healing must involve reclaiming your own power and gaining control over your own well-being. Writing is a useful vehicle for traveling the path of healing and empowerment because it allows you the freedom to exercise your power to determine when, where, what, and how you write.

Some readers may already journal regularly. The empowerment journaling approach can be incorporated into or expand your current journaling repertoire. Some readers may have journaled in the past or tried journaling but felt it did not work. Empowerment journaling is likely a different approach from the journaling that you have tried previously. Trying something new or with a fresh perspective can be tremendously helpful. For those readers who have never kept a journal, empowerment journaling allows you start from wherever you are and go where you need to go. The method is quite flexible and is compatible with many different writing approaches and strategies. There are only three guidelines:

1. Write when and where you choose.
2. Write what and how you choose.
3. Stop when you choose.

The core process is choice. Nothing is forced upon you. There is no single way to do it right and there is no way to do it wrong. There are no hard-and-fast rules for how often you write, how much you write, or how long you write. You can write daily, weekly, randomly once a year, or somewhere in between. No one is going to give you a grade or impose their opinion on what you have written. Penmanship, grammar, punctuation, and spelling are not important. It doesn't have to happen in a bound leather book with lined pages. You can journal on a napkin or on a Post-it or in your smartphone. You can use a calendar, a composition book, a binder, or even keep journal entries in a file folder. If you like electronic media, you are free to use a word processing program or a private account with a blogging platform such as LiveJournal, Blogger, or WordPress. You can choose to use specific structured journaling strategies or just write freely. The primary goal of the empowerment journaling approach is liberation from what is keeping you chained to your past and blocking you from the life you are capable of living. Empowerment journaling promotes freedom from the "should," the fears, and those critical and judgmental voices in your head. The only requirement is that you make an effort to open your mind and your heart and let your truth guide your hand.

THE CORE EMPOWERMENT JOURNALING METHODS: FREE WRITING, FLOW WRITING, EXPRESSIVE WRITING, AND INTEGRATIVE WRITING

"Fill your paper with the breathings of your heart."

—William Wordsworth

The common element in the core empowerment journaling methods is the process of writing your "stream of consciousness" as it occurs from moment to moment. In *free writing* you simply write your thoughts and feelings of the moment and follow where the writing takes you. Adams offers a variation on free writing that she calls *flow writing*.[23] Flow writing is inspired by an initial image or metaphor that can emerge during meditation. Ira Progoff, a psychologist and pioneer in the use of journaling, refers to these prewriting meditations as *entrance meditations*.[7] The purpose of flow writing is to help you connect with your truth in the process of making meaning of your thoughts, feelings, and life experiences. It enables you to access your intuitive knowledge and your survivor's voice and to uncover meanings through the associations you make with the stimulus. A guided meditation is often helpful to bring you to a relaxed and open state of mind where the image or felt sense of what you need to write about emerges. However, just closing your eyes and taking a few deep breaths can help you to visualize or discover the stimulus for your writing. The basic process is that you start with the image or metaphor and then just "go with the flow," letting the authenticity of your thoughts and experience guide your hand. With both free writing and flow writing you can choose to set a timer to establish some boundaries for how long you write, which can serve to increase feelings of safety and containment. The timer creates a writing context that balances freedom and safety. An example of flow writing would be to start with an entrance meditation that transports you to a place or time where you have felt safe and peaceful, such as a comfortable chair or a stream in the forest or during a hymn at church. You would begin by writing about the place and just go from there. There are endless possibilities of where the writing takes you, and your task is just to create an opening to allow what needs to be expressed or explored to come through you to your journal.

One specific, evidence-based, and well-researched application of stream-of-consciousness writing was developed by James Pennebaker and is sometimes referred to as the expressive writing paradigm. Pennebaker's expressive writing method has been extensively researched with multiple studies finding support for its use in helping with the trauma recovery process.[9] The process is described in detail in James Pennebaker's book, *Writing to heal: A guided journal for recovering from trauma and emotional upheaval.*[19] Basically, the instructions are to write for twenty to thirty continuous minutes for four consecutive days, describing a traumatic or stressful event as well as your thoughts and feelings about the event. It does not have to be your experience of sexual violence, and you can write about different events on different days. The requirement is that you write about some stressful experience, situation, or circumstance. Expressive writing is a powerful process that sometimes results in a short-term increase of negative emotional experiences.[9] However, research has consistently demonstrated that these initial feelings subside and most people experience longer-term symptom relief and an increased sense of well-being. The process may be best used if you have previous experience writing about painful thoughts and feelings. For newcomers to journaling, I recommend using this process with Pennebaker's book or guided by a therapist. Recent research has explored modifications to the initial written expression paradigm instructions, and initial results suggest that writing for briefer period of time (e.g., two minutes) has positive effects. This suggests that a good entry point to expressive writing may be to keep writing times initially very short and monitor how writing about stressful or traumatic events affects you.

Writing freely about whatever comes to you is a time-tested approach with the evidence-based strategy of expressive writing serving as a prototype. However, the unstructured nature of flow writing or expressive writing is not everyone's cup of tea. Sometimes it is helpful to use a specific structured process so that your writing feels more directed and the purpose and value are clearer to you. It is always important to center yourself in the core element of the empowerment journaling method: choice. Even when you use a structured journaling process, you are making an intentional choice to follow a particular strategy. If you decide to push yourself to write in a way that is outside of your comfort zone, make sure that you are actively choosing the strategy and not doing it because you feel that you have to.

The signature writing strategy for empowerment journaling is a structured three-phase variation of flow writing I have developed with my clients over the years, which I am calling *integrative writing*. Integrative writing is best used when you are feeling overwhelming emotions, when your mind is racing, or when you feel that you are about to lose control. It is those times when you have lost touch with your own power, and writing can help you to channel and focus your energy toward psychological empowerment, particularly at those times when you have impulses to engage in risky or self-sabotaging behavior. While integrative writing shares common ground with the previously discussed methods by emphasizing free writing, or writing whatever comes to you, it is more comprehensive and involves more structure than flow writing or expressive writing. The intent of the structure is to provide a process that allows you to work through the intensity of your thoughts and feelings of that moment. A guiding principle of the integrative writing process is "this too shall pass," which means that you center yourself in the knowledge that you can and will get beyond what you are going through. This strategy involves your taking an active role in the process of connecting to your power rather than giving your power over to the thoughts and feelings of the moment. There are three writing phases: release, recognize, and reset.

Release. When you first start writing, the goal is just to get it all out, to release it. Write with as much vivid detail about what you are experiencing, thinking, and feeling. Write about what you feel like doing at the moment or what you might want to say to someone. You can write the same thing over and over if you choose. The important thing is to write until the intensity of your emotions lessens. It is important to remember that overwhelming or negative thoughts and feelings are not the enemy. Having them does not make you "bad" or "wrong" or "weak." However, they also don't define you or an ultimate truth, only the truth of your experience in that moment. Think of your emotions as providing a signal that something within you needs attention. The pathway to relief from distress is to choose to accept intense emotional experiences as part of the scenery of your healing journey so that you can see them clearly. What you don't see can take you by surprise. Writing is a safe method for releasing your emotions from the darkness and shining a light on them so that you can see them more clearly and engage with them proactively. Writing them down is also a way of demonstrating that your thoughts and feelings of that moment don't define you, but rather you have the power to name and define them. Sometimes it can feel like waves of intense feelings are taking over, and you may initially try to just push them out of consciousness. However, trying to suppress them lessens your ability to see them clearly and increases the likelihood that they will control you. Releasing intense emotions in writing helps to place them in the scenery rather than allow them to be the driving force. The distressing thoughts and feelings are only what you are experiencing in that moment; they need your attention and compassion, but they are not YOU. This first stage of the integrative writing method facilitates empowerment by releasing some of what may be blocking you from experiencing and living from your own power. Once you have released the intensity of your thoughts and feelings onto the paper and see them clearly, it is time to attend to them.

Recognize. What is it that you are recognizing during this phase? Basically you are recognizing the meaning and function of the intense emotions that you just released. Writing has given you the opportunity to look at them clearly and with compassion. You can recognize them by writing about your understanding of where they come from and the consequences they have had for you. You can recognize them by writing about ways that they have helped you, as well as ways that they have potentially hurt you. You can recognize them by writing about their relationship to aspects of your identity development including gender, race/ethnicity, sexual orientation, and religion/spirituality. It is important to engage in a process of actively seeking to understand your emotional experience in the context of its origins, how its presence is a normative response to the sexual violence and related situations that you have survived, and how they have contributed to the person you are becoming. This is a very important phase of the integrative writing process. Some people may want to stop after they have experienced the initial catharsis of the release phase. However, ongoing healing and empowerment comes from actively engaging with the thoughts and feelings that were just released. Of course you should take a break if you need one, but it is strongly recommended that you come back to this next phase of the integrative writing process as soon as you can. The complete process is not optimally effective without the recognition phase. Flow writing can be incorporated during this phase, as imagery and metaphor can facilitate the recognition and meaning-making process. You can also engage the recognition phase by speaking directly to a feeling or problem. The journaling strategy of dialogue writing is often very helpful during this phase.[7,23] For example, you can write a dialogue with your anger by taking on the voice of caring and compassion toward "anger." Externalizing the feeling or problem through dialogue reinforces your position of power to name and proactively construct its meaning in your life. However, you can also recognize other significant representations and internalizations that are relevant to the intense emotional experiences you may have. Progoff's Intensive Journal Process workshop offers an in-depth description of multiple ways of utilizing this method to dialogue with persons, activities or projects, the body, events and circumstances, society, and even your inner wisdom.[7] These written dialogues can help you understand, accept, and feel more in control of your emotional experience. Recognizing these emotional aspects of your internal world involves relating to them with affirmation and compassion as you explore them through writing.

Reset. The final phase of release writing is to reset your emotional equilibrium by creating a role for the distressing thoughts and feelings in the form of an empowerment story. Writing is a documentation of your healing process, and each time you write you are establishing elements of your unique empowerment story. Current research suggests that expressing experience in the form of a coherent narrative has psychological benefits.[22] Therefore, writing a *reset narrative* involves telling the story of your emotional experience (that includes a beginning, a middle, and current endpoint) by incorporating the understandings that you developed in the previous recognition phase. The theme of the reset narrative is related to survival, growth, lessons learned, healing, power, voice, and/or transformation. The story can be quite short or it can be a longer and more autobiographical. An example of a brief reset narrative might look like this: *"I started hyperventilating and I really thought I was going to die. But I didn't. I survived that like I have survived so many things in my life. Hyperventilating is my body's way of making me stop and pay attention to my feelings. It reminds me that something is not working and I need do something different. I used to ignore my fear but now I know that it is a message I have to listen to."* Writing a reset narrative related to a particular overwhelming or distressing emotional experience establishes a reset point that you can return to as documentation of your healing and empowerment story. This phase of the writing does not have to be done immediately but is ideally done within twenty-four hours of the release writing. More importantly, if you are unable to construct a reset narrative on your own, it can be very helpful to talk it through with someone. Others can often see our strengths and our progress when we cannot.

The integrative writing process, like the written expression paradigm, is often best begun with some level of guidance from a qualified therapist, counselor, life coach, or journal therapy facilitator. While many clients have reported positive experiences with the three phases of integrative writing, it is a depth-oriented process, and each person should evaluate issues such as appropriateness, timing, and the availability of a support system. This is particularly important since the process is just beginning to be subjected to a systematic evaluation of its effectiveness through research. Also, keep in mind that empowerment journaling is ultimately about choice and freedom. You can experiment with parts of the integrative writing process that appeal to you, just as you would experiment with different journaling strategies so that you can find the best fit for you in terms of characteristics such as degree of structure, depth of emotional processing, and your personal goals and objectives for writing.

As mentioned above, many different strategies can be found in books on journaling and writing.[5-7,23-30] Different strategies will work for different people at different times, and the empowerment journaling approach, with its emphasis on choice, is compatible with multiple approaches. I encourage you to try out several strategies so that you will have multiple resources for journaling to fit different moods and needs. There are also many variations of journaling with respect to style and atmosphere. Writing is both an expressive and a creative process; however, it is not only the content that involves personal expression. Choices that you make with respect to what you will write on, where you will write, what you will write with, and how you will write are all expressions of you at that moment. You can choose to write in a particular place in your home, or in a café, in nature, with

Table 21.1.   Summary of the Core Empowerment Journaling Methods: Top Four Supplemental Strategies for Empowerment Journaling. "Writing is an exploration. You start with nothing and learn as you go." –E.L. Doctorow

	PURPOSE	FOCUS	PROCESS
Free writing	Consciousness	Thought	Write whatever comes to mind from moment to moment
Flow writing	Connection and meaning making	Imagery, theme	Entrance meditation to identify stimulus and then write your associations and connections using your intuitive knowledge and authentic voice
Expressive writing	Expression and processing	A stressful event	Write twenty minutes for four consecutive days about a stressful event
Integrative writing	Affirmation and working through	Intense emotions	Three phases of writing: release, recognize, reset

music or candles or incense, or sitting at the kitchen table. You can write with a pencil, a ballpoint pen, or a marker. I sometimes like to write with a set of colored pencils and choose different colors to express the various thoughts and feelings that I have as I am writing. With respect to how you write, you can choose to use one of the core empowerment journaling methods described above (i.e., flow writing, expressive writing, integrative writing). However, you can make other choices regarding how you write and the approach that you take. I have selected five strategies to present here that are particularly compatible with common challenges experienced by sexual violence survivors. These are strategies where many of my clients have reported experiencing an increase in psychological empowerment as a common result of the writing. All are flexible and meant to be modified to fit the style and needs of the writer. As you experiment with different approaches, you will likely find ways of journaling that are a particularly good fit for you in their ability to facilitate your healing and transformation process. I also encourage you to explore some of the resources at the end of this chapter for additional ideas for journaling.

For many people, getting started is the hardest part. The "one-word" pre-journaling method that I used with Kayla is a very effective way to gently break down barriers to writing with people who don't like to write or are resistant to the writing process. For some survivors of sexual violence, emotions and needs have been held in and blocked off for many years. It has been a way of coping with pain and an effective way of keeping up with the demands of daily life. Over time, however, a person can come to believe that their feelings are dangerous, that they will fall apart if they look within. The more the feelings are held in, the more reinforcement the person gets for their belief that their feelings will destroy them. It is like the monster under the bed. The monster gets bigger and bigger and scarier and scarier because as long as you don't face it directly, your mind can create the scariest of monsters. However, if you push through your fear and get down on the floor and peek under the bed, you will never find a monster that is quite as scary as what you had imagined, and you can sleep much easier. The one-word prewriting method gives you an opportunity to peek under the bed while still honoring the coping and the strength you have demonstrated throughout your life. Diving into the depths of your feelings may not be the best way to begin. The following five supplemental strategies describe journaling alternatives when there is a specific writing goal or when the core empowerment journaling methods seem too big or daunting.

Empowerment Journaling Strategy #1: List Writing

Making lists is a familiar activity for most people. Grocery lists, to-do lists, Christmas gift lists, baby name lists, and lists of pros and cons are among the most common. Lists are a way for us to organize, evaluate, and modify something we want to accomplish, as well as a way to get that feeling of accomplishment when an item has been completed and can be checked off. A list allows us to see something in a comprehensive way, to get "the big picture." However, lists are not only helpful for their functionality, but the process of creating and making a list also has value. The brainstorming process involved in list writing can be an empowering experience. List writing can also facilitate empowerment through the identification of elements of the target issue that leads to greater clarity and understanding. Adams suggests making long lists (e.g., 100 items), writing quickly, and not evaluating along the way for phrasing or even to determine if it makes sense. She emphasizes that it is fine to repeat items, because the emphasis is the continuous listing of the next thing that comes to mind even if it has appeared previously.[23] As an empowerment journaling strategy, topics that are related to clarifying thoughts, venting feelings, or developing coping skills can be particularly helpful. Here are some example lists that I have found to be useful journal entries for survivors of sexual violence.

1. 100 things I want to say to the person(s) who perpetrated violence on me
2. 100 reasons why I avoid commitment in relationships
3. 100 ways that I have demonstrated my inner strength

4. 100 ways to nurture and take care of myself
5. 100 things I can do when I am feeling distressed about the sexual violence experience

Empowerment Journaling Strategy #2: Positivity Writing

Recent research has demonstrated the benefits of writing about something positive. Keeping a "gratitude journal" was popularized several years ago by Oprah Winfrey and is a well-supported intervention to enhance positive emotions and decrease negative emotions.[31] Research conducted by Fredrickson and colleagues has found support for what she calls the broaden-and-build theory. Positive emotional states create expanded cognitive processes and create opportunities for additional positive experiences.[32] This means that intentional focus on positive aspects of life can contribute to the development of cognitive and emotional strengths and resilience.

A JOURNAL ENTRY YOU CAN DO RIGHT NOW
Simply Positive
Purpose: To practice directing your attention to what is good and documenting it so that you can remind yourself later.

Think of one positive thing that you have seen, done, or heard about within the last twenty-four hours. It should be something simple like hearing a favorite song on the radio, or someone letting you merge in front of them in traffic, or finding out that your favorite team won last night's game. Your journal entry is a simple, but detailed, description of what happened. Example: "I went grocery shopping after work and my absolute favorite orange juice was on sale. I bought four of them." That's all. No reflections or feelings; the description is your entry.

Empowerment Journaling Strategy #3: Daily Monitoring

The daily monitoring strategy focuses on a specific behavior or feeling that you want to understand better or modify in some way. The purpose of the monitoring is to heighten your awareness of the behavior or feeling so that you can better target how and what you might want to change. For example, I worked with a client once for whom the use of foul language was woven into his everyday speech. He recognized that this was not appropriate in some situations and decided that he needed to modify how he expressed himself. I suggested daily monitoring of the times he used curse words in an inappropriate situation supplemented by reflections every few days on what he observed from the monitoring. This meant that he noted the time, place, and words that he used in his calendar. The process of monitoring disrupts the "automatic pilot" that we often function on, where we just do what we have always done. Many people tend to operate in a default mode rather than making conscious and intentional choices. The activity of monitoring serves to maintain constant conscious awareness of the target behavior. For my client, monitoring strengthened his ability to pause and think before speaking and ultimately resulted in a decrease in his cursing. This is a natural journaling strategy for people who regularly keep a calendar anyway. However, a pocket-sized calendar can easily be purchased, or you can use the calendar function in your cell phone. Through increased self-awareness and consciousness, as well as observation of positive changes, daily monitoring can contribute to greater psychological empowerment.

Empowerment Journaling Strategy #4: Springboard Writing

This is an in-between kind of writing that merges structure with a free-writing approach. It is one of the strategies I use most frequently. Adams describes the springboard approach as most commonly centered on a sentence stem or question.[5,23] Examples include prompts like "I remember the time when_____" or "What masks do I wear?" This is a very flexible writing strategy that can be tailored to the issues or themes you want to explore. She suggests quotations and song lyrics as extensions of this strategy.[23] The guiding idea is that a springboard is anything than can serve as a jumping-off point and launch your writing in a particular direction. In addition to sentence stems, questions, quotations, and songs, a journaling springboard can also come from a book you are reading, a movie you just saw, an observation you made in nature, a conversation you had with someone, a current event, or just about anything else. The springboard is whatever catches your attention and gives you pause. A song that you find repeatedly going through your mind can serve as a great springboard for writing.

Example: "I can't get M.C. Hammer's song 'Can't Touch This' out of my mind. I don't really know the words, so I just kind of hum it in my head and then say, 'can't touch this.' Why is this song in my head? I really don't even like it. But it makes me kind of laugh because since first hearing it, I always respond to the lyric 'can't touch this' with 'don't want to.' I feel good when I say this, so maybe it has something to do with being able to be clear about my wants and needs. . . ."

I love quotations and proverbs and often use them as a springboard for encouraging clients to explore the ideas or wisdom in the quotation in terms of how it applies to their own life experience and self-understanding. I developed a process for working with quotes called QQM (quotation, question, mantra/affirmation) that is available on my daily quotation website, www.empoweredeveryday.com. You can search for a quote by keyword that focuses on a theme that you want to explore, or just choose a random date from the archives and use the associated QQM. Some clients have found it useful to subscribe to a daily quote site such as mine and write a few minutes every day on the application of the quote to their own lives. Springboard writing contributes to empowerment by providing a forum to actively process a focus issue that can create a greater sense of self-understanding. Self-knowledge is an important foundation for the development of psychological empowerment. The more one knows and understands themselves, the more empowered and confident one feels to manage life's challenges.

Empowerment Journal Strategy #5: Mindful Writing

Mindfulness is a particular kind of awareness that involves the self-control of attention toward being fully present in the experience of the immediate moment with openness, acceptance, and compassion for the thoughts, feelings, and sensations that arise from one moment to the next.[33-35] Mindfulness exercises are integrated into a number of evidence-based therapies that target stress and overwhelming emotions.[36-37] Training in mindfulness meditation, or insight meditation, is becoming more commonly available as numerous books and research studies are being published that provide support for its multiple benefits and basis in neuroscience (the science of the brain). Available research suggests that some of the benefits of mindfulness practice include increased concentration, positive emotional experience, improved immune functioning, decreased distress, and better regulation of emotions.[34] Powerful stuff. Mindful writing is a way of bringing yourself into present-moment awareness by describing your environment, body sensations, passing thoughts, and moment-to-moment distractions in a way that does not judge the acceptability of anything that enters your awareness. Mindful writing can be empowering through its effects on the ability to practice intention, attention, and awareness. Mindful writing can be done with your eyes open, closed, or a combination of both. Recommendations for closed-eye mindful writing include using unlined paper and just writing freely without concern about neatness or accuracy. Open-eye mindful writing can be done immediately after meditation or prayer to document your process. The following example is from a combination open- and closed-eye mindful writing session.

"I am laying in my bed propped up on my elbow so that I can write. The only light is coming from my bedside lamp and when I just looked at the light I spun off into thoughts about how it is good that I am conserving electricity . . . good for the environment and good for my bank account. I'm closing my eyes and getting centered now. I'm trying to just observe those thoughts passing by and bring my attention back to my awareness of myself, my breathing, and this moment. My dog is barking . . . again I'm trying to bring myself back to the present moment as I let the sound of the barking fade into the background. In this moment I am focusing

my awareness on the feeling of the sheets and the pillows and the mattress of my bed. The sheets feel . . . ."

A JOURNAL ENTRY YOU CAN DO RIGHT NOW
  Quick Body Scan
  Purpose: To establish awareness and connection to your body in the service of cultivating mindfulness and empowering you to listen to what your body tells you.

Take a deep breath and place your attention on the physical sensations you are feeling right now. How is your body positioned? What is the temperature of your body? Notice any particular sensations, good or bad, in your body starting with your head, moving to your neck, shoulders, arms, and hands, to your chest and abdomen, to your back and hips, and down through your legs, knees, and feet. Just write what you notice. *Example: "I am sitting slightly hunched over in my computer chair with my legs curled under the chair. I am neither hot nor cold but maybe a little clammy. My head feels like it's swirling . . . etc."* The body scan is a technique to develop mindfulness. If you choose to do this exercise, remember that sensations in our body change constantly and the scan is less for evaluation (i.e., positive or negative) but to heighten awareness, practice self-regulation of attention, and lessen any disconnectedness from your physical body.

Important Considerations

Journaling is not the best healing pathway for everyone. Some people find it too difficult to write without evaluating and criticizing themselves. Sometimes people may truly not be able to write more than a few words. For others, writing raises anxiety or is a negative experience for one reason or another. If you feel strongly that writing is not for you then you should not do it. Period. While it is sometimes important to push yourself beyond your comfort zone, this should be done carefully and with full respect for your needs at any given point in your healing process. It may not be the right time to travel the journaling pathway. Or writing just may not be a strategy that works for you at all. Acceptance of yourself and your needs is an important element of empowerment, and that may mean that one of the many other healing paths may be more effective for you.

Exploring painful experiences and feelings is difficult in any mode of expression, and some discomfort should be expected. However, it is important to be mindful of what Pennebaker calls the flip-out rule. The rule states, "If you feel that your writing about a particular topic is too much for you to handle, then do not write about it. If you know that you aren't ready to address a particularly painful topic, write about something else. When you are ready, then tackle it. If you feel that you will flip out by writing, don't write." (p. 23)[19]

Some days may be good writing days and other days may not. The bottom line of the flip-out rule is that you are in control and you don't have to write. Adams offers a wave-riding metaphor for journaling that is very appealing. Think of the journaling process as an experience riding the waves of your inner world, and if you get a sense that you have gotten too far from the shore, then you just bring yourself back. Finally, if you do find yourself too far from shore and you are having trouble getting back to safety, it is time to find someone who can travel the healing pathway with you.[23] Seeking help from a therapist or counselor can be an important step in the process and is strongly recommended at some point in your journey to well-being and empowerment.

CONCLUSION

"Be patient toward all that is unsolved in your heart."

—Rainer Maria Rilke

There are multiple pathways to healing and empowerment for survivors of sexual violence. Many sexual violence survivors just want to get past what happened and live a "normal" life. The desire to put it behind you is natural. However, part of the process of getting to the life you want is to accept where you've been, face where you are now, and make movement toward transformative growth. I often tell my clients, "you have to go through it to get to it." This means that the path to getting beyond the experience of sexual violence and its effects may not be smooth or easy. There will likely be rough terrain, obstacles blocking your way, and storms that slow you down. Journaling can take you "through it" and help you get closer to an optimal place of well-being and empowerment.

With the growing body of research documenting the positive effects of writing on health and well-being, journaling is a method of intervention that is increasingly evidence based.[13] Journaling can be a helpful addition to your toolbox of resources for your healing journey. The empowerment journaling approach described here is an orientation that places emphasis on the freedom and choice aspects of journal writing. Four core journaling options are variations and modifications of stream-of-consciousness writing, and five supplemental methods are more structured and give you additional options. It is recommended that you experiment with different strategies and assess which ones are a good fit for you. Journal writing can be thought of as an act of empowerment that essentially and fundamentally involves your voice speaking your experience in your own way at your own time. As you travel the path where journaling takes you, it is important to establish an internal foundation of compassion for and patience with yourself and your process. Ultimately, journaling requires a leap of faith—faith in the writing process and faith that there is a peace and power within you that wants to emerge and become stronger. Journaling is a process that can help you connect to and live from that peace and power.

SUGGESTED ONLINE RESOURCES

www.empoweredeveryday.com (Dr. Shelly Harrell's daily quotations with journaling prompts)

www.journaltherapy.com (Kathleen Adams's site, The Center for Journal Therapy)

www.createwritenow.com (Journaling ideas and tips)

www.peerspirit.com (Christina Baldwin's site for writing workshops and circle groups)

www.lifejournal.com (*LifeJournal* software for electronic journaling)

www.davidrm.com (*The Journal 5* software for electronic journaling)

REFERENCES

1. Herman, J. (1997). *Trauma and recovery: The aftermath of abuse—from domestic abuse to political terror.* New York: Basic.
2. Briere, J., & Scott, C. (2006). *Principles of trauma therapy: A guide to symptoms, evaluation, and treatment.* Thousand Oaks, CA: Sage.
3. Cori, J.L. (2007). *Healing from trauma: A survivor's guide to understanding your symptoms and reclaiming your life.* Cambridge, MA: Marlowe and Company.
4. DeSalvo, L. (1999). *Writing as a way of healing: How telling our stories transforms our lives.* Boston: Beacon.
5. Adams, K. (1998). *The way of the journal: A journal therapy workbook for healing.* Lutherville, MD: Sidran.
6. Baldwin, C. (1990/2007). *Life's companion: Journal writing as a spiritual practice.* New York: Bantam.
7. Progoff, I. (1975/1992). *At a journal workshop: Writing to access the power of the unconscious and evoke creative ability.* New York: Tarcher/Penguin.
8. Lepore, S.J., Greenberg, M.A., Bruno, M., & Smyth, J.M. (2002). Expressive writing and health: Self-regulation of emotion-related experience, physiology, and behavior. In S.J. Lepore & J.M. Smyth (Eds.), *The writing cure: How expressive writing promotes health and emotional well-being* (pp. 99–118). Washington, D.C.: American Psychological Association.
9. Pennebaker, J.W. (1997). Writing about emotional experiences as a therapeutic process. *Psychological Science, 8,* 162–166.
10. Thompson, K. (2004). Journal writing as a therapeutic tool. In G. Bolton, S. Howlett, C. Lago, and J.K. Wright (Eds.), *Writing cures: An introductory handbook of writing in counselling and therapy* (pp. 72–84). New York: Routledge.

11. Baikie, K.A., & Wilhelm, K. (2005). Emotional and physical health benefits of expressive writing. *Advances in Psychiatric Treatment, 11*, 338–346.

12. Kacewicz, E., Slatcher, R.B., & Pennebaker, J.W. (2007). Expressive writing: An alternative to traditional methods. In L. L'Abate (Ed.), *Low-cost approaches to promote physical and mental health: Theory, research, and practice.* (pp. 271–284). New York: Springer.

13. Nazarian, D., & Smyth, J. (2008). Expressive writing. In W.T. O'Donohue and N.A. Cummings (Eds.), *Evidence-based adjunctive interventions* (pp. 223–243). San Diego, CA: Academic.

14. Lepore, S.J., & Smyth, J.M. (2002). The writing cure: An overview. In S.J. Lepore & J.M. Smyth (Eds.), *The writing cure: How expressive writing promotes health and emotional well-being* (pp. 3-14). Washington, D.C.: American Psychological Association.

15. Lowe, G. (2004). Cognitive psychology and the biomedical foundations of writing therapy. In G. Bolton, S. Howlett, C. Lago, & J.K. Wright (Eds.), *Writing cures: An introductory handbook of writing in counselling and therapy* (pp. 18–24). New York: Routledge.

16. Nicholls, S. (2009). Beyond expressive writing: Evolving models of developmental creative writing. *Journal of Health Psychology, 14*, 171–180.

17. L'Abate, L, & Kern, R. (2002). Workbooks: Tools for the expressive writing paradigm. In S.J. Lepore & J.M. Smyth (Eds.), *The writing cure: How expressive writing promotes health and emotional well-being* (pp. 239–253). Washington, D.C.: American Psychological Association.

18. Bolton, G., Field, V., & Thompson, K. (Eds.) (2006). *Writing works: A resource handbook for therapeutic writing workshops and activities.* Philadelphia: Jessica Kingsley.

19. Pennebaker, J.W. (2004). *Writing to heal: A guided journal for recovering from trauma and emotional upheaval.* Oakland, CA: New Harbinger.

20. Rappaport, J. (1995). Empowerment meets narrative: Listening to stories and creating settings. *American Journal of Community Psychology, 23*, 795–807.

21. McAdams, D.P., Josselson, R., & Lieblich, A. (Eds.) (2006). *Identity and story: Creating self in narrative.* Washington, D.C.: American Psychological Association.

22. Singer, J.A., & Rexhaj, B. (2006). Narrative coherence and psychotherapy: A commentary. *Journal of Constructivist Psychology, 19*, 209–217.

23. Adams, K. (1990). *Journal to the self: Twenty-two paths to personal growth.* New York: Warner.

24. Baldwin, C. (2005). *Storycatcher: Making sense of our lives through the power and practice of story.* Novato, CA: New World.

25. Cameron, J. (1998). *The right to write: An invitation and initiation into the writing life.* New York: Tarcher/Putnam.

26. Grason, S. (2005). *Journalution: Journaling to awaken your inner voice, heal your life, and manifest your dreams.* Novato, CA: New World Library.

27. Jacobs, B. (2004). *Writing for emotional balance: A guided journal to help you manage overwhelming emotions.* Oakland, CA: New Harbinger.

28. Myers, L.J. (2006). *Becoming whole: Writing your healing story.* Berkeley, CA: Iaso.

29. Pipher, M. (2007). *Writing to change the world.* New York: Riverhead.

30. Rainier, T. (1978/1994). *The new diary: How to use a journal for self-guidance and expanded creativity.* New York: Tarcher/Penguin.
31. Seligman, M.E.P., Steen, T.A., Park, N., & Peterson, C. (2005). Positive psychology progress: Empirical validation of interventions. *American Psychologist, 60,* 410–421.
32. Fredrickson, B.L. (2009). *Positivity: Groundbreaking research reveals how to embrace the hidden strength of positive emotions, overcome negativity, and thrive.* New York: Crown.
33. Kabat-Zinn, J. (2005). *Coming to our senses: Healing ourselves and our world through mindfulness meditation.* New York: Hyperion.
34. Siegel, D.J. (2007). *The mindful brain: Reflection and attunement in the cultivation of well-being.* New York: W.W. Norton and Company.
35. Hanson, R., & Mendius, R. (2009). *Buddha's brain: The practical neuroscience of happiness, love, and wisdom.* Oakland, CA: New Harbinger.
36. Hayes, S.C., Follette, V.M., & Linehan, M.M. (Eds.) (2004). *Mindfulness and acceptance: Expanding the cognitive behavioral tradition.* New York: Guilford.
37. Baer, R.A. (Ed.) (2006). *Mindfulness-based treatment approaches: Clinician's guide to evidence base and applications.* Burlington, MA: Academic.

Conclusion

Thema Bryant-Davis

Sexual violence is pervasive across demographic lines and can have long-term psychological, social, physical, economical, and spiritual consequences. The contributors have provided a wide range of potential pathways to recovery and empowerment. These pathways cover a range of issues that survivors of sexual violence are often left to confront, including the survivor's thoughts, feelings, behaviors, and relationships. Included in the described recovery pathways are those that focus on challenging unhealthy thinking, uncovering unconscious thoughts, learning new coping strategies, developing positive spirituality, building helpful relationships, regulating a range of emotions, caring for one's body, and expressing the unspoken experiences. These recovery processes have empowered numerous survivors to move from victim to survivor and even from survivor to thriver.

It is important for therapists, survivors, and their support persons to gain a more inclusive view of the possibilities that may enhance the recovery process. While this focus on intervention is highly important, it is also critical for the reader to remember the necessity of prevention. There is a need to prevent first-time violations and also to prevent the repeated violations that survivors often experience across the life span. In other words, although there are pathways to recovery, this does not eliminate the need for the eradication of sexual violence. The larger aim is to empower survivors such that their risk for future violation is reduced and to intercede such that potential perpetrators do not engage in violent and abusive behaviors.

I would like to mention the limitations of this text. There are actually numerous healing pathways and, due to space constraints, I could not include chapters on all of them. There are three that I believe warrant your attention and consideration that are not included in this text: psychopharmacology, wraparound services, and expressive arts therapies. Medication has been an integral part of the recovery process for many survivors and is one pathway that survivors should be open to considering when needed and under the care of a psychiatrist or primary care physician. For those who make use of psychotropic medications, I would recommend their use in conjunction with therapy, not as a replacement for therapy. The second important approach is the use of wraparound services. This is especially beneficial for survivors of human trafficking and intimate partner violence. In addition to counseling, one may be in need of residential, vocational, legal, medical, and educational services. It is very difficult to get to a place of empowerment when one's basic needs are unmet. Getting assistance with these needs while in a therapeutic environment is a core component of recovery for many survivors. Finally, while this text includes the use of expressive writing and yoga, there are a number of expressive arts therapies that survivors should consider. These include, but are not limited to, poetry therapy, drama therapy, dance therapy, art therapy, and music therapy. If you do not find the pathway that works for you in this text, it doesn't mean that there is not a pathway for you. Continue to research and engage in different processes until you find one that is helpful for you.

Survivors have also healed through activism and social justice work. There are survivors who find empowerment in part by working to combat sexual violence. These survivors may work as rape crisis counselors, neighborhood watch volunteers, therapists, advocates, police officers, educators, or engaged parents. It is important to recognize that while social justice is laudable work, it is not a substitute for doing one's personal work. After one has worked through their personal experience (possibly through one of the pathways described in this book), a next step to consider may be working to eradicate sexual violence in its various forms. This is one example of posttraumatic growth. The trauma or violation does not make us become better people, but the choices we make in our recovery can help us to grow and facilitate growth in the communities around us.

General Sexual Violence Recovery Resources

In addition to the books and journal articles mentioned in the chapters of this guidebook, please consider the following resources:

WEBSITES

➤ National Sexual Violence Resource Center
http://www.nsvrc.org

➤ Sexual Assault Training and Investigations
http://www.mysati.com/resources_new.htm

➤ The National Child Traumatic Stress Network
http://nctsn.org/nccts/nav.do?pid=hom_main

➤ Rape, Abuse, and Incest National Network
http://www.rainn.org

➤ Prostitution, Research, and Education
http://www.prostitutionresearch.com

➤ Human Trafficking
http://www.humantrafficking.org

➤ Office for Civil Rights: Addressing Sexual Harassment
http://www2.ed.gov/about/offices/list/ocr/sexharassresources.html

➤ Feminist Majority Foundation: Addressing Sexual Harassment
  http://www.feminist.org/911/harass.html

➤ National Coalition Against Domestic Violence
  http://www.ncadv.org

➤ An Abuse, Rape and Domestic Violence Aid and Resource Collection
  A not-for-profit volunteer organization dedicated to fighting partner
  and family violence; includes resources for male survivors and partners
  of sexual assault survivors and lists of support services by state.
  http://www.aardvarc.org

➤ Hot Peach Pages
  An international directory of domestic violence agencies
  http://www.hotpeachpages.net

➤ Male Survivors
  Information and resources for male survivors of sexual traumas, including locations of support groups by state
  http://www.malesurvivor.org/default.html

➤ Office of Veterans Affairs: Veterans' Support Groups
  Information about different veterans' organizations and services for
  veterans
  http://ova.dc.gov/ova/cwp/view,a,1403,q,635841,ovanav,|32451|,.asp

➤ Office for Victims of Crime
  Description of national organizations and services they provide for survivors of violence
  http://www.ojp.usdoj.gov/ovc/help

➤ Women's Law
  A list of organizations and groups, predominantly based in the United
  States, who provide services to individuals after sexual exploitation/
  prostitution/sexual trafficking
  http://www.womenslaw.org

Films
➤ *Rape is...* (An educational film about sexual assault including personal
  testimonials)
  http://www.cambridgedocumentaryfilms.org/rapeis.html

➤ *No!: The rape documentary* (A dynamic film about rape in the African American community)
http://notherapedocumentary.org

➤ *Born into Brothels* (and nine other recommended films on human trafficking)
http://humantrafficking.change.org/blog/view/10_human_trafficking_films_to_watch

Index

About the Editor

Thema Bryant-Davis is director of the Culture and Trauma Research Lab and associate professor of psychology at Pepperdine University. She is past president of the Society for the Psychology of Women and a former representative to the United Nations for the American Psychological Association. She is the author of the book *Thriving in the Wake of Trauma: A Multicultural Guide*. Dr. Bryant-Davis is associate editor of the peer reviewed journal *Psychological Trauma*. She was awarded the Emerging Leader of Women in Psychology Award and served on the Committee on Women in Psychology for the American Psychological Association. Dr. Bryant-Davis is a licensed clinical psychologist and maintains a private practice where she works with individuals, couples, and families, most of whom are trauma survivors. She earned her doctorate in Clinical Psychology from Duke University and completed her postdoctoral training at Harvard Medical Center. Dr. Bryant-Davis has been a media consultant on trauma recovery and has provided training for judges, police officers, community advocates, therapists, medical personnel, and religious leaders on interpersonal trauma.

About the Contributors

Janet C'de Baca, Ph.D., (University of New Mexico, 1999) is a staff psychologist in the Women's Stress Disorder Treatment Team (WSDTT) Program within the Behavioral Health Care Line at the New Mexico Veterans Administration (VA) Health Care System. Dr. C'de Baca works with the WSDTT team in offering a variety of services to the female veteran population, as well as supervising psychology interns and offering consultation to other VA departments. She is active in conducting funded research on posttraumatic stress disorder at the VA. She came to the VA from the Behavioral Health Research Center of the Southwest, a center of the Pacific Institute for Research and Evaluation where she conducted research funded through the National Institutes of Health. Her research there focused on alcohol and drug addiction, screening and intervention programs for impaired drivers, and prevention programs for high-risk, substance-using juvenile offenders. She has coauthored a book on sudden personal transformations and authored/coauthored several other publications.

Leanne R. Brecklin, Ph.D., is an associate professor of criminal justice at the University of Illinois–Springfield. She received a Ph.D. in criminal justice at the University of Illinois at Chicago. Her research interests focus on the prevention of sexual and physical violence against women, with emphases on substance abuse, self-defense training, and the development of college rape prevention programs. She is currently conducting a study involving female participants of the rape aggression defense (RAD) program (a women's self-defense training class) with a main focus on women's psychological and behavioral changes resulting from training participation.

Richard P. Brown, M.D., associate professor of psychiatry at Columbia University, graduate of Columbia University College of Physicians and Surgeons (1977), gives more than two hundred lectures and courses every year. Since 1998, Dr. Brown has taught full-day courses on complementary and alternative medicine for the American Psychiatric Association and other conferences. He coauthored many scientific articles, books, and chapters, including *Stop Depression Now* (1999); *The Rhodiola Revolution* (2004); "Complementary and Alternative Treatments in Psychiatry" in *Psychiatry* (2003, 2007); "Alternative Treatments in Brain Injury" in *Neuropsychiatry of Traumatic Brain Injury* (2004, 2009); and *How to Use Herbs, Nutrients, and Yoga in Mental Health Care* (2009). Dr. Brown and Dr. Patricia L. Gerbarg developed a comprehensive neurophysiological theory of the effects of yoga breathing on the mind and body, particularly its benefits in anxiety, depression, and post-traumatic stress disorder. He is a certified teacher of aikido (fourth Dan) yoga, qigong, and Open Focus meditation. Dr. Brown and Dr. Gerbarg provide Breath~Body~Mind workshops for health care professionals, yoga teachers, research studies, and the general public. Sponsored by Serving Those Who Serve (www.STWS.org), their workshops are helping people overcome emotional and physical aftereffects of the September 11 World Trade Center attacks. Their disaster relief programs have been used in Haiti, Sudan, and Rwanda. Information, resources, lectures, and workshops on integrative psychiatry are available at www.haveahealthymind.com.

NiCole T. Buchanan, Ph.D., is an associate professor in the Department of Psychology at Michigan State University and a core faculty affiliate in MSU's Center for Multicultural Psychology Research, Center for Gender in Global Context, and the Violence Against Women Research & Outreach Initiative. Her research examines race and gender in workplace and academic harassment. Dr. Buchanan received the 2008 Carolyn Payton Early Career Award for research making "a significant contribution to the understanding of the role of gender in the lives of Black women," the 2008 International Coalition Against Sexual Harassment Researcher Award, the Association of Women in Psychology's 2007 Women of Color Award for empirical research contributions, Michigan State University's 2007 Excellence in Diversity Award in the category of Individual Emerging Progress for outstanding research and teaching accomplishments in the areas of diversity, pluralism, and social justice, and two Clinical Faculty Awards from the National Institutes of Health.

Rebecca Campbell, Ph.D., is a professor of community psychology and program evaluation at Michigan State University. Her current research includes studies funded by the National Institute of Justice and the National Institute of Mental Health on the community response to rape, vicarious trauma among violence against women researchers and service providers, and the evaluation of sexual assault nurse examiner programs. She is the author of *Emotionally Involved: The Impact of Researching Rape* (2002), which won the 2002 Distinguished Publication Award from the Association for Women in Psychology. Dr. Campbell is on the editorial review boards of several peer-reviewed journals including *Journal of Interpersonal Violence, Violence Against Women,* and the *Journal of Forensic Nursing.* She is the methods section editor of the *American Journal of Evaluation.* Dr. Campbell received the 2002 Emerging Leader Award from the Committee on Women in Psychology of the American Psychological Association, the 2006 Scientific Achievement Award from the International Association of Forensic Nurses, and the 2007 Distinguished Contributions to Psychology in the Public Interest (Early Career) Award from the American Psychological Association. Dr. Campbell has been active in the antiviolence social movement since 1989 and has spent ten years working as a volunteer rape victim advocate in hospital emergency departments.

Diane T. Castillo, Ph.D., is a psychologist and the coordinator of the Women's Stress Disorder Treatment Team at the New Mexico VA Health Care System, in Albuquerque. She holds an adjunct assistant professor position in the Psychiatry Department and is an associate professor (clinical) in the Psychology Department at the University of New Mexico. Dr. Castillo has developed and provided programmatic, evidence-based treatment for women veterans, is the principal investigator on a Department of Defense–funded study, conducted research, and published in the area of post-traumatic stress disorder, Hispanic veterans, and ethics. She is a consultant and trainer in prolonged exposure for PTSD through the National Center for PTSD. She received her bachelor's degree from the University of New Mexico and her Ph.D. from the University of Iowa.

Diane Clayton, LCSW, is a practicing eye movement desensitization and reprocessing therapist, consultant, and Basic EMDR Trainer certified by EMDR International Association. In her thirty-two years of practice she has worked with victims of sexual assault and other traumas. As an administrator she has developed programs for substance abusers, addressing comorbid issues.

A. Monique Clinton-Sherrod, Ph.D., is a research psychologist in the Risk Behavior and Family Research Program at RTI International. Dr. Clinton-Sherrod's expertise includes the areas of intimate partner violence (IPV), substance abuse prevention, and women's and minorities' health, with particular focus on evaluating the effectiveness of interventions at all levels. Her research experience has involved investigations of IPV and substance use issues among various populations, including adolescents, college students, the military, and couples with a partner in substance abuse treatment. Before coming to RTI, Dr. Clinton-Sherrod served as an adjunct faculty member and taught classes in statistics, research methods, and psychology. She has authored and coauthored book chapters and several journal articles for such publications as the *Journal of Interpersonal Violence, Journal of Substance Abuse, Journal of Black Psychology, Violence Against Women,* and *Journal of Family Violence.*

Michelle Contreras has provided assessment and therapy services to international survivors of human trafficking in the United States for over five years. Contreras is currently completing a participatory action research project with service providers attending survivors of human trafficking in Guatemala, which aims to strengthen international collaborations around this issue. At Project Reach, a program funded by the U.S. Department of Justice, Contreras is a consultant who provides nationwide trainings on the psychological needs of trafficking survivors to mental health professionals, attorneys, law enforcement, immigration officials, and medical personnel among others.

Sannisha Dale is a Ph.D. candidate in clinical psychology at Boston University. Prior to attending Boston University she completed a master's degree in human development and psychology at the Harvard Graduate School of Education and a bachelor's in psychology at Boston College. Her interests are in (a) studying the psychology of individuals who undergo traumatic experiences, as well as the strategies and methods they employ to cope with or overcome adversity; (b) exploring the relationship between psychological factors and health outcomes of individuals infected with or at risk for HIV; and (c) learning and developing effective prevention and intervention strategies to promote resilience among survivors of trauma and individuals with HIV. For the past five years she has provided supportive listening, safety planning, and crisis intervention to survivors of domestic violence and sexual assaults who called the Massachusetts domestic violence statewide hotline. Sannisha was also a rape crisis counselor/medical advocate volunteer for the Boston Area Rape Crisis Center for one year, and in that role she supported rape survivors in hospital emergency rooms following assaults. Currently Dale is completing practicum training at the Bedford Veteran Administration's Center for Psychotherapeutic Change. Beyond her practical experiences Dale is extremely dedicated to research and is currently supported by an American Recovery and Reinvestment Act National Institute of Allergy and Infectious Disease research diversity supplement. She is the primary research assistant in the Emotion, Gender, Culture and Health Lab led by Dr. Leslie Brody at Boston University. The lab's current research study seeks to provide a clearer understanding of factors that may contribute to the health outcomes of ethnic minority women with and at risk for HIV infection, many of whom have histories of trauma, including violence and abuse.

Jessica Henderson Daniel, Ph.D., ABPP, is director of training in psychology in the Department of Psychiatry and associate director of the LEAH (Leadership Education in Adolescent Health) Training Program in the Division of Adolescent Medicine, both at Children's Hospital Boston. She is an associate professor of psychology in the Department of Psychiatry at Harvard Medical School and adjunct associate professor in the clinical psychology program at Boston University. She has served as the psychologist on the Child Protection Team at Children's Hospital for thirty-eight years. In the American Psychological Association (APA), she is a past president of the Society for the Psychology of Women and a former member of the board of directors. She currently represents the Society for the Study of Ethnic Minority Issues on the APA Council of Representatives. Her publications have focused on child abuse and neglect, media images of women, racial trauma in the lives of Black women and children, adolescent mental health, and mentoring.

Kelly Cue Davis, Ph.D., is a clinical psychologist and research assistant professor in the School of Social Work at University of Washington in Seattle. She obtained her master's and doctoral degrees in clinical psychology from the University of Washington. Her current research focuses on the effects of alcohol consumption on sexual aggression, sexual risk-taking, and violence against women. Most recently, she has studied the effects of alcohol use on sexual violence and HIV/STI-related risk behaviors under grants from the National Institutes of Health and the Alcoholic Beverage Medical Research Foundation. Dr. Davis has served as a consulting editor for *Psychology of Addictive Behaviors* and ad hoc reviewer for numerous psychology journals, in addition to chairing the Committee on Violence against Women and Girls under the American Psychological Association's Society for the Psychology of Women (Division 35).

Joanne L. Davis, Ph.D., is an associate professor of clinical psychology, director of undergraduate studies in psychology, codirector of the Center for Community Research and Development, and codirector of the Tulsa Institute of Trauma, Abuse, and Neglect at the University of Tulsa, Oklahoma. She was recently appointed an associate editor of the *Journal of Traumatic Stress.* She received her doctorate from the University of Arkansas and completed an internship at the Medical University of South Carolina and a two-year postdoctoral fellowship at the National Crime Victims Research and Treatment Center in Charleston, South Carolina. Her research interests include the assessment, treatment, and prevention of interpersonal violence and its effects. In recent years she has focused on the assessment and treatment of chronic nightmares and other sleep disturbances.

Carolyn Zerbe Enns, Ph.D., is professor of psychology at Cornell College, where she teaches a wide range of undergraduate courses in psychology, women's studies, and ethnic studies. Her scholarly interests include multicultural feminist perspectives on psychotherapy and pedagogy, and feminist therapy in both North America and Japan. She has published approximately fifty articles and chapters on topics that focus primarily on gender, pedagogy, and feminist theory and therapy. She is the author of *Feminist Theories and Feminist Psychotherapies: Origins, Themes, and Diversity* (2004) and the coeditor (with Ada L. Sinacore) of *Teaching and Social Justice: Integrating Multicultural and Feminist Theories in the Classroom* (2005). Dr. Enns was one of three cochairs of the task force that developed the American Psychological Association (APA) Guidelines for Psychological Practice with Girls and Women. She has received the APA Division 35 (Society for the Psychology of Women) Heritage Award (2008), a Committee on Women in Psychology Distinguished Leader Award (2009), and the Section for the Advancement of Women (of Counseling Psychology) Foremother Award (2010).

Melissa Farley has written twenty-four peer-reviewed articles on prostitution and trafficking, and two books, *Prostitution, Trafficking & Traumatic Stress* (2004) and *Prostitution and Trafficking in Nevada: Making the Connections* (2007). Farley is studying sex buyers in research interviews with 700 johns in five countries. An article with three coauthors will soon be published in *Psychological Trauma: Theory, Research, Practice, and Policy*. Her research has been used by governments in South Africa, Canada, New Zealand, Ghana, Sweden, United Kingdom, and United States for education and policy development. At nonprofit Prostitution Research and Education (PRE) in San Francisco, Farley addresses the connections between prostitution, racism, sexism, and poverty. The PRE website is a widely used resource (www.prostitutionresearch.com). PRE is affiliated with Center for World Indigenous Studies and Pacific Graduate School of Psychology.

Patricia L. Gerbarg, M.D., assistant clinical professor in psychiatry at New York Medical College, graduated from Harvard Medical School (1975) and the Boston Psychoanalytic Society and Institute (1992). She has written many scientific papers and has lectured on alternative treatments for anxiety, depression, and post-traumatic stress disorder (PTSD) at the American Psychiatric Association Meetings and other conferences. Dr. Gerbarg's research focuses on integrative psychiatry (combining standard and complementary treatments) for anxiety, PTSD, and depression in survivors of trauma, military service, and mass disasters such the Southeast Asian tsunami, September 11 World Trade Center attacks, 2010 earthquake in Haiti, and genocide survivors in Sudan. With her husband, Dr. Richard Brown, she coauthored *The Rhodiola Revolution* (2004); "Complementary and Alternative Treatments in Psychiatry" in *Psychiatry* (2003, 2007), and other publications. Her chapter "Yoga and Neuro-Psychoanalysis" was published in *Bodies in Treatment: The Unspoken Dimension* (2007). Dr. Brown, Dr. Gerbarg, and Dr. Philip R. Muskin describe many innovative treatments using integrative psychiatry in *How to Use Herbs, Nutrients, and Yoga in Mental Health Care* (2008). See www.haveahealthymind.com.

Shelly P. Harrell, Ph.D., is a licensed clinical psychologist and professor of psychology at Pepperdine University's Graduate School of Education and Psychology with more than twenty-five years of experience helping, teaching, and mentoring others. She received her undergraduate degree at Harvard University and her master's and doctorate degrees from UCLA. Her primary areas of scholarship include multicultural psychology and interventions with diverse populations. As a psychotherapist, coach, and consultant, she also maintains a private practice where she works with individuals, groups, and organizations emphasizing the application of strengths-based interventions. She actively integrates meditation, music, quotations, and journaling into her work with clients. She can be found on the web at www.empoweredeveryday.com and www.focusandflow.net.

Zaje A. Harrell, Ph.D., is an assistant professor of psychology at Michigan State University. She is trained in both psychology and women's studies and is affiliated with the Ecological Community Graduate Program. Her work focuses on gender, race/ethnicity, and mental health specifically in the context of addictive behaviors. Her expertise is the relationship between college students' mental health and legal substance use (i.e., tobacco, alcohol, prescription drug use). She has recently completed an intramurally funded project on racial/ethnic differences in college student alcohol use. She has published on the relationship between addictive behaviors and depression as well as the sociocultural context for understanding women's mental health risks. She is currently the cochair of the Women's Health Special Interest Group of the Society of Behavioral Medicine. Dr. Harrell has also served as a grant reviewer for the National Institutes of Health.

Tamara G. J. Leech earned her Ph.D. in sociology from the University of Michigan, Ann Arbor. Dr. Leech is currently an assistant professor of sociology and principal investigator for the Institute for Social Research in the Indiana University School of Liberal Arts at Indiana University-Purdue University Indianapolis. She has published in areas that include violence, risky sexual behavior, and sexual violence among urban youth. She also works closely with the MidNorth Public Safety Committee and Senior 1000 Coalition to promote the health and well-being of Indianapolis residents. Dr. Leech's current research project focuses on urban neighborhood and community investment in positive youth development.

Marci Littlefield earned a Ph.D. in sociology from the University of Texas at Austin, master's of public affairs from the Lyndon B. Johnson Graduate School of Public Affairs, and a bachelor of arts from Oberlin College. Littlefield is currently an assistant professor of sociology and research fellow for the Center for the Study of Religion and American Culture at Indiana University-Purdue University Indianapolis. She has published in areas including Black women, the media, and the Black church and has been funded to research faith-based organizations in Indianapolis and Chicago. Dr. Littlefield's current book project investigates marriage in the African American community.

Shannon M. Lynch, Ph.D., is an associate professor at Idaho State University and a licensed clinical psychologist. Her research is focused on violence against women and survivors' use of resources to cope with and to recover from traumatic events. Most recently, she has been assessing incarcerated women's trauma exposure, treatment needs, and the effectiveness of trauma-focused interventions with women in prison. Dr. Lynch completed her doctorate in clinical psychology at the University of Michigan in 1999 and then held a two-year postdoctoral fellowship with the Victims of Violence Program, part of Cambridge Health Alliance/Harvard Medical School.

Melissa L. McVicker, M.S., is currently a doctoral student in the marriage and family therapy program at Antioch University New England. She earned an M.S. in marriage and family therapy from Purdue University Calumet and an undergraduate degree from the University of Texas at San Antonio. She is an adjunct faculty member and supervisor-in-training in the Department of Applied Psychology at Antioch University New England, where she teaches marriage and family therapy and master's-level courses on sexuality and sex therapy and supervises master's-level therapists in professional seminar and first-year practicum courses. McVicker is currently a clinician at the Antioch Couple and Family Therapy Institute in Keene, New Hampshire, as she works toward becoming a licensed marriage and family therapist and an American Association for Marriage and Family Therapy Approved Supervisor. McVicker has published articles related to coparenting after divorce, sex abuse factors, female sexual identity and social constructionism, and the use of narrative therapy with specific populations.

Heidi S. Resnick, Ph.D., is a professor of clinical psychology at the Medical University of South Carolina and a senior investigator at the National Crime Victims Research and Treatment Center. Dr. Resnick has conducted epidemiological and treatment outcome research related to the behavioral and mental health impact of sexual assault and other traumatic events. Her research has included development and evaluation of secondary prevention approaches implemented within primary care settings targeting problems of drug use and symptoms of post-traumatic stress disorder or other distress following sexual assault.

Z. Seda Sahin, M.S., received her bachelor's degree in psychology from Ege University, Izmir, Turkiye. Her graduation thesis was titled *The influence of age, sex, marital status and education in the dimensions of TCI in Turkish sample.* After working in the field with mentally disabled children and their families, she completed her master's degree at Purdue University Calumet in marriage and family therapy. Her master's thesis was titled *The relationship of differentiation, family coping skills, and family functioning with optimism in college age students.* She is currently enrolled in Purdue University's marriage and family therapy Ph.D. program, working as a research assistant at the Relationships and Healthcare Lab at Purdue University and as a clinician at Family Services in Lafayette, Indiana. Z. Seda Sahin has published articles related to positive psychology, resilience, divorce process, compassion fatigue, and differentiation.

Jessica Shaw is a graduate student in the ecological-community psychology doctoral program at Michigan State University. She is interested in violence against women, the rape culture, gender inequities, all-male groups, sociopolitical development, and change processes. She has been active in the movement to end violence against women since 2006. Shaw has worked with local rape crisis centers to provide crisis intervention and medical advocacy. She spent several years providing primary prevention programming to grades K-12 and organizing community events and activism. She has also worked with college students and campus communities extensively, facilitating workshops and workshop series on sexual assault, dating violence, supporting survivors, bystander intervention, and the rape culture. She received her B.S. with highest distinction in psychology from the University of Illinois at Urbana-Champaign in 2009.

April Sikes, Ph.D., is clinical assistant professor of school counseling in the Department of Counseling and Psychological Services at Georgia State

University. She is a licensed professional counselor and a certified school counselor in Georgia and a national certified counselor. Her research interests focus broadly on issues in counselor education and school counseling, with particular attention to child abuse and neglect, substance abuse and dependence, counseling children and adolescents, and ethical and legal issues in counseling. She has served as a school counselor in elementary and middle school settings, investigated reports of child abuse and neglect as a case manager, and provided therapeutic and clinical services for families of abused children. She has presented and copresented at national, regional, and state-level conferences on a variety of subjects, including child abuse and neglect and ethical and legal issues in school counseling. She is an active member of several professional organizations, including the Association for Counselor Education and Supervision, the American School Counselor Association, and the American Counseling Association. She is also an editorial review board member of the *Journal of School Counseling* and *Counselor Education and Supervision*.

Anneliese A. Singh, Ph.D., L.P.C., is an assistant professor in the Department of Counseling and Human Development Services at the University of Georgia. Her clinical, research, and advocacy interests include investigating the resilience and coping of transgender survivors of trauma; lesbian, gay, bisexual, transgender, queer, and questioning (LGBTQQ) bullying and violence prevention; and South Asian American survivors of child sexual abuse. Dr. Singh has particular expertise in qualitative methodology with historically marginalized groups and is the author of *Qualitative Inquiry in Counseling and Education*. Dr. Singh is a past president of the Association of Lesbian, Gay, Bisexual, and Transgender Issues in Counseling—a division of the American Counseling Association—where her presidential initiatives included the development of counseling competencies for working with transgender clients, supporting queer people of color, and ensuring safe schools for LGBTQQ youth. She has received numerous awards for her scholarship and community activism on violence prevention and intervention, including American Counseling Association awards (O'Hana Social Justice and Kitty Cole Human Rights) and the Ramesh and Vijaya Bakshi Community Change Award. Dr. Singh is a founder of the Georgia Safe Schools Coalition, an organization that works at the intersection of heterosexism, racism, sexism, and other oppressions to create safe school environments in Georgia.

Rachael M. Swopes holds a master's degree in clinical psychology and is currently pursuing her doctoral degree at the University of Tulsa, Oklahoma. Her interests focus broadly on researching interpersonal violence and the effectiveness of trauma-focused interventions. Under this broad umbrella, she is currently interested in minimizing the effects of trauma on subsequent risky behaviors, such as substance use and criminal behavior, as well as in identifying predictors of post-traumatic stress disorder in survivors of sexual assault and other interpersonal violence.

Shaquita Tillman, M.A., is a doctoral student in clinical psychology at Pepperdine University. Tillman received her B.A. in psychology at the University of California, Los Angeles, and her M.A. in psychology at Pepperdine University. In 2007, Tillman earned a three-year fellowship, the Substance Abuse and Mental Health Services Fellowship, from the American Psychological Association. Tillman's clinical and research interests include the cultural context of trauma recovery, the association between mental health disorders and substance abuse, and the specialized treatment needs of culturally and ethnically diverse populations who present with these co-occurring disorders. Currently Tillman is a member of Pepperdine University's Culture and Trauma Research Lab, directed by Thema Bryant-Davis, Ph.D.; as a part of this lab she researches how ethnocultural and race-related variables impact the nature and quality of resources available to trauma survivors, their willingness to access those resources, and the treatment they receive when help is actively sought out.

Pratyusha Tummala-Narra, Ph.D., is assistant professor in the Department of Counseling, Developmental and Educational Psychology at Boston College. She is a teaching associate at the Cambridge Health Alliance/Harvard Medical School. Dr. Tummala-Narra received her doctoral degree from Michigan State University and completed her postdoctoral training in the Victims of Violence Program at the Cambridge Hospital in Cambridge, Massachusetts. She founded and directed (1997–2003) the Asian Mental Health Clinic at the Cambridge Health Alliance and was an assistant professor in psychiatry at Georgetown University School of Medicine (2003–2005). She was also on faculty at the Michigan School of Professional Psychology (2006–2009) and in clinical practice for more than twelve years. She is the recipient of the Scholars in Medicine Fellowship from the Harvard Medical School. She has presented nationally and published peer-reviewed journal articles and book chapters on the topics of immigration, ethnic minority issues, trauma, and psychodynamic psychotherapy. Her research concerns the areas of racial and ethnic discrimination and mental health care disparities among ethnic minority communities. Dr. Tummala-Narra is currently the chair of the Multicultural Concerns Committee for Division 39 (Psychoanalysis), a member of the Committee on Ethnic Minority Affairs in the American Psychological Association, and a member of the American Psychological Association Presidential Task Force on Immigration.

Amy Tuttle, Ph.D., LMFT, is a licensed marriage and family therapist and assistant professor of psychology at Pepperdine University in the Graduate School of Education and Psychology. She is an American Association for Marriage and Family Therapy (AAMFT) Approved Supervisor, serves on the elections council for the AAMFT, and is chair of the Early Career Membership Committee for the American Family Therapy Academy. Dr. Tuttle's clinical and research interests include multicultural and diversity issues, postmodern and contemporary family therapy theories, intergenerational experiences of race-related trauma, family and play therapy, and working with disadvantaged, multistressed populations. She maintains a clinical practice in Southern California serving disadvantage youth and their families. Dr. Tuttle coauthored *Theory Based Treatment Planning for Marriage and Family Therapists* (2003) and *Relational Orientations: A Contextual Framework for Assessment and Practice* (2009) and published research in *Family Process* on collaborative and relational therapies.

Jennifer Hardison Walters, M.S.W., is a research analyst at RTI International, Behavioral Health and Criminal Justice Research Division. Hardison Walters has over ten years of research experience in the areas of intimate partner violence, sexual assault, child maltreatment, prisoner reentry, and juvenile assessment instruments. Her prior experience includes participatory evaluation work with programs serving minor victims of human trafficking, evidence-based reviews of sexual assault prevention interventions, and study site coordination with national studies of sexual victimization in correctional facilities and prisoner reentry. Before joining RTI, Hardison Walters served as evaluator, trainer, and project coordinator with a statewide child welfare initiative. She also has provided direct services to victims of domestic violence and sexual assault and taught English to middle school students in Mexico.